D1714981

SWINDLER SACHEM

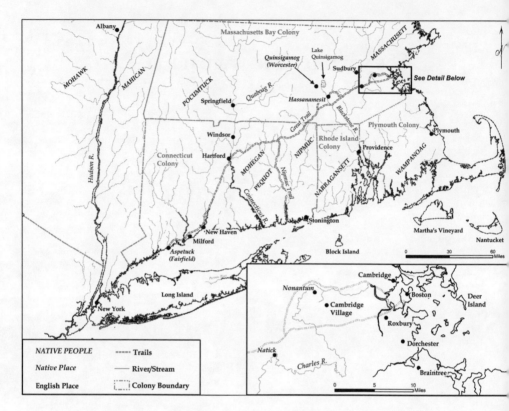

Albany

Massachusetts Bay Colony

MASSACHUSETT

MOHAWK

MAHICAN

Quinsigamog (Worcester)   Lake Quinsigamog   Sudbury

See Detail Below

POCUMTUCK

Springfield   *Quaboag R.*   Hassanamesit

Blackstone R.

Windsor

Great Trail

Plymouth Colony   Plymouth

Connecticut Colony   Hartford   *MOHEGAN*   *NIPMUC*   Rhode Island Colony   Providence

Hudson R.

PEQUOT   *Nipmuc Trail*

NARRAGANSETT

WAMPANOAG

Connecticut R.

Stonington

New Haven   Milford   Martha's Vineyard   Nantucket

Aspetuck (Fairfield)

Block Island

Long Island

New York

0   30   60
Miles

Cambridge

Nonantum   Boston   Deer Island

Cambridge Village

Roxbury

Natick   Dorchester

Charles R.   Braintree

0   5   10
Miles

Sites connected to the lives of John Wompas and Ann Prask Wompas
[Map by Jen Macpherson]

SWINDLER
SACHEM

The American Indian Who Sold His
Birthright, Dropped Out of Harvard, and
Conned the King of England

JENNY HALE PULSIPHER

Yale

UNIVERSITY PRESS

New Haven and London

Yale University Press books may be purchased in quantity for
educational, business, or promotional use. For information,
please e-mail sales.press@yale.edu (U.S. office) or sales@yaleup.co.uk
(U.K. office).

Set in Janson type by Integrated Publishing Solutions.
Printed in the United States of America.

ISBN 978-0-300-21493-2 (hardcover : alk. paper)
Library of Congress Control Number: 2017960676
A catalogue record for this book is available from the British Library.

This paper meets the requirements of ANSI/NISO Z39.48-1992
(Permanence of Paper).

10 9 8 7 6 5 4 3 2 1

For my parents,
Barbara and Phillip Hale

Contents

Acknowledgments

I HAVE SPENT A decade of my life on this project, but I can honestly say I will miss John and Ann Wompas and their world. I have incurred many debts in the course of researching and writing this book, and it is a pleasure to acknowledge them here. Alden Vaughan gave me the first nudge in the direction of this project when he asked if I planned to do anything more with John Wompas, who had appeared in a vignette in the penultimate chapter of my first book, *Subjects unto the Same King*. After his prompting, I started digging for more information, found some eye-opening documents, and was hooked.

For someone who loves research as I do, it has been a delight to hunt for information on John and Ann Wompas and their far-flung acquaintances and kin on both sides of the Atlantic. I thank the helpful staffs at the National Archives in Kew, England, and the British Library and London Metropolitan Archives in London. I thank the staff of the Maine Historical Society (where I first encountered John Wompas in a petition that had made its circuitous way there from the files of the Suffolk County Court), the American Antiquarian Society, the Newberry Library, the Massachusetts State Archives (especially Elizabeth Bouvier, Michael Comeau, John Hannigan, and Caitlin Jones), the Connecticut Historical Society, the Connecticut State Library and Archives, the New England Historical and Genealogical Society, Jennifer L. Betts at the Brown Library Archives, Elizabeth Rose at the Fairfield Museum and History Center, Heidi Fowler at the Grafton Public Library Special Collections, and Nancy and David Thierren and Mary O'Hara at the

Grafton Historical Society. At the Massachusetts Historical Society, I've found many treasures, none more welcome than John Wompas's copy of Cicero's *De Officiis*. I mentioned my search for it to a librarian on one visit, and the next thing I knew, she was placing it on the desk before me. I thank her (although I failed to catch her name!), as well as Peter Drumy, Conrad Wright, and Kate Veins. At the Mashantucket Pequot Museum and Research Center, Jason Mancini, Kevin McBride, Laurie Pasteryak Lamarre, and others dug up sources, answered questions, and allowed me to tag along on a fascinating dig at the site of the Mystic Fort massacre. I also benefited enormously from the growing availability of digital archives during my work on this book. Foremost among them is the Yale Indian Papers Project, spearheaded by Paul Grant-Costa, who has been unfailingly generous with his time and expertise. Albert Winkler, at the Harold B. Lee Library at Brigham Young University, has worked hard to procure databases useful to me and my students, most recently the invaluable Colonial America and Colonial State Papers collections from the U.K. National Archives. Digitized Suffolk County and Middlesex County, Massachusetts, deeds, available through the LDS Church's FamilySearch website, have also been incredibly helpful.

I have presented papers on this project at many different conferences, seminars, workshops, and invited lectures, and I thank the organizers, panelists, and commentators for engaging helpfully with my work. Among my favorite venues is the annual Front Range Early Americanists Consortium, a truly collegial gathering of early Americanists. At one FREAC meeting, Ann Little made a prescient suggestion that helped me locate Ann Prask where I never would have thought to look for her. I was fortunate to participate in the seminar on biography sponsored by the Early Modern Studies Institute (EMSI) and the Omohundro Institute for Early American History and Culture (OIEAHC) at the Huntington Library in 2012, where I benefited greatly from two days of rich interchange with fellow participants, organizers, and attendees. In particular, Gregory Nobles offered an insightful critique of my paper, and Susanna Shaw Romney prodded me to look at John Wompas from a different perspective, which proved to be game changing. I returned to the Huntington in 2016 to present a chapter at the EMSI/Huntington American Origins Seminar, where comments from Peter Mancall and Bethel Saler helped me refine a chapter. Invitations from Michael Goode, Michelle Orihel, and Jonathan Fairbanks to present aspects of my research at their universities and at the Historic Fairbanks House in Dedham, Massachusetts, helped me sharpen my thinking, as did the comments of fellow panelists, commentors, and audience members at the OIEAHC Conference in 2007 and 2012, the conference on Seventeenth-Century Warfare, Diplomacy & Society in the American Northeast in 2013, the Pacific Coast Conference on European Studies in 2011, and a conference on Exploring the Red Atlantic in 2010.

Like John Wompas, I have relied a great deal on the generosity of friends, colleagues, and institutions. My wonderful writing group —Kate Holbrook, Amy Harris, and Rachel Cope—read the entire book more than once, offering praise and encouragement and expecting progress. My colleague Chris Hodson and Chief Cheryll Toney Holley of the Nipmuc Nation also read the entire manuscript and gave me valuable, timely feedback. Eric Hinderaker gave helpful advice on writing early on, and on publishing later on. A number of colleagues read portions of the book or book proposal and provided useful comments, including the late, sorely missed Caroline Cox, Benjamin Irvin, Julie Fisher, Susan Rugh, Virginia Anderson, and members of the Brown Bag group at BYU's History Department. Glen Cooper translated John Wompas's probate and Latin doodles for me. Elizabeth Smart and Mandy Oscarson at BYU's Lee Library helped me set up a digital archive to share my findings and materials with other scholars and students. I've had the pleasure of hiring a series of bright, hard-working students as research assistants over the years, including Megan Coplen, Sherilyn Farnes, Chelsea Henrie, Emma Baker, Taylor Finnell, Perris Neilson, and Emma Chapman. I thank them for their assistance and hope they will enjoy learning what became of John and Ann Wompas. Brigham Young University, where I have taught happily for nearly twenty years, provided funding through the Mary Lou Fulton Young Scholar award, the Alcuin award, and a faculty grant. California State University, Los Angeles, generously provided a year-long research professorship that allowed me to complete this book.

I am also grateful to fellow scholars who have given me advice, shared their work or experience with me, answered specific questions, or pointed me to helpful sources. These include Virginia Anderson, Tad Baker, Kathleen Bragdon, Brian Carroll, Joseph Cullon, Jim Drake, Julie Fisher, Linford Fisher, Paul Grant-Costa, Holly Herbster, Eric Hinderaker, Chris Hodson, Ben Irvin, Jane Kamensky, Wayne Lee, Ann Little, Gloria Main, Peter Mancall, Jason Mancini, Kevin McBride, Josh Piker, Ann Plane, Daniel Richter, Brett Rushforth, Claudio Saunt, Nancy Shoemaker, David Silverman, Coll Thrush, the late Danny Vickers, Jace Weaver, Brian Weiser, and undoubtedly others I failed to mention. I thank Jessie Little Doe Baird of the Wampanoag Nation for advising me about Algonquian languages, and Nipmuc Nation members Rae Gould, Thomas Doughton, and Chief Cheryll Toney Holly for sharing their work, thoughts, and time. This book recounts the efforts of John Wompas and other Nipmucs to preserve and defend their homeland of Hassanamesit, a legacy carried on by the Hassanamisco Nipmucs today. Nothing would please me more than this book's being of value to them.

At Yale University Press my editor Chris Rogers has been a great champion of my work, a careful reader and perceptive editor. I also thank Karen Olson and Phillip King at the press for answering questions and keeping me on track, and my copy editor Beverly Michaels for her keen eye and good sense. The anonymous outside readers gave me just what I needed to revise the book, and I thank them for their comments. Jen Macpherson, whom I met at the 2016 Hassanamisco Nipmuc Powwow, provided the maps and was a pleasure to work with.

My family has lived through this book with me, cheering my discoveries and commiserating with me in my disappointments. Several have read chapters or sections, including my mother, Barbara Hale, my daughter, Annie Pulsipher, and my husband, Michael Pulsipher. My son, Jonathan Pulsipher, read the whole book, told me what he liked most, and came up with my title. Katie Pulsipher Brown, Jeff Brown, and Sam Pulsipher were patient and encouraging. Ethan, Isaac, and Dylan Brown provided welcome distraction. My husband Mike was most supportive of all, reading, listening, and providing neck massages as needed. Like John Wompas, I was born to parents who loved me and sought to do me good. Both are gifted wordsmiths and storytellers who raised me to love words and stories. For so enriching my life, I dedicate this book to them.

A Note on the Text

THIS BOOK PRESENTS A moving canvas of unfamiliar names and places. To add to the confusion, some people used both English and Native names, and some place names changed over the time period covered in this book. Recognizing the potential for confusion, I have included an appendix with a list of people and places connected to John Wompas as well as a chronology of key events to aid the reader. As a way of honoring the indigenous past, some historians have chosen to use only Native versions of names for people and places. For the subject of this biography, however, exclusively using "Wompas" seems to be the wrong choice. A key aspect of his story was his life-long insistence on using the tools and claiming the rights of both English and Indian cultures. This can clearly be seen in the names he used separately or in combination throughout his life—Wompony/Wompas, John Wompas, and John White. Following John Wompas's practice, I use English and Nipmuc names interchangeably and in combination—Wompas, John, or John Wompas.[1]

When referring to Native people in this book, I use tribal names, such as Nipmuc or Massachusett, when appropriate. "Indian" was the term most commonly used by both Native peoples and English in the seventeenth century, and many modern Native people continue to use "Indian" in spite of its erroneous origin. John Wompas frequently chose that term to refer to himself. I also use "Indian" or "Native" interchangeably with tribal names in reference to individuals and groups.[2]

A final word on apparatus: I have modernized all dates, converting them from the Julian to the Gregorian calendar. Under the Julian calendar used in New England in the seventeenth century, the new year began on March 25, so dates from January 1 to March 24 fell in the previous year, often indicated with a slash: 1675/76. In this book, a date such as March 5, 1675/76, will be given as March 5, 1676. I have also made minor changes to some quotations, spelling out abbreviations and, when necessary for clarity, modernizing spelling and adding punctuation.

SWINDLER SACHEM

Introduction

"Have you never seen an Indian before?" John Wompas addressed this aggressive, oddly modern-sounding challenge to a crowd of frightened English villagers in 1677. Wompas, a Nipmuc Indian, and the others had gathered near the meetinghouse in Cambridge, Massachusetts Bay Colony, to seek news of an Indian attack the previous night on the frontier town of Sudbury. It was September 27, 1677, nearly a year after colonial officials had declared the end of King Philip's War, the brutal conflict between the Wampanoag, Narragansett, and Nipmuc Indians and the English settlers of Plymouth, Massachusetts, Connecticut, and Rhode Island colonies. Despite the officials' hopeful proclamation, fighting continued on the fringes of English settlement. Scarred by two years of hostilities, the colonists milling around the Cambridge meetinghouse were on edge, alert for renewed attacks.

John Wompas, also known as John White, the Nipmuc man brash enough to taunt the townspeople, was a familiar, even notorious figure. A decade earlier, he had attended the grammar school in Cambridge and then spent several years at Harvard College. Work as a sailor since then had made him something of a stranger, but in the past four months he had made up for lost time, "travil[ing] up and downe in a vagrant Idle way, among English & Indians" in Cambridge, Boston, and surrounding towns, delivering scathing critiques of the Massachusetts government's military and political misdeeds and their abusive treatment of local Indians. In the imme-

I

diate aftermath of the previous night's alarm at Sudbury, the Nip-
muc man's presence unnerved the colonists, and some openly stared.
Feeling their eyes upon him, he asked whether they had ever seen an
Indian before. Two colonists replied that yes, of course they had.
Then, in what one Englishman claimed was a "surly manner," John
Wompas declared, "You shall feel them too."[1]

This was an open threat, made under circumstances that could
not have been more perilous: John Wompas was the only Indian in
a throng of anxious English colonists. They had yet to learn that the
alarm raised at Sudbury was a false one, but they had heard plenty of
confirmed reports of Indian attacks in the previous weeks. Just five
days earlier Indians had raided the frontier town of Hatfield, and
news of continuing Native assaults on settlements in Maine and
New Hampshire had arrived with sobering frequency for over a
year. The obvious discomfort of the English seemed only to em-
bolden John Wompas, and he began to tell them a tale that could
only distress them more. He had been in London just six months
earlier, at the same time the Massachusetts Bay Colony's agents
were there seeking renewal of the colony charter from the king.
Unlike the Cambridge villagers, John Wompas knew just how badly
the agents had fared. As the colonists listened, he told them how he
had accompanied the agents on their first visit to the king. He had
watched the king chastise them for disobedience and rebuff their
pleas to renew the colony charter, telling them that "his grand father had [given] them their patent but they had forfeited it" by passing statutes contrary to English law. While the king had rebuked the
colony's agents and declared their charter forfeit, he had honored
John Wompas, acknowledging him as his loyal subject. When one
of the Cambridge villagers angrily retorted that "they were his majesties subjects as well as he," John Wompas scoffed at the claim. In
his view, the colonists' disobedience had deprived them of that status; they "were not legal subjects to his majesty."[2]

This incident, a lone Indian taunting and threatening a crowd of
English colonists, upends common wisdom about the defeated and
subjected Natives of New England in the aftermath of King Philip's
War. Upsetting expectations is emblematic of John Wompas's entire
life. He was a Harvard-educated scholar who became a sailor; he

called the Nipmuc village of Hassanamesit his home but spent his adult life dwelling among the English of Roxbury, Boston, and London; he claimed the right, by inheritance, to lead the Nipmucs, but elders of his tribe insisted he was "no sachem"; he cheated his kin of their lands by selling thousands of acres of Nipmuc Country to the English, then bequeathed all of Hassanamesit to his Nipmuc kin in his will; he secured an audience and letters of support from the king of England, who called him his "loyal subject," and he was derided as a drunk and vagrant by Massachusetts officials, who threatened to sell him into foreign slavery.

The contradictions in John Wompas's life reflect a gap between expectations and reality, not just among readers of history, but among those who lived it. Colonial leaders and the English Crown made promises to John Wompas and other Natives about equal status, education, and royal protection that far exceeded what Indians actually received under the political and social reality in place by the last quarter of the seventeenth century. This book, a biography of John Wompas, offers the opportunity to examine that gap, explore the contradictions of his life and, in the process, revise our understanding of Native New England and the emerging English empire that engulfed it.[3]

The times in which John Wompas lived were fraught with change, including the devastating impact of English settlement on Native societies, the colonial reverberations of political crises in England, and the efforts of some English to fit Indians into their vision of the colony's religious destiny through missionary work and education. In the early days of English settlement, many colonists embraced the possibility of "raising" Indians by introducing them to Christianity and the benefits of Western civilization. Of course, the very suggestion of raising Indians shows that the English saw them as needing to be raised. Civilizing the Indians was a paternalistic notion, but it was sincere, articulated in the colony charter and numerous other documents, and acted upon through Christian missions to the Indians, educating Indians in grammar schools, and supporting a handful of Native scholars, including John Wompas, at Harvard College. The English king Charles II invited Indians to bring their grievances to him and addressed them as subjects deserving his protection, implicitly on an equal level with colonial English subjects.

This, too, offered the promise of equality, and Indians paying attention could not be blamed for taking such invitations to heart, and for
believing that they could, in fact, share in the benefits of the English
empire. John Wompas did just that. He believed the messages of
colony leaders and the Crown, seized the opportunities offered to
him, and then suffered the consequences when both promise and
possibility ended in the aftermath of King Philip's War of 1675–
1678.[4]

John Wompas, who chose for himself the role of mariner, navi-
gated the customs, languages, institutions, and legalities of both his
Native society and the nascent English empire at a time when it
seemed possible to enjoy the privileges of both worlds. The very
names John used represent this possibility: Wompas, or Wampooas,
was his father's name and represented his Nipmuc heritage; John
was an English name, arising from his family's choice to embrace
the Christian religion and live in a "praying town"; White was a
name John chose for himself as an adult entering a period of active
participation in the English commercial and maritime world.
"White" is also a loose translation of "Wompas," which means "it is
white" in Nipmuc. It was customary for Native people of the Northeast to take on a new name at a significant life stage, and the name
John chose was meaningful, perhaps even intentionally ironic. It
represented his belief that he could move easily between worlds,
translating, ordering, and combining his name to suit his audience:
John White or John Wompas, John White alias Wompas or John
Wompas alias White.[5]

The lives of John Wompas and his wife Ann Prask encompassed
a surprising number of the pivotal events, processes, and movements
of the seventeenth-century English imperial world, many of which
affected them personally. These included the Pequot War of 1636–
1637, in which Ann Prask was captured, enslaved, and sold to an
English family in Roxbury, Massachusetts; and the destructive impact of European diseases on Native peoples, which led to the deaths
of John Wompas's parents and many of his friends and kin. John's
parents were among the first converts in John Eliot's missionary
work to the Indians, and they offered their son to an English family
to take advantage of the "civilizing" efforts of the English charitable
organizations that sponsored Native education. John's and Ann's

lives also encompassed a period of dramatic transformation in the relations between colonists and Indians. King Philip's War shook the region to its core. Ann lived in Boston during that war, when many Indians were publically executed and hundreds were marched through the town as captives and sold into slavery. War, disease, and exile reduced Indian numbers in the region from around 12,000 to 6,000, and the Natives who remained faced increased restrictions on their freedom and legal and social discrimination, the beginnings of institutionalized racism. John Wompas witnessed these changes and became an ardent opponent of colonial governments and a self-appointed spokesman for Indian rights. The postwar confinement of surviving Indians to a handful of villages led to a rush to purchase Indian land from the defeated Natives of the region, a process John Wompas turned to his own benefit. At the same time, the financial, physical, and emotional demands of fighting King Philip's War also traumatized the English settlers of the region, and the colony's weakness gave the Crown an opportunity to tighten control. Wompas's strategic exploitation of this situation through his appeal to the Crown underscores the significant role Indians played in the colony's loss of its charter authority, and also reveals the Crown's failure to match its expressions of support for its Native subjects with commensurate defense of indigenous rights.[6]

John Wompas's life allows us to see how an ingenious Native man could successfully navigate the shifting spaces of the emerging English empire and colonial economy. In these unsettled decades of the seventeenth century, racial identity, political authority, and land jurisdiction were changing, enough so that a figure like Wompas, who moved with ease across cultures and between systems of power, could appear and flourish. But his story also encompasses the end of that unstable period, when changes on both sides of the Atlantic led to the hardening of social, legal, and racial boundaries. Under that new reality, even a man as ingenious as Wompas found his agency—his ability to move freely between two worlds—stymied.

While the story of John Wompas is unknown to the general public, or even to most American historians, some of the more striking aspects of his life have led to brief mentions in histories from the mid-nineteenth century to the present. Early historians focused on the anomalies of his life—things that made him distinct from other contemporary Indians: his ownership of an English house in Boston, his attendance at Harvard, and his appeals to King Charles II. Others focused on Wompas's career selling Indian land. Land loss is one of the primary issues raised in the New Indian History, a field of scholarship that has placed Indians at the center of American history, but whose depictions of Native people have swung between the poles of victimization and agency. Writers of that history condemn Wompas's actions, declaring that he "served as [an] agent for English encroachment" and that instead of defending Native interests, he "betrayed the community." This betrayal, in turn, contributed to the breakdown of Native communities in Massachusetts. But, as we will see, the story is more complicated than this telling suggests.[7]

John Wompas's life offers a broad window into the seventeenth-century English imperial world, but it also offers a more narrowly focused view into the history of a Native place—Hassanamesit, the seat of the royal line of Nipmuc sachems, or rulers, and the only plot of land in Massachusetts that has remained in the possession of its original Native proprietors to the present day. Nipmuc scholar Rae Gould, who helped secure the listing of the Hassanamisco Reservation on the National Register of Historic Places, calls the reserve "an important mnemonic device that connects Nipmuc people to their past, serves as a reminder of our endurance and continued presence throughout these centuries, and is culturally, politically, and historically significant." John Wompas came from Hassanamesit, claimed nearly two hundred square miles of Nipmuc land as his own property, and sold much of that land to English speculators, to the dismay and protests of his Nipmuc kin. Through his land deeds and bequests from 1676 to 1679, John Wompas was at the heart of the postwar dispossession of Nipmuc land. However, John Wompas also played a crucial role in preserving his homeland. The acreage held by the present-day Hassanamisco Nipmuc Indians was claimed repeatedly by English speculators in the seventeenth century, but colony courts consistently denied those claims, preserving Hassanamesit for the Nipmucs. That preservation rested largely on John Wompas's will, which ensured that Englishmen could not claim land he deeded to them without acknowledging Nipmuc ownership of Hassanamesit. John wrote this will as an English legal document, and it was proved, registered, and upheld in English courts, thus demonstrating that a canny indigenous person could use the tools of colonialism to benefit the colonized.[8]

Finally, this book is a biography, an attempt to trace the life and puzzle out the motivations of a single consequential character who straddled the border between Indian and English cultures. Traditional biographies rely on an abundance of personal records—diaries, letters, memoirs, and other writings—to flesh out their subjects. The privileged position of wealthy, educated white men through much of American history meant that they were more likely than other early Americans to produce such records and to have them preserved after their deaths. Not surprisingly, few biographies have been written about American Indians of the seventeenth century, very few of whom left any personal records. Scholars desiring to write biographies of Indian men or women have had to be creative in their sources, reading between the lines of accounts written by other, usually non-Native people, examining sources such as court and government records, and crossing disciplinary boundaries to borrow insights from fields such as anthropology, archaeology, and sociology. In addition, they have sought the input of modern descendants of Native peoples who have preserved oral histories and cultural practices. Biographical studies of the Niantic sachem Ninigret, the Powhatan sachem's daughter Pocahontas, and the Mohegan sachem Uncas follow this pattern and have added significantly to our understanding of these individuals. But, again not surprisingly, all of these Indian subjects of biography were elites—either leaders or children of leaders.[9]

This biography is unique in attempting to tell the story of an ordinary Indian. John Wompas was, according to his relatives, "no sachem." He did not participate in any wars or official diplomacy. He left no diary, no letters, no memoir, and only a handful of documents written or dictated by himself. It might appear impossible to reconstruct a life given these constraints, but I have found the sources that do survive surprisingly rich. John Wompas left marginalia in a book he owned while attending Harvard College. He composed two petitions to King Charles II. He executed many land deeds and participated in a number of court cases, some of which preserve testimonies of what he did and said. Some people who knew him wrote or spoke of him during his life or remembered him after his death. All of these sources have provided a fairly clear outline of John Wompas's actions.[10]

Biographers also try to uncover their subjects' motivations, and that has been a particular challenge for this biography. Only a few of the sources listed above give a hint of what John Wompas was feeling or suggest why he did the things he did. Readers will note that I frequently use "perhaps" and "may have" in these pages. Because most of the documents that concern John Wompas were produced after he reached adulthood, I have had to rely on historical context and scholarship about Nipmuc history and culture for the earlier years of his life. Readers will catch only fleeting glimpses of John Wompas and his wife Ann Prask in the first two and a half chapters of this book, which are intended to lay the historical background for their lives, but both John and Ann emerge more fully in the chapters that follow. All history relies on interpretation of the available sources. I have drawn conclusions about what drove John Wompas based on my best reading of the sources and their historical context. Others might come to different conclusions, and I have placed exact transcriptions of my manuscript sources, extensive tables compiled during my research, and a full bibliography on a website, which readers may consult in order to evaluate the story for themselves, at http://hdl.lib.byu.edu/1877/3945.

CHAPTER ONE

"The Place of Their Desires"

Hassanamesit

Hassunnimesut is the next Town in order, dignity, and antiquity; sundry of our chief Friends in the great work of Praying
to God, came from them, and there lived their Progenitors,
and there lieth their Inheritance, and that is the place of their
desires.

—JOHN ELIOT, 1671

For Native people . . . land has always been much more than a
wilderness to be conquered or a commodity to barter with. It
has been an anchor for kinship relations, tribal identity and,
more recently, definitions of sovereignty.

—RAE GOULD, Nipmuc anthropologist, 2010

JOHN WOMPAS'S ANCESTORS CAME from Hassanamesit, a Nipmuc
Indian town nestled in the wooded hills forty miles inland from the
coastal lands of the Massachusett Indians, in what is today Grafton,

Massachusetts. Although John spent little of his own life there, he claimed it as his own. But Hassanamesit was a place others desired as well; their conflicting wishes for its lakes and streams and thousands of acres of trees and meadows would powerfully shape John Wompas's life and reputation and divide him from his closest kin.[1]

John Wompas was born around 1637 into a world very different from the one his ancestors had known. A century earlier, the Ninnimissinuok, or "the people," in the region English settlers would later call New England, numbered over 125,000. By the time John was ten years old, epidemic disease had reduced their population to around 15,000. In the wake of this devastation, many Natives fled their widowed homelands to join forces with other ravaged Native communities or to seek assistance from the English newcomers. Some allowed their children to live with the English, perhaps to acquire their knowledge and apparent resistance to disease. John Wompas was one of those children, born to walk the precarious way between a powerful past and drastically diminished present.[2]

John Wompas's ancestors were named for their homeland: *Nipmuc* was an Algonquian word meaning "people of the freshwater fishing places." They lived between the seacoast and the Connecticut River valley, in a broad upland carved by rivers and dotted with freshwater lakes and ponds that provided a rich harvest of fish. Many Nipmuc communities occupied different sites throughout the uplands and moved from season to season, taking advantage of the various resources of the land, lakes, and sea. Their shelters, called *wétus* or wigwams, were adapted to this seasonal mobility. The mats that covered the bentwood frames were woven by Nipmuc women, who packed and carried them along on each move, leaving the frames behind to await their return. The Nipmucs' regular moves—to the woods to hunt for deer and other large game, to the seashore to gather clams, to the falls of a river to net a run of alewives swimming upstream to spawn—made them familiar with the entire region, from eastern to southern coast and far to the west. Each Nipmuc community had a home place where they planted their crops, returning for "hilling time" and harvest. For Wompas's father Wampooas, home was Hassanamesit, the "place of small stones." Situated along the Great Trail, an ancient Native route leading from

the eastern shore to the Connecticut River valley, Hassanamesit was
a frequent stopping place for travelers who relied on the hospitality
of the village. Indians carrying messages or trade goods used this
road; later, English settlers passing between Massachusetts Bay Colony and Connecticut Colony used it as well. Hassanamesit boasted
good fishing and was surrounded by acres on acres of corn. Daniel
Gookin, the Massachusetts Bay Colony's longtime superintendent
of Indians, reported that Hassanamesit was "not inferiour unto any
of the Indian plantation for rich land and plenty of meadow, being
well tempered & watered. It produceth plenty of corn, grain and
fruit."[3]

Hassanamesit was also the seat of the "royal line" of Nipmuc
rulers. Popular conceptions of northeastern Indian polities have
stressed their consensual nature, but Native societies also contained
strong rulers, hereditary elites, and clear status distinctions. While
individual communities of Nipmucs had their own rulers, or *sachems*,
they also recognized a chief or paramount sachem, whose seat was at
Hassanamesit. The paramount sachem's residence there guaranteed
a steady stream of visitors seeking protection or counsel and bringing tribute. Visitors also brought news. Long before Wampooas saw
his first Englishman, he would have heard tales of strangers appearing
on moving islands covered with leafless trees, of the "coat-men"
wearing their endless layers of skins, of the fur hiding their faces.
Coat-men had been coming since Wampooas's great-grandparents'
time, stopping to fish and trade with coastal Indians, and leaving bits
of brass, glass beads, copper pots, and coins behind them. One such
remnant, a French coin dated 1596, turned up in a shovelful of dirt
hefted by a Puritan digging a foundation in Boston in 1631. Coins
and European goods also found their way inland along the Great
Trail, traded from hand to hand and cut into pieces until copper
pots became amulets, beads, or earrings, their rareness making them
fitting adornments for sachems and others of high status. But European visitors were rare, and their trade goods were quickly adapted
into existing Native social and cultural patterns. Even as an increasing number of European fishermen and traders frequented the
coasts, the familiar current of Wampooas's life flowed on. He fished
and hunted with his brothers, helped break the ground for women
to plant corn, and traveled from season to season with his kin—to

sheltered valleys for the winter, home for planting, to the rivers and shore for fishing, home for harvest, and back again.[4]

Although trade with Europeans initially changed little in Wampooas's life, the exchange of germs that accompanied trade had a profound impact on him and all the Natives of the region. It is likely that coastal traders shared some diseases with Native peoples long before the first permanent English settlement, but the "extraordinary plague" that struck several years before Puritan separatists arrived in 1620 was the only one Natives described to the English. It was likely leptospirosis, carried by rats on European ships and causing the kind of symptoms Natives later described as headaches, nosebleeds, and jaundice—"the bodies all over were exceedingly yellow." Indeed, the Algonquian word for the illness, *wesauashaûmitch*, meant "a bad yellowing." The contagion spread rapidly and the mortality rate was staggering. Disease killed virtually everyone in the Wampanoag town of Patuxet southeast of the Nipmuc homelands; when the Plymouth colonists arrived in 1620, they found "skulls and bones . . . in many places lying still above the ground where their houses and dwellings had been." The epidemic was so horrific that children of the survivors were still telling the story over a century later. In 1730 the Indian John Thomas recounted his father's experience: "His father told him that when he . . . was about 16 or 18 years old he lived with his father at the place now called Boston, and that there was then a very great sickness and that the Indians lay dead in every wigwam: and his father went about (as he said) and found only a few alive, and they got together and lived in a wigwam by themselves: at length an Indian came to them from Dorchester Neck, and carried them thither, where they found the Indians almost all dead. And that both in Dorchester and in Boston the dead were so many that they never were buried."[5]

Age-old European plagues such as leptospirosis, smallpox, and influenza were new to North America, and the Indians lacked the adaptive immunity that previous exposure provided to Europeans. Environmental and social factors, including malnutrition brought on by the disruption of the initial plagues and the pressures of English colonization, increased Native vulnerability. As a result, when European diseases struck Indian communities they often killed over half of those taken sick, sometimes wiping out entire towns. Daniel

Gookin recorded Indian estimates of Native population before the epidemics. Based on this report, the Indians of southern New England dropped from between 126,000 and 144,000 at the start of the seventeenth century to around 15,000 by mid-century. Minister John Eliot, who preached to the Indians for forty years, described them in 1647 as only "a remnant; for there be but few that are left alive from the Plague and Pox."[6]

While disease laid waste to eastern coastal Wampanoag, Massachusett, and Pennacook communities, the Narragansetts to the south—traditional enemies of the Massachusett and Wampanoag Indians—escaped unscathed. Indian survivors of the coastal epidemic told the English that the Narragansetts "had not been at all touched with this wasting plague." They were "a strong people and many in number, living compact together" only a few dozen miles from the Wampanoag homelands. The Narragansetts' escape left the weakened Wampanoags and Massachusetts more vulnerable than ever to their attacks. In the aftermath of the epidemic, survivors banded together, abandoning some villages and combining others. Given this perilous new reality, the ravaged tribes strategically sought friendship and alliance with the English when they arrived, as protection against their Native enemies. Early accounts from both the Plymouth settlers of 1620 and the Massachusetts Bay colonists of 1630 note frequent Indian visits to English towns and homes, seeking friendship and trade.[7]

Like the Narragansetts, the Nipmucs were spared first-hand exposure to the epidemic of 1616, but it affected them nonetheless. With so many dead—and so suddenly—the balance of power among the Indians of the region was disrupted. The Nipmucs had long been weaker than coastal groups such as the Massachusetts and Wampanoags, paying tribute to them to acknowledge their superior strength and seek their protection. Failure to pay tribute could lead to armed attack and the forced surrender of their corn or goods. With these coastal tribes nearly destroyed, the Nipmucs may have seen the newly arrived English as potential allies against the Narragansetts. This possibility may explain the first recorded interaction between Nipmucs and the English in 1630, the year colonists began arriving in Massachusetts Bay forty miles east of Hassanamesit. They came in much larger numbers than the Plymouth English had, and although they sent men ahead to build houses and plant crops, the numbers of new arrivals overwhelmed their preparations. Men and women in half-finished houses on the Shawmut peninsula (later Boston) or across the river in Charlestown were starving, and within the first year of settlement 20 percent of them died. The Massachusett Indians sent word to surrounding Native groups that the English wanted corn and would pay well for it. No doubt the Massachusetts had already supplied the English with as much corn as they could spare. After receiving this message, Nipmuc John Acquittamaug and his father, along with several other Nipmucs, carried corn on their backs to Boston to sell to the English. It was Acquittamaug's first view of the new town, at a time when there was "but one cellar in the place."[8]

The Nipmucs' willingness to trade with the English was a clear signal that they wanted friendship. In the Native view, trade confirmed ties of friendship and alliance between people and conferred obligations. Natives of the Northeast expected reciprocity in their relations with other people, Indian or European. The Nipmucs had been generous to the English; they expected generosity and friendship in return. Just over a decade later, several Nipmuc sachems submitted to the English government at Boston, explaining that they did so because they "crave[d] the benefit . . . of protection." They must have found the authority of the coastal chiefdoms burdensome if they were willing to trade it for submission to the English, to whom they also paid tribute. Or perhaps they wanted a direct relationship with the new arrivals, who had valuable trade goods to offer, rather than one mediated by other Indians. Undoubtedly, other Nipmucs followed John Acquittamaug's path to Boston, out of a desire for trade or merely to satisfy their curiosity. But the Indians who carried lifesaving corn to the English may have returned to Nipmuc Country bearing the seeds of deadly disease. When an epidemic struck again, it did not spare the Nipmucs.[9]

The next plague arrived late in the year 1633. English settlers, who had seen it before, identified it as smallpox. In November 1633, Massachusetts governor John Winthrop reported "a great mortality among the Indians" surrounding Boston. Massachusett sachem Chickatabut of nearby Neponset died of the disease, along with "many of his people." In early December Sagamore [Sachem] John and "almost all his people" died; his brother Sagamore James and his village succumbed soon afterward. Many of the Indians, including Sagamore John before his death, turned to the English for help. A few were cured, but most died, and the English cared for their orphaned children until most of them died as well. As the weeks progressed, the disease spread to other settlements. A runaway English servant hiding from his master among the Indians twelve miles west of Boston returned after more than half of the Natives he lived with died of smallpox. To the south, at least seven hundred Narragansetts died. The disease spread as far north as an Indian settlement near the Piscataqua River, "where all the Indians (except one or two) died."[10]

No one at the time recorded how smallpox affected the Nipmucs. Living so far to the west of the first English settlements, the Nipmucs were virtually unknown to the English. As late as 1632, Massachusetts Colony assistant governor Thomas Dudley summed up his knowledge of the Nipmucs with a vague allusion to the "Nipnett men, whose sagamore we know not" living seventy or eighty miles to the west. "They are the only people we yet hear of in the inland country," Dudley wrote. While we have no sense of how many Nipmucs died in the 1633 epidemic, we can see hints of its impact on Wampooas's family. Wampooas's wife bore a son, later known as John Wompas, around 1637, four years after the smallpox epidemic. She had two older daughters from another marriage, and it is possible that her previous husband died in the epidemic. Young John Wompas, who spent as much time living among the English as any Indian of his generation, never contracted smallpox. If his mother had enough resilience to survive the disease in 1633, she could have passed that trait on to him, which would explain his continued health in succeeding waves of smallpox, when so many Indians around him died.[11]

To many of the providentially minded English, the destruction of the Indians by disease was God's work. John Eliot said that "God sent [disease] into those parts," and others claimed God had afflicted the Indians to clear the way for English settlement, much as he had cleared the land of Canaan for the children of Israel. A speaker at Harvard's first commencement commended God's Providence in "sweeping away great multitudes of the Natives by the small Pox a little before we went thither, that he might make room for us there."

Some English seemed to take grim satisfaction in the Indians' destruction, seeing it as punishment for their sins: one colonist noted that local Indians had argued with the English "about their bounds of Land, notwithstanding they [the English] purchased all they had of them, but the Lord put an end to this quarrell also, by smiting the Indians with a sore Disease, even the small Pox; of which great numbers of them died." Others, like Daniel Gookin and John Eliot, saw the plague as horrifying but with some positive effects: The Natives who survived would be humbled by the tragedy, and perhaps more open to religious conversion.[12]

Natives, of course, saw the epidemic differently. Indians believed in multiple gods and spiritual forces, some beneficent and others malevolent or whimsical, requiring appeasement through prayers and offerings. Among the Ninnimissinuok, two gods were predominant, one associated with creation and light known as Mannitt or Woonand, and one associated with death and darkness, known as Hobbomock or Chepi. In Native belief, Chepi usually caused disease and misfortune, so it made sense to appeal to him when afflicted. As one powwow (Native religious leader) explained to a disapproving Englishman, "all the Corn would die without rain and Chepi the Evil Power withheld that—now said he, If I was to beat you, who would you pray to? to me, or to your Father Ten miles off? you would pray to me to leave off and not beat you any more." The epidemic probably increased Native prayers to the god they believed had afflicted them, at least initially.[13]

Like the epidemic a decade and a half earlier, the plague of 1633 decimated some Indian communities and built up others from the survivors. One of those built up in the aftermath of 1633 was a community of Christian Indians. Waban, a Nipmuc who claimed land rights in Hassanamesit, moved his family to the outskirts of Cambridge Village (later Newton) sometime before 1646, perhaps driven to seek English assistance by disease or by the deaths of family members. Other Nipmucs from Hassanamesit gathered at Waban's wigwam, and they too may have been refugees from disease. Among them were John Wompas, his parents, and his paternal uncles Anthony and Totherswamp (later called Thomas Tray). While visiting among his English neighbors in Cambridge Village, Waban adopted

Christian teachings and practices; he seems to have been a man of some influence, and both his urging and his example encouraged other Natives to follow suit. A similar process took place among the Massachusett Indians of Chickatabut's village, Neponset. Ponompam and his mother moved from Neponset to a nearby English village after the winter of 1633/34, when "almost all our kindred dyed." Living among the English, they learned of the Christian god, and in time they, too, "pray'd to God."[14]

The examples and admonitions of neighboring Christians, which seem to have influenced the conversion of Ponompam and his mother, were the closest thing to missionary work English colonists attempted in the first years after settlement. English tardiness in fulfilling the "main end" of their plantation—"to bring the Indians to the knowledge of the Gospel"—exposed them to harsh criticism from some visitors to the colonies. It is likely that John Eliot's praise of the "Godly Counsels, and Examples [the Indians] have had in all our Christian Families" was an attempt to deflect this criticism. Eliot also justified the delay by arguing that bringing the Indians to "civility" was a necessary preparation for the Christian message, and "gather[ing] them together from their scattered course of life, to cohabitation and civill order" took time.[15]

Indians living near or visiting among English Christian families in the early years of colonization seem to have been very common, if the Indian conversion narratives John Eliot and his colleagues later recorded are representative. These narratives appear in a series of letters Eliot, Thomas Mayhew, and other English missionaries wrote to supporters in England, and undoubtedly played a role in Parliament's approval in 1649 of a charitable organization to fund their work, the Society for the Propagation of the Gospel in New England, later known as the New England Company. As first-person narratives of seventeenth-century American Indians, these conversion accounts are rare and valuable sources, but they are also problematic ones. In the narratives Indians speak for themselves, but their words were translated from Algonquian by English missionaries whose cultural biases undoubtedly affected the translations. The missionaries also coached the Indians to conform their stories to a confessional pattern that reflected a Puritan worldview, not a Native one. Finally, the missionaries' purpose in publishing the narratives—to solicit funds for the continuation of their work—probably shaped their selection of details.[16]

While the narratives are mediated rather than direct and must be used with caution, the fact that some of the narratives include observations unflattering to the English should increase our confidence that they are not entirely biased. For instance, many narratives tell of English colonists encouraging the Indians to become Christians but also recount the Indians' striking aversion to the suggestion. Both of John Wompas's uncles reported visiting English homes where the colonists urged them to "Pray to God"; John's uncle Anthony added that "when the English did bid me pray unto God, I hated it, and would go out of their houses, when they spake of such things to me." Like Anthony, most of the Indians who mentioned colonists preaching the Christian gospel said they "hated" it at first. Even John Eliot admitted ruefully in a letter to English supporters that Indians "so disliked" English colonists speaking about Christianity "that if any began to speake of God and heaven and hell and religion unto them they would presently be gone. So that it was a received and knowne thing to all English that if they were burdensome, and you would have them gone, speake of religion and you were presently rid of them."[17]

The question of what caused the Indians, many of whom initially hated Christianity, to convert has long been a contentious one, some arguing that Indians freely chose Christian conversion out of sincere belief in the new religion, and others that Natives converted for material or political reasons following the devastation of European contact. More recently, scholars have suggested that "convert," which implies a complete transformation from one religious worldview to another, may be an inappropriate term for the "testing, sampling and appending to existing customs and practices" Indians engaged in when they chose to "pray to God." An estimated 2,500 Indians became Christian in New England over the course of the seventeenth century, and while this is a significant number, Christian Indians always remained a minority among Natives of the region, and often a despised one. Most Indians who were introduced to Christianity rejected it, which suggests that pressures to conform to English wishes were not so overwhelming that they removed Indian agency. Those Indians who did choose Christianity did so for a variety of reasons, from sincere belief to a strategy for ensuring survival.[18]

Our earliest accounts of Indian conversion come from the English who preached to them, chiefly John Eliot on the mainland and Thomas Mayhew at Martha's Vineyard. As Puritans, these men understood Christian conversion as a process in which listeners heard the "Word" (the Christian gospel), recognized their sinful state, gained faith in Jesus Christ, and eventually received an assurance that he had saved them. English missionaries looked for signs of this process in the Indians, taught the steps of conversion to their proselytes, and coached them to follow the sequence in their conversion accounts. Thus, Thomas Mayhew reported that after the Indians were reproved for practices such as "having many gods" and "going to Pawwawes," they became "sensible" of their sins. In other words, they recognized and regretted them. The English rejoiced in this recognition; for them it signaled the first step on the path to Christian conversion. But the Indians understood their choice to accept Christianity within a Native construct, not a Christian one.[19]

A Native perspective on conversion is discernible alongside the English perspective in Mayhew's account. Mayhew reports that the Indians invited him to preach to them, and when he arrived, their sachem Towanquatick said, "A long time agon they had wise men, which in a grave manner taught the people knowledge; but they are dead, and their wisdom is buried with them, and now men live a giddy life, in ignorance." Mayhew adds, "He told me that he wondered the English should be almost thirty yeers in the Country and the Indians fools still; but he hoped the time of knowledge was now come; wherefore himself with others desired me to . . . make known the word of God to them in their own tongue." In this telling, Towanquatick informs Mayhew that his people once had "knowledge" but lost it, and that he saw the English as a means to recover ancient Native knowledge, not to give them something new. Speaking in the metaphorical language traditional to Native orators, Towanquatick declared to Mayhew that he "should be to them as one that stands by a running river filling many vessels." Mayhew interpreted this phrase for his English readers as, "even so should I fill them with everlasting knowledge," but he may have been unaware of a meaning that would have been evident to Native listeners. Within Native cosmology, the border between dry land and water was liminal, a threshold from one world to another. Native graveyards were often located near water, which was associated with the underworld and its god Hobbomock, or Chepi. When Towanquatick used the metaphor of Mayhew standing at that threshold filling vessels with water, he was placing Mayhew within a Native spiritual construct, making him the bearer of knowledge from those long dead to living Native people.[20]

Both Mayhew and John Eliot gave multiple accounts of Indians who, like Towanquatick, believed that "Christianity was less a new faith brought by the English than a colonist-spurred revival of ancient Indian practices." The sense of familiarity Towanquatick expressed may have arisen from similarities between Native and Christian beliefs, which included shared concepts of an afterlife, a creator god, punishment for bad actions and reward for good ones. The English noted these parallels with gladness, because they thought they would ease conversion, and they probably did. But belief was not the chief hurdle to Christian conversion. Practice was. The English consistently conflated religious and cultural practice, insisting that the Indians not only learn to pray and believe in Christ, but that they abandon Native cultural ways the English viewed as "superstitious" and embrace patterns of English "civility," including permanent dwelling in one place, laboring six days in the week, and adopting English clothing and hairstyles.[21]

These cultural expectations, and the divisions they created between Christian and non-Christian Indians, proved hard for many Natives to accept. Incurring the anger of leaders and alienating friends was one reason Natives gave for resisting conversion. Another was the pleasure they took in their traditional patterns of living. Waban, the Nipmuc who was instrumental in converting John Wompas's uncle Totherswamp, confessed that before becoming Christian he "did in my heart love wandering about, and our wild courses always." His choice of words clearly reflects English disapproval of "wandering" and "wild courses," as well as his own difficulty in giving up these patterns for the sedentary lifestyle of the English.[22]

Evidence suggests that even Natives who identified themselves as Christians preserved some cultural practices and beliefs frowned on by the English. Natives placed great store in dreams, believing that they were a source of true knowledge conveyed to them by spirit beings. Some even claimed their dreams had prompted them to accept Christianity, thus confirming the old cultural belief within a new Christian practice. English Puritans were ambivalent about dreams; while they acknowledged that some dreams might come from God, they saw such "extraordinary revelation" as a rare exception and they associated Native dreams with the "diabolical" practices of powwows. Archaeological evidence also reveals continuing Native cultural practices among Christian converts, such as burying meaningful Native or English items—"grave goods"—with their dead. Grave goods appear in Christian Indian burials at close to the same rate as in non-Christian Indian graves. Preservation of such practices is consistent with the way many Natives approached Christianity, determining what to embrace based on the practical question, was it "profitable"? In other words, were the ceremonies pleasing, and did the religion benefit its adherents? As Thomas Mayhew observed, many Indians preferred "their own meetings, wayes and customes, being in their account more profitable then ours, wherein they meet with nothing but talking and praying." Mayhew also recounted a visit from Massasoit, sachem of the Wampanoag Indians on the mainland, who challenged Christian Indians to tell "what earthly good things" Christianity offered.[23]

One of the "good things" Natives found in their own tradition was the ministration of powwows. In addition to being religious leaders, powwows provided the benefit of healing the sick. They communicated with the spirits, or *manitou*, that animated all creation. Gifted with unusual spiritual sensitivity, powwows practiced "soul flight," in which their "dream souls" left their bodies and traveled to the spirit realm to gain the assistance of spirit beings. Powwows were also experienced in applying plant and herbal remedies. Brought to the bedside of an ailing person, powwows administered medicines and summoned spirits by burning tobacco, dancing, and praying aloud. Entering a trance state, powwows might embody a spirit and use its power to "suck" sickness out of the afflicted. Powwows also called in friends and relatives to join in their rituals, praying and singing with them. John Wompas's uncle Anthony recalled such experiences, saying "my father and mother prayed to many gods, and I heard them when they did so; and I did so too, because my parents did so: and in my childhood . . . I did delight in it, as dancing and Pawwau[in]g." Daniel Gookin acknowledged the effectiveness of the powwows: "Sometimes broken bones have been set, wounds healed, sick recovered." That effectiveness made many Indians resist conversion, declaring, "if we once pray to God, we must abandon our powows; and then, when we are sick and wounded, who shall heal our maladies?"[24]

The devastating epidemics before and after English settlement underlined the need for supernatural help. Daniel Gookin lamented that Indians prayed more to the mischievous Chepi, whom he and other English colonists identified with the devil, than to the benevolent Mannit, whom they associated with the Christian god. But Native belief in multiple gods provided room for Indians to turn to other gods when their powwows' prayers to Chepi failed. In the midst of the smallpox epidemic of 1633, Natives observed that fewer English became sick, and among those who did catch the disease, fewer died. This suggested that the English god had answered colonists' prayers for help; some Natives hoped he might answer Indian prayers as well. Winthrop reported that Sagamore John promised if he recovered "to live with the English and serve their God" and that "Divers [others], in their sickness, confessed that the Englishmen's God was a good God."[25]

Other material reasons—the desire for English protection, assistance, or access to trade goods—could also prompt conversion. Even in the first years after English settlement, Indian depopulation from epidemic disease placed the English in a position of dominance. The power disparity became even more dramatic after the English conquered the powerful Pequot Indians in the war of 1637–1638, leading many Indian polities to seek English friendship. Accepting Christian instruction was included in the terms of some Indian submissions to the English; Indians desiring to demonstrate their loyalty to the English could have found few better signs than Christian conversion. Contemporary critics speculated that "all this [missionary] worke among them is done and acted thus by the *Indians* to please the *English*, and for applause from them." Indians readily acknowledged a desire to please the English in their conversion narratives. John Wompas's uncle Totherswamp admitted that "at first

I did not think of God, and eternal Life, but only that the English should love me." Others confessed that a desire to protect their land drove their decisions: a Native convert from Nonantum, an Indian settlement near the falls of the Charles River, admitted, "I saw the English took much ground, and I thought if I prayed, the English would not take away my ground." In truth, Christian converts did gain a degree of protection for their land that other Indians did not enjoy, although it came at the cost of accepting a sedentary English lifestyle and, in some cases, agreeing to give up claims to other lands. The Indian converts at Nonantum asked Eliot to petition the General Court to set aside the land they lived on for the exclusive use of their new Christian town, and the court granted the request in 1646. The court later granted land for what came to be called "praying towns" at Natick, Punkapoag, and Hassanamesit, and hedged the grants with restrictions against sale without the express consent of the General Court.[26]

While some Christian Indians acknowledged that material and social considerations influenced their choice to pray like the English, they claimed that these were merely initial attractions, later replaced by spiritual motivation, or faith. When Massasoit challenged Christian Indians to show what "earthly good things" they had received by accepting Christianity, one answered, "We serve not God for cloathing, nor for any outward thing." The movement from outward things—behavior and material considerations—to inward things —faith in Christ—was the goal of conversion. Missionaries admitted that "many" of their Native proselytes remained at the level of outward motivation, but they argued, "certainly 'tis not so in all, but that the power of the Word hath taken place in some, and that inwardly and effectually, but how far savingly time will declare."[27]

In Eliot's view, two of the Indians who had clearly moved from outward action to inward belief were John Wompas's parents. Wampooas and his family moved from Nipmuc Country to Nonantum by 1646. The town had long been a gathering place for Natives who came to catch fish migrating upstream to spawn. But in 1646 Indians gathered there for a different purpose: to hear the Christian preaching of the English minister John Eliot. There was no formal Christian mission yet. Those Indians who considered themselves Christian had acquired their faith by visiting in English houses and listening to Puritan sermons. Foremost among these early believers was Waban, who actively recruited fellow Nipmucs to come learn about the English religion.[28]

Eliot made his first, halting effort to preach the gospel to a group of Massachusett Indians at the Indian settlement of Neponset near Dorchester in September 1646. The timing of this attempt seems to have been influenced both by Indian interest and by outside pressure, including criticisms of the long delay in preaching to the Indians and the 1643 appearance of Puritan minister Roger Williams's *Key into the Language of America*, which seemed to herald Williams's imminent entry into Indian missionary work. Although Eliot had studied the Algonquian language of Massachusett for over two years, aided by a Pequot War captive named Cockenoe, he still could not speak the Native tongue fluently, and the Neponset Indians "despised" his effort. Eliot blamed himself for this failure and increased his efforts to learn to speak Massachusett. By late October 1646, he felt ready to try again. This time, Eliot spoke at Waban's village, Nonantum. Eliot and his colleagues—his Roxbury neighbors Daniel Gookin and Isaac Heath, and fellow minister Thomas Shepherd—met with the Indians in Waban's large wigwam. There they found "many more *Indians*, men, women, children, gathered together from all quarters round about, according to appointment, to meet with us, and learne of us." The Indians Eliot addressed this time were much more open to his message. News of Eliot's preaching seems to have spread widely, and this second attempt likely found Wampooas and his family in attendance. Eliot preached for an hour and a half in Massachusett, with assistance from his Indian interpreter Cockenoe, and then asked if his listeners understood him. It was a valid question; given his recent learning of the language, his vocabulary must have been limited and his pronunciation poor. Whether in truth or out of charity, a "multitude of voices" replied that "they all of them did understand all that which was then spoken to them."[29]

Eliot and his colleagues visited Nonantum again two weeks later, on November 11, 1646, and found "many more Indians met together than the first time we came to them." Children were present with their parents, and Eliot and his colleagues turned to them first, teaching a simple catechism, or series of questions and answers on key points of Christian doctrine. Young John Wompas, about nine years old at the time, would have been seated among the other children. Eliot turned to each child in turn and asked a question in Massachusett, "Who made you and all the world?" Their answers came individually and then in chorus: "God." For this first catechizing, Eliot asked only two additional questions:

"Who doe you looke should save you and redeeme you from sinne and hell?"

"Jesus Christ."

"How many commandements hath God given you to keepe?"

"Ten."[30]

Down the row of children he went, receiving each child's reply, until the last of them could answer without prompting.

Eliot's third meeting with the Nonantum Indians on November 26, 1646, seems to have had a profound effect on John Wompas's father Wampooas, leading to a lifelong commitment to the Christian religion. John's mother, too, became an ardent convert. Hers was the first question Eliot's ministerial colleague Thomas Shepherd recorded at a lecture at Nonantum on December 9, 1646. Speaking in Nipmuc, which Cockenoe assisted Eliot in translating, she wondered if her silent agreement with her husband's vocal prayers—"if I like what he saith, and my heart goes with it"—also qualified as prayer. Shepherd noted with approval her belief that prayer should be "an inward action of the heart," not just an "externall action of the lips." John Wompas's aunt, Totherswamp's wife, was the second to ask a question, "Whether a husband should do well to pray with his wife, and yet continue in his passions & be angry with his wife?" Here again, Shepherd was struck with the wisdom and "modesty" of the question, which indirectly offered both approval and rebuke to her husband, the former for beginning to pray, the latter for past and apparently continuing bad temper.[31]

Totherswamp's wife's question alludes to the forceful demonstration of male authority within northeastern Indian societies in the contact era. Although there were a number of female sachems near the time of English settlement in New England, men usually held political office, and their authority extended to family as well as community life. In some instances, Native men exerted their authority through physical dominance of their wives. Although Englishmen wielded authority in political and cultural life too, the Puritan colonists considered wife beating sinful. Indian converts, under pressure from the English, made a strict law against wife beating. In September 1647, a court was held at Nonantum, attended by all the Indian converts, the Massachusetts colony's governor John Winthrop, and many other English colonists. Wampooas was one of the Indians presented for judgment. He made a public acknowledgment and apology for having beaten his wife. Clearly remorseful, Wampooas made no excuses for a behavior that Eliot claimed was "in former times . . . very usuall" among Native people. When an English visitor pointed out that abusing his wife was, in the Christian interpretation of marriage, "cruelty to his own body, and against Gods Commandement," Wampooas turned his face to the wall and wept. Eliot, clearly moved, considered this such "modest, penitent, and melting behavior" that he and the other English immediately forgave him. The Indians conducting the court, however, still required Wampooas to pay a fine.[32]

Wampooas was fortunate to have the support of his wife and brothers in his new faith, but he acknowledged the difficulties many converts faced. During a question and answer period following Eliot's lecture, Wampooas said: "Because wee pray to God, other Indians abroad in the countrey hate us and oppose us, the English on the other side suspect us, and feare us to be still such as doe not pray at all." Suspicion and resentment flourished on both sides of the religious divide. Many Indians were offended by the exclusivist approach of the English, who said the Christian god was the only god and therefore Indians worshiped the devil. Even some Natives who later converted, such as Waban, were initially put off by such a brazen claim. For their part, the English seemed unable to see distinctions among believing and unbelieving Indians and were quick to ascribe any reported wrongdoing to all Indians. Unconverted Indians, particularly sachems, saw conversion as a rejection of their authority, fought against it, and derided and harassed Native Christians.[33]

Family members of John Wompas's mother were among those who seem to have hated the new religion. In 1647, she lay dying of an infection she contracted while recovering from childbirth. As her family gathered at her bedside, she urged her daughters and her son John to maintain their commitment to Christianity after she was gone. "I shall now dye," she declared, "and when I am dead, your Grand-Father and Grand-mother, and Uncles, &c. will send for you to come live amongst them, and promise you great matters, and tell you what pleasant living it is among them; But do not believe them, and I charge you never hearken unto them, nor live amongst them; for they pray not to God, keep not the Sabbath, commit all manner of sins and are not punished for it: but I charge you live here, for here they pray unto God, the Word of God is taught, sins are suppressed, and punished by Laws; And therefore I charge you live here all your days." True to her prediction, soon after her death her family sent messengers and came in person to urge her two grown daughters to come live with them, but Wampooas, their stepfather, refused, "not only as adjudging it evil, but because of their mothers charge." His wife's dying speech, like the sachem Towanquatick's metaphor of filling vessels by a river, reflects both Native and English cultural patterns. The story, recounted by John Eliot, is typical of the English genre of deathbed speeches intended to inspire readers to reform their lives before death caught them unawares. Crafted to fit that genre, the account carries the implicit message that Wampooas's wife's prediction came from the Christian god, evidenced by both its fulfillment and its Christian purpose. But the prediction also fits into Native patterns of divination. When a Native person received knowledge in a dream or vision, she or he conveyed that knowledge to another person, thus "performing" and completing the dream. By telling her husband and children what would happen after her death and bidding them to remain among the Christian Indians, John's mother followed a Native pattern for a Christian purpose, simultaneously demonstrating and helping to create a uniquely Native Christianity.[34]

His mother's death may have provided the occasion for young John Wompas to move to Roxbury to live with the English colonist Isaac Heath. Wampooas had sought such a move for his son the previous year. Just days after Eliot's third sermon at Nonantum in November 1646, Wampooas visited Eliot's house in Roxbury and asked the preacher to take his nine-year-old son and five other Indian children and youths into English homes "to be trained up among the English." The request startled Eliot, coming so close on the heels of Wampooas's own conversion. Eliot asked why he wanted the children to be raised in Roxbury, rather than by their own parents, and Wampooas answered, "because they would grow rude and wicked at home, and would never come to know God, which they hoped they should doe if they were constantly among the English." Eliot praised Wampooas for his devotion and agreed to find homes for the two young men, but he suggested that the younger children stay with their parents a little longer. It is not clear exactly when John made the move to Roxbury, but he was there by 1651.[35]

Wampooas's attempt to send John to live with the English strikes the modern reader as strange, just as it did Eliot. Indians usually declined to place their children with the English, citing the harshness they observed in English child-rearing practices. Indeed, it is unlikely that Wampooas intended the placement to be permanent. It is possible that concern for John's physical welfare guided his father's decision. He may have believed John would be safer among the English, who seemed shielded from the ravages of disease that had decimated Native communities. The reason Eliot provides—apparently the only one Wampooas expressed aloud—is that Wampooas wanted John to "come to know God" and he thought such knowledge was more likely to be found among the English. Eliot seized on that reason as a welcome demonstration of Christian conversion, an additional sign of the commitment Wampooas and his wife had previously shown when "out of desire to live where the word of God was taught . . . [they] fetched all the corne they spent, sixteen miles upon their backs from the place of their planting" and resettled in Nonantum.[36]

Eliot recorded Wampooas's hope that, once John learned the religious ways of his English hosts, he would return to teach his Native kin and friends about the Christian god. Other Native converts expressed similar hopes. Piambow, a fellow Nipmuc of Hassanamesit, recalled that after hearing the English preach, "we resolved we would pray to God, and carry our children to *Roxbury*, that they might learn to pray." Converts like Piambow knew that Puritan parents were expected to provide both physical and spiritual care to all who lived in their household, their own children as well as servants or apprentices living with the family. They may also have hoped that

Roxbury would be a haven from disease and a place where children could gain English allies, knowledge, and skills that would help them and their families survive the turmoil English settlement had brought. Isaac Heath, John's host in Roxbury, was the ruling elder of Roxbury Church, a sort of lay assistant to ministers John Eliot and Samuel Danforth. He was also Eliot's close friend and a supporter of his missionary work. For these reasons Heath likely felt an obligation to ensure that his young charge received regular religious instruction in his home.[37]

In April 1651, just four years after his wife's death, Wampooas himself lay dying. Epidemic illness runs a bleak thread through the records of John Eliot and his colleagues' ministry among the Indians. Both of John Wompas's parents died of disease, as did many other converts, their spouses and children, and others at school or working among the English. Wampooas left no record of what led him to convert or which aspects of Native belief he discarded and which he retained, but both his actions and his words indicate that he maintained his commitment to Christianity up to the time of his death. Eliot wrote that his calm acceptance of death—a model of Christian submission—"hath greatly strengthened the Faith of the living to be constant." He also wrote down and translated a sermon Wampooas preached from his sickbed, declaring "that God giveth us three mercies in this world; the first is health and strength; the second is food and cloaths; the third is sicknesse and death; and when wee have had our share in the two first, why should wee not be willing to take our part in the third?"[38]

Eliot went to sit with Wampooas in his final days of life and was deeply affected by the visit, declaring, "nor am I able to write his Storie without weeping." Eliot was not alone with Wampooas when he died. Crowds of Native Christians came "to heare his dying words," an event Eliot considered remarkable because Indians—probably responding to the wave of contagious epidemics—"flie and avoyde with terrour such as lye dying." Eliot recorded that after speaking to the Indians, Wampooas turned to Eliot and charged him to continue the Christian education of his son John and other Native youth, saying, "Foure yeares and a Quarter since, I came to your house, and brought some of our Children to dwell with the *English*, now I dye, I strongly intreate you . . . that you would strongly intreate Elder *Heath* . . . and the rest, which have our Children, that they may be taught to know God, so as that they may teach their Countrymen, because such an example would doe great good among them." Next, Wampooas turned back to the assembled Indians and urged them to continue the work he had supported but not seen fulfilled: the gathering of an Indian church at Natick. "I now shall dye," he declared, "but Jesus Christ calleth you that live to goe to Naticke, that there the Lord might rule over you, that you might make a Church, and have the Ordinance of God among you, believe in his Word, and doe as hee commandeth you." As Wampooas was one of the "first and principall men" among the Christian Indians, his dying words carried great weight with the Indians gathered at his bedside. Eliot reported that "they could not heare [his words] without weeping." Indeed, Eliot claimed that long after his death they repeated his counsel among themselves, so that, in Eliot's judgment, "he did more good by his death, then he could have done by his life."[39]

Whatever good Wampooas's dying speeches did for those who gathered in his final hours, his death left young John Wompas without father or mother, a casualty of the epidemic diseases cutting a deadly swath through the Indians of seventeenth-century New England. John was no more than fourteen years old at his father's death, bereft of both parents and living with an elderly English couple in Roxbury. Born into one world, raised in another—is it any wonder that John Wompas sought a place in both and found one in neither?

CHAPTER TWO

"Prask That Was Wife to John Wompas"

The Pequot War and the Enslavement of Ann Prask

The Indian Netorah in the Court . . . owned that the Pequit Indians came to them as they fled before the English, and that the Sasqua and the Paquamuck Indians went into the swamp along with them; and the English offering of them quarter, they came out of the swamp and resigned themselves and their deer-skins and wampum to them. Also says that he knew neither the mother nor grandmother of this Prask that was wife to John Wompas.

—Examination of Netorah, Fairfield, Connecticut Colony, September 21, 1683

ANN PRASK WAS BORN in Mahican Country—Mawhegemuck— near present-day Albany, New York, at least five years before John Wompas's birth in Nipmuc Country. Like John, Ann came from a

Native community and was raised in an English one, and like him she lost her mother and father at an early age. The first loss came through her mother's premature death. The second came through her violent separation from her father as a captive in the Pequot War, the first major Indian-English clash following colonization of the land of the Ninnimissinuok. Ann and John shared the common experience of straddling Indian and English worlds, but Prask entered English society as a common slave—the polar opposite of John Wompas's privileged position as an Indian scholar. One day, the enslaved girl would marry the Native scholar, bringing him an endowment of land vast enough to launch his sales career. Ann Prask would also bring John her experience of war and Indian slavery. Although the impact of these experiences is more difficult to trace, it must have informed John's attitude toward the English, particularly after both scourges resurfaced during King Philip's War of 1675–1678.

When Sassacus, paramount sachem of the Pequot Indians, arrived at the site of one of the two great Pequot forts near the mouth of Connecticut's Mystic River on May 26, 1637, he found a smoldering ruin. Mystic Fort had held over seventy Indian wigwams, each normally housing five to ten people. An additional one hundred and fifty Native soldiers had arrived at the fort the day before, after learning that the English army was marching against the Pequots. This brought the total number at the fort to over five hundred. Now at least four hundred occupants of Mystic Fort lay dead in the ashes of their houses—men, women, and children.[1]

The English burning of Mystic Fort was the awful climax of several years of sporadic violence and failed negotiations. Once the most powerful nation in the region, the Pequots had first tried to harness and then to resist the rising English power. Pequots had killed an English trader and his crew and then refused to surrender the killers to the English, a condition of their trade agreement. Tensions between the Pequots and the English escalated in the impasse; after English soldiers under John Endicott slashed and burned their way through Indian villages on Block Island and the southeastern Connecticut coast, the Pequots laid siege to Saybrook Fort at the mouth of the Connecticut River, killing any Englishmen who ven-

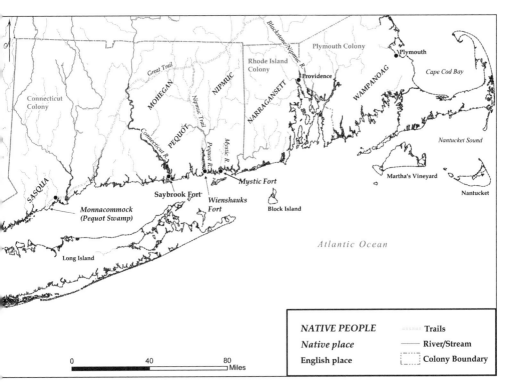

Figure 1. Key sites in the Pequot War, 1637 [Map by Jen Macpherson]

tured outside. On May 16, 1637, Connecticut Colony declared war on the Pequots, and on May 26 a force of seventy-seven English soldiers backed by several hundred Mohegan and Narragansett Indian allies attacked the Pequot stronghold of Mystic Fort. The English army made little headway in the initial fight. Outnumbered and afraid that at any moment more Pequots would arrive, the English were quick to embrace Captain John Mason's suggestion that they burn the village. Mason set the first fire himself: "Entering into a Wigwam, [he] brought out a fire-brand, after hee had wounded many in the house, then hee set fire on the West-side where he entered." From the other entrance to the fort, Captain John Underhill laid a line of powder: "The fires of both meeting in the center of the Fort blazed most terribly, and burnt all in the space of halfe an houre."[2]

The scale of the destruction was staggering. Sassacus and three to four hundred Indian soldiers had marched that morning from the main Pequot fort of Weinshauks, a few miles to the southwest. They may have heard gunshots from the initial skirmishes and shouts from the English and Pequots fighting between the wigwams before Mason's order to burn everything. They could scarcely have missed the smoke billowing from the burning fort, or the dying cries of hundreds of people trapped in collapsing houses, barred by English guns from exiting the inferno. Only a handful escaped. The acrid smell of smoke and charred flesh would have reached the Pequot soldiers approaching Mystic Fort long before they arrived, dread dogging their steps, but they could not have realized the full extent of the disaster until they saw it for themselves.[3]

The English had retreated to the base of the hill on which the Indian fort sat, and from there they watched Sassacus and his men approach the scorched palisades, look inside, and then, as if suddenly struck mad, stomp their feet and tear clumps of hair from their heads. Spotting the English nearby, the Pequots careened down the slope toward them. The English fired their guns to warn them off, and the Indians veered away, but they continued running, back and forth, shooting wildly aimed arrows into the sky, crazed with horror and grief. Three times over the next few hours Sassacus's army would attack the English near the destroyed fort, and then harry them all along their six-mile path of withdrawal to the sea. In the fierce skirmishes of that day, the English added another one hundred and fifty Pequot deaths to the hundreds burned in the fort before reaching the safety of their ships in the harbor. English casualties were relatively few: two men killed, and about forty wounded.[4]

The Mystic Fort massacre was the pivotal event of the Pequot War. In their unrestrained violence, the English succeeded in quelling a foe that had boldly defied them for over a year. The Pequots had intimidated other Indians throughout the region for well over a decade, cowing many of them into submission by their threats or attacks. They had threatened the English as well, vowing "wholly to roote them out of the land, & to fish their corne with their carcasses." In the end, the English proved far more savage.[5]

The burning of Mystic Fort, which took the lives of men, women, and children, was a violation of Native norms of warfare. Among Indians of the Northeast, warfare was a limited business—

Europeans mocked it as "more for pastime, than to conquer and subdue enemies." But it was limited for a reason: killing was not the primary aim of Indian warfare. Indians were not trying to obliterate their enemies or seize their land; rather, they fought to defend their rights, to take captives to replenish their population, and, particularly for young men, to win prestige for their military exploits. It would be unthinkable to simply massacre people wholesale. Even the Narragansett Indian allies of the English protested against the slaughter at the fort, declaring that it was "*mach it*" (bad) because "it is too furious, and slays too many men." Such destruction was not only savage but wasteful, because it also killed the women and children that Indian victors normally incorporated into their population or used as gifts to create or cement alliances.[6]

Among Europeans, too, women and children were generally spared in warfare, which was supposed to be waged far from civilian areas. That ideal was not always met; the horrors of the previous century's religious wars testified to that. In the early years of English settlement, Indians were unsure whether the English followed norms similar to their own or not. Recorded Native statements before the Mystic Fort massacre show the Indians probing English military practice, trying to ascertain if they would behave in the manner Natives expected of one another. Through their neighbor Roger Williams, a Puritan minister exiled to Rhode Island after clashing with Massachusetts authorities, the Narragansetts sent a message to the English preparing for war "that it would be pleasing to all natives, that women and children be spared." During the siege of Saybrook Fort in March 1637, Pequot soldiers parlaying with Lieutenant Lion Gardiner asked if the English "did use to kill women and children?" Gardiner's ominous answer—"they should see thereafter"—signaled to the Pequots that the English played by different rules. Angrily, the Pequots declared that they would kill women and children too. Gardiner's bit of bravado may have been responsible for the fact that just weeks later, on April 23, 1637, Pequot attacks on Wethersfield, Connecticut, led to nine English deaths—including three women.[7]

In the days that followed the conflagration at Mystic Fort, the stunned survivors of the Pequot nation—those who had escaped the attack, and hundreds of others from the fort at Weinshauks—debated what to do. Sassacus was "all for blood," but few others shared his desire to keep fighting. Some called for the sachem's death, blaming him for bringing the English down on their heads, but Sassacus's counselors dissuaded them. Most, appalled at the willingness of the English to kill so indiscriminately, wanted to get far, far away, and the largest body of Pequots began traveling westward, aiming for the Hudson River valley. They moved slowly, hampered by the need to forage along the way and to allow the elderly and small children to keep up. By early July these Pequots had gotten as far as present-day Fairfield, Connecticut, about sixty miles west of the Mystic Fort.[8]

This was the territory of the Sasqua Indians, whose village lay next to a dense swamp called Monnacommock. If the Sasquas were one of the many groups the Pequots had brought under subjection in the previous decade, they would have been obligated to offer shelter to them. But the Sasquas may simply have given the Pequots refuge as an act of Native hospitality. Either way, joining their fate to the Pequots would alter the Sasquas' lives forever.[9]

The English, now joined by soldiers from Massachusetts, determined to make a "final destruction" of the Pequots; they boarded pinnaces and began to sail westward. Like the fleeing Pequots, they went slowly, stopping frequently to send out parties of men to scout for any signs of their fleeing enemies. Near the Quinnipiac River the English captured and executed several Pequot soldiers but promised one his life if he would search and bring news of Sassacus's whereabouts. The captive located the sachem and his people, stayed with them a few days, then slipped away to report to the English. His disappearance raised Sassacus's suspicions, and he and twenty or thirty men broke off from the slower group and sped north. Acting on the intelligence brought by their Pequot captive, the English continued westward. On July 13, a small party of Englishmen discovered the Sasqua village sheltering the Pequots, but an Indian sentinel spied them first and gave an alarm. Before the English could fire their weapons, all of the Indians, "Pequods [as well] as Natives of the Place," had retreated into the boggy depths of the swamp.[10]

No one could blame the Sasquas for joining the Pequots in Monnacommock Swamp. The refugees must have told the Sasquas about the English destruction of Mystic Fort, the wholesale slaughter of men, women, and children. To the Pequots, the English must have appeared monstrous and unpredictable, an opinion they would likely have shared with their Sasqua hosts. Joining the Pequots in the refuge of Monnacommock, whose thick undergrowth and unstable ground would significantly hamper an English attack, must have seemed the Sasquas' only option.

Among those Indians taking refuge in the swamp were a man called Romanock and his daughter Prask, who would later marry John Wompas. Romanock was originally from a place called Pachequage near the Hudson River, about a three-day journey from the seashore. A noted military leader, Romanock had traveled far from his birthplace, serving as a "captain" among various Native groups from his homeland to western Connecticut and picking up wives along the way. One wife, the mother of Prask, lived in Mahican Country. When she died, leaving Prask motherless, Romanock traveled there to retrieve the child and brought her to Sasqua to live with him. Given rumors that Prask's mother and grandmother had rights to land at Sasqua, this move may have been a return to her ancestral homeland. Prask was reportedly about five years old when she came to Sasqua. No one recorded how long she resided there before the Pequot exiles arrived, but it was most likely a short time. In fact, Prask may not yet have learned the local Algonquian dialect, which would have made the next series of events doubly terrifying for her.[11]

In the swamp, Prask, Romanock, and the other Indians—eighty men and two hundred women and children—waited for the English to attack. The scouting party's alarm had brought the rest of the English soldiers running, and they began to form a circle around the swamp. The Pequots and Sasquas sheltered inside could hear the English outside, shouting orders in their odd, barking language. Indian soldiers patrolled the edges of the refuge as women and children huddled together in the deepest brush, listening: A rustling sound, twigs snapping, then shouts as several English soldiers broke through the maze of undergrowth. More shouts, then loud cracks and a burning smell, as if lightning had struck nearby. Screams of pain and struggle carried back to the waiting women and children for long minutes, then quieted. A dozen English under Lieutenant Richard Davenport had plunged into the swamp ahead of orders and been attacked by the Indians on guard. Several Indian soldiers were killed and three English were badly wounded before they withdrew. Rather than attempt to enter the swamp again, the English stood guard outside all through the night. The recent addition of 160 Massachusetts soldiers under Captains Stoughton, Trask, and Patrick had swelled the English ranks to two hundred. With so many men, they could entirely surround the swamp, standing only twelve feet apart to prevent any escape.[12]

The continuing siege and the deaths of Native defenders brought the reality of their peril home to the Sasquas. As Puritan minister and war chronicler William Hubbard put it, the "Indians of the Place, who had for Company sake run with their Guests the Pequods into the Swamp, did not love their Friendship so well as to be killed with them also for Company sake." Instead, the Sasquas sent a message to the English that they "desired a Parley, which was granted." Thomas Stanton, a skilled interpreter, volunteered to enter the swamp alone to treat with the Indians, promising them mercy if they surrendered, so long as none of them had shed English blood. After only a short time he returned, bringing with him the Sasquas' sachem, plus several other men and their families. Over the next two hours, nearly two hundred old men, women, and children, Pequots as well as Sasquas, emerged and surrendered, leaving only male Indian soldiers, including Prask's father Romanock, behind.[13]

The male soldiers had good reason to stay behind in the swamp. In both Native and European practices of war, male combatants unfortunate enough to be captured were executed. Indians executed male captives because they were considered dangerous and difficult to assimilate. They kept women and children alive, incorporating them into their society as slaves or sometimes as replacements for deceased kin. Europeans, too, executed male captives guilty of shedding blood in an unjust or unconventional war. English forces had already executed a large number of male combatants captured in the days after the massacre, including twenty-three Pequot captives taken aboard Captain John Gallop's ship, executed, and dumped into the sea. The Pequots sheltered in Monnacommock Swamp almost certainly learned of this brutal execution from the Pequot warrior spared execution if he would pursue the fleeing Pequot refugees and bring news back to the English. Although Romanock was not a hostile Pequot deserving death if captured, he could not count on the English making that distinction. He remained inside the swamp when the women and children—including Prask—surrendered.[14]

Securing the captives nearby, the English kept a chain of guards around the swamp. If Indians approached the circle, the English fired on them, hoping to keep them penned in until morning. Just before daybreak, a group of Indian soldiers tried to force themselves through the guards commanded by Captain Patrick, whooping and yelling to intimidate the English, who beat them back once, and then again. The Indians shifted their attack to another point in the circle, shouting even louder. The noise and commotion grew so intense that the alarmed English on the other side of the swamp broke their siege and raced to the point of attack, firing "small shot" to drive the Indians back. At that, the Indians wheeled about, "pressed violently upon Captain Patrick," and broke through the English line—a successful feint. Sixty or seventy Indian soldiers—Romanock among them—escaped at once. Others remained in the swamp. English soldiers later found several clumps of Indian men within Monnacommock, sitting and apparently awaiting their deaths, which they received at English hands. English chronicler William Hubbard wrote disdainfully that these Natives were "killed in the Swamp like sullen Dogs, that would rather in their Self-willedness and Madness sit still to be shot through or cut in Peices, than receive their Lives for the asking."[15]

The English pursued the escaped Indians for a short time, finding several dead of their wounds along the way, but the large number of captives they had taken made an extended chase impossible. Abandoning the pursuit, they returned to the site of the battle. The English had taken nearly two hundred captives in the swamp fight. They sent eighteen of them, two women and sixteen boys, out of the country as slaves, one to England, and seventeen to the English colony of Providence Island, part of an archipelago between present-day Jamaica and Costa Rica. The rest would be distributed among the English and their Indian allies as domestic slaves or, in the words of Uncas's agent Foxon, "under people." This was the meaning of surrendering to "mercy"—being allowed to live, but as slaves.[16]

The child Prask was among the nearly fifty captives sent to slavery in Massachusetts. The Massachusetts soldiers had come to Connecticut in at least four watercraft—a pinnace, a pink, and two boats.

They put one hundred captives aboard these vessels along with forty-five English soldiers and sailed eastward to Saybrook Fort at the mouth of the Pequot River. The boats had carried only ninety men from Massachusetts; they were returning with nearly 150 passengers and would have been horribly cramped. In addition to suffering from overcrowding and possible seasickness, young Ann Prask must have been miserable with grief. Romanock's escape had left her bereft of father as well as mother, and she may also have lacked the usual comfort of Native kin. Depending on how recently her mother died, Prask may not have known any of the Sasqua Indians well. In fact, she may not have been able to speak with them; the Mahican language of her homeland was a different dialect than those spoken by the Sasquas or Pequots.[17]

   After leaving the fort, the boats likely carried the captives and their guards eastward through Long Island Sound and northeast through the maze of islands in Narragansett Bay to Providence, where Massachusetts exile and religious radical Roger Williams lived. He had served as a key negotiator in securing Indian allies for the English and had offered shelter and provisions to the English army returning from the Mystic fight in June. Troops returning from Connecticut in July may have used Williams's home as a way station as well. The child Prask must have been in a fog of confusion and misery during this last stage of her long journey from her Mahican homeland. But not knowing the Pequot or Sasqua languages had one advantage: it spared her from the speculation of her fellow captives, who must have been sick with fear at what would become of them once they reached Boston.

What actually happened to the captives taken in the Pequot War remains a question nearly four hundred years after the event. Almost three hundred were taken captive in the fighting of 1637. Eighteen were sold out of the country as slaves. The remainder were also enslaved, but in New England. One hundred and forty-eight were sent to Massachusetts, one hundred remained with the English in Connecticut, and thirty-three were distributed to Native allies. Around two hundred Pequots later surrendered themselves to the Narragansetts and Mohegans. These captives, in addition to the thirty previously given to the Narragansetts, remained with their

Native captors. Thus, there were close to five hundred captives of the Pequot War in all, half residing among the Mohegans and Narragansetts, who were expected to send yearly tribute on their behalf to the English, and half among English families in Massachusetts and Connecticut. Although this is a substantial number of captives, neither English nor Native records give specifics about the exact nature or intended length of their enslavement. Almost no reference to Pequot captives appears in English records after about 1646. Historians have concluded that most of the captives ran away from the English within a few months or years of their capture, echoing Captain John Mason's claim that the English "intend[ed] to keep them as Servants, but they could not endure that Yoke; few of them continuing any considerable time with their Masters."[18]

Mason used the term "servant" rather than "slave" to describe the captives, but the terms were inexact in the early seventeenth century, when the status of slavery itself was somewhat fluid. One could be an unpaid "servant" for life or a "slave" for a set term of years. Race was not yet indelibly associated with slavery, as it would be in the eighteenth century. Europeans as well as Africans and Indians could be enslaved, permanently or temporarily, for various reasons, including voluntarily selling themselves into slavery to relieve debts, pay for boat passage to the colonies, or secure material support. Massachusetts Bay Colony would frame its law on slavery in 1641, just a few years after the Pequot War and likely in response to the influx of war captives. The law declared that there would "never be any bond slavery, villenage or Captivity amongst us," with three exceptions: those that "willingly sell themselves or are sold to us," those whose crimes led to judicial sentences of enslavement, and "lawful Captives taken in just wars."[19]

Christian notions of justice infused early modern Europeans' discussions of "just war." Going to war without just cause would bring God's wrath upon an army and a people. Just cause might include being repeatedly attacked or provoked; even then, the victim was not justified in counterattacking without first seeking peace. As representatives of the New England colonies asserted, "The English engage not in any warr before they have full and satisfying evidence, that in all respects and considerations it is just, and before peace upon just termes hath been offered and refused." The English believed that these requirements had been met in the Pequot War; the Pequots had refused repeatedly to fulfill the terms of their treaty with the English—turning over the murderers of the English trader Captain Stone—and the Pequots had besieged and attacked English communities in Connecticut, killing or capturing a number of colonists. Thus, the English felt justified in responding with the full force of arms, destroying their enemies in battle or after capture, and seizing their lands by right of conquest. Because those who provoked war deserved death according to theories of just war, perpetual enslavement of guilty combatants was considered a "mercy." The fact that the English applied just war thinking to captives in the Pequot War can be seen in a letter sent to John Winthrop Jr. in 1647. Begging Winthrop's assistance in securing the return of his runaway Pequot maid servant, the writer declared, "be pleased to understand she was a child of death, delivered to him by the Bay in the time of the Pecod ware." In other words, as the child of hostiles in a just war, she was subject to either death or mercy, defined as perpetual enslavement. Hugo Grotius, whose *De Jure Belli* was well known to contemporaries, claimed that the right to make war captives into perpetual slaves was common to all nations, and that it applied to women and children of the warring society as well as combatants. It also applied to their descendants.[20]

Whether or not the English intended the status of perpetual slavery for all the captives of the Pequot War is unclear from the 1641 law or other surviving records. The law of 1641 said nothing about the length of enslavement, but contemporary records of people who sold themselves or were sentenced to slavery show that their terms rarely exceeded ten years. Forty years after the Pequot War, laws governing the Indians taken in King Philip's War distinguished between captive Indians who had "imbrued their hands in English blood" and those caught up involuntarily in the fighting who surrendered themselves to the English. Those who had killed English colonists were executed, and their enslaved children were "at the disposall of their masters," as long as those masters took care to instruct them in "civility & Christian religion." In other words, they were perpetual slaves who could be retained or sold, subject to their owner's wishes. Children of surrendered or friendly Indians who had not killed English colonists in the war also served as servants in

English households, but they were to be released at the age of twenty-four. The fact that release did not always occur is evident in at least one case in which a Native captured as a child and still held to service as late as 1720 challenged the enslavement in court.[21]

Messages sent between Governor John Winthrop of Massachusetts Bay Colony and Roger Williams of Rhode Island suggest that in the weeks after the Pequot War's end, the captives' status was a subject of debate, not just between the two men, but also between English and Indian leaders. In June 1637, one month after the Mystic Fort massacre, Roger Williams wrote to John Winthrop to report a visit from Assotemuit, a messenger from the Narragansett sachems Canonicus and Miantonomi. The messenger was reluctant to discuss the sachems' wishes for the captives outright, but based on the "hints" Williams was able to gather, Williams reported that the Narragansett sachems "incline to mercy and to give them [the Pequots] their lives." Apparently conscious of the English belief that captives guilty of killing Englishmen merited death, Assotemuit insisted that none of the Pequot captives among the Narragansetts had done so. Instead of death, the Narragansetts "liked well that they should live with the English and themselves as Slaves." Such a result was consistent with traditional Native practices of incorporating war captives into the victors' society. Men, who were troublesome captives, were killed; women and children were enslaved or adopted. While the Narragansett sachems "liked" the idea of enslaving the Pequots, their version of that enslavement was a comparatively gentle one: they should be "used kindly, have howses and goods and fields given them."[22]

Roger Williams made a similar plea for "merciful" treatment of the captives. Drawing from his study of the Old Testament, which was full of "Types," or examples of how to deal with aggressors in a war, Williams admitted that those guilty of shedding English blood merited execution: "If they have deserved Death, tis Sinn to spare." But those who were drawn innocently into the conflict—women, children, and subject peoples like the Sasqua—deserved mercy. Distributing these captives to service among the English and their Indian allies was prudent as a way to "weaken" and "despoil" the enemy. By incorporating captives, the Narragansetts would strengthen their own people and deprive their enemies of "all comfort of wife and children." But Williams believed the service should be temporary: "I beseech you well weigh if after a due time of trayning up to labour, and restraint, they ought not to be set free: yet so as without danger of adjoyning to the Enemie."[23]

No reply from Winthrop survives. He may have agreed with Williams that a short term of slavery was best. A letter to Winthrop from another correspondent suggests this possibility. Patrick Copeland, a colonist in Bermuda, wrote to Winthrop of his intention to "have trained . . . up" the Pequot captives sent to him "in the principles of Religion; and so when they had been fit for your Plantation, have returned them againe to have done God some service in being Instruments to doe some good upon their Country men." This arrangement sounds very similar to the plans John Eliot and his missionary colleagues had for John Wompas and other Indian children, plans that Wampooas apparently set in motion by bringing his son and other Nipmuc youth to Roxbury. Once these youths had become thoroughly acquainted with English ways and taught the Christian religion, they could return home to "doe some good" to their Native kin. On the other hand, Winthrop may have thought that "perpetuall servitude" was an appropriate, even positive, condition for the Pequot women and children. It would weaken the Pequots, preventing them from regaining the power that had allowed them to threaten and raid surrounding Indians and the English, while at the same time giving them access to the "principles of Religion" and the benefits of English culture.[24]

Of course, concern for the well-being of the captive Indians was not the only, or even the primary, consideration for Winthrop, Williams, and other English people. Massachusetts colonists were desperate for labor, particularly domestic help, which was very hard to come by in the first decades of settlement. Indian women were known as diligent workers, and Indian children could easily be taught to perform the myriad household tasks burdening English women. English eagerness for domestic help is evident in the clamor for captives that began almost immediately after the Mystic Fort massacre. Israel Stoughton, captain of the Massachusetts forces, sent Governor Winthrop a letter reporting that "48 or 50" women and children would be arriving in Boston by boat and asking for a particular Indian woman as a servant, "the fairest and largest that I saw amongst them, to whom I have given a coat to cloathe her." At the same time, Stoughton passed along the appeals of his steward Richard Callicot, Lieutenant Richard Davenport, and their Massachusett Indian ally Sassamon for young female captives. The fact that those requesting captives had fought in the Pequot War suggests that officers and even soldiers may have had some claim on captives. Roger Williams added his voice to the chorus of wishes, writing Governor Winthrop "to request the keeping and bringing up of one of the children. . . . I have fixed mine eye on this litle one with the red about his neck." John Winthrop's and Hugh Peter's letters also mention having or requesting captives.[25]

Such a request may have been how Joshua Hewes of Roxbury, Massachusetts, obtained the young Prask. Hewes was a prominent settler in Roxbury. Though only twenty-five years old, he was sergeant of Roxbury's militia company and was one of the largest landholders in his community. Ten unnamed men from Roxbury served in the Pequot War, and Hewes may have been one of them. Like Israel Stoughton, he may have examined the captives while they were still in Connecticut and later requested a particular one from the colony government. If Hewes had not been one of the Roxbury soldiers, he could have purchased Prask later from among the unclaimed captives who arrived in Boston in July 1637 and taken her home to Roxbury to assist his wife Mary with her household chores. Prask, soon renamed Ann, joined the Hewes household very early in Joshua and Mary's married life; she was there for the birth and death of their first child, the births of their next two children, and the sickness and death of Mary in 1655, when the surviving children were thirteen and nine years old. Child rearing and tending to the household for an ailing mistress were precisely the kinds of domestic tasks that made the labor-poor English so eager to claim Pequot War captives.[26]

As domestic servants, Pequot captives seem to have experienced the same range of treatment as other servants in colonial New England. Massachusetts's law of 1641 declared that slaves, including captives of just wars, "shall have all the liberties and Christian usages which the law of god established in Israell concerning such persons doeth morally require." The English defined "Christian usage" as bodily care and religious instruction through household

devotions and weekly church services. For Puritans, religious instruction also meant teaching servants to read, so that they could
take in God's word themselves. Two Pequot captives who died of
sickness in Roxbury in 1646 suggest that this standard was being
met: both were considered "hopeful," meaning they were on the
path to church membership. One of them could read. Another captive in Dorchester learned to both read and write and became a
member of the town's congregational church. Later in her life Ann
Prask signed legal documents with a clearly formed "A," which suggests that she may have received some formal schooling.[27]

Records indicate that efforts to educate and evangelize Indian
captives were widespread but not always welcome. John Winthrop
reported in February 1638 that the Indians "which were in our families were much frightened with Hobbamock (as they call the devil)
appearing to them in divers shapes, and persuading them to forsake
the English, and not to come at the assemblies, nor to learn to read,
etc." The fact that Indian servants in English households reported
seeing Hobbomock is striking. While the English saw Hobbomock
as "the devil," Natives had a more nuanced view. In Native cosmology, Hobbomock, or Chepi, was associated with death, darkness,
and misfortune, but he was also the being who most often appeared
in dreams and visions to convey spiritual knowledge. Did seeing
Hobbomock, the god of the underworld, convince these Indians
that they would die if they embraced English religion and culture?
Certainly, of those who stayed among the English for long, a good
number did die. Fear of such an outcome probably influenced many
captives to do as Hobbomock instructed and "forsake the English."[28]

Of course, not all captives were treated well. One was raped and
beaten by fellow servants, and then punished by her master, who
burned her with a hot poker for allowing herself to be abused. Another was raped by a Dutch colonist after she ran away from her
Connecticut mistress. Horrible as this treatment was, it does not
seem to have been common, and it was as likely to afflict English or
African servants as Indian ones. Simply stated, involuntary servitude
was an odious status. The overwhelming number of runaways—
most with no evidence of abuse—testifies to that.[29]

Pequot captives seem to have had the same freedom of movement as English servants to run errands or visit friends. Unlike

English servants, however, the Indian servants had somewhere to go. The woman burned by the poker fled to the Narragansetts, along with two other Pequot slaves, one of whom denied any mistreatment but said she had been "enticed" to run by her companion. Adhering to their agreement with the English, the Narragansetts returned these runaways to Boston, where authorities branded them on the shoulder as proof of their enslavement. But branding was not enough to keep Pequot servants in their new English homes. A decade after the Pequot War, almost all of the enslaved Natives were free, not because colonial officials opted for a more merciful policy, but because most had run away or died of English diseases. The running away began almost immediately. As early as July 31, 1637, Roger Williams wrote to John Winthrop that he had not yet heard "of any of the runnaway Captives amongst our neighbours." By August 12, Williams wrote of "many runn away," and by October he reported that "all the Runnawayes [are] harboured" with the Pequots in subjection to the Niantic and Mohegan allies of the English. John Winthrop's letters recount the loss of his servant, a young male captive he called Reprieve, in the months following the war. Knowing the Connecticut and Rhode Island areas well, Reprieve was a useful and trusted messenger between the Bay and those other plantations. But his knowledge of the region also allowed him, and many others, to return home with ease. Granted an extended visit to his wife in October 1637, Reprieve disappeared. Despite sending repeated inquiries to Roger Williams and others about whether they had seen the young man, Winthrop never saw him again. This was true of many other captives, in both Connecticut and Massachusetts. A steady stream of letters passed between English officials in Boston and the Narragansett and Mohegan sachems reporting runaways and demanding their return. A few, like the woman who fled a cruel master, were sent back to the English, but as more and more Pequot slaves fled, the Narragansetts and Mohegans began resisting or ignoring English demands that they return them.[30]

In succeeding years, English leaders continued their efforts to retrieve runaways, and to obtain possession of the nearly two hundred Pequot refugees who had surrendered themselves to the Mohegan, Narragansett, and Niantic sachems, with little success. Winthrop reported that Narragansett sachem Miantonomi returned a few runaway Pequot women, but, overwhelmingly, the flow of captives went the other way. By June 1638 Winthrop conceded that the Pequots who submitted to the Mohegans and Narragansetts could continue to live with them and pay the English tribute. However, the surrendered and runaway Pequots chafed under the authority of their Indian overlords, and in 1647 they petitioned for the right to establish independent towns. The leaders of the United Colonies initially balked, reminding the petitioners that they "should not be suffered (if the English could help it) either to be a distinct people, or to retayne the name of Pequatts, or to settle in the Pequatt country." But by 1654 the English relented, declaring that Pequot leaders Wequashcook and Cassasinnamon and their followers were free of their subjection to the Mohegans and Narragansetts, "taken under protection of the English and freed from Tribute." Contrary to their previous insistence that the very "name of Pequatts" should be extinguished, the English referred to these now independent Indians as "Pequots," a term they continued to use in subsequent years. Indeed, Cassasinnamon's mark would one day become the symbol for the modern Mashantucket Pequot Nation. In all likelihood, the captives whose fates are unknown ended up with one or the other of these Pequot groups.[31]

Only a handful of captives stayed with the English longer than a few months or years. Two died in 1646 in Roxbury, Massachusetts. One was sold in 1648 by Edward Winslow of Plymouth to an Englishman in Barbados. Three ran away after nine or ten years living with their masters in Massachusetts, Connecticut, and New Hampshire. By ten years after the war, there were only two documented captives still in service to the English: One was an unnamed slave belonging to John Latimer of Wethersfield, Connecticut, mentioned in his 1662 will. The other was Ann Prask.[32]

While the Pequot captives in Roxbury, Dorchester, Boston, and other English towns escaped back to their homelands or died, Ann Prask remained in Roxbury. Unlike Winthrop's Pequot servant Reprieve, Prask could not have found her way home. Indeed, Sasqua may have been less familiar to her than Roxbury was. As a Mahican speaker and recent arrival to Sasqua, she may not have had strong ties to the other Indian slaves in the town. Instead, she seems to have developed a strong attachment to the English family she lived with, particularly her master Joshua Hewes. In 1676, after Hewes's death and long after her service to him had ended, Ann Prask would declare, "what estate soever she had she would give to Mr Hughes his children after her death for the love that their father had shown her." Some of this attachment must be attributed to Ann's situation; a child traumatized by war and separated from her kin in a strange new environment would have had a desperate need for stability and connection. The phenomenon of captives developing strong ties of affection and identification with their captors has been labeled "Stockholm Syndrome," and this phenomenon may explain Ann's strong connection with her captor. But evidence also suggests that Joshua Hewes was a kind man who fulfilled the obligations laid out in colony laws regarding bond slaves, including care, education, and Christian nurture. Ann Prask's declared affection for her master and her apparent ability to write testify to the care and opportunities Hewes provided. She may even have been the "one gerle" among the nine Native scholars who attended grammar school in Roxbury in 1656. Another of these scholars lived just across the green from the Hewes family, in the home of Isaac Heath and his wife. His name was John Wompas, and he would one day marry the child taken captive at Monnacommock Swamp.[33]

CHAPTER THREE

"To Bee Trained Up Among the English"

John Wompas and the Civilizing Project

The Saturday night after this third meeting . . . there came to his house one *Wampas* . . . a wise and sage Indian, as a messenger sent to him from the rest of the company, to offer unto him his owne sonne and three more Indian children to bee trained up among the English, one of the children was nine yeares old, another eight, another five, another foure: and being demanded why they would have them brought up among the English, his answer was, because they would grow rude and wicked at home, and would never come to know God, which they hoped they should doe if they were constantly among the English.

—THOMAS SHEPHERD, 1647

Then we resolved we would pray to God, and carry our children to *Roxbury*, that they might learn to pray.

—THOMAS WUTTASACOMPONOM, 1659

THE TOWN OF ROXBURY, where John Wompas spent much of his youth, was thirty-two miles and a world away from Hassanamesit. William Wood, writing in 1634, described it as a "handsome country town, the inhabitants of it being all very rich." Among Roxbury's English founders were some of Massachusetts Bay Colony's leading citizens: a future governor, magistrates, and prominent merchants. By the time young John Wompas arrived there to live with the Heath family, Roxbury had grown to a thriving village of 120 houses with an English population of at least five hundred.[1]

Although Roxbury was an English town, it had a decidedly Indian side. It sat on a well-worn Native road, and Indians continued to use the route after English settlement to carry trade goods to the English in Boston, or to visit friends and kin living in Roxbury or nearby towns. Because Roxbury was the home of John Eliot, the "apostle to the Indians," the town was a destination as well as a way station. It stood at the heart of the English effort to bring "civility" and Christianity to the Indians, a project that would frame much of John Wompas's life. John Eliot, Daniel Gookin, and colleagues from surrounding towns used several different approaches to converting and "civilizing" the Indians, including establishing Christian Indian towns, preparing Indians to form their own Puritan congregations, recruiting Indian children to live and work within English families, and shepherding a small number of Indian children through English grammar school to enroll at Harvard College.[2]

Eliot's missionary work with the Indians assumed that civility must precede conversion. Civility included being settled in one place, adopting English patterns of agriculture and animal husbandry, and learning to read. The English saw these behaviors as necessary precursors to accepting the Christian gospel. Indians' traditional pattern of moving from one place to another as the season dictated prevented weekly worship in a gathered church, so the English insisted that it be replaced with a sedentary existence and intensive agriculture to provide sufficient food for that new lifestyle. Because all Christians needed to read the scriptures—"every man for himselfe"—Indians must also attend school and learn to read. To keep these habits in place, young Indians needed to be trained in English skills, educated, and prepared to take positions of authority in church and civil life.[3]

Establishing the praying town of Natick, fourteen miles west of Roxbury, was a key step in Eliot's plans for civilizing the Indians. John Wompas's father Wampooas had died too soon to become a part of that community, but John must have known of his father's eagerness to see Natick rise. Established in 1651, Natick was home to Massachusett and Pawtucket Indians as well as Nipmucs like Wampooas's family, who had moved to Nonantum in the aftermath of the great epidemics. One of the first tasks of the residents was to construct a meetinghouse, a one-story rectangular building set within a palisade. Once that was completed, Eliot began preparing Natick's townspeople to gather their own church.[4]

The process of gathering a church followed a familiar pattern in early New England. Leading men from surrounding communities selected at least seven men from the new town to serve as founders of the new church. These founders, or "pillars," composed the first membership of the church, and they extended a call to a minister and saw to the election of lay officers, such as a ruling elder and deacon. With the church's officers in place, town residents could seek admission to the church by submitting narratives of their religious experience—how they had come to recognize their sinful state and accept God's saving grace—to the minister, elders, and other leading men. If these men approved, the applicants would present their relations to the entire congregation and answer questions probing their religious experience and knowledge of church doctrine. Finally, the congregation voted on whether or not to accept applicants to full membership, which would allow them to take communion. It was a grueling process, a much higher bar for membership than existed even in the reform churches of England. This approach to gathering a church came to be known as the "New England way," and it was required of Indians as well as English.[5]

Because the Indians had limited acquaintance with the Bible, Eliot and his colleagues spent two years schooling them in doctrine before requesting visitors to come to Natick to hear their conversion stories and assess their understanding of Christian doctrine. Some Indians pushed Eliot to speed up the process, saying they wanted to be baptized and receive "Ordinances in a way of Church Communion," but Eliot "declared unto them how necessary it was, that they should first be Civilized, by being brought from their scattered and wild course of life, unto civill Co-habitation and Government, before they could . . . be fit to be betrusted with the sacred Ordinances of Jesus Christ, in Church-Communion." Eliot involved his Roxbury congregation in fasting and praying for Natick's success, and after the initial attempt to gather a church failed to secure the approval of the visiting ministers, Eliot used his Roxbury meetinghouse to host subsequent rounds of conversion narratives and doctrinal examinations.[6]

Preparations for gathering a church and the associated business of running the praying town led Indians to make the fourteen-mile trek from Natick to Roxbury regularly to seek advice or assistance from Eliot. When trouble visited Natick, Indians brought news of it. Eliot shared his news with Isaac Heath, his ruling elder, and it would be surprising if John Wompas, who lived with the Heaths, would not have caught wind of it.[7]

And there was trouble from the very beginning. Natick was carved out of land the General Court had granted to the town of Dedham in 1635, and Dedham's residents deeply resented the incursion. Never mind that, as the Indians insisted, Natick was built upon land "where some of the Praying Indians then planted, & had done of old, even beyond the memory of the oldest man alive." Although the General Court ordered Dedham to allow the Indians to remain where they were, the dispute continued to simmer for decades. Such tensions made it easier for some local English to hold the Indians in contempt and to suspect them of disloyalty. Nishoukou, a Native Christian, recalled how English soldiers burst into the Indians' meetinghouse at Natick during worship services and ordered them to carry their guns to Roxbury and turn them over to town authorities. This event was connected to a threatened Narragansett uprising in 1653. But Nishoukou and his friends must have wondered what that had to do with them. If the English could not trust allied Christian Indian neighbors, whom could they trust? That night, Nishoukou recalled, "my heart was broken off, my heart said, God is not, the Sabbath is not, it is not the Lords Day, for were it so, the Souldiers would not have then come."[8]

Trouble came from inside the Indian community as well. Although the site of Natick was welcomed by the Indians who considered it their ancestral home, the Neponset Indians resented the choice, preferring a site closer to their own lands. Job Nesutan, who would become Eliot's longest-serving translator, was from Neponset, and it is possible that the location dispute had something to do with an incident that arose a few years after Natick's settlement.[9]

In June 1654, Job Nesutan and two other young Natives endangered the life of an eleven-year-old and humiliated his father Totherswamp, a ruler of Natick and John Wompas's paternal uncle. Nesutan and his companions—whom Eliot characterized as "three of the unsound sort of such as are among them that pray unto God"— purchased several quarts of alcohol and got drunk somewhere near Watertown. Totherswamp's son went to the same place on his father's bidding to get "a little Corne and Fish." When he ran into the men, whom he undoubtedly knew, they gave him "t[w]o Spoonfuls of Strong-water, which was more then his head could bear." Then one of the men began to pour liquor directly down the boy's throat, revealing his reason for doing so by saying, "Now we will see whether your father will punish us for Drunkennesse . . . seeing you are drunk with us for company." It seems that these men, who "had been severall times Punished formerly for Drunkennesse," probably by Totherswamp, were hoping to revenge themselves on their ruler.[10]

Writing of this affair, Eliot revealed the fractures in Natick society. Not only land but governance pitted some parts of the community against others. The offending men lived in Natick and were subject to its laws, but they chafed under the restrictions. They may have been old enough to remember an approach to child rearing very different from the strict discipline the English practiced, and that new converts had begun to follow. Nearly all English observers of Native family life in the early days of English settlement noted the Indians' great love for their children. They also noted—with disapproval—"the evill of their too indulgent *affections*"—what they saw as failure to properly discipline their children. Among the Native converts of Natick, English rules applied, apparently to the whole community. By setting Totherswamp's son up for punishment, the young men highlighted the contrast between old ways and new, daring their ruler to apply his new strictness to his own young son. Would he punish a child who was essentially force-fed alcohol, or would his love for the boy hold him back?[11]

In the end, Totherswamp chose strictness. The decision to punish the three adult offenders was easy: they were guilty of drunkenness, fighting, reproaching their rulers, and endangering a child by leaving him outdoors all night in a drunken state. Totherswamp ordered them to sit in the stocks "a good space of time" and then receive twenty lashes each. While Totherswamp agreed with the pleas of some that his son was not as culpable as the three men, he argued that the boy "was guilty of sin, in that he feared not sin, and in that he did not believe his counsells that he had often given him, to take heed of evill company; but he had believed Satan and sinners more then him, therefore he needed to be punished." He ordered the boy to sit in the stocks a short time and then to be whipped a few lashes in the schoolhouse in front of his peers—undoubtedly as an example to them of the consequences of drinking and bad company.[12]

This experience was an excruciating one for Totherswamp, forcing him to confront the harsh approach to parenting in his chosen religion. By Eliot's report, Totherswamp was "greatly grieved" and saw his decision as a test of his faith: "Now God tryeth me whether I love God or my Child best." Indian efforts to dissuade Totherswamp from punishing his son show that the incident was traumatic for the entire Christian community, as well as their English mentors. Eliot was packing for his twice-monthly stay in Natick when news of the event arrived, and it nearly paralyzed him: "I began to doubt about our intended work: I knew not what to doe, the blacknesse of the sins and the Persons reflected on, made my very heart faile me." A long-planned examination of Native converts' understanding of Christian doctrine—a prelude to gathering the Natick church—was only ten days away. One of those to be examined was Job Nesutan, whose role in getting Totherswamp's eleven-year-old son drunk demonstrated his unworthiness for church fellowship. Nesutan had been under Eliot's personal supervision for four years; if he could backslide, who could be trusted to hold firm? The incident also cast discredit on Totherswamp, "a Principall man in the [Christian] work," for failing to keep his young son under control.[13]

Nowhere in the records are the other two men involved in debauching Totherswamp's child named. They seem to have been Natick residents, or at least subject to Natick governance. John Wompas would have been about seventeen when the incident occurred, and he was living in Roxbury, not Natick. Totherswamp was his uncle—his father's brother—and the child was his cousin. Years later, Wompas would himself be punished for similar behavior—drunkenness and fighting. If Wompas did not participate in the incident, he undoubtedly knew of it, and even at this early stage he may have been one of those who felt "hemmed in . . . to doe that which [his] heart love[d] not."[14]

While the business of gathering a church at Natick involved many at Roxbury, so did the project of training and educating young Natives. Writing to the governor of the New England Company, a United Colonies commissioner explained the need for both work training and education for Indian youth, saying, "[to] bring them to a course of labor is the readiest way to their civilizing and that a good preparation to the religion." Christianized Indians like Wampooas seem to have sought English training for their children for religious reasons, but they also saw practical benefits in it. In a rapidly changing world, English training gave Native youth access to tools, trades, and allies that could help them and their families survive. Throughout his years of education and his later career, John Wompas would be a striking example of acquiring and applying English tools for his own benefit. Having Native Christians learn skills and trades benefited the English as well as the Indians by preparing them to provide labor—always a scarce commodity in seventeenth-century New England.[15]

In 1646 John Wompas's father Wampooas brought two Indian youths from Nonantum to Eliot and asked him to place them in English homes in Roxbury. Job Nesutan was likely one of these youths; Monequasson, of Neponset, may have been the other. Both were educated in Roxbury, to the point that they were qualified to serve as schoolmasters in Natick, whose town school had thirty Indian pupils by 1653. Indian parents also brought their own children to Roxbury to be educated. John Wompas was one of these children, and there were at least eight others by 1656. Church and town records make it clear that the civility project applied to all of the Indians living in Roxbury—slave or free. Among the slaves brought to Roxbury after the Pequot War were Egborn and Nan. Both learned to speak English, and Egborn also learned to read English by the time both of them were accepted as members of the Roxbury church.

Ann Prask's apparent literacy suggests that she too may have received some schooling. She may also have joined Roxbury's church. An unnamed "maid servant" associated with the Hewes household and not an "original inhabitant of the town" was admitted to the church before 1650. This "_____ Hues, a maid servant" might have been Ann Prask.[16]

Within a few years of Nesutan and Monequasson's arrival in Roxbury, other young men agreed to become servants in Roxbury families, probably motivated not only by what Thomas Shepherd called a hope "to know Jesus Christ," but also by their (or their parents') desire to acquire knowledge and skills from the English. Learning an English trade was the reason John Wompas's uncle Anthony gave for yielding to his brothers' urging that he go live with the English. Anthony was not yet a convert to Christianity, although he had heard many sermons and been urged by his brothers Wampooas and Totherswamp to accept the English faith. At the coaxing of one of these brothers, Anthony joined a group of young Indians going to live in Roxbury, hoping it might give him the chance to learn the blacksmith trade. But when Roxbury's English blacksmith heard that Anthony wanted to learn smithing, not just be a general servant, he protested: "I may not teach him my Trade, lest *Indians* learn to make Locks and Guns." Deeply stung, Anthony refused to live with the blacksmith and "thought to cast off praying and . . . forsake my brothers."[17]

Anthony's bitter response to the blacksmith's rebuff brings the clash between English ideals and actions into stark relief. Ministers might proclaim that Indians were the biological and spiritual equals of the English—"Nature knowes no difference between Europe and Americans in blood, birth, bodies, &c. God having of one blood made all mankind"—but the people of Roxbury and other English towns did not always share these lofty sentiments. The Roxbury blacksmith's fear that Anthony would learn to make guns shows that he saw him as a potential enemy who could not be trusted. Sometime later, after Anthony had cooled down, his brother persuaded him to spend just one year living with an English family other than the blacksmith's, and he finally relented. He even attended church during that year but, by his own account, it was "in vain, for I understood not one word."[18]

English and Indian fears for personal safety clearly contributed to mutual distrust, but the unfamiliarity of each other's culture also played a role. In the early years of colonization, English and Indians interacted frequently. Although epidemics had greatly thinned Indian numbers, there were still many thousands. Colonist John Dane reported passing forty or fifty Indians at once on the road from Ipswich to Roxbury. They hailed each other, Dane calling out, "Good cheer!" and the Indians laughing and throwing his "good cheer" back to him. On the same journey, Dane passed two more Indians, one of whom grabbed his bag and looked into it. Flustered by this familiarity, Dane pulled the bag away from him, made an angry face, and hurried off. Dane's uncomfortable response was a common one. The differences between Indian and English habits of interaction often led to misunderstanding. The English placed a high value on respect for private property and social rank, signaled by the quality of one's clothing. Indians placed a high value on generosity and hospitality. Thus, "naked" Indians would enter English homes and expect to be welcomed and fed, and the English would shoo them out, decrying their "insolence," a word associated with disrespect for one's superiors. Indeed, Roxbury's earliest records list many sums paid "for driving away Indians"—a verb more commonly used for cattle or wolves than people.[19]

This mutual incomprehension and distrust undoubtedly flavored the experience of Indian youths living in Roxbury, such as John Wompas and his uncle Anthony. To the English, all the Indians, whether sachems or commoners, were culturally inferior to them by virtue of their uncivilized condition. That did not necessarily mean all English viewed Indians with contempt, though many did. For John Eliot, pity more aptly described his attitude toward them. Eliot, Daniel Gookin, and others involved in missionary work referred to the Natives as "poor Indians," not because of their material poverty (although they had little), but because they lacked the Christian gospel. Pity was a more compassionate emotion than contempt, but it still assumed English superiority. It is worth noting that Eliot and Gookin saw this superiority as cultural, not biological. Gookin declared that the Indians were, like the English, "Adam's posterity, and consequently children of wrath; and hence are not only objects of all christians' pity and compassion, but subjects upon which our faith, prayers, and best endeavours should be put forth." By offering Indian children places in their homes, giving them access to religion, literacy, and civility, the English intended to raise them "from barbarism to civility," much as the Romans had raised up the savage Picts, ancestors of the English. If they could benefit from their labor at the same time, so much the better. Isaac Heath, Eliot's close friend and colleague in the Indian work, shared Eliot's enthusiasm for the effort to civilize the Indians, which is no doubt why he and his wife Elizabeth agreed to accept John Wompas into their household.[20]

John Wompas moved to Roxbury sometime between 1646, when his father first asked Eliot to place him in an English home, and 1651, when Wampooas stated that John was living with the Heaths. When the Heaths took in John, they were long past their own child-rearing years. Elizabeth, fifty-six years old in 1651, had only one living child, a daughter also named Elizabeth, who married John Bowles in 1650. Isaac Heath was sixty-six. As ruling elder of Roxbury's church, he was one of the most prominent residents of the town; he was also among the largest landowners, with over 250 acres. Without sons of his own, Heath would have needed servants to help him farm and care for his land. John Wompas would have been around fourteen years old in 1651, old enough to be of considerable help to Heath. John probably did work in Heath's fields and farmyard, but like other servants he also spent time being instructed in Christian doctrine and learning to read, write, and in John's case, to speak the English language. By Eliot's report, John's father Wampooas's dying wish was that John and the other Native children in Roxbury "may be taught to know God, so as that they may teach their Countrymen." John's master Isaac Heath was a close personal friend of John Eliot and a man of noted piety; it is probable that he made sure that Christian instruction as well as labor occupied John Wompas's time.[21]

A Native adolescent like John would already have received a great deal of instruction from his parents and community before he began his education with the Heaths and an English schoolmaster. From as young as two years old, he would have been taught to fish, shoot a bow, recognize animal signs, and know the constellations.

He also would have learned about Native gods and viewed rituals performed by religious leaders, or "powwows," although his parents' embrace of Christianity before he was ten years old may have made Native religious practice a distant memory, charged with taboo. While both English and Indian education were designed to fit children for the world they lived in, their manner of instruction was strikingly different. English observers often noted that Natives loved their children and allowed them great freedom in speech and action. Of course, English parents also loved their children, but in their view good parents curbed their children, following the maxim, "spare the rod and spoil the child." Some sent their children away to receive training at the hands of relatives or friends, fearful that their parental affection would prevent them from properly constraining them. John's training from his parents and kin, at least in his earliest years, would have involved learning by practice and example, and little or no punishment or restraint. However kind Isaac and Elizabeth Heath may have been, it is likely that John would have found their parenting harsh compared to his previous experience.[22]

John's instruction in the Heath household would have included the daily devotions expected of all Puritans. One of John Eliot's sermons outlined this expectation: "We perform family-duties every day . . . wherein having read the Scriptures to our families, we call upon the Name of God, and ever now and then carefully catechize those that are under our charge." A catechism was a set of religious questions and answers that laid a foundation for understanding religious doctrine. Massachusetts officials considered this introduction to Christian learning so important that they made it the subject of a law in 1648: "All masters of families doe once a week (at the least) catechize their children and servants in the grounds and principles of Religion." While there were many catechisms the Heaths could have used to instruct John, it is likely they selected the one Eliot wrote for his Roxbury congregation in 1654. To measure the religious progress of the congregation's youth, the Roxbury church elders themselves examined the young men "every sab[bath] after the evening exercize, in the Pub[lic] meeting house" about what had been preached that day in church or "any fit poynt" of doctrine from their catechism. The elders met with the young women for the same purpose the following day.[23]

Besides family devotionals, there was church twice every Sabbath, with prayer, scripture reading, singing, and preaching that could last three to four hours each time. Children usually did not attend church until they were old enough to sit still throughout the lengthy exercises, sometime in their late adolescence or early teens. Once he reached that age, John Wompas would have attended church with the Heaths, but he would not have shared a bench with them. Elizabeth Heath sat in a seat of "dignity" among the women, and Isaac, the ruling elder, sat on a seat prominently raised between the deacons' bench and the pulpit. John likely sat on a bench at the back of the main room or gallery, with other single young men and servants. Female Indians like Ann Prask and "Joane the Indian maid" would likewise have sat at the back, on the women's side of the meetinghouse. In addition to John, there were eight other Indian scholars living and working in Roxbury households, as well as household servants like Ann and Joane. Some were slaves; others—the students—were boarders who probably did some household work in return for their keep. Either way, they had none of the status associated with family position or church office that earned the Heaths the right to sit in the best seats at the front of the congregation.[24]

Parents and masters were also responsible for teaching their charges to read, a vital skill in Puritan New England, where studying the Bible was expected of every resident. The Heaths could have purchased a primer for John at a store in Roxbury where they sold for two pence each, or they could have used one of those sent for the use of Indian students by the New England Company. Primers contained alphabets and pronunciation guides for budding scholars: A = ay / B = bee / AB = ab. The difficulty of teaching a child who spoke little or no English to read from such a book must have been apparent to Eliot, Heath's close friend. In 1669, Eliot published the *Indian Primer*, which provided alphabets and pronunciation guides in both English and the Algonquian language of Massachusett. This came too late for John, who was well advanced in his schooling by then.[25]

Many colonial children never went beyond household instruction to attend a school, and many New England towns lacked formal schools until later in the century. Roxbury was fortunate to have a grammar school early on, as well as an excellent schoolmaster, Daniel Weld. Roxbury's grammar school sat in the center of town on a triangular lot opposite the common, surrounded by the homes of its most prominent citizens. These included the town's two ministers, John Eliot and Thomas Weld, the ruling elder Isaac Heath, and the merchant Joshua Hewes, Ann Prask's master. Hewes, Heath, Weld, and Eliot all pledged annual funds to support the school, and this support, as well as the school's central location, are clear evidence that education was important to the town's founders. Education was equally important to the colony's leaders, who passed a law in 1648 ordering every town with more than fifty families to support an English school and every town with one hundred families to establish a Latin grammar school. Latin grammar schools were necessary to prepare students for Harvard College, which, despite its frontier surroundings, had exacting standards for admission: scholars had to be able to translate Cicero or some other Latin writer on the spot, write and speak "true Latine in Verse and Prose," and "perfectly decline paradigms of nouns and verbs in Greek." Students typically began grammar school at age seven or eight, after years of instruction at home. John was between ten and fourteen years old when he began his home education with the Heaths, and he would have had to master both speaking and reading in the new language of English before he could begin his classical education. John was very bright, later described as a "towardly lad & apt witt for a scholler," so he likely picked up these skills quickly.[26]

Roxbury's schoolhouse was a rough affair, as were most New England schoolhouses—indeed, most buildings—of the period. Typically, town schools had one main room, with the teacher's desk and a large fireplace at one end and students' desks attached to and facing the other three walls. Backless benches served for seating. Providing firewood was one of the responsibilities of parents, and when they neglected it, students froze—or tore up the floorboards for fuel, as Roxbury's pupils did in 1681. Daniel Weld and Elijah Corlett, who taught the grammar schools in Roxbury and Cambridge, educated the vast majority of Indian pupils. Both men received salaries from their respective towns, but they charged extra for any students who enrolled from outside the town. The fees of the Indian students were paid by the United Colonies commissioners, colonial magistrates who acted as agents for the New England Company. In 1656, when Weld had nine Indian scholars, he received eighty-five pounds from the New England Company for feeding and teaching Native students and an additional fifty pounds for clothing he provided for them. Such additions to Weld's paltry salary led him to actively seek Indian students. Until his death in 1666, Weld had anywhere from four to nine Native students studying with him at all times.[27]

It is intriguing that Weld's group of Indian scholars in 1656 included "one gerle." Who was she? The historical records are frustratingly sparse on Indian education, rarely attaching names to the students. Most likely she was "Joane the Indian Mayde," who was boarding with Daniel Weld in 1658. The fact that an Indian girl was among the group receiving a Latin grammar school education is unusual; few girls of any race attended such schools in seventeenth-century New England. All children were expected to learn to read in order to study the Bible for themselves, but they could learn reading at home or in "dame schools"—classes held by neighborhood women for local children. Grammar school went beyond reading instruction to teach Latin, Greek, mathematics, and handwriting, skills boys would need for their professions or to qualify for admission to college; girls were not expected to need these skills at all. However, the 1650s and 1660s were a time when the likelihood of a girl attending grammar school may have been higher than at the end of the century. Dame schools did not become common until 1670, and the New England towns that had grammar schools could not afford to have separate English schools. Thus, in those towns, girls who had outgrown home education may have attended grammar school for a short time. Many girls, like Ann Prask, learned enough to sign their name or initial. Indeed, the Indian girl in Roxbury's school could have been Ann, although she would have been at least twenty-five years old in 1656.[28]

From 1655 to 1672, anywhere from two to ten Indian scholars were enrolled in the grammar schools at Roxbury and Cambridge almost constantly—at least twenty over the entire period. The large number of Native students in Roxbury's grammar school while John was there provided several advantages to him: he would not stick out so baldly as an older student among the typical seven-year-old entrants to the school, and he would be able to preserve his Native connections and language. Most of the Indian students would have had parents or kin who took them to hear Eliot preaching; some were Nipmucs, like John. They would share much in common in both experience and language. Unlike the Indian boarding schools of nineteenth- and twentieth-century America, the schools enrolling Native students in seventeenth-century Massachusetts actually encouraged students to retain their first language. Writing in 1660, the United Colonies commissioners assured an English supporter that the Indian students "have so much exercise of their owne language, as there is no feare or danger of their forgetting it." Forgetting their primary language would have completely undercut the reason they were being educated—so that they could become messengers of the gospel to their own people.[29]

While the number of Indians studying in English schools was quite large in the 1650s and 1660s, it quickly dwindled, for the same reason the Indian population as a whole fell off dramatically in the seventeenth century: disease. Epidemics continued to cut through both Indian and English communities. John Eliot reported "much sicknesse at Roxbury & greater mortality then ever we had afore" during the winter of 1645. Two years later another "great sicknesse epidemical" struck Roxbury, "scarce any escaping English or Indian." Smallpox, which had so decimated the Indians in 1634, struck the colony again in 1649, "whereof many dyed," including Elizabeth Bowles, the only child of Isaac and Elizabeth Heath. She left a husband and three small children. Smallpox would hit again in 1666. Severe episodes of "colds, coughs, agues, & fevers" arrived in 1659 and 1660, leading to the death of Isaac Heath. This last epidemic may have been what killed a number of Indian students. In 1660, the United Colonies commissioners reported that one of Corlett's five Indian students at Cambridge and two of Weld's four at Roxbury died the previous summer—a 30 percent mortality for Indian students overall. Such a high mortality suggests another reason why the numbers of Indian scholars may have dwindled: Native parents who learned of these repeated epidemics may have chosen to keep their beloved children at home.[30]

John undoubtedly knew the two students who died at Roxbury, and he probably knew the one who died in Cambridge, where he relocated to complete his preparation for Harvard. This move most likely occurred sometime after 1657, when the United Colonies commissioners recommended that the Indian students most "capable of further improvement" shift from Weld's Roxbury schoolroom to Corlett's Cambridge one. Corlett's grammar school prepared more students for Harvard than any other school in the colony. He was also apparently more successful than Weld in teaching classical languages to Native students like John Wompas.[31]

Another reason for the decline in Native scholars was discouragement with the lengthy educational process. Daniel Gookin, the superintendent of Indians in Massachusetts Bay Colony, reported that some Indian scholars "were disheartened and left learning, after they were almost ready for the college." The United Colonies commissioners assumed responsibility for helping the Natives who chose to stop their education obtain apprenticeships instead. Apprenticeships were a long-established English practice for training youth in a trade. Established by a legal contract between a child's parents or guardians and a master, an apprenticeship bound the child to serve the master for a period of years in exchange for training, room, and board. Children were typically in their teens when beginning an apprenticeship and rarely continued longer than seven years.[32]

The United Colonies commissioners considered apprenticeships, like schooling, civilizing experiences, and they actively encouraged Indian parents to send their children "to be brought up in English families as Covenant servants or apprentices." To encourage Native families to place their children with English masters, the commissioners promised to provide the parents with an English coat every year their child remained in an English home. To ensure that English homes did, in fact, further the civilizing project, the commissioners revised their apprenticeship policy, stating explicitly that Indian children should be placed "with godly masters, such as will engage to teach them to read well, and bring them [up] in Christian nurture." For the Indians who had formerly been scholars in grammar school or at Harvard College, the commissioners were willing to bear some expense in setting up job training arrangements. For example, the commissioners spent two pounds—over half a month's wage for an English laborer—to outfit an Indian youth named Job before he began his apprenticeship with a carpenter. In September 1660, the commissioners reported that two of the young Indians

"formerly brought up to Read and writ[e]" had been "put apprentice," one to a carpenter, and the other—undoubtedly the Nipmuc
James Printer—to the Cambridge printer Samuel Green. Three years
later the commissioners directed Thomas Danforth, who lodged a
number of Indian scholars in his Cambridge home, to secure a contract to train one of them "to some meet Imployment for his future
good."[33]

As an Indian scholar residing among the English, John was exposed
to more than an academic education. He was also schooled in the
politics of power in the British Empire. John's last years at the Cambridge Grammar School were a time of increasing political tension
in Massachusetts Bay Colony. We don't know how he felt, as a child
and young man, about the events unfolding around him. We know
only the barest facts of his life before he reached adulthood—where
he lived, where he went to school, the deaths of people close to him.
As an adult, however, John's actions would show an astute apprecia-
tion of the tensions between Crown and colony and a remarkable
ability to manipulate those tensions to serve his own interests. His
first exposure to the contest between Crown and colonial authority
occurred during his student days in Cambridge, in the years surrounding the visit of King Charles II's royal commissioners to New
England in 1664. Because many of the public conflicts between
Crown and colony during that time involved language and political
approaches that John Wompas would later employ for his own purposes, it is worth laying out those events in some detail.

King Charles II's Restoration to the throne in 1660 released a
backlog of complaints against Massachusetts from petitioners who
saw the king's return as the chance to have long-pending grievances
addressed. Petitioners against Massachusetts included the proprietors of Maine, New Hampshire, and Rhode Island, who protested
the colony's intrusion on their jurisdictions; Quakers and other individuals whom colony leaders had punished for religious or political transgressions; people whose economic interests were hampered
by the colony; and Indians complaining of colonial oppression.
These complaints, and Massachusetts's offensive delay in publically
acknowledging the restored king, convinced Charles II to send royal
commissioners to New England to investigate each colony's loyalty

and adherence to English law. The first two royal commissioners arrived in Boston on July 23, 1664. They went right to work, asking the Massachusetts Council to assemble to hear their instructions from the king. The council met on July 26 and the commissioners gave them the king's letter and a request that the colony immediately raise troops for an expedition against the Dutch in New Netherland. The commissioners expected instant compliance; instead, the Massachusetts Council explained that it would have to defer its response until the full General Court could gather and give its "advice, asistance, & concurrance therein." The affronted commissioners refused to wait and left for New York, warning the court in parting to "give a more satisfactory answer to his majesty." This first interaction between Massachusetts officials and the king's commissioners, characterized by defensiveness and inflexibility on both sides, set the tone for a series of fraught exchanges to come. As a scholar at Cambridge Grammar School and then at Harvard, John would have been alerted to the political turmoil each time he and fellow scholars gathered at the Cambridge Meeting House to hear the General Court's official proclamations of fast days for God's aid in "diverting such calamities as are coming upon us."[34]

Conflict between the colony's representatives and the Crown was not surprising; they held very different views on the nature of the king's authority in the colonies. The Massachusetts General Court made its position on colony authority very clear in a document created in 1661, as its members contemplated whether or not to publically proclaim their allegiance to the king. The document had two headings: "Concerning our liberties" and "Concerning our duties of allegiance to our soveraigne lord the king." Under the first, the court declared that its charter was "the first & maine foundation of our civil politye here" and that its elected officers had "full power & authoritie, both legislative & executive, for the government of all the people here . . . without appeale"—even to the king. Under the second heading, the court concluded that "the premises considered, it may well stand with the loyalty & obedience of such subjects as are thus priviledged, . . . to pleade with theire prince against all such as shall at any time endeavor the violation of theire priviledges." Thus, the court officers saw their duty of allegiance as best fulfilled by resisting any infringement on the privileges the king had granted them by charter. The royal commissioners understood this position and found it preposterous. In particular, they were outraged that Massachusetts leaders refused to acknowledge their right, as the king's representatives, to hear appeals. One of the commissioners, George Cartwright, protested, "These Gentlemen of Boston would make us believe that they verily think that the King hath given them soe much power in their Charter to doe unjustly, that hee hath reserved none to Himselfe to call them to an account for doing soe." Despite Massachusetts's prohibition on appeals, the royal commissioners openly accepted petitioners; indeed, they sought them out within the colony and in neighboring colonies. Some of those who heeded the commissioners' invitation to air their grievances were Indians.[35]

In obedience to royal command, Massachusetts leaders broadcast the king's letter of 1664 authorizing the royal commission. Whether there were sufficient copies of the king's letter to reach every literate individual or whether men were appointed to read it aloud in each town, it is unlikely that John Wompas was "ignorant of the contents thereof." The king's letter contained ideas and language that would echo in John Wompas's later petitions and declarations, including the assertion that the Indians of New England were subjects of the Crown. A subject was under the authority of a higher power, but a subject also enjoyed certain privileges, including the Crown's protection. King Charles II made his view of the status of Indians in New England clear by assigning the royal commissioners to gather "full & particular information of the state & condition of the neighbour princes to our severall colonies, from some of whome wee have received addresses of great respect & civilitie, not without some complaint, or at least insinuation, of some injustice or hard measure excercised towards them from our colonies." These "neighbour princes" were the Narragansett sachems Pessacus, Canonicus, and Mixan, who had submitted themselves, their lands, and their people to the Crown in 1644, begging the king's protection against the intrusions of Massachusetts into their sovereign territory and authority. The king directed his royal commissioners to visit these sachems and "assure them of all freindship from us, & that wee will protect them from injustice & oppression."[36]

By inviting the Indians to bring him their complaints and offering to protect them from any "injustice or hard measure excercised towards them from our colonies," the king made it clear that the Indians were not under colonial authority, but directly under the Crown. To anyone reading the king's letter or hearing about its contents, the message was clear: The English king considered the Indians of New England to be his subjects, and—as the Narragansetts had argued in 1644—that made the Indians and English colonists equal subjects of the Crown. This was a message that John Wompas would, in the future, both act on and boldly proclaim.[37]

Many Indians took notice of the king's promise to protect his Indian subjects and sought out the royal commissioners during their visit to the colonies. News of the commissioners traveled far and fast, resulting in Indian submissions and petitions from west of the Connecticut River to the northern headwaters of the Merrimack River. Sachems closer to Boston and Hartford appealed to the commissioners as well, including the Wampanoag sachem Philip (Metacom), Uncas of the Mohegans, Ninigret of the Niantics, and Josias Wampatuck of the Massachusetts. Wampatuck's petition in 1666, in which he submitted his lands to the Crown in exchange for protection, is worth noting because of a connection between the sachem and John Wompas. In 1662, while Wompas was still attending grammar school in Cambridge, he acted as a witness on two of Wampatuck's land sales. While there is no evidence that John was involved in Wampatuck's 1666 submission to the Crown, the Englishman Richard Thayer, who also had connections to John Wompas, was involved. All three men would later appeal to the king against the rulings of colonial authorities. It is unclear how and when Wompas, Wampatuck, and Thayer became acquainted, but their pattern of similar actions and attitudes suggests they may have influenced each other, even goaded each other to action.[38]

The royal commissioners remained in New England for over a year, visiting the neighboring colonies and Indian tribes, but returning in between visits to their base in Boston, the home of Thomas Bredon, a man who had previously incurred the wrath of the Massachusetts General Court by challenging their authority.[39] At Bredon's home, the commissioners received colonists with grievances against Massachusetts and heard appeals of cases previously settled by colony courts. To the Massachusetts leaders, the commissioners seemed to have set up a rebel base inside the colony's own fortress. In May 1665 the General Court's secretary Edward Rawson wrote to the commissioners, "wee apprehend our patent, & his majesties authority therein committed unto us, to be greatly infringed." The commissioners denied doing anything more than fulfilling the king's explicit instructions. When neither side would yield, the General Court took an extraordinary action. They drafted a letter of protest and had it publically proclaimed, with a trumpet to command attention, at three sites in Boston, including directly across from Bredon's house. Few people in Boston that spring day could have missed this display, and, because it was repeated three times, people from the nearby towns of Cambridge and Charlestown may have had time to come and hear the General Court's messenger proclaim, "in observance of our duty to God, & to his Majestie and the trust committed to us by his Majesties good subjects in this colony: wee cannot consent unto, or give our approbation of the proceedings of the above-said Gentlemen, neither can it consiste with our allegiance that we owe to his Majestie to countenance any that shall in so high a manner go cross unto his Majesties direct charge; or shall be their abettors, or consent thereunto. God save the King."[40]

Even if John did not witness this proclamation in person, he would have heard about it, as did everyone in the colony. It was the culmination of the battle of wills between the General Court and the royal commissioners, who departed the colony soon afterward. In parting, they informed colony leaders that they would represent them to the king in their very own words, which they considered sufficiently damning to require no further commentary. Over the course of a year, Massachusetts had been the site of a dizzying power struggle between the king's appointed agents and the colonial authorities who insisted that they represented the king within his colony. John's Cambridge education put him in position to hear the public proclamation of the king's letter inviting his subjects, English and Indian, to submit their grievances to him, and to witness colony leaders openly defy any appeal over their own authority. The discontent among both Indians and English brought to the surface by the royal commissioners' visit, and the petitions to the Crown their presence evoked, must have played a powerful role in John's emerging antipathy to colonial authority. In the future, he would align himself with others who chafed under Massachusetts's yoke and would use direct appeal to the Crown as a weapon in his own battles with colonial leaders.[41]

The pinnacle of the long civilizing project, approached by only a handful of Christian Natives, was attaining a college degree. The idea of educating Indians was even older than the push to found Natick. As early as 1636, a subscription circulated in England among friends of the Bay Colony seeking support for "erecting a place where Some may be maintained for learninge the language and instructing heathen and our owne and breeding up as many of the Indians children as providence shall bringe unto our hands." The New England Company secured funds for constructing an Indian College in 1653, and the building was completed around 1656. It was located near present-day Matthews Hall in Harvard Yard and has been the focus of several recent archaeological digs. In addition to providing rooms for Indian students, the Indian College would house a printing press that would produce translated religious works for the use of Native Christians. Most notably, the press would issue the first Bible printed in America in 1663, and that Bible would not be in English, but in the Algonquian Indian language of Massachusett.[42]

The Indian College was a two-story brick structure with enough space to house twenty scholars. For the commissioners of the United Colonies, twenty Native students did not seem an unattainable goal. United Colonies commissioners kept supporters in England apprised of the progress of construction and of the Indian scholars. In 1658 and 1659 they sent certificates testifying that "two of the *Indians* that are trained up at the Grammer-Schoole in *Cambridge* of *New-England*, whose names were *Caleb* and *Joel*, were called forth upon tryall at the publick Commencement before the Magistrates and Elders." Their "trials" consisted of translating passages from the books of Isaiah and Psalms into Latin, and Harvard College's president Charles Chauncy attested that they gave "good satisfaction" and that the other three Indian youths at the Cambridge Grammar School had "made some competent proficiency, for the short time that they have been with us." Countering claims of colonial abuse of Indians with examples of the positive good colony leaders were doing for them was one of the reasons a specially prepared edition of John Eliot's translation of the Bible into the Massa-chusett language was presented to King Charles II in 1664. When presenting it, Robert Boyle, the head of the New England Com-pany, "tooke an opportunity to . . . doe your Colony some good of-fices at Court, and to shew the exercises of your indian scollars"—which, of course, Eliot, Shepherd, and others had sent to Boyle for just such a purpose.[43]

Soon after the Indian College was begun, the United Colonies commissioners sent two of interpreter Thomas Stanton's sons to Cambridge to be educated, supported by company funds. They were to live in the Indian College, complete their B.A. degrees, and then stay on at Harvard as tutors to Indian students. Their fluency in an Algonquian language suited them to explain the intricacies of classical education to the Indians who would fill the chambers of the new brick building. Unfortunately, this plan failed. The Stanton boys proved to be lackadaisical scholars—"worthless," in the words of President Chauncy. Thomas Stanton Jr. left Cambridge early, but his brother John stayed on. In the fall of 1659, Chauncy charged him with "Intolerable negligence" of his studies as well as several other "miscarriages," including extended absence from the college without permission. Complaints about his behavior continued through 1663, when the commissioners finally removed him from the payroll and sent him home. While in Cambridge, John Stanton studied both with Master Corlett and at the Indian College, so he would have been acquainted with the college and grammar school students, including John Wompas. One of the reasons the agents for the New England Company dismissed him was his poor example to these students; they feared the Indian scholars would be "justly of-fended," or perhaps enticed to follow John Stanton's bad example. After the Stantons' departure, the tutors of the English students and President Chauncy himself took charge of the Indian students' in-struction.[44]

Like the hopes for the Stantons, the plans to produce qualified Indian ministers also failed to materialize, at least in the numbers anticipated. While at least twenty Indian students attended Latin grammar school, few persisted long enough to enter Harvard. Some abandoned their schooling while still in grammar school; others died of disease during their time living among the English, a grim reality that may have spooked other potential scholars. But some Indians did complete their grammar school training and enroll at Harvard. The earliest was probably John Sassamon, who spent a year or so at Harvard beginning in 1653, before the Indian College was completed. Job Nesutan, who acted as Eliot's translation assistant for nearly twenty-five years, may also have attended for a short time.[45]

The early 1660s were the high mark of Indian education in the Bay Colony, when at least three Native scholars were enrolled at Harvard. In 1661, two Indians from Martha's Vineyard—Caleb Cheesechaumuck and Joel Hiacoomes, the students who had demonstrated their proficiency in Latin in 1658 and 1659—began their college studies. Their ability to translate passages extemporaneously from the Book of Isaiah into Latin gave clear evidence to colony officials that they were qualified for a university education. Mastering Latin was necessary because, once students entered the college, they would receive their instruction in Latin, their textbooks would be in Latin, and they would be expected to respond in Latin during disputations—rhetorical exercises in which students took opposing sides on a question posed by instructors.[46]

Cheesechaumuck and Hiacoomes remained at Harvard longer than any other Native students in the seventeenth century. Indian Superintendent Daniel Gookin knew both of them well. John Wompas probably did too; their final years at Corlett's grammar school overlapped with John's first years. Gookin described Hiacoomes as "not only a diligent student, but an attentive hearer of God's word; diligently writing the sermons, and frequenting lectures; grave and sober in his conversation." President Chauncy, who had "instructed them in Arts and languages," acknowledged that both young men were "in some good measure fit to preach to the Indians." Cheesechaumuck graduated with Harvard's class of 1665, and one of his Latin addresses is still preserved in the university archives. Hiacoomes would have graduated the same year, but on a trip home to visit relatives his ship ran aground on Nantucket, and he was killed by hostile Indians. Cheesechaumuck spent the year after his graduation slowly wasting away from tuberculosis, undoubtedly contracted during his years in Cambridge. That left only John Wompas.[47]

Wompas left Corlett's Cambridge grammar school to attend Harvard in 1665. Writing to their supporters in England, the United Colonies commissioners noted his entrance into the college, describing him as "a towardly lad & apt witt for a scholler." While John was the only Native pupil who entered Harvard that year, he was part of a large entering class of eleven students. In addition to these first-years, there were sixteen to twenty upperclassmen, eight to ten students studying for their M.A. degrees, and five resident fellows or tutors—well over forty people living and studying in three buildings: the increasingly decrepit Old College, Goffe College, and the Indian College. While the Indian College was intended for Native students, the small number of them and the large demand for housing led to English students also being housed there as early as 1656.[48]

Harvard students, even more than grammar school students, were almost constantly together, cheek by jowl. As classmates, they shared the same tutor, went to public prayers twice daily at 6:00 a.m. and 5:00 p.m., attended lectures together at 8:00, 9:00, and 10:00 a.m. in the Old College's main hall, and shared their two daily meals and "bevers" (morning and afternoon breaks for bread and beer). In the afternoons they met in the hall for disputations at 2:00, 3:00, and 4:00. They studied with their tutors between the second public prayer at 5:00 and supper around 7:30, then studied some more until 9:00, when they retired to their chambers. On the Sabbath day there were no lectures, but President Chauncy delivered a sermon in the hall, and then the students moved in a body to the Cambridge meetinghouse to attend Sunday services, sitting all together in the east gallery built to accommodate Harvard students.[49]

Harvard rules, renewed in 1655, reminded students of the gravity and privilege of being admitted to study at the college. Students were forbidden to leave their chambers without proper academic attire, which included "modest and sober" clothing covered with an academic gown. Long hair "after the manner of Ruffians and barbarous Indians" was also banned, as well as any faddish "curling, crisping, parting or powdering" of their hair. Students were allowed some excursions from the college grounds, but these too were hedged with restraints. Vashti Bradish ran a popular bakery close to the college yard where it was possible to buy beer, but when it became clear that students were spending too much of their time and their "parents estate" at the shop, President Chauncy set limits on her commerce: students could buy beer no more than twice a week and could spend no more than a single penny each time.[50]

Harvard offered daily lessons in subordination. Its president and commissioners consciously emulated the collegiate traditions of Cambridge, Oxford, and other European universities, in which rank determined where students would have their quarters, when and how much they would be fed, where they would sit for meals, even in what order they would sit in the hall for lectures and disputations. Lest students forget where they ranked in Harvard's hierarchy, a paper posted in the Old College listed each member of the college community in order of seniority. President Chauncy was first, followed by the senior fellow, the other fellows (tutors), the fellow commoners (students who paid double tuition and were allowed to sit at the fellows' table), the M.A. students, and then each undergraduate class, with individual students ranked according to the eminence of their families. John Wompas's family—Indian, and thus absent from the social hierarchy of the colony—placed him at or near the bottom of the already low-ranking list of first-year students. First-years—most of whom would have been around seventeen years old—walked at the end of the line, got the last seats at lecture, arrived last at the half-door of the buttery to get whatever was left for "bevers," and were served last at dinner and supper. This public subordination must have been galling to a man more than a decade older than his academic peers and from a family that—at least in Native circles—was considered prominent.[51]

Living conditions reinforced the hierarchy. Harvard students were expected to live in the college, benefiting from the "*Collegiate Way of Living*" in which "learning accrue's by the multitude of persons cohabiting for Scholasticall communion." All lived together in the rooms, or "chambers," provided for students in one of the three buildings that made up the campus in the early 1660s. A single chamber was usually shared by three or four students, although first-years were occasionally housed dormitory style in one large room, such as the long chamber in the Old College. Students slept two to a bed, with trundle beds pushed beneath each four-poster for the use of upperclassmen. After the first year, students gained the privacy of a tiny study of their own; three or four of these studies lined the exterior walls of each chamber, each with its own window for light.[52]

John Wompas was no longer a youth when he enrolled at Harvard. He was about twenty-nine years old and had been married for four years. The traditional Harvard experience of sharing college chambers with fellow teenaged freshmen and older students would have been awkward for John if he lived in college. Taking chambers at Harvard was expected, and the New England Company paid for it, but it was not required. During President Chauncy's term, a number of students attended Harvard without living there. Whether or not John lived at Harvard, he had another life outside it. He and his wife Ann Prask may have rented lodgings together in or near Cambridge, or Ann may have continued living with and working for the Hewes family, who had moved to Boston, while John lived at the college. Given the company's preference for Indian students living at Harvard, and the free rent provided, the latter is likely.[53]

Wompas's presence in his class seems to have had an impact on his fellow Harvard students. Three of his eleven classmates—Daniel Gookin Jr., Joseph Gerrish, and Samuel Treat—involved themselves in Indian missionary work after they left Harvard, showing both an interest in and at least some facility with an Indian language. Gookin, whose father was deeply involved in Indian missionary work, regularly preached to the Indians at Natick while serving as minister in the nearby town of Sherburn. Gerrish, who would become minister at Wenham, Massachusetts, was known to be "zealous for the conversion of the Indians," and Treat, who became the minister at Eastham on Cape Cod, preached to hundreds of local Indians in their own language and met with the teachers of four Indian congregations once a week to provide religious instruction. Wompas must have had something to do with their choice. He was a living symbol of the aim laid out in Harvard's charter of 1650 that the university would "conduce to the education of the English and Indian youth of this Country." Even John's eventual abandonment of his course at Harvard may have spurred the English students' involvement. The United Colonies commissioners noted the difficulty of attracting young Natives to fill the shoes of the Indian scholars who gave up their schooling or were "cut off by death." If the colony was to fulfill its stated purpose "to wynn and incite the natives of the country, to the knowledg & obedience of the onlie true God & Saviour of mankinde," English ministers would have to take up the slack.[54]

John's presence gave his classmates opportunities to learn his Native language, something vitally important for ministering to the Indians. The Christian Indians who attended Roxbury or Cambridge Grammar School and Harvard came from a range of tribes and spoke different but closely related Algonquian languages. Caleb Cheesechaumuck and Joel Hiacoomes of Martha's Vineyard spoke Massachusett—what modern Wampanoags call Wôpanâak. John Wompas and James Printer spoke Nipmuc. In 1669, more than twenty-five years after John Eliot began studying Massachusett, he asserted that the language was intelligible to a wide range of other Algonquian speakers, from the mouth of the Connecticut River to Cape Cod, and north to Pennacook. The language spoken in Narragansett country was, Eliot said, "all one" with Massachusett. Eliot acknowledged "some variation" of dialect and vocabulary in the other locales but claimed that the Bible and other religious works published in Massachusett were "readily understood" there.[55]

Although it is possible that Eliot's need for continuing support for his publication projects led him to exaggerate non-Massachusett-speaking Indians' ability to understand that language, modern linguists agree that Nipmuc and Narragansett are very closely related to Massachusett. Regardless, Eliot's claim that Massachusett was understood across a large area was based more on political and cultural realities than linguistic similarities. He asserted that the Massachusetts' and Narragansetts' political dominance over surrounding tribes and the Narragansetts' monopoly on the production and distribution of valuable wampum beads made Massachusett something of a lingua franca in the region. Because Massachusett was also used in Eliot's religious translations, he believed that "these books will be a meanes to fix, and extend, this language." John Wompas's childhood residence among a mix of Nipmuc and Massachusett-speaking Christian Indians would have prepared him to use Massachusett to bridge any gaps in understanding. Such a sharing of language skills was one of the explicit goals of the New England Company, whose governors declared their desire of the Indians' "preserving theire owne languige [so] they may attaine the knowlidge of other tongues and disperse the Indian tounge in the colledge." Samuel Treat's fluency in the Massachusett language and Daniel Gookin Jr.'s partial acquaintance with it were undoubtedly helped by having an Algonquian speaker—John Wompas—with them every day.[56]

While being ranked among—or beneath—the teenaged students must have been humiliating to the adult Wompas, there were other aspects of the college experience that must have rankled as well, aspects related to his status as an Indian scholar. Charles Chauncy, Harvard's president during John's time there, had a low opinion of Native students—not their intellectual abilities, but their persons. When the Stanton boys' failure to complete their schooling left the task of preparing Indian scholars to the other tutors, President Chauncy wrote to the New England Company requesting extra funds for these tutors, who would "have to deale with such nasty salvages, of whom they are to have a greater care and diligent inspection."[57]

"Savage" is a charged word in the modern world, indelibly associated with colonialism, the subjugation of Native peoples by invading populations. Europeans used the word to describe those whom they considered beneath them, lacking in education, government, religion, manners—in civility. To Europeans, this made savages naturally inferior to "civilized" people like themselves, from whom Indians could learn the arts of literacy, government, and religion and progress upward on the scale of civilization. As John Eliot put it, the English had themselves moved from heathen ignorance to enlightened Christianity "by reading his [Jesus Christ's] booke, and hearing his word, and praying to him . . . and just so shall the *Indians* know him if they so seeke him also, although at the present they bee extremely ignorant of him." If the English were once like the savages, the savages could one day become like the English. Belief in such an outcome was the reason the New England Company paid for John Wompas and his fellow Indians to attend grammar school and college. While the English concept of progression from savagery to civility seemed to promise the Indians eventual social equality, President Chauncy's description of Indians who had mastered Latin as "nasty salvages" casts doubt on whether he considered that a real possibility.[58]

If Chauncy was willing to use the phrase "nasty salvages" in a letter to the English governors of a charity dedicated to the Indians' uplift, it is hard to imagine that he would not have used similar phrases in front of those "nasty salvages" themselves, including John Wompas. "Nasty" was a clearly derogatory term, associated with filth and dirt. And this slur was directed at Indians who had received educations that qualified them for admission to Harvard, who dressed like and lived with English students, suggesting that Chauncy was disposed to see filthiness as an inherent characteristic of "salvages."[59]

One of the relics of John Wompas's time at Harvard suggests that he had heard the term "savage" often enough to begin to use it himself, in a sort of ironic self-mockery. John owned a copy of Cicero's *De Officiis*, the title page of which bears his name: "John Wompowess, 1665." On the facing page is a sketch of a congregational meetinghouse with the caption: "John Savage his meeting house the king of it I say." This phrase is in the same handwriting as the signature; in other words, Wompas wrote it himself and probably also drew the sketch. With its gabled roofline, its open turret and bell, the building appears to be the Cambridge meetinghouse, clearly visible from the Indian College at Harvard. John and his fellow students would have spent hours every Sunday sitting at attention in the east gallery reserved for Harvard students. The meetinghouse was the heart of English public and spiritual life, presided over by the exalted figure of the minister, or "king of the meetinghouse." In John Wompas's drawing, this lofty position was held not by an Englishman but by "John Savage," an educated Indian. It is as if Wompas were echoing—and darkly mocking—Chauncy's point that Christian, classically trained Indians were still "nasty salvages." But John's irony may have run deeper. By the time he sketched this meetinghouse and penned its caption, he must have known that no Indian minister would ever be "king" of a building like the one sketched in his book. The Cambridge meetinghouse, presided over by Rev. Jonathan Mitchell, was forty by forty feet square and could seat over eight hundred people on its main floor and second-floor gallery. Each person who attended church was expected to contribute to the salary of the minister or ministers, who typically received sixty to eighty pounds per year. In contrast, Natick's meetinghouse was a one-level structure, just twelve feet high. At twenty-five by

Figure 2. John Wompas's signature, title page of Cicero's De Officiis *(London, 1629) [Massachusetts Historical Society]*

fifty feet in width and length, it could seat several hundred worshipers, many more than Natick's hundred or so residents. But those residents had little to spare for a minister's support. Instead, the New England Company paid the salaries of Natives who acted as teachers and interpreters in the praying towns. The highest pay any of them received was ten pounds per year—one fifth of the sum the company paid Eliot for his twice-monthly visits to Natick. John Wompas must have concluded that no Indian minister—Harvard-educated or not—would ever preside over an English congregation or make a living wage ministering to an Indian one. Bitterness over the unequal prospects for students of equal educational preparation and aptitude may have prompted his sketch.[60]

Whether that inequality inspired John's doodles or not, he was clearly unhappy at Harvard. Evidence of this appears on another

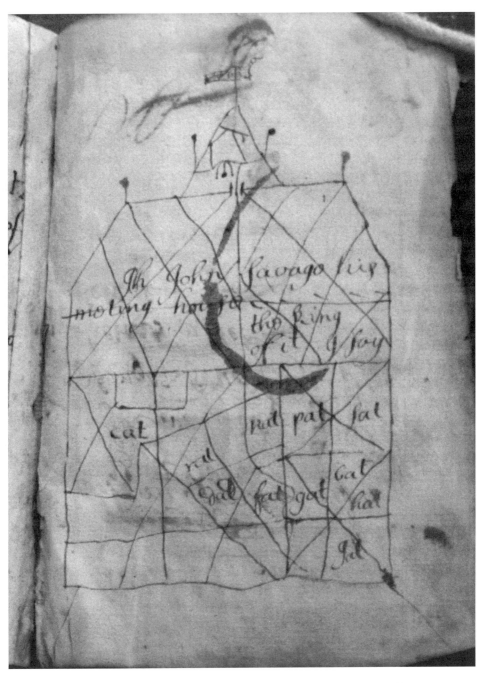

*Figure 3. John Wompas's sketch of the Cambridge meetinghouse, endpaper,
Cicero's* De Officiis *(London, 1629) [Massachusetts Historical Society]*

blank page of his copy of *De Officiis*. At the top of the page are these words in Latin, hastily scrawled by John Wompas:

> *fungor fruor*
> *cetaris affectu*
> *Cetare*

This translates as, "I cherish a desire to be at sea." Ironically, John used Latin, the language of scholarship, to express his wish to be doing something decidedly less erudite. Beneath his words, in a different hand, are six more lines of writing, the first one nearly obliterated with a maze of loops. Dimly visible underneath the scrawl are the letters "Joh," which must go on to spell John Wompas. Including this first line, then, the passage translates:

> John Wompas
> is a fool
> for writing
> *fungor fruor*
> *hetaris affectu*
> *Cetare*[61]

The fading words on this page vividly evoke John Wompas's experience at Harvard. Wompas sits with his book, not studying it, but staring out the window, doodling, uncomfortably shifting his weight, wishing he were somewhere else. Finally, he scrawls at the top of a blank page, *Fungor fruor cetaris affectu Cetare*—"I cherish a desire to be at sea." John's tutor, Joseph Browne, is making his rounds, supervising and correcting his students. On this particular day, he peers over John's shoulder to see what he has written. He frowns, takes the book, and writes, in larger letters than John's and with pressure born of disapproval, "John Wompas is a fool for writing *fungor fruor hetaris affectu Cetare*." The tutor substitutes "hetaris" for "cetaris," but "hetaris" is not a correct Latin word. Has he misread Wompas's "c" as an "h," and that perceived mistake is the reason he writes that John is a "fool"? Or does he think John is a fool for wishing to leave Harvard? Maybe both. When Browne steps away to check the progress of his other pupils, John puts his pen

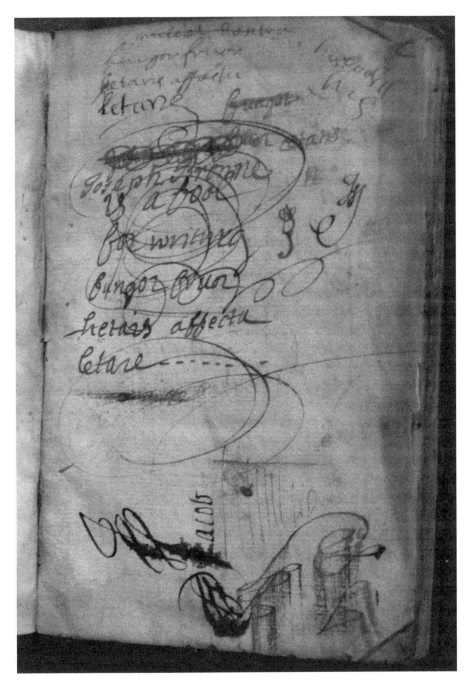

Figure 4. John Wompas's Latin doodling, endpaper, Cicero's De Officiis
(London, 1629) [Massachusetts Historical Society]

back to the paper, vigorously scribbles over the "John Wompas" that Browne has written, and in place of his own name pens "Joseph Browne" in large letters. Now who was the fool?[62]

By September 1668, John had had his fill of Harvard. Writing to the governor of the New England Company, the commissioners for the United Colonies reported that "of those Indians at the Colledge one of them being wholly indisposed to follow learning wilbee took of & put upon some other occupation by sea which he mostly desires." This Indian was undoubtedly John Wompas, who identified himself as a "seaman" on a document in 1671. Perhaps, as the commissioners' letter implied, going to sea was simply a matter of preference, a choice that seemed more attractive to John than the life of a scholar or minister. But John's own writings suggest another possibility. His mockery of the ministerial life—"John Savage the king of the meet-inghouse I say"—suggests bitterness, perhaps over the constrained opportunities he, as a Native scholar, would have compared to other Harvard students. His response to the tutor who belittled him— "Joseph Browne is a fool"—shows his growing anger at the subordi-nate position he occupied at the college, corrected and outranked by students years younger than he was, from families who held no sta-tus in Indian society. If an honorable and well-paid position within the colony was simply a pipe dream, why not find out what another life had to offer? By 1668, John abandoned Cicero and the daily round of readings, disputations, prayer, and study; he left behind Joseph Browne's disapproval and President Chauncy's disdain and followed his desire to sea.[63]

CHAPTER FOUR

"My Proper Right & Inheritance"

John Wompas and the English Land Market

John wampus of Boston . . . Indian & Seaman . . . Have given
& granted . . . Thomas stedman of New-London in the
Coloney of Conecticutt . . . Marriner . . . one hundred acres
of upLand ground . . . being one part of fourteen miles Square
of Land appertaineing unto me the afore Said John wampus as
my proper right & Inheritance.

—Deed of sale, Suffolk County, Massachusetts, November 20,
1671

"Wee think it but Reason that we . . . our selves should sett
the price on our own Land."

—OWANECO, Mohegan sachem, May 13, 1680

JOHN WOMPAS LEFT HARVARD because he had a life outside the schoolroom, one that seemed more promising, certainly more lucrative, than a career as a minister to his Indian kin. Working as a mariner gave John connections to people across New England and the larger Atlantic world, and soon after leaving Harvard, John began to sell, mortgage, or grant these people Indian land. John's life experience in both Native and English worlds gave him the knowledge and skills to navigate between them, borrowing the legal practices of both to lend legitimacy to his transactions. John's land deals provided him with a source of income, occasionally even wealth. His strategic use of English and Indian land ways allowed him to push back against the growing dominance of English law and authority that permitted colonists to secure vast tracts of land from Indians for a pittance.

John Wompas's acquaintance with Ann Prask may have served as the initial inspiration for his career selling Native land; it certainly provided the funding he needed to entrench himself firmly in the English commercial world. Wompas married Ann Prask in 1661, four years before he began studying at Harvard College. In some ways the marriage seems like a natural outgrowth of their acquaintance, but in others it seems more like a business proposition than a marriage, an arrangement entered to facilitate John Wompas's acquisition and sale of a vast tract of land. At the time of their marriage, Ann and John had known each other for nearly a decade. They were two of the small but constant number of Indians living in Roxbury. Their homes faced each other across the green on which the grammar school sat, along the town's main road. The cluster of houses around the green belonged to many of the leading citizens of the town, people who supported the grammar school and were involved in efforts to educate and evangelize the Indians, including Roxbury's ministers John Eliot and Thomas Weld, its schoolteacher Daniel Weld, the ruling elder Isaac Heath, and Ann's master Joshua Hewes. Other leading citizens, including colony magistrate Thomas Dudley and the Denison family, lived close by, and town business led to frequent interactions among these families. John and Ann attended church together, and it is possible that Ann attended grammar school with John as well.[1]

Ann and John shared the same Roxbury neighborhood until the

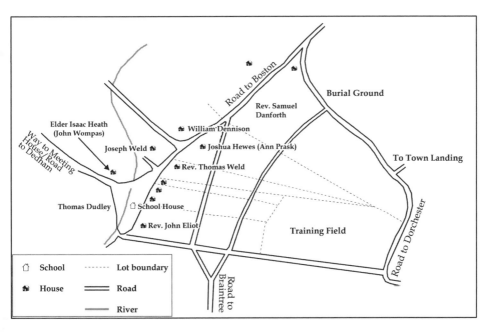

Figure 5. John Wompas and Ann Prask's neighborhood in Roxbury, Massachusetts Bay Colony, around 1651 [Map by Jen Macpherson, based on a map in Lieutenant Joshua Hewes: A New England Pioneer and Some of His Descendants, *ed. Eben Putnam (Privately printed, 1913)]*

Hewes family moved to Boston after the death of Joshua's wife Mary in 1655. Joshua Hewes undoubtedly took Ann to Boston with him; she was needed to care for his surviving children, Mary and Joshua Jr., who were thirteen and nine years old when their mother died. While this relocation removed Ann from the immediate neighborhood of John Wompas, he was not far off. Roxbury lay just two miles to the south of Boston. Cambridge, where John later attended school, was also close, just across the Charles River from Boston. It could be reached by land, boat, or the Charlestown ferry.[2]

John and Ann apparently stayed in close contact, close enough to allow John to participate in the arrangements surrounding a significant land transaction in 1660. On September 11 of that year, Romanock, an Indian living in southwestern Connecticut, granted a piece of ground "commonly called by the name of Aspitock" to his daughter Prask, "called by the English Ann." Aspetuck was named for a group of Indians who lived along the Aspetuck River to the north of Monnacommock Swamp, where Prask was taken captive during the Pequot War of 1637. After the war, the English claimed Aspetuck and the surrounding lands by conquest and built the town of Fairfield on the site. The English record of Romanock's grant does not provide the specific bounds of the land, but John Wompas believed that, because Romanock was "sachim of Aspatuck & Sasquanaugh," the grant included all the lands of the Sasqua and Aspetuck Indians and encompassed "those Tracks of Land, upon which the Town of Fairfeild in Conecticut Colony is built." After John's marriage to Ann Prask, which took place within months of Romanock's grant, the land became legally his under the English practice of coverture. By his own report, John would later sell a portion of this land to a group of men from Stonington, Connecticut, for the enormous sum of 530 pounds. There are many twists and turns and some missing pieces to this story, but it is worth exploring in detail because of what it reveals about John Wompas. It demonstrates both his astute manipulation of Indian and English land ways for his own benefit, and his wit and engaging personality, which enabled him to persuade a series of Englishmen, over a sequence of years, to trust and assist him.[3]

To profit from Romanock's land, John Wompas first needed to reunite Ann Prask with her father. Brought to Roxbury as an enslaved child, Ann may have assumed her father was dead, killed in his attempt to escape from Monnacommock Swamp. For his part, Romanock's escape from the swamp before the end of the English attack kept him from learning where Prask had been taken, or if she had survived the Swamp Fight at all. But perhaps, as a trickle and then a flood of enslaved Pequots fled their masters' homes and returned to Connecticut, Romanock learned of Prask's whereabouts. He may have sent her a message by way of an Indian or English traveler. He may even have come in person or sent someone else to seek her out. Other parents or kin of children enslaved in the aftermath of the Pequot War had done just that, traveling as far as New Hampshire to visit or rescue an enslaved child. Indians had worn highways from one end of the region to the other, and they and the English used the roads constantly to travel and carry messages and goods between settlements. The Bay Path ran in an unbroken line between the homeland of the Sasqua Indians and Boston; a spur of the Great Trail broke from the Bay Path at Hartford and ran directly through Roxbury. It would not have been surprising if Romanock had taken one of these familiar routes to travel to Roxbury, looking for his daughter.[4]

But the search may have gone the other way. Word that Romanock still lived may have reached Ann Prask, and she may have gone searching for him or asked someone else to find him. Hints in surviving records suggest that John Wompas may have filled such a role. John was not bound to service as Ann was, so he had freedom to travel should the need arise. In December 1656 an "Indean Called Womponege" spoke with Thomas Minor, a settler in Stonington, Connecticut, who recorded the encounter in his diary. "Womponege" is very similar in sound to "Wampony," a version of John's name documented in 1661, raising the possibility that Womponege and Wompas were the same person. Another indication that "Womponege" was John Wompas is Thomas Minor's later testimony that he assisted Wompas with the sale of Indian land belonging to Romanock, the father of Ann Prask. This 1656 visit, then, may have been John Wompas's attempt to find Romanock and begin the process of acquiring his land. Thomas Minor was one of the best English speakers of Algonquian dialects in Connecticut Colony; he and his neighbor Thomas Stanton had spent considerable time as translators and negotiators between the English and local Indians. Both were well known in the Bay Colony as well. If John Wompas had asked the residents of Roxbury, Cambridge, or Boston who could help him locate a Connecticut Indian named Romanock, Stanton's and Minor's names would most likely have been volunteered. In addition, John Wompas knew Stanton's son John, who studied with him in Roxbury and then went on to the grammar school at Cambridge. If no one else had directed John Wompas to John Stanton and Thomas Minor, surely John Stanton Jr. would have.[5]

Tellingly, Womponege spoke to Minor like the wit John Wompas was known to be: Minor recorded in his diary Womponege's joke that the "2 blue streaks" on "the fore finger and the greate finger" of his left hand were "eache a bottell of lichuor as he said from Thomas Stanton." An archaic meaning of "blue" is drunk; Womponege seemed to be claiming that he had earned his "blue streaks" by consuming two bottles of alcohol purchased from Thomas Stanton, who lived to the east of Minor. John's later land dealings with Minor, the similarity of his name to the one Minor recorded, and his fluency with the English language—enough to make puns in it—argue that Womponege was in fact John Wompas. This identification is important, because Thomas Minor's diary gives us the only physical description we have of John. In addition to the two blue streaks on John's left hand, Minor described a "wen" on John's wrist. Given the location, the "wen" was probably a ganglion cyst, the most common growth on the hand, usually appearing on the back of the wrist. Such cysts were not malignant, but they could grow quite large. Sometimes they were called "Bible bumps," because folk medicine treatment consisted of slamming them with a Bible or another weighty tome. With information gathered from Minor and perhaps also from Stanton, John Wompas could have continued west to Fairfield, Connecticut, located Prask's father, and then returned home armed with the information that Romanock was still alive and claimed "the whole tract of land in and about Sasquage," the home of the Sasqua and Aspetuck Indians and the location of the English town of Fairfield.[6]

There is no evidence that Ann Prask accompanied John Wompas on his 1656 trip to Connecticut, but four years later she made the trip to visit Romanock herself. On that visit, September 11, 1660, Romanock conveyed his land to Ann. Thomas Minor was there to witness the deed, which makes it probable that John Wompas was there, too. In fact, John probably facilitated the entire affair. His presence provides the most logical explanation for an event that otherwise seems highly unlikely. Why would Thomas Minor witness a land transaction that he was not a party to and that was located some seventy miles distant from his home? Why would Romanock choose to deed land to his daughter at this time, rather than leave it to her at his death? Most pointedly, why would Ann Prask marry John Wompas just eight months later? John's career in Indian land sales provides an answer to all of these questions.[7]

John Wompas was in an ideal position to negotiate Indian land sales. He was intelligent and persuasive, fluent in both Indian languages and English, and familiar with both cultures. As a result, he was able to lend legitimacy to his transactions by drawing on the practices of both, a tactic scholars call "legal code switching." In Native culture, sachems had the right to distribute land. John acknowledged this by seeking out Romanock, sachem of the Aspetuck and Sasqua Indians, and having him convey land to his daughter Ann Prask. The fact that Romanock did so demonstrates that Prask, and by extension other Native women, could own and inherit land. Minor later testified that Indians told him Prask's right to the land came through her mother and grandmother, evidence of a Native pattern of matrilineal inheritance. Wompas invoked English land ways by ensuring that Romanock's grant of land conformed to legal patterns that would be recognized in English courts. Having a prominent Englishman available to testify that English norms were indeed followed gave additional weight to the transaction, which explains Thomas Minor's appearance as a witness to Romanock's deed of land. To secure Minor's assistance, John Wompas probably promised him a share in the eventual sale of that land, which would explain Minor's willingness to testify to Wompas's legal possession years later, in the face of considerable opposition from Fairfield's English population. Minor, a leading citizen of Connecticut Colony and a frequent deputy to the General Court, testified that he saw Ann Prask "take possession" of the land and witnessed Romanock perform a version of the traditional English "turf and twig" ceremony used to transfer land to another person: Romanock "cut a stake, drove it into a hole, said, 'Mee narrowe,'" then "cut up a turf" and repeated the words. Even as early as 1660, the turf and twig ceremony was considered archaic. Romanock used it in addition to, not in place of, a formal written deed. The fact that he used the ancient English ceremony as well as official registration of his deed demonstrates Romanock's—or John Wompas's—determination to use every English tool available to ensure the validity of the title. The ceremony also appears in several other Indian land sales in this period, including one for which John Wompas ("John Indian") may have acted as interpreter. Throughout his land sales career, Wompas would follow a similar pattern, using English law to legitimize his sales, securing deeds, registering them with English officials, and marking the bounds of his land in the English manner by carving his initials into trees, as Thomas Minor did on his own land.[8]

In addition to securing a prominent English witness, recruiting Minor offered other advantages. For one thing, Minor owned a boat, which he used for frequent trips to Boston, New Haven, and other towns. That boat may have provided Wompas and Ann Prask with transportation from Boston to Fairfield. According to Minor's diary, he traveled to Boston at the end of August 1660 in order to take some things to his son John Minor, who was studying at Harvard. Like John Stanton Jr., John Minor was supported at the college by the New England Company to prepare him to assist with the Indian mission. Given that goal, John Minor probably spent time working on his Algonquian language skills with the Native scholars in Cambridge, including John Wompas. Thomas Minor's visit to his son in Cambridge in August 1660 would have provided John Wompas and Ann Prask an opportunity to sail with him when he returned to Stonington, Connecticut, and later they could have gone on to Fairfield to execute the transfer of Romanock's land.[9]

Besides persuading Minor to assist him, Wompas needed to convince Romanock to grant his land to his daughter. Romanock may have considered it pointless to do so, as most of the land was already occupied by English settlers. The English believed that conquest in the Pequot War justified their possession of Native land, but in some parts of Connecticut, the English had also paid the conquered Indians for their land, as insurance against future disputes. Fairfield was not one of those places, at least not in 1656. But by early 1657 something changed. Beginning on March 20, 1657, just three months after Wompas's probable visit with Romanock, Fairfield's English residents began taking steps to make their title more secure, obtaining their first recorded deed from the local Indians. The deed was prefaced with the statement, "there have beene Severall Indians have made claime to much of the Land that the Towne of fairefeild have & Doe possesse." The timing of this deed and its announcement of recent Native claims suggest the possibility that Wompas encouraged Romanock to assert his ownership of Fairfield land in 1656. In March 1657, other local Indians claimed ownership and secured payment, and in 1661 Fairfield residents obtained two more deeds to their town lands from the surrounding Indians.[10]

Romanock's name does not appear on any of these deeds. It is possible that John Wompas had something to do with that omission as well, convincing Romanock that he should wait and make over the land to his daughter rather than join with the other Indians in signing away their land for what seem to have been paltry amounts of money or goods. Only one of the early Fairfield deeds actually lists the amount paid to the Indians: thirteen English coats or blankets of two yards each and an unspecified amount of wampum to be divided among five sachems. All the other deeds declare that the English gave a "valuable consideration" or an unstated amount of "money already paid" to the Indians in exchange for their land. Most likely, these considerations were similar in value to the thirteen coats and un- specified amount of wampum. John Wompas, armed with his educa- tion and bicultural experience, would later secure a much higher price selling Ann Prask's right to this same tract of land.[11]

Before John could sell the land, of course, he had to obtain title, and that meant he had to persuade Ann Prask to marry him. At the time of their marriage Ann was at least twenty-nine years old and could have been as old as her late thirties. John, on the other hand, could not have been any older than twenty-four and may have been as young as nineteen. This was a large age gap in a marriage, espe- cially one in which the woman was the older partner. That and the fact that John and Ann's marriage was apparently a troubled one sug- gest that the chance to acquire land may have motivated the union. Under the English legal practice of coverture, all of a wife's goods became her husband's at marriage. By marrying Ann, John Wompas gained title to the land that Fairfield, Connecticut, sat on—at least under English law. John Wompas's sales of Fairfield land would pro- vide a dramatic jump start to a long career selling Indian land. He would later claim that he sold a portion of Prask's land to a group of men from Stonington for 530 pounds—a fabulous sum, equivalent to the entire value of two or three householders' estates. One of these Stonington investors was undoubtedly Thomas Minor. The difference between the price five sachems received for their rights to Fairfield land and the price John Wompas received for only a por- tion of Prask's right to that land is startling. If he truly received 530 pounds, it may be the highest amount ever paid for Indian land in seventeenth-century New England, and it demonstrates just how well the bicultural John Wompas could play the land game, particu- larly compared with other Natives.[12]

While the benefit to John of marrying Ann is obvious, it is less obvious how the marriage benefited Ann. After living with the English for so long, Ann must have understood that men controlled marital property, even if that property had been brought to the marriage by the woman. A *feme sole*, or single woman, had legal rights that a married woman lacked; she could make contracts, buying and selling her own property. Why not do that herself, rather than marrying John Wompas? The answer is that she may not have been able to. Ann was likely still a slave when John went looking for Romanock. Even if she had not been a slave, being female and Indian placed her in a doubly dependent position that would have made selling land across colony borders very difficult. In addition, she may have seen John Wompas as a good marriage prospect, and why not? Ann Prask, who had known Wompas since he was a boy, must have known that he had unusual gifts. He was intelligent, he had an "apt witt," as demonstrated by his jocular exchange with Thomas Minor, he was bilingual and culturally savvy in both English and Indian worlds, and he was on his way to obtaining a Harvard degree, something that only an elite few of any race achieved in seventeenth-century New England. Such a man might be able to offer her something she could not obtain for herself—her freedom. By selling the land Romanock granted Prask, John might have been able to pay Joshua Hewes to release her from slavery. No record of such an agreement exists, but it is telling that, after the deaths of Joshua Hewes and John Wompas, Joshua Hewes Jr. became one of the claimants to the land John acquired by virtue of his marriage. It is possible that in return for Ann's freedom, Wompas had promised some of the land at Fairfield to Joshua Hewes Sr. Such a promise would conform to a pattern Wompas followed repeatedly in his later land sales—promising land in exchange for an immediate loan or service. Joshua Hewes Jr.'s appearance as a claimant to Fairfield land could have been an effort to collect a long-promised payment.[13]

When Ann Prask and John Wompas did marry, they did so under English law, mirroring the publicly observed, legally binding contract Romanock used to convey his land to his daughter. The marriage took place on May 21, 1661, in Boston. It was performed by Major Humphrey Atherton, a colony magistrate, in accordance with the Bay Colony practice of marriage as a civil, not a religious, contract. Only two words indicated that the marriage was any different from the other marriages performed in Boston that year: "an Indian" following John Wompas's name. Being married under English law at Boston, rather than in Indian Hassanamesit or Natick, was evidence that Ann and John were already deeply enmeshed in English culture. John was English in religion, English in education. He would take up English employment as a seaman, traveling with English sailors on English ships. For her part, Ann had lived among the English most of her life and had formed strong bonds with the Hewes family, which helps explain why she remained a slave in Roxbury when so many of her fellow captives escaped to their homelands. An English marriage had practical value as well. It created an official record proving that Ann Prask was John Wompas's wife, combining their estates into one, and thereby giving John access to her land.[14]

The possibility that John Wompas married Ann Prask for what she could bring him in land, or that Ann married John to gain her freedom, creates a rather unflattering portrait of their marriage. But such a pragmatic marriage was by no means uncommon among English or Indians. And such a marriage does not preclude the possibility that Ann and John had an affectionate relationship, not just a business arrangement. On February 7, 1664, Ann Prask Wompas gave birth to a child, a daughter named Anna. Boston town officials recorded the event this way: "Anna of John (the Indian) and Ann White, Feb. 7." This entry is striking for several reasons. Like the Wompases' marriage—the only one recorded in seventeenth-century Boston that involved Indians—this birth record was one of a kind, the only one recorded in seventeenth-century Boston involving Indian parents or children.[15]

The official record of Anna's birth is also striking as the first recorded example of John or Ann Wompas using the surname "White." John would continue to use that name in addition to or in place of "Wompas" for the rest of his life. In Native culture, taking a new name heralded a significant life stage, such as entering adulthood, marrying, or taking on a new role or responsibility. That may explain why John added White to his name at the time he became a husband and father. Given John's penchant for irony, he probably relished the knowledge that in the Algonquian languages of the region, *wompi* meant "it is white." Thus White was a rough translation of Wompas, a sort of pun that worked in English as well as in Algonquian. By adding the name White to Wompas, John may have been making a joke that turned on racial irony, much in the way that he joked about being "John Savage" at Harvard. He may also have used White to signal his entry into the English commercial world, marking a new life stage and easing his interactions with English businessmen, who could more easily pronounce and remember White than Wompas. Just as John used both Native and English land ways strategically, switching from one to the other or combining them according to the demands of his audience and situation, he used the names Wompas and White strategically, giving precedence to one or the other to suit his circumstances. So, as early as 1664, the Wompases were also known as the Whites. And Ann, who had spent much of her life raising other people's children, became a mother herself.[16]

John Wompas's involvement in the acquisition and sale of Romanock's land at Fairfield seems to have whetted his appetite. For the rest of his life, he participated in the English land market, using his knowledge of both English and Indian land ways to steer the most profitable routes between them. The notion that the English colonists acquired land primarily by seizing it from Indians persists in popular culture. Even Francis Jennings, a bitter critic of the English "invasion" of Native America, acknowledged that taking land without purchasing it was rare and, when it did occur, was often challenged in court. Less attention has been paid to patterns of land acquisition that were far more damaging and widespread: the English practice of granting land before paying Indians for it, which pressured them to sell; and English insistence on setting prices for Native land that were far too low to provide Indians with economic subsistence once the land that supported their traditional way of life was gone. John Wompas knew these patterns and responded to them with tools and knowledge from both Indian and English cultures. Wompas was not unique in doing this. Both Indians and English had recognized and—to a certain extent—employed each other's land ways since shortly after English settlement. The relative equality of Indian and English populations at that time, and the benefit each saw in maintaining a relationship with the other, pushed them toward a mutual tolerance of differences, a "creative misunderstanding" that turned a blind eye to conflicts and encouraged the creation of new practices that combined aspects of both cultures. But as the English population and power grew, English ways increasingly took precedence. Creative adaptation, including legal code switching, became largely a Native tactic, employed by people like John Wompas to push back against English dominance of the legal, political, and commercial systems of the region. By the early 1680s, even as culturally and politically savvy a person as John Wompas could not resist the tide of English dominance that swept most Indian land into the outstretched hands of the English colonists.[17]

To understand this transition, we need to start with the land ways of each culture at the time of their initial encounter. Indian land use patterns in the Northeast, sometimes described simply as communal ownership, actually involved both group and individual rights to land use. Before the English arrived, the Algonquian-speaking Indians of the region, including the Nipmuc, claimed specific tracts of land, with distinct, recognized boundaries. Within these boundaries, Indian groups used different parcels of land at different times of the year. They wintered, planted, and harvested in one location, fished and hunted in others. From time to time, they shifted the locations of their villages and planting fields to allow the soil to replenish itself. Sachems, or Native leaders, had the right to distribute land within these bounds, but this right was constrained by the traditional use a particular family made of a piece of land, a right that could be associated with a family over many generations. Holding land within a sachem's domain placed people under the authority of that sachem, and they were expected to pay tribute to him. An aged Wampanoag Indian testified of these traditional rights in 1686, when he precisely described the boundaries of his sachem Ossamaquin's lands, declaring that "all this land was, after Wassamakins death, [his son] Philips land; & all the Indians that lived there when Philip was alive, called him sachem, & paid tribute to him." While particular Indians had the right to use the land, some uses, such as access to hunting grounds, were shared with other Natives. Having the traditional right to use a particular piece of land did not confer the right to sell that land, something that required the sachem's consent. Likewise, the sachem could not dispose of land traditionally used by specific Natives without their support for his action. Another constraint on the sachem's ability to distribute land was the consent of the elders of the tribe, who acted as his counselors. Ignoring the wishes of either of these groups would alienate them, undermining the sachem's authority.[18]

In the first years of English settlement in Massachusetts, the Indians gave the English land to build on because they saw benefit in doing so. According to their cultural preconceptions, extending a gift of land brought the recipient into their sphere of authority. The gift established a relationship of obligation that could yield military alliance and favorable trade relations, a boon at a time of real crisis. By the 1620s and 1630s, much of Indian land that had formerly been the traditional property of particular persons or families was vacated by death from European diseases, so securing other Natives' consent to give land to the English was probably not difficult, especially considering the benefits the Indians expected from English proximity. Of course, because the Indians gave the land according to their own land ways, they were only giving the English the right to use the land—to plant and build on it. They kept their own rights to plant and build on certain parts of the land, and to use all of the land for other traditional uses. Shared use of the land was what made the gift useful to the Indians: they wanted the English nearby for trade and alliance.[19]

Wittingly or not, in the early years of their settlement, the English signaled conformity with Native land ways by accepting gifts of land but allowing the Indians to continue living, planting, fishing, and hunting on it. The English also conformed to Native land ways by giving the Indian sachems gifts such as English peas, coats, cloth, and other trade goods. While the English perceived these gifts as payment, it is likely that the Indians perceived them as tribute from a people who had accepted their authority and lived on their land. Indeed, on the peripheries of New England, where Native power remained substantial much longer than it did in Massachusetts Bay, Indians continued to expect—and receive—tribute from the English who settled their land well into the 1680s.[20]

The land ways of the English differed significantly from those of the Indians they encountered. Among the English, land was commonly held in fee simple absolute, meaning that the owner of land had the right to all of its uses as well as the right to sell the land and its uses to someone else. It was also common among the English for a single person to hold title to land, rather than the multiple claimants in Native society. English land ways also provided colonists newly arrived on the shores of Massachusetts with justifications for claiming land. Among those justifications were a royal grant from the king by right of discovery, and conquest, as in the Pequot War. Colonists also appealed to the European concept of natural law embodied in legal principles such as *terra nullius* or *vacuum domicilium*, and in God's commandment to Adam to "replenish the earth." By this understanding of natural law, no one had the right to unused land; the earth belonged to those who would subdue and improve it by planting crops, grazing livestock, and building houses and barns. Colonial promoter Robert Cushman expressed this judgment in its baldest terms: "This then is a sufficient reason to prove our going thither to live lawful: their land is spacious and void, and there are few [people] and [they] do but run over the grass, as do also the foxes and wild beasts. They are not industrious, neither have art, science, skill or faculty to use either the land or the commodities of it, but all spoils, rots, and is marred for want of manuring, gathering, ordering, etc. As the ancient patriarchs therefore removed from straiter places into more roomy, where the land lay idle and waste, and none used it, though there dwelt inhabitants by them, (as Gen. 13:6, 11, 12, and 34:21, and 41:20), so is it lawful now to take a land which none useth, and make use of it."[21]

Not all English were so certain of the lawfulness of taking Native land they considered unimproved. Roger Williams famously protested that the Massachusetts Bay Colony had no right to land by virtue of their royal grant "except they compounded with the natives." This criticism may have prompted the Massachusetts General Court's enactment in 1634 of a set of laws regarding Indian lands. These laws prohibited the sale of Indian land without permission from the General Court and acknowledged the "just right" of the Indians to lands that they "have possessed and improved, by subduing the same." In practice, English courts determined "just right" both by improvement and by Indian testimony of their traditional possession. Similar laws requiring General Court permission for the sale of Indian land were enacted in other New England colonies as well. It is important to note that these laws were not put in place solely for the protection of the Indians. By publishing the laws, colony officials asserted their authority over Indian as well as English residents of the region. Requiring colonial permission for Indian land sales was a public declaration that even the chief sachems of the Indians were under the authority of the governors of the English colonies.[22]

During the years that Indians retained power relative to the English, it made sense for the English to tolerate the Native concept of shared use of land and to respect Native land ways. It smoothed relations between groups and, particularly where the English were few in number, lent legitimacy to their land transactions. The Indians could assume that English gifts of goods and food were tribute, while the English could consider them payment for land. The Indians could assume that they had granted only use of their lands to the English, and the English could assume the land was theirs and that the Indians would move on once it got too crowded for comfort.

Had English and Indian power remained relatively equal, they might have continued to tolerate one another's precepts and practices, ignoring conflicting interpretations because of the benefits each gained from the other. But power did not remain equal. Within a generation the balance tipped toward the English because of their explosive population growth and the Indians' continued population decline. By the time John Wompas came of age in the late 1650s, the English population of New England had grown from one thousand to nearly twenty thousand, well exceeding the disease-decimated population of approximately fifteen thousand Indians. The expanding English population created increased demand for the lands shared by Indians and English, leading to the breakdown of the creative misunderstanding that allowed Indians and English to practice their distinct land ways in the same area.[23]

In response to this shift, Indians sought ways to preserve their remaining lands or, if that was not possible, to profit from them. John Wompas entered the English land market at this transitional time. One tactic Indians used was to employ the English court system to fight English trespasses or to secure legal recognition of Native ownership of lands. Romanock's use of English deeds and English land transfer ceremonies when conveying land to Ann Prask is a clear example of that tactic. Indians also sought the assistance of knowledgeable persons to help them use the English legal system to preserve or profit from their lands, as the Mashpee Indians did when they employed Englishman Richard Bourne to record deeds to their lands in a Plymouth Colony court. John Wompas's long tenure among the English and experience with the land market made him an obvious resource for other Indians. There is evidence that he filled official roles in land transactions as early as 1659, when he may have been the "John Indian" acting as the interpreter for a large transfer of Nipmuc land. In 1662 Wompas appeared as a witness on two deeds for land that Massachusett sachem Josias Wampatuck sold to the English. These were lands the English had held for many years; the sale simply formalized the transaction and added payment, much like the flurry of transactions in Fairfield beginning in 1657. Given this similarity in circumstances, it is likely that John Wompas advised Wampatuck on this sale, and perhaps on later sales as well. The fact that Josias Wampatuck later appealed to royal authority to defend his land sales from English challenge—a tactic that John Wompas also used—is further evidence for an advisory relationship between the sachem and John.[24]

John Wompas also served as an advisor to his own Nipmuc kin, who recruited him "To inquire after & in our name & for our use to declare & endevor to get setled & Recorded, the indians title & Right to those lands." The Nipmuc elders explained that they chose John because he "spake English well & was aquainted with the English." In the October 1672 session of the Massachusetts General Court, Wompas "alias White," his uncle Anthony Tray, and fellow tribesman Piambow petitioned the court over land in dispute between Indians and English, with John Wompas apparently acting as an agent to defend the Nipmucs' right. Two years later, John acted on the Nipmucs' behalf again, initiating a lawsuit against the English trader Ephraim Curtis, who resided in the heart of Nipmuc Country. Curtis had purchased grant rights from another colonist, but neither the original grantee nor Curtis had ever paid the Indians for the land.[25]

These court cases provide evidence of the consequences of a particular English land practice—granting lands for new plantations before purchasing the land from the Indians. Colony charters gave English governments the authority to grant land, and the Massachusetts General Court typically gave eight or nine miles square of land to any group of people who desired to settle a plantation and agreed to gather a church there in a timely manner. Grants did not confer title. Colonists were still expected to pay Indians for the lands within any grant. But grants often preceded purchase, and English efforts to lay out lots and even to build houses and barns on them effectually forced Indians to agree to sell their lands. Once the English had possession, it was very hard for the Indians to refuse to sell. English grants of land proved to be an enormous wedge opening the door to Indian land sales.[26]

Controversies over English settlement at Quinsigamog (later Worcester) in Nipmuc Country illustrate the consequences of colony grants preceding purchase from the Indians. In 1667 the General Court granted land to establish an English plantation near Quinsigamog Pond, although it overlapped with some older grants. The English trader Ephraim Curtis had purchased rights to one of these earlier grants, and he built and lived at a trading post in the center of the new plantation of Quinsigamog. While English colonists had exchanged good money for grant rights among themselves, there is no evidence that anyone had yet paid the Nipmucs. Competing English grants to the region and Curtis's settlement at Quinsigamog before title had been secured from the Indians are probably what prompted the Nipmucs to hire John Wompas to defend their title. When Wompas and the other Nipmucs appeared before the Massachusetts General Court in 1672, they used legal code switching, citing English colonial laws that declared "that what Lands any of the Indians in this Jurisdiction have possessed and improved, by subduing the same, they have just right unto." Quinsigamog land was "improved" land. Early records of the English plantation of Quinsigamog mentioned the "Indian broken up lands" (planting fields), which proved that Indians had cultivated the land. Thus, colony law stipulated the Indians had a "just right" to it. The Quinsigamog plantation committee itself acknowledged the need to obtain title from the Indians "then numerous in the vicinity, that neighbors so dangerous and powerful might be propitiated." But while English surveyors, traders, planters, and builders had been present at Quinsigamog to some degree since 1650, there is no evidence that the English paid the Indians for any of the land until 1677, by which time King

Philip's War had cut like a scythe through the Native population. By 1677 there was no question of resisting sale, merely of how much the Indians would be paid.[27]

The English did pay for the land at Quinsigamog—*after* the court granted it to them—but they paid very little: twelve pounds for eight miles square, or 3,153 acres per pound. In contrast, Ephraim Curtis bought grant rights to five hundred acres of the very same land in 1670 (six years before the Nipmucs were paid) for fifty pounds, or ten acres per pound. Inconsiderable payments were standard practice in Native land purchases, the English often expecting to secure absolute title for the price one might pay for a year's tribute. The most destructive element in the long history of Indian land sales was the English ability to set land prices that were far too low to sustain a Native population increasingly dependent on English goods and unable to continue their traditional land uses in the face of English expansion. The Mohegan sachem Owaneco complained bitterly of this practice, declaring "wee think it but Reason that we . . . our selves should sett the price on our own Land." The settlers of early New England may have had statutes informed by Christian ethics and democratically expansive concepts of natural law, but they were also hard-headed businessmen, willing to pay as little as the market would bear. Colonist Nathaniel Saltonstall illustrated this approach in his narrative of King Philip's War. Defending Plymouth Colony against the implication that its inhabitants had provoked the war by taking Native lands, he declared, "The English took not a Foot of Land from the Indians, but Bought all, and although they bought for an inconsiderable Value; yet they did Buy it."[28]

While the initial reason for such "inconsiderable" payments may have been the creative misunderstanding that allowed Indians to construe English coats and cloth as tribute while the English considered it payment for land, the pattern of token payments persisted throughout the seventeenth century, with few exceptions. Englishmen would not pay Indians more than what they themselves considered a "fair" price, and that price was much, much lower for lands purchased from Natives than for lands sold between Englishmen. Because Native people saw exchange as something that renewed social ties between people, the stingy prices the English paid for land must have also convinced Indians that the English had little regard for sustaining the relationship. An illustration of this pattern, and its justification, appears in a striking extract from a 1650 deed conveying the land of the Tunxis Indians of Connecticut to the English. After detailing the terms of the exchange, the English writer of the deed proceeded to explain to the Indians why their land merited only a small purchase price: "It is Clear that all the Lands the English have is Little worth till the Wisdom, Labour, and Estates of the English be Improved upon it." The English writer admitted that "the Increas of theyer Company," that is, the growth of the English population, would require them to "hire" more and more Indian land, but he argued that the English presence gave the Indians more advantages "then ever they Enjoy'd Before the Comeing of the English, when all the Land was In theyer own dispose." These advantages included protection and trade, and the Englishman asserted that "Now Corn & Skins will Give a Good Price," forgetting that both growing corn and hunting for skins required land.[29]

The colonists' belief that the Indians had no need for the kind of sums typically commanded by land sales between two English buyers betrayed their view that their own civility made them fundamentally different from the Indians. English buyers needed payments that would sustain a "civilized" lifestyle, one replete with houses, barns, plows, domestic animals, pillows, bolsters, bedsteads, linens, plates, knives, spoons, undergarments, clothing, stockings, shoes, books, and candles to read them by. Indians, in the eyes of most English, were uncivilized. They did not need or want most of these things, so it followed that they did not need large sums of money. The Englishman who went to such lengths to explain to the Tunxis Indians why they did not need to be paid well for their land concluded the deed by reasoning, "therefore the Indians have Reason to Live loveingly among the English by whom theyer Lives are preserved and theyer Estates & Comforts advantaged." Signing their names to the deed, the Tunxis Indians engaged to "make no Quarrels about this matter," thus providing evidence that they, and other Indians, had already raised objections to the terms of previous land sales to the English.[30]

John Wompas had a first-hand view of how land was exchanged among the English and what it was worth. It is very clear from his transactions that he believed that the Indians were paid far too little for their land, and he demanded much more, as demonstrated by his sale of a portion of the land his wife received from Romanock for the sizeable sum of 530 pounds. But if Wompas was truly able to command such a payment, it was a rare occurrence. Over time, as Native power continued to wane, even the culturally and politically savvy John Wompas would receive less and less for his land sales.[31]

Both the difficulty of preserving land once the English had acquired a town grant and the paltry amounts that Indians were paid for their land may explain why John Wompas began selling land on his own. Over and over again he must have seen Indians receive tiny payments for vast tracts of land. And because Native land tenure practices required the consent of multiple Indians to a sale, those tiny payments were divided among many individuals, diluting their benefit. At times, Indians responded to these small sums by returning for payment multiple times, either by producing new claimants to the land or by requesting confirmations of earlier deeds. By doing so, they invoked the Native pattern of tribute payment, although under the English label of "confirmation." Indians also included specific wording in English land deeds to preserve Native uses of the land, including hunting, fishing, and even continued residence; a group of Indians near Hadley, Massachusetts, added to a deed in 1658 the right to "set their Wiggwoms at sometimes with in the tract of ground they sold." Even traditional sachems' prerogatives, such as the right to grant strangers permission to pass through the land, appeared in early deeds, but over time the English became resentful of such tactics. They complained that the Indians were "alwayes ready to sell when any man will buy what they were once or twice paid for" and sought legal remedies against Native demands for repeated payments. They also began to specifically exclude some or all reserved rights and shared uses from land deeds. Most tellingly, the English continued to pay very little for Indian land. English courts did entertain Indian complaints, and they frequently voided land sales that violated legal protections on Indian land, but they did nothing to address the issue of unfair land prices. Given this situation, John Wompas seems to have decided to make the best of a bad system by selling land on his own for the highest price he could get.[32]

Wompas's sale of a portion of Prask's land is the earliest surviving example of his selling Indian land. It probably took place around 1667, when Romanock's deed to Prask was registered in Connecticut. The next surviving deed is Wompas's sale to Thomas Stedman in 1671 of 110 acres of land in Nipmuc Country between Marlborough and Mendon, Massachusetts, for an undisclosed amount of money—"divers other good causes and considerations." In the deed, Wompas declared himself the owner of a fourteen-mile-square tract of land "appertaineing unto me . . . as my proper right & inheritance." The deed is intriguing for several reasons beyond John's claim to a sizeable portion of Nipmuc Country. It also reveals John's use of a hybrid identity, visible in how he signed the deed. His signature consists of both English initials and a symbolic mark, akin to the marks used by other Natives to sign land deeds. In contemporary English practice, "I" and "J" were interchangeable; a number of Englishmen named John regularly signed documents with the first initial "I," as John Wompas did here. John's mark, three circles in a triangle formation with a tail trailing beneath, is also striking. It appears on this deed as well as a 1677 deed, both registered in Suffolk County. The Suffolk County Clerk took great care to trace signatures and marks into the record just as they appeared. In Middlesex County, where John Wompas also registered a number of deeds, the clerk simply recorded signatures in his own hand. It is possible that John used his unique mark on deeds registered there, too, but they were not preserved. We have no way of knowing what meaning John attributed to his mark, but its distinctive shape and artistic elegance suggest that his adoption of it, paired with English initials, was more than haphazard. John knew many other Nipmucs who consistently used a distinctive mark, including his uncles Thomas and Anthony Tray. Other Nipmucs, chiefly those who received English schooling, used an English signature. None that we know of other than John Wompas used both. His choice to combine a mark and a signature could be read as an assertion of his dual identity, his right to sell land, and his expertise in the ways of doing business in both English and Indian worlds.[33]

John Wompas's dual legal expertise is apparent in the wording of his 1671 deed to Thomas Stedman. Although Wompas was the only land owner listed on the deed, it contains additional wording

Figure 6. John Wompas's initials and mark, as traced by Suffolk County clerk. Top: John Wampus of Boston, Indian and seaman, to Thomas Stedman of New London, Mariner, Nov. 20, 1671 (SD 8:421). Bottom: John Wompas to Joshua Hews, Mary Lambe, Hannah Hews, June 2, 1677 (SD 10:112). [Courtesy of Massachusetts Archives]

that suggests that John knew his exclusive right could be challenged. In the court clerk's copy of the deed, the phrase "or one third part thereof" is inserted after the words "my proper right & inheritance." Wompas's father Wampooas had died twenty years earlier, but his father's brothers Thomas Tray and Anthony were still living in 1671. John's acknowledgment that his inheritance only extended to "one third part" of the tract shows that he knew that according to Native land ways, the land was not his exclusive property. In fact, the acknowledgment ("or one third part thereof") suggests that the court official, Edward Tyng, questioned John's right to sell the land without the consent of other Indians.[34]

A number of Indians had successfully challenged sales of Indian land that lacked proper Native consent, something that Tyng, a colony magistrate, certainly knew. By reducing his claim from the whole to a third, John Wompas acknowledged the claims of Anthony and Thomas Tray. Why not just ask his uncles for their consent? Wompas may have asked and been refused. Or he may have decided that, given the vast expanse of land claimed by the three men, he could sell a tiny fraction (110 out of 125,540 acres) without consulting his kin. John also knew that involving his uncles in the sale would not increase whatever price he got for the land. By using the English legal pattern of partible inheritance, Wompas could claim the entire profit for himself. And, should his uncles object to the sale, they could always demand additional payment from the buyer later on, an action that appears frequently in English court records. Given John Wompas's advisory role to his Nipmuc kin and other Natives, he was undoubtedly aware of this. It would have been easy for John to justify his actions through his knowledge that Indians were paid far too little for their land, a practice that forced Natives to respond with demands for multiple payments for the same piece of land. In addition, through his work defending Nipmuc land titles, Wompas knew that English courts had already granted considerable Nipmuc land to English colonists who had settled on but not yet purchased it. Why not get paid for land that would soon become impossible for Indians to hold?[35]

Witnessing the English buying and selling Indian land—or even grant rights—between themselves for prices hundreds of times larger than they paid Indians, and profiting from those sales long before Indians were paid at all, John Wompas began to sell and bequeath Nipmuc lands at the disputed plantation of Quinsigamog himself. He knew that the land he was selling was already granted and, in some cases, settled and sold between English buyers, but he seems to have concluded that if the English could profit from land they did not actually own, he could too. Over a three-year period from 1676 to 1679, Wompas sold or mortgaged 11,300 acres plus eight miles square (66 square miles) of land at Quinsigamog—essentially the entire plantation. That total includes existing deeds as well as descriptions of sales in other records, but it is likely that there were other transactions—perhaps many others—for which no evidence survives. John Wompas's profit from these transactions was seventy-eight pounds and an undisclosed amount in loans, nearly five times more than the Nipmucs were paid for the same land in 1677. But that higher price was still far, far less than the unimproved land could fetch on the English market. In 1682 Joseph Dudley and other English speculators paid a group of Nipmucs ten pounds for half of a tract of land five miles square southwest of Quinsigamog Pond. Before the end of the year, Dudley sold a mere 2,000 acres of that same land to Thomas Freake of London for 250 pounds.[36]

John Wompas's Indian land transactions are striking for a number of reasons. They demonstrate his skillful use of English patterns of land tenure—securing deeds, using partible inheritance, and working through the English court system to secure title. But they also show his concerted effort to subvert the pattern of small and divided payments the English expected Indians to accept. By selling land that had already been granted or sold to the English, Wompas pushed back against that practice, obtaining payments for himself alone that were equivalent to or higher than the payments that large groups of other Nipmucs shared for similar parcels of land. Some of these Nipmucs would decry Wompas's actions, calling him "an evil instrument to disquiet them." But John seems to have considered his sales justifiable. He knew that other Nipmucs could likewise demand and receive payment for themselves, and some of them later did. Wompas's actions also threw a wrench into English efforts to settle new plantations. His sales, which overlapped with English grants and later Nipmuc sales, created decades of legal wrangling and delayed the establishment of several English plantations, and that may have been his intent.[37]

Another reason Wompas's sales of Indian land are striking is that they give clear evidence of his participation in a transatlantic economic network. Land sales were not all that kept Wompas busy in the years after he left Harvard. He also realized his "desire to go to sea," and the bulk of his land deeds were made over to men he met in the course of his travels. Of the twelve surviving deeds of land he mortgaged or conveyed in his life, five were to fellow mariners, and two were to men engaged in supplying the maritime trade. Most strikingly, seven of Wompas's twelve documented land sales were to residents of London's maritime neighborhoods. John's career as a sailor introduced him to an entire Atlantic world of new acquaintances, and his claims to Native land gave him something to sell to them.

CHAPTER FIVE

"I Cherish a Desire to Be at Sea"

John Wompas and the Maritime Atlantic

Of those Indians at the Colledge one of them being wholly indisposed to follow learning wilbee took of & put upon some other occupation by sea which he mostly desires.

—UNITED COLONIES COMMISSIONERS, September 10, 1668

JOHN WOMPAS SPENT HIS life straddling two worlds, so there is harmony in the fact that he sought the companionship of a group of men who spent half of their lives at sea and half ashore. From 1668 until his death, the maritime community—on sea and land—was where John seemed most at ease. He addressed a number of fellow mariners as close friends, expressed his love for them, and turned to them for assistance when his life on land began coming apart. Being a mariner was an indelible part of John Wompas's identity. "John White, alias Wompas, mariner" was the title he attached to deeds, petitions, and even his last will and testament.

Perhaps it is not surprising that John "cherish[ed] a desire to be at sea"; water was central to both his Indian and English worlds. The Nipmucs were the "freshwater people" because their lives and livelihood centered on the large lakes that dotted their homeland.

They set their wétus near the lakes and their feeding streams, carved long, heavy canoes, called *mishoons*, from hollowed-out tree trunks, and used these craft to fish in the waters of Quinsigamog Pond and other lakes. But the Nipmucs were at home on the sea as well as on freshwater. When the warm season came, they moved their wétus to the coast, gathered clams, and fished the great waters of the Atlantic Ocean. Some of their seagoing mishoons could carry as many as forty men at a time. As a child, John may have witnessed Nipmuc fishermen paddling their mishoons so far out to sea that they vanished over the horizon. He may have ridden in one himself and been seduced by the rush of sea-cooled air on his face.[1]

John Wompas's years in the English world, in Roxbury, Cambridge, and Boston, also showed him the centrality of seafaring to the English. Evidence of the colony's maritime economy was everywhere, in the warehouses, docks, and shops, and in the watercraft on each river and bay. Walking the streets of Boston, John could look up to see masts raised above Boston Harbor, beckoning him to places far from the stifling schoolrooms of Cambridge, and he could scarcely avoid running into the local ropewalk, where strands of hemp stretched nearly one thousand feet before being tightly wound, coiled, and sold to shipmasters or local maritime retailers to be made into rigging. At least one in every twenty-five male colonists was employed in maritime work, and a large percentage of the rest depended on regular shipping commerce for their mercantile or farming livelihoods. Massachusetts shipbuilders had begun supplying their own fleet almost as soon as the colony was settled, and by 1662 half the ships carrying trade goods to the colony had been built there. By 1674, Boston and the other New England port towns could boast twelve ships of one hundred tons or more, and 14,000 tons of ocean-going vessels of all kinds. While Boston's late-seventeenth-century population was only around five thousand, its location on a peninsula within a sheltered harbor was an ideal setting for maritime trade. Dozens of wharves lined the northern and eastern shores of the peninsula; some were beginning to creep around the shore to the south. In another generation, wharves would themselves spawn wharves, jutting out at all angles. One of them, aptly named "Long Wharf," stretched over a quarter mile into the bay, with landings on each side. By 1702, Boston's fleet of ships would be the second largest in the empire, after London's.[2]

In January 1666 John took a step that fully integrated him into Boston's growing maritime community: he purchased a house bordering on Boston Common, just a few blocks away from the major town docks. John was still a Harvard student at this point, but he seems to have already become acquainted with local sailors and taken a voyage or two. That would explain how he came to buy a house owned by a couple then living in Connecticut—Robert and Sarah Wyard. In fact, the deed to the house was executed in Hartford, with Connecticut's governor John Winthrop Jr. as a witness. Such far-flung connections are evidence that John's "desire to be at sea" had already led to significant absences from his studies at Harvard.[3]

Buying their own home was yet another unique event associated with John and Ann Wompas—the only English home owned by Indians in all of seventeenth-century Boston. The site of the home still borders Boston Common but is now occupied by St. Paul's Episcopal Church. A number of writers have commented on the fact that St. Paul's stands where an Indian once held title to an English house. Nathaniel Bowditch, reflecting nineteenth-century attitudes toward Indians, marveled at the juxtaposition: "The light of Gospel truth emanating from a truly heathen source!" But the purchase does not seem to have attracted much attention in 1666. The original deed did identify John as "an Indian of Boston." But the mortgage from 1668 and the sale of the property in 1677 identified the owners only as "John Wampus" and "Ann Wampus." John and Ann's occupation of the home for nearly a decade evoked no official notice, despite the fact that they resided there during two Indian uprising scares and a devastating Indian war.[4]

The process of purchasing the Boston house reveals John Wompas in both the flush of new money and the bluster of not having enough. The Wompases made their purchase on January 28, 1666, two years after the birth of their daughter Anna. The house's selling price was 78 pounds and 4 shillings—a substantial sum. At the time of purchase, John was still a student. Ann, who had likely been freed from slavery by this time, could not have earned more than a few pounds a year as a domestic servant, even if caring for her own child gave her the freedom to work for others. That they were able to buy the house at all suggests that John had already sold some of Romanock's land at Fairfield, Connecticut. Wompas later testified that "some time" after Romanock's grant in 1660 to Ann Prask he sold a portion of Aspetuck to a group of men from Stonington, Connecticut. John claimed that these men paid him 530 pounds for the land, more than enough to purchase a home in Boston—indeed, enough to purchase four or five homes. While no deed of such a sale survives, Romanock's gift to Prask was registered in Connecticut on October 14, 1667, nearly two years after John and Ann purchased their Boston home. John may have made up the story of being paid 530 pounds for Romanock's land. He may have paid for the house in Boston with funds obtained through other sales or labor. Or he may have secured payment for Romanock's land on the strength of the deed alone, before it was registered in an English court.[5]

If John did receive the entire 530 pounds for Fairfield land before purchasing his Boston house, he did not manage it very well. When he signed the deed for the home, he laid down thirty-seven pounds and ten shillings, promising to pay forty pounds and ten shillings more by September 29, 1666, "without fraud or farther delay." This phrase in the deed suggests that the purchase involved some kind of unfulfilled promise. John may have claimed to have the full purchase price but only produced half the required money when it came time to sign the deed. As a result, the sellers, Robert and Sarah Wyard of Hartford, Connecticut, assigned the collection of the remainder of the purchase price to the merchant John Richards of Boston. Apparently, John and Ann failed to meet the deadline of September 29, 1666, because in August 1668 they took out a mortgage of thirty-seven pounds and five shillings on the home, payable again to John Richards. This time, Richards was acting on behalf of Major Robert Thomson, an English merchant and benefactor of the New England Company, who must have loaned the money for John Wompas to complete his payment to the Wyards. The mortgage's 8 percent interest rate covered "one whole yeare then expired," dating back to February 1666, shortly after the original payment had come due. It is unclear how much money, if any, the Wompases paid on this mortgage, but it was still outstanding a decade later.[6]

Being short of cash, evidenced by his failure to come up with the full purchase price of his home, must be one reason why John chose to leave Harvard and take up work as a sailor. Although a typical sailor worked only six months a year, during the months when he did work the wages were fairly good. An "ordinary seaman"—the lowest rank on a ship, aside from boys—was paid nineteen shillings a month in the mid- to late-seventeenth-century English Navy. An "able seaman," one with at least four years' experience at sea, was paid twenty-four shillings per month. In labor-poor New England, wages were higher. Pay depended on experience, but ordinary and able seamen averaged over thirty shillings per month on merchant ships sailing in the 1650s–1680s. Sailors did not have to pay for their food or lodging while aboard ship, so their wages were comparable to those of day laborers in New England, who earned one and a half to three shillings a day. Indian day laborers earned less than the going wage for English laborers, only one shilling a day in the 1670s. The same disparity of pay probably existed between English and Indian sailors, but the records are too scanty to generalize. The few records that do exist show Indian mariners earning twenty to twenty-two shillings a month—a wage comparable to that of the least experienced English sailors. With free room and board on top of the wage, becoming a sailor might have been an attractive alternative to day labor on land, where Natives could earn only a shilling a day and had to take Sundays and fast days off. John Wompas had a family to support, and he seems to have run through the profits from his initial land sales rather quickly.[7]

Another reason John Wompas chose to leave Harvard for the sea may have been the influence of his new maritime neighborhood. As residents of Boston, the Wompases had many neighbors who were sailors, merchants, and maritime tradesmen. John Blake, a sailor whom John Wompas called his "very loveing freind," lived in the block just west of him. Ship captain Edward Ellis lived two doors away, and Captain William Wright lived just across the Common, in a home that his wife and her son operated as the Three Doves tavern. John could have met all these men in the street or in a tavern, and Captain Wright or Captain Ellis could have offered him a position on his crew. Wright's and Ellis's wives were friends of Ann Prask Wompas, possibly as a result of John's employment. John had other mariner friends and acquaintances who rented lodgings in the neighborhood as well.[8]

Only a year after purchasing his Boston home, John Wompas made his break from Harvard complete. In September 1668, the United Colonies commissioners wrote that "of those Indians at the Colledge one of them being wholly indisposed to follow learning wilbee took of[f] & put upon some other occupation by sea which he mostly desires." John was the only Indian scholar at Harvard known to have pursued a career as a sailor, so the commissioners' letter undoubtedly refers to him. As they had done for other Native scholars who abandoned their studies, the United Colonies commissioners assumed the responsibility of helping John find an "occupation by sea." They most likely gave preference to ships owned and captained locally, by men they knew and trusted to be good examples of Christian living. A godly shipowner or captain would do his best to ensure that the environment aboard ship mirrored the godly society on land. Boston merchant and shipowner John Hull, a devout Puritan, showed his commitment to nurturing such an environment in his instructions to shipmaster John Harris: "We solemnly charge you to worship the Lord daily in your Vessel, & sanctify his Sabbath carefull[y] with all your company, & watch diligently against all those sins & temptations that easily assault & are ready to overcome yourself, & company; that by your good example they may be the better drawn to doe well."[9]

The records mentioning John Wompas's shift from scholarship to sailing say nothing about whether an apprenticeship or indenture was involved. John was around thirty years old in 1668, fifteen or twenty years older than a typical starting apprentice. He was also a husband, father, and home owner, which would likewise have made a formal apprenticeship unusual. In the maritime trades of New England, which suffered from the same labor shortages as the rest of the colonial economy, apprenticeships were usually informal. New recruits learned their professions on the job, receiving ship-room and board the first few years, drawing pay as ordinary seamen for the next few, and then advancing to able seamen. That is most likely the path John Wompas followed.[10]

If a New England sailor steadily took employment in the same community, he had a very good chance of eventually becoming a shipmaster; nearly half of those who began as ordinary sailors became masters by their late twenties. John Wompas never advanced

into the officer ranks. He first described himself as a "seaman" in
1671, although he probably first went to sea several years earlier. In
1679, the year of his death, John still described himself as a mariner
or seaman, not a master or other officer. His advancement may have
been stalled by any number of things. As an Indian, he would have
been seen as an outsider among the overwhelmingly European sailors who manned the Atlantic fleet in the mid- to late seventeenth
century. His late start in the profession and his lack of family connections could also have been factors, as well as his sporadic employment. John seems to have gone to sea only when it suited him,
viewing it as one of several moneymaking options. He may have
found selling land a more profitable employment than sailing.
Spending time in other pursuits would have led to long breaks in his
service as a sailor, which was known to hinder promotion. Race may
have been a factor in John Wompas's lack of advancement; sporadic
employment almost certainly was.[11]

A generation after John went to sea, Indians joined New England whaling and fishing crews in large numbers. In the seventeenth century, however, John was one of only a handful of Natives
employed in the English maritime world. That did not mean Indians were unfamiliar with European sailing techniques. Indians were
keen observers and early adopters of European technology. In the
first decade of the seventeenth century, French and English explor-
ers along the northeastern American coast reported a number of
Native seamen manning abandoned or stolen European ships and
expertly wielding their sails. Early colonists also described several
instances of Indians who were essentially pirates, using captured
English boats to take other vessels. After English settlement, Indians served as hired sailors on boats owned or captained by English
colonists. As early as 1636, a "coaster," a small boat designed to stay
close to the shore, was reported to have a crew of two English boys
and two Indians. In 1667 another Indian, called Thomas, was listed
as a seaman in colonist William Weekes's small vessel, probably also
used for coastal trade. Indians were also the primary laborers in the
first New England whaling business, which began in the 1670s at
Easthampton on Long Island. But these were local enterprises, with
boats rarely going more than a day's journey from shore. The first

recorded evidence of an Indian in the transatlantic sea trade was John Wompas.[12]

As a seaman, John would have found himself yet again in the company of men five to ten years younger than himself. And just as his age made him stand out among the undergraduates at Harvard College, his age and education would have made him unique among the new recruits of a merchant ship crew. He may have been the only common sailor in the maritime Atlantic who could recite and read Latin and Greek, along with a smattering of Syrian, Chaldaic, and Hebrew. Few of the officers could claim as much. But seamen had little need for Latin or Greek in their daily round of duties, and it is doubtful that John got any special consideration for his years toiling with the intellectual elite of New England. When sailors were not serving one of their endless rounds of watches by day and night, they were busy cleaning and maintaining the ship: they scrubbed the deck to remove brine and refuse; they spun and knotted yarn for repairs, and they inspected and repaired weak or fraying sails and lines. After a long voyage, the bottom or hull of a ship would need scraping, or "graving," to remove barnacles and seaweed that could weigh down and slow the ship; that required sailors to haul the ship onto the shore and, after the tide had receded, scrape and clean the hull and seal the seams with tallow—an exhausting process. When sailors had gained more experience, they could also help repair the ship itself and assist in sailing it. An "able seaman," one with at least four years' experience, could "hand, reef, and steer." In other words, he knew how to handle lines and sails; he could "reef" or shorten sails in storms or high winds, and he could take a turn at the helm.[13]

On large ships, many crew members would share these tasks. The size of a ship was given in tons, reflecting how much weight or "burden" it could bear. A ship of 240 tons typically employed up to thirty sailors. But ships of that size rarely came into Boston Harbor. In a list of twenty-seven ships arriving and departing Boston Harbor in 1661, only three were as large as 150 tons. Over half ranged between sixty and ninety tons. That may seem like a perilously small craft to be out on the open sea, but many of the ships traveling across the Atlantic in 1661 were even smaller. The *Blessing* of Boston, which regularly made voyages to Barbados and London, had a burden of 50 tons and carried a crew of only five men.[14]

The sailors' life was highly dangerous. As Samuel Johnson put it, "No man will be a sailor who has contrivance enough to get himself into a jail; for being in a ship is being in jail with the chance of being drowned." Four out of every hundred ships at sea in any given year were lost to storms or other maritime disasters, often with all hands. If a ship was not sunk, it could be attacked by French, Dutch, or Spanish ships during one of the many European wars that plagued the seventeenth century. During the first Anglo-Dutch War in 1653, *The New England Merchant*, en route from London to Boston, was attacked by a Dutch ship. In the fight, a common seaman named James Makins was wounded and died four days later. The five-man crew, captain, and single passenger of the *Blessing* of Boston were captured by a Spanish ship in the Caribbean in 1683. The Spanish stripped the men "stark naked," tied them to half-submerged trees on the shore, and left them to perish in the tropical sun. Barbary pirates were a common and greatly feared hazard of sea life. At least 20,000 Englishmen and women were captured and imprisoned or enslaved by Barbary pirates during the seventeenth and eighteenth centuries. Many New Englanders shared this fate, and lurid tales of the cruelty of the "Turks" chilled the spines of listeners in Boston and other colonial ports.[15]

If death or slavery did not take you, disease very likely would. Scurvy was the bane of long-distance voyages. After five or six weeks without the vitamin C provided by fresh fruits and vegetables, sailors' teeth loosened, their skin acquired the look of a pimply adolescent, and they became so weak that they could not get out of bed. Death soon followed. While seafarers had noted the effectiveness of citrus fruit in preventing this malaise as early as the sixteenth century, it was entirely up to shipowners or captains whether or not to provide it for their crews. The medical establishment failed to confirm and recommend the practice until the end of the nineteenth century, by which time tens of thousands of sailors had died. Travel also exposed sailors to tropical diseases such as malaria, and many picked up syphilis and other venereal diseases in their ports of call. In the port towns of Salem and Boston, 12 percent of women were widows in 1754, a "rough index of the death rate among resident mariners."[16]

Life as a sailor was not only dangerous, but physically and emotionally punishing. Sailor Edward Barlow wrote that sailing was "one of the hardest and dangerousest callings . . . all the men in the ship except the master being little better than slaves." Barlow complained that some stingy merchants and shipowners put only enough food and drink aboard their ship to last through the quickest possible voyage. If ships were "a little longer in their passage and meet with cross winds," the supplies ran out, "so that many times in long voyages men are forced to spend half their wages in buying themselves victuals." Merchants were known to make up the costs of cargoes that were spoiled or damaged in passage by subtracting the losses from their crew's wages.[17]

John Wompas's voyages as a mariner would have taken him away from the familiar streets of Boston for long stretches of time. Signing on for a voyage on a merchant ship meant many months away from home, and then many more waiting either at home or abroad while the ship was loading freight, being repaired, or safely docked for the winter. Voyages on merchant ships sailing round trip from Boston might take six weeks (to Newfoundland), two to four months (to Virginia), three to five months (to the West Indies), or five or six months (to England or Europe). But ships frequently made several stops rather than a simple return trip. In the list of ships trading to Boston for 1661, over a third registered their intent to stop at least twice before returning home, selling goods and loading new freight in each port. On a typical voyage, a ship might load pipe staves and fish in Boston for sale in Madeira. In Madeira, wine was loaded for sale in London, and in London finished goods were loaded for sale in the shops of New England. The entire voyage could take a year. If the ship was laid up for repairs or the weather was bad, it could take much longer.[18]

All this is to say that with a sailor for a husband, Ann Wompas spent a great deal of time on her own. Mariners' wives, then and later, could count on long stretches without a husband to assist in family labor, and without his income to pay the rent or purchase food, clothing, or other necessities. A provident husband might leave enough money to see his family through until his return. However not all husbands were provident, and many seamen's wives looked to other sources for income. Options for lone women to support themselves in colonial New England were few, but they did exist. Women ran taverns alongside their husbands, and when those husbands were away or died, wives could and did carry on without them. Boston granted licenses to sell liquor to a number of widows as part of an informal welfare system. By allowing a woman to continue the business in her husband's place, town leaders kept the widow and her children from becoming a burden to their neighbors.[19]

Many mariners' wives also took in boarders to supplement their husbands' income, and Ann Wompas may have done that as well. Because Boston was the English colonies' major port in the late seventeenth century, many foreign sailors disembarked there for a few weeks or months between voyages and spent their wages freely in the city's lodging houses and taverns. Boston's Castle Tavern and the King's Arms were closest to the Town Dock and likely hosted hundreds of mariners, but the Horseshoe, the Three Doves, the Bluebell, and the Anchor were all within a mile of the Town Dock and got their share of the sailors' business as well. If a ship's home port was Boston, many of the crew would be New Englanders, and their wives and mothers might regularly rent rooms to the friends and fellow crewmen of their kin. As shipmates lodged together at home, aboard ship, and in distant ports, they formed a community that moved seasonally much like the Nipmucs and other Natives of New England.[20]

As John Wompas became tied into this transatlantic community, making friends and acquaintances at distant ports as well as at home in Boston, he found new opportunities to sell land. The most consistent characteristic of Wompas's land deeds from the time he became a sailor to his death in 1679 is their connection to the maritime Atlantic world. Some of John's deeds have been lost, but of the eleven surviving deeds drawn up between 1671 and 1679, six were to mariners, four from New England and two from London's dockside neighborhoods of Ratcliffe and Stepney. Four more were to men involved in London's maritime trades and living in its maritime neighborhoods. In every case, John deeded or mortgaged land in return for immediate loans of from ten to fifty pounds or to repay previous, undisclosed loans of money, food, or other assistance. While John paid these men with deeds to Nipmuc land, their assistance to him was not entirely mercenary. These were his friends, not just opportunists. They took care of him, even when he wasn't around to reward them for it. For instance, on one occasion, John skipped town still owing seventeen shillings to Boston's town jailer. He entrusted his friend and fellow seaman John Warner to pay it. Warner had his Boston landlady Katharine Franklin (whose husband was also a mariner) take the payment to the jailer, adding the expense to Warner's debts to the Franklins. John Wompas—long gone from Boston by that time—was off the hook.[21]

The exchange of debts between John Wompas and his friends reveals the complicated interconnections of the maritime Atlantic world that John traveled in. John Wompas had met John Warner in the London suburb of Ratcliffe, along with his father, Nicholas Warner. Nicholas Warner assisted John with some loans and favors, and John paid him with deeds to Nipmuc land. John probably introduced the Warners to other New Englanders, such as John Cole of Charlestown. Cole was another mariner John Wompas deeded land to, and Cole testified to visiting Nicholas Warner's house in Ratcliffe. John may also have introduced the Warners to Benjamin Franklin (uncle to the statesman of the same name), who worked as a cooper, supplying barrels for Boston's sea trade. When that didn't keep him busy, he shipped out as a mariner, going to sea on the same crew as John Warner at least twice. Back home in Boston, Franklin's wife Katharine provided food and lodging for seafarers, including the Warners. She also facilitated various maritime trading ventures, renting shop space to Nicholas Warner so that he could ply his trade as a tobacconist, and supplying the younger Warner with a barrel of pickled mackerel to sell after reaching port on one of his sailing voyages. And, as mentioned, she paid her lodgers' debts if they were suddenly called to sea. All of these people—the Franklins, the Warners, and John Cole—interacted in multiple locations, in New England, in Old England, in other port towns, and aboard ship, demonstrating the pervasive reach of the Atlantic maritime community. The assistance and loyalty of that community would become increasingly necessary to John Wompas as his relationships on land unraveled.[22]

While the seafaring life created financial opportunities for John, it also gave him more occasions to spend the wages he earned. It is a stereotype that sailors were spendthrifts, prone to drink. Seventeenth-century English diarist Samuel Pepys, who worked for the British

Naval Office, declared that sailors were the "most adventurous creatures in the world, and the most free of their money after all their
dangers." During the months when winter storms could prove
deadly to ships, most vessels were laid up in port, leaving their crews
to while away their time at home or abroad. A group of restless sailors left to winter over in New London, Connecticut, managed to set
a house on fire, causing more than one hundred pounds in damages.
The latent danger of mariners stuck ashore was captured in "Nep-
tune's Raging Fury," the most popular mariners' song of the era:

> When we return in safety with wages for our pains,
> The tapster and the vintner will help to share our gains;
> We'll call for liquor roundly and pay before we go,
> Then we'll roar on the shore when the stormy winds do blow.[23]

Roaring on the shore was something sailors were notorious for in
every port of the Atlantic world. With no regular daily employment,
and no wives or mothers to keep them in line, it is no wonder that
sailors far from home were known for idleness, heavy drinking, and
"bad exploits," being "left at leisure to exercise their dissolute manners on the inoffensive passenger in the public street." Idleness and
drunkenness were jailing offenses in Puritan Boston, not only because they disturbed public order but because of the example they
set, "where by such persons as attend their duty, & spend their time
in that service, are discouraged."[24]

The stereotype of drunkenness was associated not only with sailors
but also with Indians. Like most Europeans of the era, sailors drank
large amounts of alcohol every day, and some violated public behav-
ioral norms by becoming drunk and disorderly. In seventeenth-
century New England most Indians drank neither socially nor daily.
Instead, they drank occasionally, and when they did, they usually
drank to the point of inebriation. That was, in fact, the point of
drinking. Rather than share limited amounts of alcohol among an
entire group, Natives would often pool their supplies, allowing a
small number of individuals to become drunk. In this way, they
treated the "altered spiritual state" induced by alcohol as an end in
itself rather than a by-product of social drinking. For the English,

such an approach to drinking reinforced their notions that Natives were uncivilized. Alcohol-fueled sociality, not its consequences, was what Europeans valued.[25]

Both colony laws and Native leaders recognized the temptation and destructive potential of alcohol for Indians. It wreaked havoc in Indian communities, not only among those who indulged, but among family members and friends who suffered abuse from drunken friends and kin. In one particularly tragic case, a group of English traders illegally supplied alcohol to a Native community in Connecticut. An Indian man became drunk, then beat his wife "and stamp'd upon her in his mad fitt." When he came to himself and learned that he had harmed his unborn child, his remorse was so extreme that he killed himself. Both Indians and English placed the blame for this terrible incident solely on the unlawful traders, whom the English rushed to apprehend "that the greate Name of God might not suffer and blood crye not against us." Laws forbidding the sale of "stronge water to any Indean" appeared as early as 1633. As English magistrates perceived that "the sinn of drunkeness amongst the Indians doth much increase," new laws were added, punishing both the Indians who became drunk and those whose illegal trade facilitated it.[26]

There is widespread evidence that English colonists violated laws against selling alcohol to Indians to access the lucrative fur trade or simply to make some extra money on the side. By some accounts, even government officials colluded in using Native desires for alcohol to their own advantage. According to an English ship captain who spent three months in Massachusetts in 1673, colony leaders passed a law stipulating "that every Indian coming into their towns . . . who was drunk should pay 10 [shillings], or be tied to a gun and whipped." Needing laborers to help build a defensive fort on Castle Island in the bay, the magistrates replaced the punishment of whipping with ten days' forced labor. Reportedly, after nine days someone would send rum and brandy to the island, and when the Indians became drunk they were sentenced to ten more days of labor. The captain claimed that hundreds of Indians were consigned to work on the island, some for the entire three months of his stay, "which barbarous usage made not only those poor sufferers, but the other Indians, to vow revenge." Despite complaints by Native leaders and their English supporters and increasingly harsh penalties for Indian drunkenness and the illegal trade of alcohol, abuses continued.[27]

The increase in drunkenness in Massachusetts Bay Colony was not just an Indian problem. In November 1675 the Massachusetts General Court, recognizing the "shamefull and scandelous sin of excessive drinking," tightened regulations on public houses and their proprietors and laid a penalty of five shillings for every offense. At the same time, Increase Mather preached that "strangers had reported seeing more drunkenness in New England in half a year than in England in all their lives." When Governor Leverett objected to the statement, Mather groused, "As for the Governor, He hath bin the principal Author of the multitude of ordinaries [taverns] which be in Boston, giving licences when the townsmen would not doe it. No wonder that N. E. is visited, when the Head is so spirited." Indians who served alongside English soldiers in King Philip's War of 1675–1678 were influenced by the English approach to alcohol and the "multitude of ordinaries" that sprang up during the war. John Eliot noted: "The successe of our Indians was highly accepted with the souldiers, & they now welcomed [them] where ever they met them[. T]hey had them to the ordinarys, made them drink, & bred thereby such an habit." Eliot claimed that acquiring the habit of social drinking led to debt, drunkenness, fighting, and other "sad effects of strong drink" among former Indian soldiers. Undoubtedly, it also strengthened English tendencies to associate drinking and social disorder with Indians.[28]

In John Wompas's case, the stereotypes of the drunken sailor and drunken Indian held some truth. It is possible that his long residence among the English had led him to adopt the English practice of drinking on a daily basis. He was arrested for public drunkenness in 1673, and his relatives and English officials described him as frequently drunk. For his wife Ann, John's drinking became a wedge that split their marriage apart. Of course, the marriage may have been troubled before his drinking became an obvious problem. The large age difference between the two may have bothered either or both of them, and John's extended absences may have been hard on Ann. The marriage also may have been weakened by a traumatic event— the death of their child. Boston death records are missing for the years 1665–1688, so it is unclear exactly when their daughter Anna died. She probably survived at least through her first year, as her name does not appear in the existing death records for 1663 and 1664. Town records do not show the birth of any other child to Ann and John. It may be that Ann was too old to conceive again, that Anna's death and the couple's other troubles alienated them from each other, or that John responded to the tragedy by staying away from home.[29]

John's drinking affected not only his marriage, but other relationships as well. His Nipmuc relatives had entrusted him to defend their landholdings in the early 1670s, so they must have considered him responsible at that point. Within a few years, however, Wompas lost their trust. In 1677 a delegation of leading Nipmucs, claiming that "all hee aymd at was to gett mony to be drunke & spend upon his lusts," asked Daniel Gookin, the superintendent of Indians, to prevent Wompas from acting in their behalf or interfering in any way in their business. This does not seem to have been their first complaint to the authorities. Massachusetts officials had begun to prohibit John's land sales three years earlier, leaving him entirely reliant for money on his wages or the generosity of his seaman friends.[30]

In the spring of 1673, John's drinking landed him in jail. The Suffolk County Court charged him with drunkenness and his wife Ann with "abuseing and strikeing of her husband." These words evoke a troubling scene, one that must have taken place in public, perhaps at one of the taverns close to their house. Had Ann gone to fetch him and found him drunk and unwilling to come home? Had John spent money on ale that she needed for food or some other purpose? Whatever the cause, Ann raised loud and public complaint against her husband, "abusing" him verbally and then "striking" him with her fists or whatever else she had at hand. Someone must have reported the disturbance to court officials, because they issued a summons for both John and Ann to appear in court and collected a bond for their appearance from John.[31]

When John did appear in court on April 29, 1673, he was alone. Ann failed to appear, whether because she was away or because she simply refused to share her husband's shame. Because she did not come to court as ordered, the magistrates retained the bond John had posted for her appearance (probably ten or twenty pounds), fined John ten shillings, imposed a forty-pound bond for good behavior on top of the other charges (twenty pounds for John himself, and ten pounds for each of two sureties), and committed him to prison until the charges were paid.[32]

Ann did not appear in court herself until six months later, on October 28, 1673. There is no indication that John was with her, and the court treated her with remarkable gentleness. The magistrates admonished her for "abuseing and strikeing" her husband but did not fine her, assign any corporal punishment, or commit her to prison; they simply dismissed her with the standard requirement that she pay court fees. It seems likely that the court viewed Ann with sympathy. Perhaps the magistrates saw her response to her husband's carousing as improper but understandable given the circumstances.[33]

Court records offer valuable insight into the daily events of the past, but they can't help but skew our perceptions as well. In the case from 1673 and other legal records, John comes across as a drunkard, but this may not accurately depict his life as a whole. The complaints against John for drunkenness may have been exaggerated because of stereotypical associations of Indians with alcohol or because of other grievances people had against him. It is worth noting that in two other court depositions about John Wompas's behavior, English witnesses specifically described him as "sober & not in drinke." In the 1673 court case, we see John drunk and fighting with his wife, but there were undoubtedly happier times that did not come to the attention of the court. John must have known of his wife's anger over his drinking and may have tried to make it up to her. The inventory taken of Ann's estate in 1676 suggests the possibility that John bought her presents. Ann, the Indian wife of an Indian sailor, owned luxuries comparable to those in the best families in Boston, including a feather fan with a silver handle, two pairs of leather gloves, a silver bodkin, and a pair of silk stockings. If these were gifts and not her own purchases, they could have been tokens of apology from John. Or perhaps they served as unpleasant reminders of his spendthrift ways.[34]

John's frequent appearances in colony records from 1671 to 1674 suggest that he did not take maritime employment (or collect seaman's wages) for some time, or if he did, it was only for short voyages. Instead, he seems to have focused his efforts on Indian land sales. The magistrates' prohibition of those sales sometime in 1674 cut off that source. He had to either return to sea to earn money or find some way to overcome the magistrates' ban. Or he could do both—taking a berth on a ship to England and appealing to the king to restore his freedom.

One hint that John had such an appeal in mind when he left Massachusetts in 1674 is the appearance of a set of debits and credits for "John Indian" in the account book of Boston merchant Robert Gibbs. Gibbs owned an extensive piece of property on the slopes of Fort Hill, just half a mile south of John Wompas's Boston house. He built a "mansion" there in 1671, and the property also contained a warehouse and a wharf for his own use. Gibbs's shop, from which he sold goods mostly in exchange for work or produce brought in by his customers, probably sat on the property as well. Starting in May 1674, John Indian put in thirty-three and three-quarter days of labor for Gibbs, at a rate of a shilling a day, earning a total of one pound, thirteen shillings, and nine pence. This wage was significantly below the rate Gibbs offered to other workmen in the same period. The Gibbs account book shows five other men hired for day labor in 1672 and 1673, at tasks such as cutting wood, bringing goods from the wharf, fetching "corn and pease" from town, or working in his garden. Four of the men were paid two or two and a half shillings a day. The fifth workman, "Goodman Hollys man," meaning his servant, was paid a shilling and a half a day. Gibbs also employed three women in this period, each of whom received one shilling a day, the same rate Gibbs paid John Indian. Women received lower wages than men for their labor in this time and place, often less than half, a practice justified by their supposed physical weakness and the types of labor they performed. The fact that Gibbs paid John Indian a woman's wage, a third less than a male English servant, for doing a man's daily labor speaks volumes about the status Gibbs accorded to Indians. Apparently, Gibbs was not alone in placing such a low value on Indian labor. A shilling a day was the same rate the Massachusetts government paid the Indians recruited to build a fort on Castle Island.[35]

Although we cannot be sure that John Indian was John Wompas, there are a number of factors that make it likely. One is the proximity of Gibbs's warehouse to Wompas's home—just half a mile away. Another is the fact that, like John Wompas, John Indian was not a servant. If he had been a servant, Gibbs's account book would have listed his master, as it did for "Goodman Hollys man" and "John Wells Mr Peacocks servant." But the most persuasive evidence that John Indian was John Wompas are his purchases, which were particularly fitting—one might say tailor-made—for what John Wompas planned to do next. In exchange for his labor early in the summer of 1674, John Indian bought three and a quarter yards of white cloth and thirteen and a half yards of black woolen frieze, befitting a formal occasion. He would need to hire a tailor to make this into a suit, and that would cost him another one to two shillings a day for up to a week of sewing. John also purchased a shirt and rented a "gown," a loose outer garment worn by men, spending just under two pounds for the whole—nearly thirty-four days' wages, plus some debt he would have to repay at a later time. How it must have galled him that he was earning less than a servant! It was a great deal of effort and expense for a set of new clothes, but it was necessary. John Wompas was going to visit the king.[36]

CHAPTER SIX

"New England Hath Lost the Day"

John Wompas Protests to the English Crown

John Wompus Indian beeing at my house in cambridge village
. . . saying that hee cume from England lately. . . . & said hee
saw mr Stoughton deliver the letter upon his knees to his
majestie, & said wompus they petitioned the king that . . . the
king would please to renewe their pattent. The king answered
that his grand father, had [given] them their pattent, but they
had forfeited it & acted contrary to it.

—DAVID MEADE, 1677

JOHN WOMPAS LEFT MASSACHUSETTS at a time of personal trouble, but it was also a time of trouble for the colony, with worse still
to come. Massachusetts had been under a cloud of royal disapproval
for the past decade, since the king sent royal commissioners to investigate the colony's loyalty and adherence to English law in 1664.

Those commissioners returned to England with damning reports, urging the Crown to rein in the defiant colony and replace its stubbornly independent leaders with appointed royal officials. Only a series of imperial crises, including two wars with the Dutch and political standoffs between King Charles II and Parliament, had kept the king from revoking the colony's charter long before 1674, and Massachusetts officials knew they were on borrowed time. Within a year of John's departure from Massachusetts a more immediate crisis struck the region: a devastating war broke out between the English colonists and their Indian neighbors the Wampanoags and Narragansetts, as well as many of John's Nipmuc kin. Away from the colony during the outbreak of King Philip's War, John would nevertheless have learned of it, if not from the broadside hawkers who shouted the news on the streets, then from his New England contacts on ship and shore. By the time he returned to Massachusetts in 1677, he would find a way to use both the war and the colony's political disgrace to his own advantage.[1]

John's purchase of a white shirt and black wool for a suit suggests that visiting the king was the immediate purpose of his voyage. Such a possibility may have been planted in John's mind as early as 1662, when he heard Charles II's invitation to his "loving subjects" "to receive any aplication or addresse from them which may concerne their interest." We do not know if the voyage John took in 1674 was his first visit to London. He may have crossed the Atlantic soon after becoming a mariner in 1668, or he may have made shorter journeys to Virginia, the West Indies, or Newfoundland, all of which were frequently visited by New England ships. London-bound merchant ships, like the one bearing John Wompas, entered the channel of the Thames River at Gravesend, twenty-five miles east of the city. There they would wait for the tide and prevailing southwest winds to carry them in to the wharves lining the banks on the east end of London. The hours or days John would have spent in the Thames channel before finally stepping ashore may have brought to his mind Native ideas about the liminality of such shore spaces, which functioned as thresholds between the world of the living and the world of spirits. Some Indians seem to have made the connection between London and the world of spirits explicit; one Native story told of a servant who overheard his English mistresses using witchcraft to travel

to another world. Repeating the spell, the man was instantly trans-
ported to a "crowded street" in London, where he saw his mistresses
walking. Frightened that they would be angry with him, the man
hid. Later, he tried to remember the spell in order to return home,
but he failed and was forced to spend the rest of his life in a city of
strangers. Undoubtedly the story echoes the sense of loss Native
people felt for friends and kin who went to London and died there,
thus making it a clear metaphor for the world of spirits. If Wompas
had heard an early version of this tale, he may have had it in mind
when he stepped ashore. Would he die in London, as so many Native visitors had done before him? Would he ever be able to return?[2]

When John's ship passed Greenwich on its trip up the Thames,
he could have seen the distant peaks of church spires and towers and
the monument to London's Great Fire of 1666 soaring above the
houses and shops of the city. From the docks on the east end of London, he could have looked west just over a mile to see the crenel-
lated walls of the Tower of London, its massive bulk looming over
the river. London was certainly daunting in appearance, with its
countless buildings crowding in on the Thames. Some features of
the city would have felt familiar to a Nipmuc man. Nipmucs planted
near lakes and streams; hence their name, the "freshwater people."
Like the Nipmuc River, which was the pulsing heart of Nipmuc
Country, the Thames River connected rural England to the outer
world and carried a constant supply of food and goods to sustain the
city. Nipmucs favored hilltop locations for their towns; London,
too, rose from the banks of the Thames to Ludgate Hill, where
St. Paul's Cathedral sat. But the scale of London greatly exceeded
any place John had seen before. By the 1670s, London had a population of between 300,000 and 400,000 persons—a tenth of the entire population of England and Wales. Hassanamesit was tiny in
comparison. Even Boston, the leading town of colonial America, had
a population of only 12,000, and its largest structure was the Town
House, which was sixty feet long, thirty-six feet wide, and not quite
thirty feet high. That building—imposing by colonial standards—
could have fit nearly eighteen times over within London's White
Tower.[3]

It was not just the scale of buildings or the size of the population
that distinguished London from the towns of John's homeland, but

the noise, turmoil, and pollution they produced. So busy and crowded were the streets of London that walkers were jostled as they went, a "bustle [that] wearies the body and giddies . . . the head." Native visitors like John often found the crowds overwhelming. Accustomed to the clean air of Massachusetts and the open sea, John must have felt his eyes itch and burn as he approached London. A contemporary English diarist lamented the "horrid smoke which obscures our churches and makes our palaces look old, which fouls our cloths and corrupts the waters." Tens of thousands of households burning coal were responsible for the haze. New England households burned wood—an even dirtier fuel than coal—but there were far, far fewer of them. London's residents, like Boston's, habitually dumped their refuse in the street or in the Thames, where it sloshed around the wharf pilings and raised a stink. Although scavengers descended on the riverbanks at low tide to cart away anything of value, noisome things remained that nobody wanted, including dead rats, waste from riverside tanneries, and raw sewage. Another English diarist even reported a human corpse floating dockside for four days.[4]

London and Boston shared the English legal tradition, and justice was on fierce display in both places. The head of an Indian man executed for murder in 1671 was set on a pike on the narrow neck of land leading to Boston, the only land route into the town. Similarly, even a few days in London would have brought John Wompas face to face with the moldering heads of traitors fixed above the entrance to the Tower of London, on the turret at the south end of London Bridge, or arrayed over one of the city gates. The bodies of criminals executed at various public sites within and outside of London were often left dangling from their nooses until they rotted and fell of their own accord.[5]

While some of London's sights, sounds, and smells must have been oppressive, others could have been exhilarating, displaying a variety far beyond what Boston had to offer. London was home to thousands of shops. Each bore a wooden sign advertising its wares in a colorful language of symbols: unicorn horns and dragons for an apothecary, a cupid and torch for a glazier, a man made of green leaves ("jack-in-the-green") for a distiller. Hawkers of produce and merchandise roamed the narrow streets, shouting, "Buy a mouse trap, a mouse trap!" "Lilly white vinegar!" "Have you any brass pots, iron pots, or frying pans to mend?" Milk sellers clanked their pails, and cart drivers shouted at their horses and at careless passersby.[6]

The London that greeted John Wompas in 1674, with its din and confusion and tight-packed lanes, was a city reborn. For three days in September 1666, fire had swept through the crowded streets within the ancient walls of the city. The flames leaped easily across the houses leaning toward each other over the narrow lanes. Although King Charles II ordered entire blocks to be blown up as firebreaks, most of London inside the city walls and a large swath outside the walls to the west was incinerated. Only a few neighborhoods in the northeast of the city escaped the flames. When the fire burned itself out on September 6, 1666, more than thirteen thousand houses had been destroyed, as well as eighty-five of the 107 parish churches, fifty-two livery halls, and such prominent public buildings as the Guildhall, Newgate Prison, and the Royal Exchange. Even the massive stone cathedral of St. Paul's, standing since the twelfth century, lay in ruins.[7]

The rebuilding of St. Paul's would take a mammoth effort and over a quarter century to complete, but the homes, shops, and smaller churches of London rose from the ashes with startling speed. "Three short years completes that which was considered the work of an age," proclaimed the inscription on the monument to the fire, erected by order of the king and completed in 1677. Workers poured into London from outlying towns and were soon swarming over scaffolding throughout the old city. Men and women who would once have gone to the colonies as indentured servants stayed in London instead, where there was more than enough work to go around. The royal government encouraged rapid reconstruction with both carrot and stick: The king temporarily suspended taxes on the city's inhabitants; Parliament placed a tax on coal and used its proceeds to fund the rebuilding of St. Paul's Cathedral and the parish churches; and the government threatened to repossess the land of any owners whose previous structures had not been rebuilt within seven years of the fire. By 1671, much of the housing of the ruined city had been restored. When John Wompas arrived, eighteen of the eighty-four churches destroyed in the fire had been rebuilt, and ten more were under construction. St. Paul's was still in ruins, but work on the new cathedral began in 1675. Walking past the site, John would have seen charred walls still looming above the construction barriers erected to keep the curious out and building materials safely in.[8]

Much of the clutter and squalor of the old city was swept away in the flames. As eminent a talent as Christopher Wren drafted a plan for a newly ordered London, with wide, straight avenues radiating from the centers of commerce and worship. It would be a capital worthy of a rising empire, fit to stand with the grand cities of the continent. But no one, from the city fathers to the king, could face the herculean task of negotiating with owners of the thousands of individual land parcels that would need to be reallocated to carve a truly new London out of the old. The maze of curving streets, lanes, and alleys remained and served as the template for the new city. Wren's ideal city remained unbuilt, and the new London looked much as it had before, although many buildings, by royal decree, rose in brick or stone to prevent future fires.[9]

One of John Wompas's first tasks after landing was to secure lodging. Among his shipmates, there were doubtless several who knew London well and could guide John to a suitable boarding house or tavern where he could clean up before seeking an audience with the king. He may have thought he had merely to present himself at the palace to secure a royal audience, following the Thames River west until he reached Westminster, where Whitehall Palace stretched along the riverbank. If that was the case, he surely was disappointed. By 1674, King Charles II had reduced access to his royal person from what had formerly been a flood to a trickle. Frustrated with the emerging Whig party's persistent opposition to his efforts to loosen religious restrictions, the king began admitting only his political allies to his presence as a reward for their loyalty. To enforce these new constraints, the king issued regulations to Whitehall's ushers, directing who could approach him, when, and how, and reducing the number of entrances visitors could use in the sieve-like palace, and stationing guards there. If John presented himself at Whitehall without a specific invitation secured from someone with Court connections, he would have been brusquely turned away, new clothes or not.[10]

John was not easily discouraged, however; he was still in London two years later in 1676, still trying to get the attention and assistance of the king. His efforts would undoubtedly have taken him to the place that attracted every New Englander seeking assistance or news—the Royal Exchange. The Royal Exchange was a magnet for New Englanders in the city. Many visiting merchants or agents took lodgings on streets adjoining the Exchange: Cornhill, Cheapside, Leadenhall, and Coleman. Indeed, many of Boston's leading merchants had lived near the Exchange before migrating to Massachusetts, and they named streets in their new home after those in their old one.[11]

First known as "The Burse," the Royal Exchange was erected in 1566 on land donated by the City of London. By 1570, it had become a popular enough center of commerce to merit a visit from Queen Elizabeth, who ordered that it be renamed the "Royal Exchange." Due to the Exchange's prominence, it was one of several locations where trumpet-bearing heralds proclaimed public business and pillories were set up for malefactors to be publically shamed. Events at the Exchange reflected the political turmoil of seventeenth-century England. Early in the century, a statue of King Charles I graced the entrance. During the English Civil War of 1648, supporters of the Parliamentary faction pulled down the statue and put up in its place a plaque declaring *Exit tyrannorum ultimus:* the tyrants' last exit. In 1661, after the Restoration of the monarchy, the public executioner burned Parliament's "Acts for constituting a Commonwealth" at the same spot, thus publically repudiating the era of "unkingship" proclaimed thirteen years before.[12]

Like most buildings inside the old walls of London, the Exchange was destroyed in the Great Fire of 1666, but as a vital engine for economic growth, it was rebuilt much faster than St. Paul's. In 1669, just three years after the fire, a new Royal Exchange was completed. Like the former building, this one contained a large interior courtyard with wide covered galleries surrounding it on every side where merchants, agents, and traders could continue their business even in bad weather. Businessmen from particular regions met every day in the same parts of the Exchange, under the protection of the galleries or along the paths that crisscrossed the courtyard. One such area was dubbed the "New England Walk," so frequently did Massachusetts merchants, agents, and other men of business gather there. This familiar haunt of New Englanders was common knowledge; when the Lords of Trade were investigating Massachusetts's obedience to the Navigation Acts, they sent a messenger to summon New Englanders to appear before the committee, informing him that four of them could be found "at the Exchange upon the New England Walk." At the Exchange John Wompas could easily have picked up news from home, discovered the names of people with royal connections, or failing that, learned which shipmasters were seeking sailors, in order to earn some money while he waited for his luck to improve.[13]

Waiting, of course, meant John needed a place to stay. The most natural place for a mariner to take lodgings in London was in the dockside hamlets east of London's city wall—Shadwell, Wapping, Stepney, Ratcliffe, Mile End, and Limehouse. The vast majority of residents of these hamlets were seamen and their families, ship's officers, or people supplying the needs of the shipping economy, providing transient mariners with food and shelter and producing the ropes, rigging, canvas, casks and barrels, and other goods needed aboard every ship. As in Boston, mariners' wives in London often rented rooms or beds to visiting seamen. The proverbial rivers of alcohol consumed by mariners newly cast ashore were well supplied in these towns as well. In Shadwell, a town of just over six hundred households, there were forty-four taverns, or one for every thirteen residents. Few tavern keepers could keep their doors open with such a ratio. Undoubtedly transients—mostly sailors—filled out the numbers. Ashore between voyages, flush with their accumulated wages from extended service, and with no work to keep them busy, seamen, local and foreign, gave the East London towns a reputation for heavy drinking and associated crime and violence.[14]

On his first arrival in London, John probably knew no one outside of his ship's crew, but by 1676 he could count several residents of the maritime hamlets as his friends, including three men from Ratcliffe. The fact that these early acquaintances in London lived in Ratcliffe makes it likely that John lived there too, at least on his first extended stay. Ratcliffe was known for its poverty, disorder, and easy access to alcohol. Speaking of the town, a magistrate of the county court declared that he and his colleagues "know well the poverty of the said hamlett, and how numerous and mutinous the poore are there." Such a reputation had one advantage—it likely made the rent more affordable.[15]

Figure 7. The Royal Exchange, interior courtyard with merchants, 1727
[London Metropolitan Archives, City of London]

Living in London could be expensive. Weekly rent cost two to three shillings, or eight to twelve shillings per month. The cost of food and drink was at least that much. A typical London pauper spent nearly two shillings a week on these necessaries alone. A "middling" laborer could afford to buy more meat, tea, and sugar, so spent around four shillings a week. John Wompas, who was known to be free with his money, probably spent closer to four shillings per week on food and drink. Coal for heating his room, clothing, bedding, or any other household items would have added two or three shillings to this total, making expenses of around eight shillings per week, or thirty-two to thirty-eight shillings per month. John's wages as a seaman may have been as low as twenty shillings per month, or half that if he drew half pay while on shore. With monthly living expenses that significantly exceeded his monthly salary, John would have burned through his money rather quickly, even if he had managed to save some from his last voyage.[16]

Beyond bare subsistence, London offered a bewildering array of other opportunities for a man to run through his wages. Two officially sanctioned theaters operated in or near the city, as well as unlicensed theaters offering "cruder type of melodrama." A number of establishments staged cock-fighting and bear- or bull-baiting, and there were thousands of shops offering clothing, foods, and goods rarely seen in Boston. Brothels were plentiful, even one conveniently located just behind the House of Lords, and taverns and pubs were almost as common as sailors, particularly in the maritime neighborhoods of East London. Any of these places could have drained away John's wages even if he only spent money on himself. But John was a man fond of extravagant gestures. His generosity or efforts to impress others may have led him to treat people to drinks or to indulge in fineries he could not afford. Whatever the reason—necessities or excess—John quickly found himself in debt.[17]

Evidence suggests that John turned to his friends for help in relieving his debts. John Cole, a mariner from Charlestown, Massachusetts, was also in England when he performed a "service" for John in 1675—likely lending him some money. John paid his debt to Cole with land, a deed for three hundred acres. Whatever service or loan Cole provided John in the year 1675, it merely slowed the financial hemorrhaging. By February of 1676 John found himself in prison "in or near London" for a debt of fifty shillings.[18]

Debtors' prison was a creditor's final resort to get a debtor to pay what he owed. The creditor could enter a suit against the debtor in the county court and obtain a warrant for his arrest. That warrant was delivered to the warden, or keeper, of a nearby prison, who seized the debtor and, if he was unable to post bail, carried him off to jail—which is what happened to John Wompas. London's Fleet and Ludgate prisons were best known for housing debtors in the late seventeenth century, but debtors also ended up in Newgate, the notorious hold of murderers, whores, and thieves, as well as in less well-known prisons set up in the "liberties" attached to various churches, hospitals, or private estates, such as the Duchy of Lancaster in the Strand, or St. Mary Whitechapel. This last prison served the manors of Stepney and Hackney; it was one of the two prisons closest to Ratcliffe, where John probably had lodgings, so it may have been where he spent nearly a year in prison.[19]

John's debt was quite small. Traditionally, debtors were not imprisoned if they owed less than forty shillings, and Wompas owed only fifty shillings, or two and a half pounds. There was a man in prison at the same time as Wompas who owed more than sixteen hundred pounds—a small fortune—as well as a woman who owed only thirty shillings. But for both debtors on a grand scale and those whose debts were measured in shillings the penalty was the same: imprisonment until the debt and all charges incurred in prison were paid.[20]

Debtors' prison was a wretched place for the poor. Even for the upper classes, being jailed for debt was a terrible predicament to be in, racking up daily fees for lodging, food, the use of linens for bedding, even for the privilege of being admitted or discharged from prison, or to have their case heard by a judge. But at least gentlemen inmates had wealthy friends and family to pay these small fees, to keep them in food and clothing, and to prevent them from being shifted from the relative comfort of the "Master's Side" of the prison to the squalor and misery of the "Common Side." A debtor who wrote an account of his imprisonment in the Fleet in 1733 described what occurred when he failed to pay for his keep: He was unceremoniously turned out of his room and "forc'd to walk the Prison to keep Warmth within him, during the Winter-Season."[21]

For the poor, or for the once-wealthy whose resources had run out, the Common Side could be a ticket to an early grave. One Englishman imprisoned in the Fleet in the 1690s reported that he and twenty-seven other Common Side inmates slept on the stone floor of the prison's dungeon and that the men there were "so lowsie that as they either walked or sat down, you might have pick'd lice off from their outward garments." Few windows lighted the wards, and poor ventilation magnified the rank odors of smoky chimneys and sick and unwashed bodies. Poor nutrition, no water or soap for washing, and the crowded conditions of the Common Side created an environment ripe for the spread of infectious disease. As many as one in four of its inmates died in any given year. For many people in seventeenth-century England, the idea of imprisoning someone indefinitely for a debt of only a few pounds was repugnant. But so was the idea of providing no recourse for creditors, who could themselves become insolvent if their bills were not paid.[22]

Parliament struck a balance between these opposing injustices by instituting a "Law for the Reliefe of Distressed Debtors" in 1671. By the terms of this act, imprisoned debtors could petition county justices of the peace for release from prison if they could take an oath that they had neither real nor personal property worth more than ten pounds. Once the debtor took this oath, the court sent notice to his creditors and directed them to appear at the next session of the county court. There, the justice of the peace asked the creditor to provide any reason why the debtor should not be released. In the vast majority of surviving London-area cases from the last decade of the seventeenth century, the creditor made no objection and the debtor was discharged.[23]

John Wompas could have used this means to obtain release, if he had known about it. The fact that he was still in prison in August 1676, at least six months after his arrest, suggests either that he did not know about this avenue of appeal, that his imprisonment happened to fall in a gap between the county court sessions that dealt with insolvent debtor petitions, or that his creditor refused to consent to his release. We don't know who Wompas's creditor was, but the most likely candidates are his landlord or his victualler, who might have been the same person. Many lodgings, particularly those associated with inns or taverns, included board as well as room. By February 1676, when Wompas was imprisoned, it was winter, and most ships were safely laid up in port until spring. He probably had not drawn pay for several months. It is no surprise that he was fifty shillings in debt.

Entering the cold stone walls of a debtors' prison in the depth of winter, John Wompas must have wondered how he would survive. Nearly forty years old in 1676, he had no money of his own and no family nearby to appeal to for help. Because little or no food was distributed without charge in the prison, many inmates relied on the charity of friends and family, or of strangers, to supply the rest. One debtor's obvious plight prompted a chemist who lived near the Fleet prison to bring him a plate of meat every Sunday for over a year. Like this Fleet prisoner, Wompas was fortunate in having at least two friends who assisted him during his time in debtors' prison. One was Nicholas Warner and the other was Anthony Mudd, both English tradesmen from Ratcliffe. Mudd was a house builder, and Warner was a tobacco cutter, someone who prepared the tobacco imported from English colonies for sale. Mudd and Warner apparently provided both material and emotional support to John Wompas. John would later describe the "love, tenderness & affection showed mee by Anthony Mud . . . while a prisoner in old England." John also noted the "kindness & maintenance, I had and reseived from Nicholas Warner" and "the Loane of severall summes of money— borrowed of the said Nicholas Warner, with out interest." "Maintenance" suggests that Warner brought him food and other necessaries, as well as providing cash. If John was imprisoned at St. Mary Whitechapel, which allowed liberty of the prison yard to debtors, these "severall summes of money" would have allowed him to post bond for his return, leave the prison, and meet with his friends. The sums may also have helped him purchase food, drink, perhaps even access to a bed in the prevailing fee system of debtors' prisons. If John was not fortunate enough to be held in a prison that granted such liberty, his friends would have to enter the prison to visit him, or pass him news, food, or money through the "begging grate," a barred opening between the prison and the street, where passersby could see and speak to the inmates.[24]

Whether John was in one of the more restrictive prisons such as the Fleet, or one with a liberty such as St. Mary Whitechapel, he needed the assistance of his friends to complete the task that had brought him to London. He meant to make another attempt to contact the king, this time by petition. For a man in prison, the obstacles to such a plan were considerable. John, who was Harvard educated, could have penned the petition himself, but there are several reasons to think that it was written by a scribe on his behalf. The first reason is that it would have been difficult for a prisoner to obtain the supplies needed to produce a formal letter—high-quality paper, pen, ink, and a clean, well-lit surface to compose it on. And John probably had no notion of the correct protocol for a royal petition. It is unlikely that either Warner or Mudd, both common tradesmen, understood the protocol either, but protocols were a professional scribe's bread and butter. Second, the penmanship of the petition does not seem to match other examples of John's hand, and it is also different from a second royal petition John submitted in 1679. The petition read,

> To the Kings most Excellent Majesty
> The humble Peticion of John Wampas alias White.
>
> Sheweth
>   That your Petitioner being a poore Indian having a certaine parcell of Land in Massy Chussit Bay the which he hath held for many yeares, he having received the oaths of Allegiance and Supremacy, and being now reduced to great distresse was cast into Prison about six months since for a debt of fifty shillings, where he hath remained ever since to his utter Ruine.
>   Wherefore your Petitioner most humbly prayes that your Majesty will be graciously pleased to grant your Petitioner your Majesty's Royall Letter to Sir John Leveritt Knight, Governor of Massy Chussitt Bay, whereby he may be restored to his said lands or else that he may [have] free liberty to make Sale thereof for his present releife and towards paying of his debts.
>   And your Petitioner shall ever pray &c

The wording of the petition is general and formulaic, as one might expect from a scribe; the few times it mentions specific details, it does so in a way that suggests unfamiliarity with the places and persons named. For instance, twice the writer uses the spelling "Massy Chussit Bay" for Massachusetts Bay. Spellings varied wildly in the seventeenth century, but this particular version looks like an attempt to phonetically spell a phrase unfamiliar to the writer. Another clue is the writer's anachronistic reference to "Sir John Leveritt Knight, Governor of Massy Chussitt Bay." Governor Leverett of Massachusetts had not been and would never be knighted, although John Wompas's petition prompted a flurry of nineteenth-century claims to the contrary. The line containing this mistaken honorific was clearly inserted later, between two lines in the completed petition. One can imagine how the process unfolded: The scribe listened to John's account of what he wanted included in the petition. He then returned to his home or workplace to write the formal document and brought it back for John's approval. At that point, John told him he should include the Massachusetts governor's name. Either John mistakenly told the scribe the governor was "Sir John Leveritt," or the scribe himself added the honorific as an extra flourish, on the mistaken assumption that any governor would also be a knight.[25]

Getting the petition written was the easiest part of the plan. Getting it into the king's hands was the real challenge. Persons of very high status could simply hand their petitions to the king or to one of his chief officers at Court. If the petitioner lacked such connections, he could deliver it to a meeting of the Privy Council by entering, kneeling, and placing the paper on the table, and then silently withdrawing. Finally, petitioners could submit petitions to one of the rotating "Masters of Request" at Court. This officer would see that petitions reached the right people, presumably at some cost to the petitioner. Confined to prison or the boundaries of its liberty, John could not deliver the petition in person without risking severe penalties. He could borrow money to pay the scribe to deliver it for him, or he could ask one of his friends to deliver it. Nicholas Warner, a man of considerable energy and persistence who later secured an audience with the Privy Council for himself, could certainly have carried out the task.[26]

On August 22, 1676, John Wompas's petition, perhaps delivered by Nicholas Warner, was raised before the Lords of Trade, a standing committee of the Privy Council. While the handwriting on the petition was probably not John Wompas's own, the idea and content certainly were. In fact, John's petition may be the first example of an Indian petitioning the king on his own initiative, without English sponsors manipulating his words for their own political purposes. His lack of such a sponsor was undoubtedly the reason John had spent two years trying to see the king and still had nothing to show for it. Other Natives had previously traveled to England in the company of colonial officials who had direct ties to courtiers or to the king himself, and the king's welcome of Native visitors was part of an imperial strategy to impress American Natives with the power and magnificence of the English Crown in order to obtain their willing submission to English authority. Of course, Indians had their own reasons for allowing themselves to be enlisted in such royal visits.[27]

John was not the first Indian to use the strategy of appealing to the king. In 1644, the Narragansett Indians of Rhode Island wrote to King Charles I, submitting themselves and their lands to his authority and begging to be taken under his protection. Similarly, in 1666 Josias Wampatuck, sachem of the Massachusett Indians, submitted himself and his lands to Charles II in return for his protection. In both cases, the Indians involved showed a clear understanding of the political advantages of submitting to the king; by doing so, they became subjects of the English Crown, on equal footing with the English colonists and thus free of their authority. But Indian submissions to the Crown also benefited English colonists. The Narragansetts' 1644 submission was penned by Samuel Gorton, an inveterate enemy of the Massachusetts government. He carried it to England with him as further proof of Massachusetts's wrongdoing and as a vital support to his effort to secure a separate charter for the colony of Rhode Island. The Massachusett sachem Josias Wampatuck's submission to the Crown in 1666 also supported an English as well as an Indian agenda. Wampatuck had leased land to an Englishman, Richard Thayer, against the wishes of the elders of his tribe. The town of Dorchester claimed the land under an earlier grant from Wampatuck's father. When Dorchester officials ordered Thayer off the property, he and Wampatuck petitioned King Charles II, giving him the land and begging for his protection. By trumping Dorchester's authority with the king's, Thayer got his land back, and Wampatuck got his rent.[28]

It is very likely that John Wompas knew about these appeals to the king. Indeed, he may have assisted with Wampatuck's appeal. John served as a witness to two of Wampatuck's land sales in 1662 and may have been acting as an advisor to the sachem. John was a student in Cambridge during the royal commissioners' visit of 1664–1666, when Wampatuck made his submission to the Crown and the Narragansetts renewed theirs. The threat that their appeals to royal authority posed to the Massachusetts leaders could not have been lost on John Wompas. Now he had a chance to petition the king and harness that authority for himself.[29]

Like previous Native petitions to the king, John's showed political astuteness, playing on his status as a royal subject to claim the king's protection and favor. In his very first sentence, in fact, John pointed out that he had "received the oaths of Allegiance and Supremacy," proof that he acknowledged the king's ultimate authority and was his loyal subject. During the royal commissioners' visit, those oaths had been a source of conflict between the Massachusetts colony and the Crown's agents. Massachusetts officials did not administer the king's official oaths; instead, they had colonists swear oaths of loyalty to the Massachusetts Bay Colony. This was sufficient, they claimed, because colony officials were the king's representatives; thus loyalty to the colony included loyalty to the king. The commissioners rejected this reasoning and insisted on an overt statement of loyalty to the king through the royally prescribed oaths, which did not mention the colony. John Wompas's claim that he had taken the king's official loyalty oath would have evoked this conflict and immediately made it clear which side he was on.[30]

John Wompas also displayed his political acuity by highlighting his identity as an Indian, probably to remind the king of his 1662 promise to receive the appeals of his Native subjects. He may also have hoped to pique the interest of a king known for his love of the exotic. In his petition to the Crown, John gave precedence to his Native identity, writing "the humble Peticion of John Wampas alias White" and describing himself as "a poore Indian," despite the fact that he had participated fully in the English world for well over a

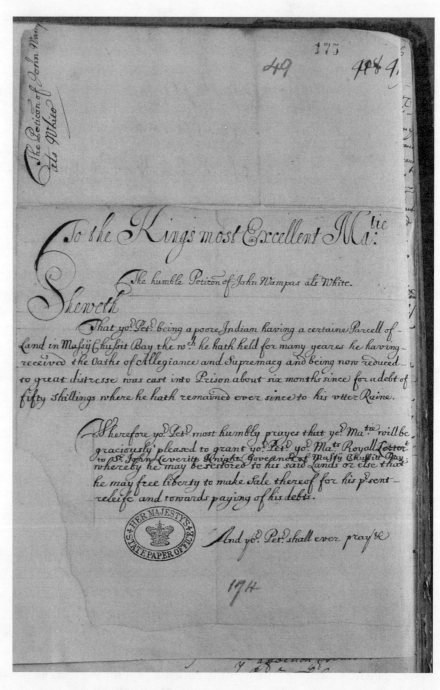

To the Kings most Excellent Ma:^tie

The humble Peticon of John Wampas als White.

Sheweth

That yor Pet.^r being a poore Indian having a certaine Parcell of Land in Massij Chusitt Bay the wch he hath held for many yeares he having received the Oaths of Allegiance and Supremacy and being now reduced to great distresse was cast into Prison about six months since for a debt of fifty shillings where he hath remained ever since to his vtter Ruine.

Wherefore yor Pet.^r most humbly prayes that ye.^r Matie will be graciously pleased to grant yor Pet.^r yor Ma.^ts Royall Letter to Sr John Leveritt Knight Gove.^r and of Massy Chusitt Bay whereby he may be restored to his said Lands or else that he may free liberty to make Sale thereof for his p.^rsent releife and towards paying of his debts.

And yor Pet.^r shall ever pray &c

174

Figure 8. John Wompas's first petition to King Charles II [The National Archives of the UK (TNA), ref. CO1/37 (49)]

decade, purchasing a home in Boston, attending Harvard College, working as a seaman, and even adopting an English name—John White. As he no doubt knew, being an Indian made him stand out from the hundreds of other supplicants to the king. While there had been Indian visitors to England before, most famously Pocahontas in the early years of the century, Indians were still an exotic rarity, interesting to nobles and commoners alike. Not for nothing did Shakespeare give Trinculo the words, "when they will not give a doit to relieve a lame beggar, they will lay out ten to see a dead Indian." This "poore Indian" had been cast into prison for a debt of only fifty shillings, "where he hath remained ever since to his utter Ruine." John begged the king to intercede in his behalf by overruling the Massachusetts Bay Colony's prohibition on his land sales. He requested a letter to the colony's governor "that he may [have] free liberty to make Sale [of his lands] for his present releife and towards paying of his debts." Like the Narragansetts and Josias Wampatuck before him, John placed himself directly under the king's authority, thereby freeing himself from the yoke of the Bay Colony.[31]

As John Wompas hoped, the king was moved by his petition and ordered his Secretary of State Joseph Williamson to pen a letter in his behalf to Governor Leverett in Massachusetts. On August 22, 1676, Williamson wrote the letter, commending John Wompas to the governor, directing "that he may have Justice done him, & what favour the matter will bear," and, significantly, referring to Wompas as "our Subject." In his letter to Massachusetts a decade earlier, the king had included Indians among his subjects by inviting "all . . . within that our plantation" to present their grievances to him. Now he had made it explicit: John Wompas, "a poore Indian," was a subject of King Charles II, and thus under his protection. Moreover, as a subject, John was equal in status to Massachusetts's governor, who was no more than a subject himself. Those words would fill John Wompas with a heady sense of his own power and independence. He would wield the status of royal subject like a sword once he returned to Massachusetts.[32]

But that time had not yet come. John was still in prison, his debts still unpaid. The king had shown his sympathy for John's plight and demonstrated a willingness to consider Indians equal to

English colonists in political status. But the king did nothing to help John get out of prison or ensure that justice actually was done to him in Massachusetts Bay Colony. In fact, the king's letter seems to have remained at Whitehall, waiting for John to get out of prison, collect it, and convey it to the governor himself. Eventually, it must have become clear to John Wompas that he was on his own.[33]

In December 1676, John finally found a way to free himself. After nearly a year in prison, his debts must have been considerable, more than the "severall summes of money" Nicholas Warner had given him could cover. John's friend Anthony Mudd had sufficient money to pay John's debts, and John seems to have convinced him to do so by promising to repay him in Nipmuc land. On December 19, 1676, John deeded one thousand acres of land in Massachusetts to Anthony Mudd in gratitude for his "getting my freedom from & out of prison" and "also for divers other good and valluable causes & considerations"—probably cash. John had persuaded Mudd to pay his debts and then some, in exchange for a tract of land that to a London tradesman must have seemed unimaginably vast. On the same day John conveyed this land to Mudd, he deeded a thou-sand-acre tract of land to Nicholas Warner and another of the same size to his son John Warner, in gratitude for the money loaned to him without interest during his stay in prison. It is likely that Wompas had long since informed both men of his struggle with Massachusetts Bay Colony leaders, infecting them with his own indignation over the unjust treatment he had suffered. The king's letter would change all that, freeing John to sell his land. Clearly, both men trusted John Wompas's claim that he was the legal heir to a large portion of central Massachusetts and were willing to stake their money on his promise that they could cash in on that wealth. Within the year, both men would sail to Massachusetts to attempt to do just that.[34]

Freed from prison and from his debts, John could plan his tri-umphant return to Massachusetts. He had only to find a berth on a ship. The berth would be simple enough to obtain: merchant ships were always in need of experienced sailors, although he might have to wait until spring before any would depart for New England. As a seaman, he could draw pay rather than expend it on his trip home, and to find a ship bound for New England, he could inquire at the

Royal Exchange. The Exchange is undoubtedly where John learned that two Massachusetts agents, Peter Bulkeley and William Stoughton, had arrived in England and were shortly to receive an audience with the king. He may even have run into them in person. Within the month, Wompas would accompany them to their first audience with Charles II.

William Stoughton had met John at least once before, and that meeting could not have left him with a positive impression. Stoughton was one of the justices at the Suffolk County Court when John was sentenced for drunkenness in 1673. Why would Stoughton and Bulkeley allow John to accompany them to their audience with the king? The most likely explanation is that they needed him as a translator for the two Nipmuc boys they brought with them as living testaments of the colony's benevolent care of their Indian neighbors.[35] The boys were the sons of Christian Indians, part of a large group of children who had been placed with English colonists as servants in the aftermath of King Philip's War. At least one of them was from John Wompas's home village of Hassanamesit. Daniel Gookin, who prepared the boys for their journey, reported spending nearly three pounds on their apparel—like John Wompas, they needed to be outfitted appropriately to visit the king—and he urged the Massachusetts Council to appoint someone to guard them lest they "slipp away being posibly affrayd to goe for England." As Christian Indians, the boys had probably attended one of the schools established in the praying towns. Their ability to read and perhaps to write the Algonquian language of the Bible may have been the reason they were chosen to go with the agents, who probably wanted them to demonstrate their skills. The colony had previously sent Charles II a copy of the Algonquian Bible, and the agents were likely counting on the king to remember his "pious intentions" in granting a new charter to the New England Company shortly after his Restoration. He had directed that company funds be put toward "perfecting the translation and printing of the Bible, partly for the maintenance of Schooles for the breeding up of the Indian children . . . whereby they be not only taught the true religion, but civilized also and brought to submitt to his Majesties gracious government." Having the boys read from the king's Algonquian Bible would be an impressive demonstration of what the colony had done to fulfill the king's wishes. But making that request of the boys would be difficult without a translator. Their education, at the hands of Native schoolmasters appointed and paid by the New England Company, had been in an Algonquian language. They probably spoke little or no English. John was Nipmuc himself, from Hassanamesit, and certainly knew the boys' families, if not the boys themselves. He could speak with them, perhaps calm them after the traumatic experience of crossing the ocean and entering the teeming metropolis of London. He could prepare them to make a positive demonstration of the colony's benevolent work to the king.[36]

That the Massachusetts agents needed to positively impress the king is a clue to the world of trouble Stoughton and Bulkeley were in. As agents of the Massachusetts government, Stoughton and Bulkeley bore the full weight of the Crown's grievances against the stubbornly independent colony, unresolved since the 1664 visit of the royal commissioners and added to since then. These included ignoring England's Navigation Acts, withholding rights from non-Puritans, and exercising illegal jurisdiction in Maine and New Hampshire. The last two of England's three seventeenth-century wars with the Dutch and a series of political crises distracted Charles II from responding to the royal commissioners' report or to subsequent petitions against Massachusetts, but in 1676 the Crown's agent Edward Randolph forced the issue of the colony's disloyalty back into the king's attention.[37]

Edward Randolph, a doggedly persistent foe of Massachusetts, was a man who had fixed on reforming New England as a remedy for his own sagging fortunes. He was also related by marriage to Robert Mason, the proprietor of New Hampshire who had been battling Massachusetts's political interference there ever since the king's Restoration. Appointed as the Crown's agent to Massachusetts, Randolph made a whirlwind visit there from June 10 to July 30, 1676. He was tasked with observing the colony's trade, their adherence to the Navigation Acts, "how the people stood affected to England," and "what Laws and ordinances are now in force there, derogatory or contradictory to those of England." He was also ordered to deliver to colony leaders a copy of a petition against Massachusetts's illegal usurpation of government in Maine and New Hampshire and to convey the king's demand that they send messengers empowered to answer these complaints. In response, Massachusetts leaders appointed William Stoughton and Peter Bulkeley as agents for the colony and sent them to England. They came armed with maps demonstrating the belief in Massachusetts that the colony's charter took in both Maine and New Hampshire, as well as petitions from inhabitants of those regions praying that they be allowed to remain under Massachusetts rule, the only shield between themselves and marauding Indians.[38]

While the Bay Colony had proclaimed a day of fasting and prayer for the success of the agents, Stoughton and Bulkeley knew that no such good wishes awaited them in England. Quite the contrary. The proprietors of Maine and New Hampshire, Ferdinando Gorges and Robert Mason, awaited them at Court, where they had spent years filling the ears of the king and council with tales of Massachusetts's abuses. Written complaints against the colony poured in as well, including a petition from English merchants arguing that Massachusetts's violation of the Navigation Acts was taking money out of their pockets, and another from the Dutch Estates General protesting the colony's expulsion of Dutch traders from the coast of Maine. Most damaging of all was Edward Randolph's stream of vitriolic commentaries on his visit to Massachusetts. He reported that several of the magistrates, as well as the governor himself, had failed to remove their hats as a sign of respect while the king's letter was being read before the council, clear evidence of their "discountenancing all affairs that come to them from the King." Randolph's return ship reached England three months before Stoughton and Bulkeley arrived there, and he had spent the intervening time haunting Whitehall, seizing every opportunity to rail against the colony and urge the revocation of its charter. Representing the colony under such circumstances was a bleak prospect.[39]

John Wompas's description of the royal audience he attended suggests that it may have been the Massachusetts agents' first meeting with Charles II. After the agents arrived in December 1676, they delivered a letter of introduction from Governor John Leverett to Secretary of State Joseph Williamson, requesting that he assist them in gaining a royal audience. Although the agents had come to London in response to the king's explicit command, they still needed a connection—someone with "interest"—to gain access to the Crown.

The agents carried official papers from the Governor and General Court of Massachusetts Bay, which they probably included in their letter to Williamson. These papers were read to the King's Council on December 13, 1676, but there is no indication that either the king or the Massachusetts agents were present at that time. Rather, the king seems to have sent for the agents shortly after their papers were read at council, and it was this meeting that John Wompas attended.[40]

By John's report, the royal audience was a humiliating experience for the two agents. Smugly recounting it to Cambridge villagers after his return to Massachusetts, Wompas told of the king summoning the agents to his presence on a Sunday. They declined to come, citing religious scruples against doing business on the Sabbath. Politically, this was a misstep. It was a distinct honor to receive a personal invitation from the king, and the Massachusetts agents' refusal was a grave breach of protocol. By placing the demands of their religion above their duty to the king, Stoughton and Bulkeley undoubtedly reminded Charles II of his ongoing struggles with Parliament over religion. Now the religious nonconformists from Massachusetts had spurned a rare invitation from their king, insisting that he adapt his schedule to their convenience. When the agents arrived at Whitehall the following day, they had good reason to fear that the king would not give them a warm welcome.[41]

The Palace of Whitehall sat on the banks of the Thames River in Westminster, to the west of the old city of London. It was an enormous, rambling assemblage of more than fifteen hundred rooms, including state rooms and private apartments for the king's family, household staff, and leading courtiers. The Massachusetts agents and their party would have entered Whitehall through the formal palace gate next to the Banqueting House. Once summoned to the king's presence, they would have passed through the state apartments to the chamber where the king was receiving visitors that day. The formal entrance and route through the state rooms were meant to convey to visitors the power and divinely appointed authority of the king, a concept embodied in many of the works of art throughout the palace, from the Banqueting House's mural depicting the apotheosis of King James I to the painting on the ceiling of the king's bedchamber showing the gods in heaven admiring a portrait of Charles II.[42]

Figure 9. Whitehall Palace, from the Thames River, 1677
[London Metropolitan Archives, City of London]

The first in the sequence of state rooms was the guard chamber, which had a staff of over one hundred yeomen of the guard, forty of whom served in each rotation. The guards wore brightly colored uniforms of red and gold and were required to be tall and strong, thus visually representing the splendor and power of Charles's court. The Massachusetts agents and their party may have been received in the king's presence room, which was adorned with Holbein's mural of Henry VIII. In it the monarch stood like an ermine-robed boxer, arms akimbo, legs widely splayed, eyes boldly accosting viewers— the ultimate power pose to greet visitors to the king.[43]

Royal audiences began with formal greetings. Visitors would

kneel and kiss the king's hand and present him with gifts. Gifts were meant to signal the wealth and status of both the giver and the recipient, so ambassadors brought the king rich treasures from their home countries suitable to a monarch's high standing. The Russian ambassador to Charles II brought sable and ermine furs, Moroccan visitors brought lions and ostriches, and the Venetian ambassador brought two gondolas for the king to use in royal processions on the Thames. The gifts brought by the agents from Massachusetts were decidedly more pedestrian, although equally representative of their home country: ten barrels of cranberries, two hogsheads of "speciall good sampe" (ground Indian corn for making porridge), and three thousand codfish. Given the expectation that gifts would befit the standing of their royal recipient, King Charles II may have felt that these presents confirmed Edward Randolph's claim that Massachusetts leaders lacked proper respect for their king.[44]

Next, the agents probably presented the Nipmuc boys for the king's inspection. The boys were dressed in their new clothes, and the agents no doubt also wore their best suits of apparel to signal their respect for the Crown. It is unlikely that the new suit of clothes John acquired before sailing to London survived his year in prison. He probably sold it to pay his debts or wore it out in jail. If John was savvy, which he usually was, he would have gotten the Massachusetts agents to buy him new clothes for the visit to Whitehall. We know nothing of the boys' exchange with the king, nor of John's. It seems likely that the king inquired, through John, about the boys' education and their experience of King Philip's War, accounts of which had appeared in London newspapers and book stalls. It seems likely, too, that John Wompas informed the king that he was the Indian man who had sent him a petition several months earlier laying out his grievances with the Massachusetts government. But John's report of the royal audience said nothing of that. It focused, instead, on the king's cold reception of the Massachusetts agents.[45]

The agents knew that the colony's charter had been in peril for years, and that the grievances that had led the king to command their presence in England would very likely end in the revocation of Massachusetts's charter authority. They lost no time, then, in falling to their knees before him and begging him to renew the colony's charter. By kneeling they hoped to demonstrate that, despite the previous day's affront, they honored him as their sovereign. It is easy to imagine the jaundiced eye the king must have cast on this tardy show of loyalty. His reply was blunt: he said that "his grand father had [given] them their patent but they had forfeited it and acted contrary to it." The king also castigated the agents over Massachusetts's usurpation of the governments of Maine and New Hampshire, and for violating their own charter prohibition on laws contrary to English law. Alluding to the 1659–1661 execution of Quakers who had returned to Massachusetts after banishment, the king declared that colony leaders had "acted contrary to [their charter] by making lawes to hang . . . men for Religion whereas they had no such liberty."[46]

Stoughton and Bulkeley's royal audience made a powerful impression on John Wompas. Describing the scene to Cambridge residents nine months later, John gloated over the humiliation of the Massachusetts agents. How the world had turned upside down! Just a few years before, Wompas had been summoned to a colony court as a malefactor and sentenced by Judges William Stoughton and John Leverett, who laid a whopping forty-pound bond of good behavior on him and, no doubt, delivered a harsh lecture on the evils of drunkenness. Now the situation was reversed: Stoughton and Bulkeley were the ones on trial, disgraced and berated by the king, while John, whose petition had been rewarded with a royal letter of support, looked on in triumph.

The agents would meet repeatedly with the king or his Lords of Trade over the next year and a half, by their own request or in response to royal summons. John Wompas may have attended some of these meetings. By his own account, he not only appeared at the Monday audience between the Massachusetts agents and the king, but at other times "hee had sene them, & spake with them." If he accompanied the agents when they delivered petitions to Whitehall in January, or when they appeared with Mason and Gorges at a hearing before the council on April 7, 1677, he would have heard a great deal more about the political troubles of Massachusetts. But he could have gotten that information from many other sources. Mason and Gorges, as well as Edward Randolph, were present at Whitehall on most of the days the Massachusetts agents were there themselves, and there was a constant flow of New Englanders, some with their own grievances against the colony, at the Royal Exchange.[47]

It is abundantly clear that John Wompas learned enough in the months before his departure for New England in spring 1677 to become an informed critic of Massachusetts politics and of the colony's ongoing war with the Indians to the northeast. Like the king whose subject he proudly proclaimed himself to be, John would yet demand, "What had the english to do to send out soldiers to the eastward or to the southward . . . both out of Massachusetts' jurisdiction?" And, confident of his own standing with the Crown, he would taunt the residents of Massachusetts with the precarious state of their political future, declaring: "New England hath lost the day. . . . and it is known in old england."[48]

CHAPTER SEVEN

"Hee Had Lost a Great Many Men in the Warr"

The Nipmucs and Ann Wompas in King Philip's War

Then fell hee [John Wompas] in to discourse what great things hee would doe if hee were to leade souldiers against the enimies: & withall spake very disparigingly & contemptuously of the English mens actings against the enimies; . . . hee spake also that hee had lost a great many men in the warr as I understood he spake of the indian enimy slaine in the warr.

—HANNAH MEADE, 1677

Mr Hughes if hee would might have made her a Slave all the dayes of her life.

—ANN WOMPAS, quoted by Milcah Wright, 1676

WHILE JOHN WOMPAS WAS laying his grievances before King Charles II in England, his kin, friends, and enemies in New England were caught up in the bloodiest conflict in the region's history. The war between the colonists and many of the surrounding Native peoples began in late June 1675. Initially, it involved only the English of Plymouth Colony and the Wampanoags under their sachem Philip Metacom, also known as King Philip, but the conflict quickly spread to Massachusetts, Connecticut, Rhode Island, and northern New England, drawing in English and Indian combatants from all of those locales, including the Nipmucs of the central Massachusetts highlands. By war's end, more than three thousand Indians and nearly a thousand English had perished, and dozens of towns, Indian and English, were destroyed and abandoned. John Wompas probably heard about the war from mariners, merchants, and other English colonists visiting London, from over a dozen accounts published in London or appearing in the *London Gazette*, and certainly from the exchange between the king and the Massachusetts agents in December 1676. The two Nipmuc boys sent to England with Massachusetts agents William Stoughton and Peter Bulkeley had first-hand knowledge of the war; they had witnessed the death and enslavement of fellow Nipmucs and endured captivity, disease, and starvation during long months of exile from Hassanamesit. Few groups suffered more during King Philip's War than the Christian Indians, caught as they were between the distrust of their Indian kin and the English to whom they had pledged their loyalty. Their treatment by the English during and after King Philip's War fueled John Wompas's growing anger against the Massachusetts government, which would explode on his return to Massachusetts Bay Colony in 1677.[1]

The Hassanamesits and their fellow Christian Indians should not have suffered in the war as they did, given their status as allies of the English. The 1644 submission of five Nipmuc and Massachusett sachems to Massachusetts Bay Colony governed the colony's relationship with all the Indians who later submitted to its authority, and the terms of the submission included mutual military assistance. To confirm that submission in the aftermath of the first clashes at Plymouth, in July 1675 Massachusetts leaders sent Ephraim Curtis to confer with the Nipmucs about whether or not they would remain faithful to the English. They could hardly have made a more offensive choice of a messenger. Curtis operated a trading post in Nipmuc Country, on land granted to the English by colony leaders but disputed by the Nipmucs, so his presence there was a continuous affront. When Curtis located more than two hundred Nipmuc soldiers and their families encamped on an island in the Quinebaug River, a large number of Nipmucs surrounded him, shouting, cocking their guns, and threatening to shoot him. Only the strenuous efforts of Curtis's Natick Indian guides succeeded in calming the tumult enough for him to deliver his message and depart in safety. This incident made it abundantly clear that there were sharp divisions among the Nipmucs over whether to maintain subjection to the English or join Philip's cause. Most of the Nipmucs from the older praying towns proclaimed their loyalty to the English and remained faithful allies throughout the war, but they found that their fidelity did little to shield them from the rising anti-Indian hysteria of the besieged colonial populace. Nipmuc Indians from the newer praying towns, all founded since 1671, broke from the English very soon after the violence at Plymouth, casting their lot with Philip. In fact, these Nipmucs carried out a devastating attack on the English town of Mendon during Curtis's negotiations with the Nipmucs on the island. This attack undermined English trust in those Nipmucs who remained English allies. For both "friend" Indians and English, fear that the other would prove unfaithful became a self-fulfilling prophecy, a fact poignantly evident among the residents of John Wompas's home village of Hassanamesit.[2]

The leading man of that village was Thomas Wuttasacomponom, or Captain Tom. He was the "ruler"—a civil leader under the government system established by John Eliot—of several of the newer praying towns in Nipmuc Country. But he was also a sachem. Indeed, he was "of the chief sachem's blood" and lived at Hassanamesit, the ancient seat of the Nipmuc chief sachems. Wuttasacomponom's English title, "captain," was given to him at the start of King Philip's War when he led a group of forty Christian Indian soldiers in the English army. There is also evidence that "captain" may have been used as an equivalent for "sachem" by Natives who observed its function as a term of honor in English society. Their English officers attested that Wuttasacomponom's men served faithfully, but ordinary English soldiers distrusted them, accusing them of being "cowards" who "skulked behind trees in fight" and "shot over the enemies' heads." After less than a month, the English released half of the Indian soldiers from military service. By the end of autumn 1675, colony leaders had sent the rest of the Indian soldiers home, yielding to English soldiers' suspicions and the rising "animosity and rage of the common people." The constant suspicion and accusations from English soldiers "who had conceived much animosity against all Indians" is evidence of the fact that English colonists believed "all Indians" would side together in the war. As the town leaders of Dorchester put it in a petition to have friendly Indians removed from their town, they feared that these Indians would turn on them if the enemy ever came near, they "being their own Nation."[3]

Returning home provided no haven for Christian Indian soldiers or their families. The "animosity and rage" that prevented the embattled settlers of Massachusetts Bay from tolerating Indian soldiers made them just as wary of Indian neighbors. On August 30, 1675, the Massachusetts Council responded to the growing outcry by ordering a halt to the "usual commerce" between Indians and English—the trade of food, goods, and labor that had become a familiar feature of colony life. This edict closed off a reliable source of income for Natives. Worse, the council prohibited Indians from hunting in the woods, either to feed their own families or in the pay of an English employer. To ensure that these rules were followed, the council ordered that all Christian Indians be confined to five praying villages, one of which was Hassanamesit. They reasoned that this order was necessary "to quiet the people" and for the security of both English and Indians. These regulations "reduced [the Christian Indians] to great sufferings, being hindered from their hunting and looking after their cattle, swine, and getting in their corn, or laboring among the English. . . . also, [they] were daily exposed to be slain or imprisoned, if at any time they were found without their limits."[4]

Even restricting the Indians to a few praying towns was not enough to appease many colonists, who continued to urge the council to take stronger measures to secure the English from Indian danger. When the council was slow to respond, some English acted on their own. In August 1675, Samuel Mosely, who led a military band of pardoned Dutch pirates, used dubious evidence from a captured Indian enemy as an excuse to round up a group of Christian Indians in Marlborough and march them to prison in Boston. There, the Indians narrowly escaped an attempt by thirty young ruffians to break into the jail and kill them. When the council later freed nine of the eleven Indians, many Bostonians condemned the action and called for the removal of all Indians from the colony. In response, the council—reluctantly, according to Daniel Gookin—ordered that the Indians of Natick, the closest praying town to Boston, be exiled to Deer Island in Massachusetts Bay. Natick drew its population from Indian villages throughout the region, including Hassanamesit. John Wompas's uncles, Anthony and Tom Tray, were residents, as was John's friend Andrew Pittimee.[5]

On October 30, 1675, with less than two hours' warning, an English officer rounded up two hundred Natick Indians and escorted them to a launch near Watertown, where boats waited to carry them to the windswept and barren island that would be their home for the next seven months. There they would be protected from the "rage" of the English and, more to the point, the English would feel safe from them. Deer Island had no large trees or sheltered valleys to offer protection from the storms scouring the bay, and the Naticks were able to bring only the barest essentials with them, leaving "much of their substance, catle, swine, horse & corn" behind. As a result, they soon found themselves starving, "exposed to great sufferings haveing litle wood for fuell, a bleak place & poore wigwams" with little food beyond the poor harvest the island provided: "clams and shellfish, that they digged out of the sand, at low water." The fearful English refused to grant Indian petitions to go to the mainland to gather corn or fuel. Worse, the Naticks' forced relocation did not prevent the more aggressive English from taking out their hostility on them. One Natick man reported that the Indians on Deer Island were "threatned to be killed. We have bene shot at . . . and have nothing to defend are selves with." Many of the exiled Indians would starve or freeze to death before the English saw fit to release them, a trauma still held in memory by their descendants today. News of the fate of the Natick Indians spread rapidly among the other Indians of the region, fueling distrust and hostility toward the English. For the Hassanamesits, this example of how the English treated their Indian allies would have profound consequences.[6]

In November 1675, a group of Christian Indians at Hassaname-sit, made up of both Hassanamesit Indians and refugees from other praying towns, gathered to bring in their harvest of corn, which had been drying on the stalk in preparation for winter storage. The bulk of the group of fifty men and 150 women and children worked close together, moving down the rows and piling the corn into woven baskets. A smaller group of Indians worked a separate field, distant enough that they were not noticed by the large Indian war party that suddenly appeared and confronted the harvesters. The Native sol-diers were well armed and three hundred strong. Many of them were Nipmucs; some were close kin to the harvesters. They made no move to attack, although their guns were clearly visible. In a loud voice, the leader of the war party announced that the Christian In-dians must join them to fight against the English. If they came along quietly, the soldiers would "spare their lives." If not, they would seize all their corn and let them starve. This was an empty threat, and the Indians must have immediately recognized it: the Native Christians would turn to the English for help rather than perish with hunger. The war party needed to undermine the Christians' confidence in that avenue of appeal, and they did so with devastating precision: "If we do not kill you, and . . . you go to the English again, they will either force you all to some Island as the Natick Indians are, where you will be in danger to be starved with cold and hunger, and most probably in the end be all sent out of the country for slaves."[7]

Wuttasacomponom was in the larger group of harvesters at Hassanamesit. As a sachem of the royal blood, he was a powerful figure among all Nipmucs. It is likely that the head of the war party addressed him when he demanded that the Hassanamesits go with them. Wuttasacomponom weighed that demand carefully against his experience, which included his own and his companions' humil-iating dismissal from the English army, their confinement to a hand-ful of praying towns, and the council's order for English soldiers to destroy many of the Christian Indians' cornfields in Nipmuc Coun-try, thus threatening starvation to friendly as well as hostile Indians. During their service with the English, Wuttasacomponom and his company had also seen hostile Indians captured and marched off to Plymouth and Boston for sale into foreign slavery. Not just captured male combatants, but their wives, children, and some Indians who surrendered into English hands were sent out of the country, which greatly alarmed Indians throughout the region. John Eliot, who regularly met with the Christian Indians, warned the Massachusetts Council that the "terror of selling away such Indians, unto the Ilands for perpetual slaves, who shall yeild up themselves to your mercy, is like to be an effectual prolongation of the warre." Knowing that some of those sold into slavery had not been combatants may have made the Christian Indians fear that they, too, were at risk, and rumors began to fly that the English intended to sell the Natick Indians on Deer Island into slavery. These circumstances were enough to convince Wuttasacomponom that the Hassanamesits had more to fear from the "rage of the English" than from the hostile Indians. He agreed to go away with the war party. The rest of the harvesters followed his example, although at least two—Hassanamesit's pastor and his father—were said to have gone with "heavy hearts and weeping eyes." The smaller party of Indians gathering corn remained in hiding until the Hassanamesits departed, then two men raced to the nearby English town of Mendon to seek help. Two English companies of soldiers, guided by five Natick Indians, went out after the Hassanamesit Indians but could not find them. The captives would remain among the hostile Indians for the next six months, some of them joining in attacks, others waiting and watching for a chance to escape.[8]

The news of the Hassanamesits' departure spread quickly through the English settlements, where it confirmed what many already believed, that the Christian Indians were loyal to their fellow Indians, not to their fellow believers. Even Daniel Gookin, who believed Wuttasacomponom was a "pious man," voiced the general sentiment that "had he done as he ought, he should rather have suffered death, than have gone among the wicked enemies of the people of God." By "yield[ing] to the enemies' arguments," the sachem "drew most of the rest" to follow him. While the Hassanamesits' harsh treatment by their English neighbors and pressure from their captors helps explain their decision to go with the hostile Indians, the English persisted in seeing their choice as a betrayal. Massachusetts officials responded with anger to news that some of the captured Hassanamesits had told the Narragansett Indians that the English intended to sell the Deer Island Indians into slavery. Writing to a Rhode Islander who reported the tale, magistrate Daniel Gookin explained, "the truth is wee have placed som of them upon an Island in order to their & our security but nott with any purpose of doing them wrong. therfor you shal do well to demand those false intellegensers to bee sent up to us or delivered to you that they may be punished for the[ir] flight & false reports." For Massachusetts leaders, reports of "cruelty" to the praying Indians needed to be suppressed to prevent other Indians, such as the still-neutral Narragansetts, from defecting to the enemy.[9]

Massachusetts officials were right to fear the consequences of such rumors. By December 1675, the Narragansetts had abandoned their neutrality, and fears of enslavement kept them from seeking peace even after devastating losses in the swamp fight in Rhode Island. Narragansett sachem Canonchet declared "that if they yielded to the English they should be dead men or slaves, & so worck for the English." Job Kattenanit and James Quannapohit, Christian Indians sent as spies among the warring Indians in January 1676, reported similar feelings among both the captured Hassanamesits and the hostile Nipmucs. Speaking to Quannapohit, Wuttasacomponom justified his decision to submit to the enemy, saying: "for if they came to the English they knew they should be sent to Deere Iland, as others were . . . & others feard they should be sent away to Barbados, or other places." Likewise, the young Nipmuc soldiers declared, "why shall wee have peace to bee made slaves, & either be kild or sent away to sea to Barbadoes &c. Let us live as long as wee can & die like men, & not live to bee enslaved."[10]

Far from their winter villages, Philip's allies suffered severely from cold and lack of food. Weakened by hunger, many, including the Christian Indians, died of disease during the long winter. Ammunition supplies were low as early as January, leading some Natives to abandon the cause. In the early spring of 1676, the Narragansett sachem Canonchet, who led the war during Philip's absence in New York, was captured and executed by Indian allies of the English, severely disheartening his followers. Reports began to filter in that the Indians were ready to give up. In response, colony leaders sent word that they would accept any who wished to surrender on terms of "mercy," which meant they would be enslaved rather than executed. Faced with the alternative of starvation, hundreds streamed in, both Natives who had been hostile in the war and Indians such as the Hassanamesits, who had been caught up in the war unwillingly.[11]

But some were afraid to come in, including Wuttasacomponom and his son, Nehemiah. Knowing that his influential decision had led the rest of the Christian Indians at Hassanamesit to yield, Wuttasacomponom feared retribution from the English. When English scouts captured him and his family in early June 1676, his worst fears were realized. He was imprisoned, and when several Englishmen testified that they had seen him among the Indians attacking Sudbury in April 1676, he was tried and condemned to death. James Quannapohit testified in Wuttasacomponom's favor, telling how "I heard som of the enimy mock Tom & some others of the indians carried captive that they cryed when they were caried away, more like squas then men. Capt Tom also told me that hee was weary of liveing among those wicked indians, & greatly desired to bee among the praying indians & english againe." Other Christian Indians also submitted petitions in his favor. John Eliot protested Wuttasacomponom's conviction to the Massachusetts Council and made a personal visit to Governor Leverett to plead for the sachem's life. To his dismay, the governor insisted on "how bad a man Tom was," to which Eliot retorted, "that at the great day he should find that Christ was of another mind." This and all other efforts to save the sachem failed. On June 22, 1676, Wuttasacomponom was hanged. To the very end, he declared that he was innocent: "I did never lift up hand against the English, nor was I at Sudbury, only I was willing to goe away with the enemise that surprised us."[12]

Wuttasacomponom was one of dozens of casualties among the Hassanamesit Indians and hundreds among the Christian Indians as a whole. Many, including his younger son, died of disease while traveling with the hostile Indians. Others, like Job Nesutan, one of the Indian scholars, were killed in battle by fellow Christian Indians. Among those who surrendered to "mercy," some were sold into slavery in the West Indies or elsewhere, including a son of Hassanamesit's pastor Tuppakuwillin. Six other Indians who were captured or surrendered to the English were executed on suspicion of aiding hostile Indians in the war. Like Wuttasacomponom, they protested that they had not participated in attacks on the English, to no avail. Speaking with the Nipmuc boys in England, John Wompas could have learned of these horrors, as well as the fate of other Christian Indians, their deaths and "desertions," the mistrust of the English for their fellow believers, and how few Christian Indians remained in the colony in the aftermath of King Philip's War. On the eve of the war, the Christian Indian population of Massachusetts had grown to over a thousand souls occupying fourteen distinct praying towns. By war's end, only four towns remained, with a total population of 567. No wonder John Wompas appeared angry and restless on his return to Massachusetts.[13]

While John Wompas was sitting in a London prison and his Nipmuc kin were suffering in King Philip's War, Ann Wompas was living quietly in Boston, contrary to General Court orders. At the very start of the war, in June 1675, the General Court banned Indians from entering or living in Boston, with the exception of Indians of "knowne faithfulnesse to the English." By October 1675, this exception was dropped. No Indians, faithful or otherwise, were allowed in Boston "unless in prison." Any Indian who wished to enter Boston had to seek explicit permission from the governor and be accompanied into town by two armed English guards. If English residents discovered an Indian without guards, they had permission to "apprehend and secure him."[14]

It is unclear how Ann managed to evade this order. Her gender was not enough to protect her; Englishmen would later attack and kill Christian Indian women from Natick even though the women carried written permission to leave their homes to search for food. Ann's appearance and speech may have helped deflect attention from herself. She dressed like an Englishwoman and probably spoke without an accent, given how young she was when she was enslaved. Her skin may have been darker than that of her neighbors, but skin color might not have been the primary factor in how they perceived her. English people in this era were as likely to attribute "Indianness" to behavior and belief as to appearance. Ann lived in an English house, shopped in English markets, and went to an English church, and she had done so for most of her life. While John Wompas was described as Indian at least half the time his name appears in court records and land deeds, the term "Indian" was never applied to Ann Prask Wompas. It is hard to account for this curious fact. Perhaps it was a matter of personality. John was outspoken and seemed to relish drawing attention to himself, traits that made him the target of disapproval and could have become associated with his race. Ann appears to have been more reserved. Other than the single incident in which she struck John for being drunk, her behavior was unexceptionable. While the Suffolk County Court sentenced John severely, it did not fine Ann at all, implicitly excusing her for behavior the magistrates may have considered justifiable. Even when King Philip's War heightened fears and prejudices against Indians, Ann's neighbors never described her as Indian. To them, she was simply Ann Wompas.[15]

Although Ann's Indian identity does not seem to have concerned her neighbors, it must have concerned her. Indeed, her situation must have become increasingly stressful each day that war persisted between Indians and colonists. From June 1675 until the autumn of 1676 a constant stream of court orders, delegations of Indian allies, news of Indian attacks, and files of Indian captives passed through Boston, and the hostility of the English populace toward Indians grew apace. Ann's home stood just two blocks from the Boston jail where Indians seized by Captain Samuel Mosely in August 1675 were held for over a month while Boston residents, convinced that all Indians were enemies, called for them to be put to death. Public executions of hostile Indians were held nearby as well, and the clamor would have been hard to miss. Wuttasacomponom's hanging in June 1676 took place on Boston Neck, a short distance from Ann's house. The Nipmuc sachem Matoonas was shot to death in Boston on July 27, and eight more Indian captives were shot on Windmill Hill on September 13. All of these events would have been bitter reminders of the war Ann experienced in her own childhood, none more so than the hundreds of Indian captives brought into Boston and sold into slavery.[16]

As in the Pequot War forty years earlier, the English followed European patterns for treatment of hostiles: Men guilty of actually killing English persons could either be enslaved or executed, "they having forfeited their lives by warring against us." Women and children among the hostiles could be enslaved within the colony or sold

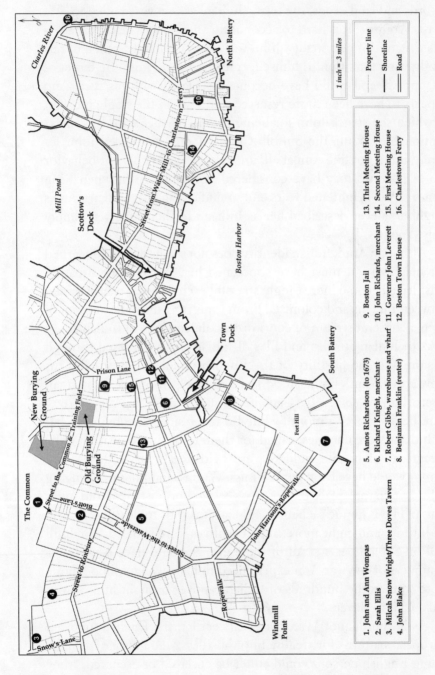

The Common

Charles River

Mill Pond

Scottow's
Dock

Street from Water Mill to Charlestown Ferry

North Battery

Boston Harbor

New Burying
Ground

Street to the Common & Training Field

Old Burying
Ground

Prison Lane

Town
Dock

Bloit's Lane

Street to Roxbury

Snow's Lane

Windmill
Point

Street to the Waterside

Ropewalk

John Harrison's Ropewalk

Fort Hill

South Battery

Ropewalk

1 inch = .3 miles

———— Property line
———— Shoreline
▬▬▬▬ Road

1. John and Ann Wompas
2. Sarah Ellis
3. Milcah Snow Wright/Three Doves Tavern
4. John Blake

5. Amos Richardson (to 1673)
6. Richard Knight, merchant
7. Robert Gibbs, warehouse and wharf
8. Benjamin Franklin (renter)

9. Boston Jail
10. John Richards, merchant
11. Governor John Leverett
12. Boston Town House

13. Third Meeting House
14. Second Meeting House
15. First Meeting House
16. Charlestown Ferry

Figure 10. John and Ann Wompas's Boston neighborhood [Map by Jen Macpherson, based on a map by Samuel Clough (Massachusetts Maps, MHS)]

outside it. Domestic or foreign slavery was the fate of hundreds of
Indian men, women, and children during King Philip's War, including Indians who surrendered on the promise of mercy and friendly
Indians grouped with the hostiles by mistake. Some were sent to the
perpetually labor-starved English colonies of Barbados, Nevis, and
Jamaica; some were shipped as far away as Fyall in the Azores, or
Cadiz, Spain, where they were sold as galley slaves on English ships
operating out of northern Africa. The wives, daughters, and male
children of hostile Indians were generally allowed to remain within
the colonies as slaves, some in English households, and some among
allied Indians. In either case, their masters were free to keep them
or sell them, and could hold that threat over their heads to ensure
good behavior.[17]

Most of the sales of captive Indians recorded by the Massachusetts colony treasurer in the summer of 1676 were for one or two
children intended for service in the purchasers' own homes, but he
also recorded some larger purchases intended for immediate resale,
clearly demonstrating English commodification of captive Indians.
Merchant Samuel Shrimpton bought fifteen Indians and sold over
half out of the country. Other merchants bought groups of eight,
thirteen, fourteen, or seventy Indians. This parade of slaves seems
to have made Ann ponder her own experience of enslavement. Forty
years earlier she had been among a group of Indians captured by the
English, classified as hostile, and brought to Boston for sale. Although no record remains telling how long Massachusetts officials
intended to keep the captives of the Pequot War in slavery, contemporaries justified the perpetual enslavement of hostile captives and
their families. Ann evidently believed that she had narrowly escaped
that fate. Speaking to a friend in September 1676, Ann declared that
if her master Joshua Hewes had wished, he could have "made her a
slave all the days of her life."[18]

Whether Boston's English population knew that Ann was an Indian but considered her harmless or whether her reserved demeanor
allowed her to go unnoticed, she apparently aroused no one's interest or alarm in Boston during the years of King Philip's War. She
was able to remain in her home and go about her business. By the
time war ended in southern New England in the fall of 1676, John
had been absent from Massachusetts for two and a half years. Ann

may have preferred it that way, given the contentious nature of their marriage. But if the marriage was a source of grief to her, it was also a source of income. Like other mariners' wives, Ann had to wait months, sometimes years, between infusions of cash from her husband's work as a seaman. If he was profligate with his wages, as John seems to have been, she might have had little to tide her over between voyages. So how did Ann Wompas get by in the years he was gone? She seems to have gone into trade for herself, selling items John had brought home from distant ports.

Early modern sailors held the time-honored privilege of shipping a certain amount of goods, free of freight charges, for personal trade. Depending on their rank, they might be allowed several barrels full of wine, finished goods, or whatever else they could buy cheap in one port and sell dear in another. Sailors could also bring home whatever they could fit into their own sea chest. A sailor with a talent for business could use his privilege to expand his income by as much as fifty percent. By having their wives or mothers sell the goods, they also sidestepped the fees tacked on to merchandise by middlemen such as merchants and shopkeepers. Sailors' limited personal baggage space made them focus on small, easily portable goods with the highest potential for profit in a given port. Ann Wompas's possession of ribbons, gloves, and other luxury items in quantities well beyond her personal needs suggests that these were items John brought home for her to sell.[19]

By September 1676, Ann's supply of saleable goods was nearly depleted. However, she still had on hand forty pieces of head and wrist linen, twelve handkerchiefs, a few remnants from a box of ribbons, and a handful of items likely intended for the high-end market: a silver bodkin, a pair of silk stockings, two pairs of leather gloves, two black scarves with hoods, and a feather fan with a silver handle. In addition, Ann had three pounds, eight shillings, and six pence in cash in the house, which was enough to keep her comfortably in food and other necessaries for some time. If she ran out, she could redeem IOUs from two Englishmen who owed her money: seventeen pounds from the merchant Mr. Robert Sedgewick, and ten pounds from Mr. Richard Knight, who kept a shop just a few blocks from Ann's home.[20]

This remarkable fact bears repeating: Ann Wompas, an American Indian woman, was owed twenty-seven pounds by two Boston merchants and supported herself for two and a half years through sales of luxury goods, with no assistance from or contact with her husband. Either she was a very shrewd manager or John Wompas had left behind cash from his land sales, enough that men like Sedgewick and Knight saw Ann as a source of loans. Few women were in such a position in seventeenth-century Massachusetts, and far fewer Indian women, perhaps none other than Ann.[21]

Ann was not wealthy, but she was comfortable. In addition to items that seem to have been intended for retail, the Wompas home held a bedstead furnished with a valance, curtains, and a featherbed; two tables, eight chairs, and all the linens and cooking wares a lone woman could possibly need. Ann's clothing was consistent with the amount and type belonging to tradesmen's wives in the same period, although some of her things were becoming "old" and worn with use. Whether she could have remained comfortable for much longer is another question. Saleable items were running short, and unless she had hidden or deposited sums elsewhere, her three pounds and change would not last more than a year. Once that ran out, what could she do?[22]

She did not have the chance to find out. In September 1676, Ann was scalded, probably by the contents of a pot hanging in the hearth, and by the twenty-eighth of that month she was dead. A severe scalding was not an unusual event in colonial New England, where cauldrons of water or soup were constantly simmering in fireplaces large enough to stand up in. A misplaced step could send one tripping into the embers or bumping against a pot whose contents sloshed out on bare skin. The resultant burn was not only extremely painful but highly susceptible to infection. Like many others, Ann did not die immediately from her burns but lingered for a week or more in great pain. As the wounds became infected, she slipped into fever, delirium, and finally death.

Ann probably lived alone, judging from the single bed in the inventory of her estate, but she did not die alone. Three women cared for her after her accident, Prudence Delany, Milcah Wright, and Sarah Ellis. The latter two were Ann's near neighbors, and both were connected to the maritime world John Wompas occupied. Milcah Wright and her husband, Captain William Wright, lived just across the Boston Common from the Wompas home, in or next to the Three Doves Tavern, managed by her son-in-law. Sarah Ellis lived with her husband Edward, also a ship captain, at the corner of Blott's Lane and the road leading to Roxbury, just steps away from Ann. Prudence Delany, an eighteen-year-old girl, appears on no record other than the depositions surrounding Ann's death; she was likely a servant working for the Wrights, the Ellises, or for Ann herself. Two of these women were with Ann when she was scalded, and their presence likely allowed her to get assistance quickly, to be helped into bed and have her burns washed and bandaged. Milcah Wright's report that she had conversed with Ann "often in her life time" suggests that their friendship was of long standing, and Ann's entrusting the keys of her house to Sarah Ellis suggests that theirs, too, was a close relationship. When Ann was injured, these women quickly stepped in to help, and the conversations they reported show that they spent significant time sitting with her and seeing to her needs. But they could do little or nothing to drive away the infection that would take her life.[23]

Ann knew that she was dying. Indeed, it is possible that she was ill even before her scalding and that this hampered her ability to fight the infection. One of the chief topics of discussion between Ann and her friends after her accident was what was to be done with her home and belongings. But this seems to have been a topic even before Ann was burned. Prudence Delany reported that about half an hour before her accident, Ann expressed the wish "that Joshua Hughes should have all the Estate she had when she dyed." This would make sense only if Ann had reason to anticipate her death, and illness would have provided that reason. Milcah Wright reported that "often in her life time and a little before she died" Ann claimed "that what estate soever she had she would give to Mr. Hughes his children after her death." Joshua Hewes Sr. had died in January 1676, just nine months before Ann's accident, but his son Joshua Hewes Jr. and daughters Mary Lambe and Hannah Hewes—"Mr. Hughes his children"—were still living in Boston. Sarah Ellis confirmed Milcah Wright's report of Ann's wishes, adding that "in the time of her sickness [Ann] gave her the keys of her house to deliver unto Joshua Hughes which she did after she was dead."[24]

The glaring absence in Ann's wishes for the disposal of her estate is, of course, John Wompas. Under English law, which was the rule the Wompases followed in purchasing and mortgaging their Boston home, the husband held full legal title to all of a couple's estate, including whatever his wife brought into the marriage. As a *femme covert*, the wife was economically, legally, and politically subsumed in her husband's identity. Thus, while Ann had the right to live in the house as John's wife, she could not sell the house without his consent. How, then, could she give it away to Joshua Hewes? The answer was that in her mind, and in the opinion of the court that oversaw the disposal of her property, John was dead.[25]

John had vanished from Boston shortly after his appearance at the Suffolk County Court in June 1674. By September 1676, he had been gone for more than two years, and there is no evidence that he sent word—or money—to Ann during all that time. Mortality among sailors was very high. The wife of a mariner would have known of many men who died of illness or injury at sea, whose ships sank with all hands, or who simply disappeared in some distant port. Ann must have imagined one of these fates for John Wompas. Otherwise, surely, he would have found some way to contact her, despite their bitter parting. The fact that she did not even mention his name to her caregivers as she lay dying argues strongly that she had given him up for dead. She and John had only one child, no longer living, and John had no known offspring by any other woman. With his death, the Wompas estate became Ann's alone, and she chose to give it to the closest thing to family that she had left: the children of Joshua Hewes.[26]

There are good reasons why Ann might have regarded the Hewes children as her family. She had joined the Hewes household as a child, orphaned by her mother and probably uncertain whether her father had lived or died in the Swamp Fight in Connecticut. Brought to Boston with other captives of the Pequot War, Ann was unusually isolated. She was neither Pequot nor Sasqua and may not have spoken the dialect of either Indian people. Young and disoriented, Ann was in desperate need of human contact, comfort, and information. Children in similar circumstances—separated from family and friends, linguistically isolated, and young enough for memories to fade—have always been good candidates for assimilation. Bonding with her captors was an understandable sequel to Ann's traumatic experience, particularly if they offered her kindness. By all reports, Joshua Hewes was a kind man, punctilious about fulfilling obligations, and one others turned to in trouble. The continuing strength of Ann's connection to him shines through her final recorded conversations with her friends. To them, she insisted that "what estate soever she had she would give to Mr Hughes his children after her death for the love that their father had shown her." Indeed, "she wished she was worth a thousand pounds for his sake, he should have it every farthing."[27]

Of course, the evidence of Ann's affection for her master relies entirely on the accounts of Ann's English neighbors, who might have benefited from her death. Sarah Ellis seems to have known who Joshua Hewes Jr. was and where to find him. Could she, Prudence Delany, and Milcah Wright have conspired with the Hewes family to secure Ann's estate? Might they even have had a hand in the scalding that led to Ann's death? There is no evidence—no trail of payments or suspicions—to support this possibility, however intriguing it might be. If we accept the evidence that exists, Ann's powerful regard for Hewes was rooted in gratitude for his freeing her from slavery. Ann believed that the law did not require her to be freed, "for she said that Mr. Hughes if he would might have made her a slave all the days of her life." By 1661 there were no other known slaves from the Pequot War remaining in Massachusetts. Some had died, victims of the European diseases that cut down so many American Indians. Others had set themselves free, using their connections with other captives and familiarity with the area to escape and make their way back home. But even if Ann Wompas had been the last remaining Pequot War slave in Boston, Hewes could have kept her in slavery or sold her out of the country. That is what Massachusetts's slavery law implied, and Ann clearly believed it.[28]

At her death in 1676, Ann's relationship with the Hewes family had come full circle. Joshua Hewes had been her benefactor by freeing her from slavery; now she bequeathed her property to his adult children, whom she had helped to raise. The estate Ann Wompas left to Joshua Hewes Jr. and his sisters Mary Lambe and Hannah Hewes must have been a tremendous boon to them. When their father, Joshua Hewes Sr., died in January 1676, he left a drastically diminished estate to his second wife Alice and his three children. He had once been among the wealthiest men in Roxbury, with significant landholdings and a promising career as a merchant and investor, but his fortunes had been in steady decline since his uncle and business partner Joshua Foote died in 1655. At the time of his own death, Hewes owned a few plots of land, but no house. His estate was valued at forty-nine pounds, but he owed debts of nearly seventeen pounds, leaving only thirty-two pounds in all. Ann Wompas's estate must have seemed princely in comparison. Aside from her house and land, which were valued at one hundred pounds, Ann's clothes and furnishings were worth twenty-three pounds and the value of her loans to Sedgewick and Knight added another twenty-seven pounds. The entire estate was valued at over 150 pounds—133 pounds more than the total worth of the estate Joshua Hewes Sr. had left his family at his death.[29]

There is a great deal of irony in Ann's final wishes for her estate. Just as John Wompas sold Indian land to English buyers without the consent of his Nipmuc kin, Ann Prask Wompas left her house to an English family without the consent of her Indian husband. She did not do this with any intent to defraud John, as she undoubtedly thought him dead. But, with such intent or without it, the property left Indian hands for English ones. John would not return to Massachusetts for another eight months. One of the many unpleasant surprises that awaited him there was a taste of his own medicine.

CHAPTER EIGHT

"The English Did Wrong Them About Their Lands"

The Political Awakening of John Wompas

Since hee came out of England in this spring about 4 months
past hee takes to no imployment but travils up and downe in a
vagrant Idle way, among English & Indians, vapouring of the
great quantity of land hee hath, offering to sell that which is
other mens possesson & improvement both English &
Indians . . . also hereby stirring up & dissafecting some
Indians his kindred as if the english did wrong them about
their lands, which practise of his is of very evel consequence.

—Testimonies against John Wompas, 1677

ALL THAT JOHN WOMPAS had to do to learn that his world had been
turned upside down was enter his own front door. His house was a
ten-minute walk from the dock where his ship completed its Atlantic voyage on May 15, 1677. It had been more than three years since
he was last at home, and his parting from his wife had been an angry
one. He may have hesitated before turning his key in the lock, fear-

ing a rebuke, but he had a much greater shock in store. An English family was living in his house—had been for eight months—and Ann Wompas was dead.[1]

Three years can transform a place, particularly if they are war years. While John Wompas was away, King Philip's War had devastated New England. Boston had been spared direct attack, but signs of military readiness were clear. On Beacon Hill overlooking the town, piles of wood stood ready to ignite in case of alarm, and townsmen took turns watching for lighted signals from surrounding towns. Watchmen also stood guard at Boston Neck, a narrow passage providing the only land access to Boston. War was not the only agent of change. Less than six months before John's ship pulled into Boston Harbor, fire had roared through the north end of town, incinerating homes, shops, warehouses, and Boston's Second Church. At least eighty families were left homeless in the bitter cold of November. The charred evidence of that disaster was clearly visible from the northern wharves.[2]

Just as striking as these visible signs was what could not be seen: Indians. Three years before, Indians had visited Boston daily, attending court, browsing the market or shops, carrying messages, or refreshing themselves in the taverns. But soon after the war began in 1675, Indian visitors were banned from Boston; even Indian servants, common in Boston households, caused enough "trouble and fear" to the anxious English colonists that the General Court ordered all Indians over twelve years of age removed from the town. When John Wompas returned from England in May 1677, adult Indians on the streets of Boston must have been an uncommon sight.[3]

John knew the colony had been at war in his absence; every New England ship brought news of the "rebellion of the Indians," and he had been on hand to hear William Stoughton and Peter Bulkeley tell the king about Massachusetts's fighting in Maine. But because Boston was never attacked, John Wompas probably thought his wife and home were safe. This expectation was shattered when he reached his house and found an English family in possession: Joshua Hewes Jr., and his sisters, Mary Lambe and Hannah Hewes. John knew them. The oldest two had been born and raised within sight of the home he had shared with the Heath family in Roxbury. Ann Wompas

became a slave in the Hewes home three years before the birth of
the oldest Hewes child, Mary. She probably helped raise Mary and
Joshua during their mother's illness and after her death in 1655.
Ann's bequest to the Hewes children confirms that her relationship
with the family continued after she married and left their service, so
it is likely that John's acquaintance with them continued as well. For
the Hewes siblings, glimpsing John Wompas's form in their door-
way must have been something like seeing a ghost. They, and the
colony courts that confirmed their possession of the house, considered John dead. Given what they stood to lose by his sudden resur-
rection, they may have felt disappointed that he had not remained
conveniently in the grave.[4]

John Wompas's experience of returning home and finding an
English family occupying his house was emblematic of the situation
facing New England Indians in the last quarter of the seventeenth
century, a situation dramatically accelerated by the recent war.
Everywhere, the English had taken possession of Indian property,
shutting Indians out with their fences, their livestock, and their laws.
Not just barriers and deeds, but also colony-wide restrictions on
Indian activity made what once had been Indian land, and what just
months earlier had been John's own house, off limits. Certainly, Indians had been restricted before during times of heightened alarm
over potential Indian attacks. But Indian regulations had always
been repealed in peacetime—until now.

The restrictions on Indians after the war made the kind of life
John Wompas had once lived, scarcely distinguishable from that of
an Englishman, virtually impossible. After the war, Indians, Christian or otherwise, were confined to four, then three, praying towns,
changing what had been refuges into reservations. King Philip's
War and the racial antipathy that sprang from it had created a new
reality in New England, completely at odds with John's view of himself as an English subject with rights equal to any colonist. Indeed,
as John would discover over the next several months, the condition
of Indians throughout the New England colonies had eroded significantly over the war years in terms of political autonomy, land
ownership, and even survival. This realization seems to have trig-
gered a radical change in John Wompas, turning him from a man
who moved fluidly between Indian and English worlds in pursuit of

his own interests to one who consistently represented himself as an Indian, championed Indian interests, and aspired to Indian leadership.

Before John could deal with any of the larger challenges facing him and other Indians, he had to decide what to do about the Hewes family occupying his house. It must have seemed obvious to him that they should move out. It was his home, after all, and he was demonstrably alive. Of course, what was good for John was bad for the Hewes family. They had lived there for eight months, and the house represented the bulk of their fortune. They were probably desperate to keep possession of it, and the colony's restrictions on where Indians could live provided significant leverage. On May 24, 1677, just after John arrived from England, the General Court had met to consider its regulations on Indians. The court voted to continue its prohibition on Indians over the age of twelve living in Boston and other English settlements and to confine Indians to four praying towns. That meant that people like John Wompas—free Indians holding property in Boston—were no longer included in the category of Indians allowed to reside in the town.[5]

Even if John Wompas's clothing and hairstyle made him hard to distinguish from the other weathered mariners in Boston, he was an Indian. The Hewes family could have seized on Massachusetts's Indian regulations as a way to strengthen their bid to keep the house. The property was legally John's, but colony law dictated that he could not legally live in it. Doing so would invite prosecution and imprisonment. It was probably these circumstances that persuaded John to quitclaim his house to the Hewes family. On June 2, 1677, he signed a deed conveying the property to them for "divers good causes and considerations" and "perticulary" for the sum of twenty pounds. Just nine months before, at Ann Wompas's death, the house had been valued at one hundred pounds, so twenty pounds was a fraction of its actual worth. But it was nothing to sneeze at either. An Indian laborer in late seventeenth-century Boston earned around a shilling a day, so twenty pounds would have been most of his pay for a year.

It is possible that the Hewes family suspected that the deed to the house was not free and clear and, as a consequence, would have been unwilling to pay more than twenty pounds. The deed itself says nothing about any lien, and the Hewes siblings had no difficulty registering the deed with the Suffolk County Clerk four days after their transaction with John. Despite the evidence that the deed was unencumbered, there was in fact a substantial outstanding mortgage on the house, which the Hewes family would soon discover if they did not know of it already. John had paid thirty-seven pounds for the house in January 1666, promising to pay an additional forty pounds within nine months. He failed to meet that deadline, and in 1668 he took out a mortgage of forty-four pounds and six shillings on the remaining amount owed on the house, due six months later in February 1669. John missed this deadline as well, and the loan was still outstanding when he conveyed the property to the Hewes siblings. There is no indication that John or Ann made any additional payments on their loan between 1669 and 1677, and if the 8 percent interest per year was still accumulating, the debt would have ballooned to over eighty-six pounds by June 1677. By January 1679, when the Hewes family paid the debt off, it would have grown to ninety-seven pounds—nearly the entire valuation of the house at Ann Wompas's death in 1676. Including the twenty pounds they paid to John Wompas in 1677, the Heweses may have been forced to invest nearly 120 pounds to secure a clear deed for the home that they had received as a bequest from Ann Wompas. John and Ann, on the other hand, may have paid as little as seventeen pounds for more than a decade of possession—thirty-seven pounds toward the purchase of the house in 1666 minus the twenty pounds John received to quitclaim it. John Wompas may have been dispossessed by the Hewes family, but he also seems to have gotten the better half of the deal.[6]

The same day that Wompas deeded his home to the Heweses, he completed an errand that he hoped would be the first step in regaining his freedom to sell land. He delivered the letter from King Charles II of England to John Leverett, governor of the Massachusetts Bay Colony. Leverett, a member of the first generation of English immigrants to the colony, was elected governor in 1673. A former soldier under Oliver Cromwell, Leverett was a stubborn defender of the colony's independence, declaring to Edward Randolph in 1676 that Parliament's authority did not extend to the English colonists living across the ocean. He was also a man not easily dissuaded from his chosen course, as his refusal to heed John Eliot's pleas for Wuttasacomponom demonstrates. The governor and John Wompas had met at least once before John's June 1677 visit; in 1668 Leverett was the officiating magistrate when John and Ann Wompas acknowledged the mortgage on their home. Leverett probably also knew John by reputation. The magistrates who blocked John's land sales would likely have warned their colleagues about John's schemes. If they failed to do so, the king's letter would have brought the governor up to speed.[7] It read:

> Trusty and well beloved, we greet you well. Whereas wee have been humbly informed by the peticion of John Wampas alias White that he was about six months since put into prison here for a small debt, where he hath since remained to his utter ruine and that he hath a certain parcell of land in Massachusetts bay, the which he hath held for many years, having taken the Oaths of Allegiance & Supremacy as our subject, and having humbly besought us to interpose with you, that he may bee restored to his said lands, or have liberty to sell the same for his present reliefe and the payment of his debts, wee taking into our gracious consideration the misrable condition of the petitioner have thought Fitt to recommend him to you that he may have justice done him and what favour the matter will fairly beare. And so we bid you farewell. Given At our Court att Whitehall the 22nd day of August 1676 in the 28th yeare of our reigne.
> By his Majesties comand
> J Williamson[8]

Leverett may have bristled at this intrusion into a colonial dispute, but he understood the seriousness of a royal missive. It embodied the king's authority. And he could not have missed the veiled threat in the king's reference to John Wompas as "our subject" who had "taken the Oaths of Allegiance & Supremacy." A subject was under the king's protection, a point the king emphasized by using the term. And taking the oaths of allegiance and supremacy meant that John had pledged his loyalty to the king and acknowledged the Crown's ultimate authority, which was more than most colonists of Massachusetts Bay could claim. The failure of Massachusetts officials to administer the proper oaths of loyalty was a longstanding bone of contention between the colony and the Crown, one that the Massachusetts agents Stoughton and Bulkeley had had to answer for. The agents were still in London, still pressing for reconfirmation of the colony's charter from the king. If they failed, the king could revoke the charter and impose a royal governor, an outcome colony leaders had dreaded for years. It may have been the possibility of royal intervention that prompted Leverett to promise John a court hearing to determine the validity of his claims. Until that court met, however, John would have no legal right to sell his land. To justify this delay, the governor latched on to a qualifying phrase in the letter—"that he may have justice done him and what favour the matter will fairly beare." These words made it clear that the "justice" John sought hinged on the merit of his case, and that merit was by no means self-evident. Either Governor Leverett or John must have spread the story of this interpretation around Boston, because residents of Cambridge would later sneer that the king's letter promised "no more than to doe him justice [as] is due to all his majesties subjects." With the pledge to have a court look into the matter, Leverett dismissed John from his home.[9]

That was not the outcome John Wompas expected. Any rational man would assume that a letter from the king would end the matter, not simply add one more item of discussion to a future hearing. John had returned to Boston in triumph, expecting the king's letter to remove all barriers to his success. Instead, he had lost his wife, his home, and his hope of resuming the business that had formerly enriched him. In addition, many of his Native friends and kin were either dead, enslaved, or so restricted in their freedoms that they might as well be slaves. A man faced with such bitter realizations might long to go home and nurse his sorrows, but John no longer had a home. He did have a few alternatives. He could sign on to another ship's crew and leave the colony. He could seek out his friends, fellow sailors who had helped him pay his debts in England—although giving John lodging would mean "entertaining" an Indian, contrary to colony law. Or he could seek shelter among his Indian kin.

The closest Indian settlement to Boston in 1677 was Nonantum, the first gathering place for Christian Indians, just eight miles and a couple of hours southwest of the town, within present-day Newton. A number of Christian Indians had returned there from their exile on Deer Island in the summer of 1676, and by autumn of that year Nonantum and Punkapoag had become the chief refuges for Christian Indians who survived the war. Wompas's uncle, Anthony Tray, built a large wigwam at Nonantum in October 1676, and this served for the community school and biweekly religious meetings with John Eliot and Daniel Gookin. Nonantum was a convenient settlement for a number of reasons: It was close to the falls of the Charles River, a traditional Native fishing and gathering spot. It also abutted the English towns of Cambridge Village and Watertown, where Natives could work for the English during harvest and have easy access to trade. Until September 1677, when the Christian Indians moved to Natick and other designated praying towns in response to the General Court order of May 1677, Nonantum was home to most of Wompas's surviving kin and friends.[10]

Because so many of the leading Christian Indians were at Nonantum or nearby, the court hearing that Governor Leverett promised Wompas took place there in June 1677, rather than at one of the county courts held in Boston or Cambridge. Indian courts had been held for decades among the Christian Indians who had submitted to the authority of the Massachusetts Bay Colony. Like the English quarterly courts held in each county, Indian courts met under the supervision of a traveling English magistrate, but their other court officers and jury were Indian. Appearing at an Indian court was a notable change for John Wompas. All his previous appearances to answer for offenses or to record deeds for property had been in English courts, reflecting his English residence, occupation, and education. He had also added an English name—John White—to his Native name, putting one or the other first to stress whichever identity suited his purpose. By June 1677 English tolerance of such a fluid approach to identity had apparently waned. Rather than send him to the county court with jurisdiction over Boston—the court where John Wompas, as a resident of the town, had appeared previously—the governor assigned his jurisdiction by race, referring him to the Indian court. In the racially charged atmosphere of post-war Boston, there was no question of "John White" moving freely between two worlds.[11]

Rogers Brubaker and Frederick Cooper argue that identity—often described as evidence of individual agency—can also be vulnerable to the "sometimes coercive force of external identifications." The Massachusetts government's regulation of Indian movement acted as just such a coercive force, triggering in John Wompas "the emotionally laden sense of belonging to a distinctive, bounded group, involving both a felt solidarity or oneness with fellow group members and a felt difference from or even antipathy to specified outsiders." John's actions and words from June 1677 to the summer of 1678 demonstrate that he had begun to embrace his Indian identity, sympathize with Native grievances, and nurture a sense of antipathy toward the English colonists of Massachusetts Bay and Connecticut.[12]

The Indian court's presiding magistrate was Daniel Gookin, the superintendent of the Indians and the leading proponent of the new English plantation at Quinsigamog. John Eliot, a longtime minister to the colony's Indians, was also present, as was John Wompas. Gathered to give testimony on the question of whether or not John had the right to sell Indian land were "all the old men the principall Indians" of the Christian Indian settlements. These "principall Indians" included John's uncles—his father's brothers Anthony and Thomas Tray—and probably his kinsmen Piambow, John Awassamog, and Waban, all of whom held positions of ecclesiastical or civic responsibility among the Christian Indians. Waban, Thomas Tray, and Piambow were rulers of the principal praying town of Natick and Anthony was a teacher in its gathered church; John Awassamog was the ruler of the praying town of Okommakamesit adjoining English Marlborough. All of them testified that they had known John Wompas since he was a child. They knew of John's strong abilities as well as the remarkable opportunities he had been given. He was one of the few Indians selected to study at Harvard College. Much of the funding provided to the Christian Indians by the New England Company had gone to support his schooling.

John's knowledge of both Indian and English law and society had fitted him to protect his people's interests, and they had employed him for that purpose. But instead of safeguarding their property, John had abandoned his obligations to the community and used his knowledge to betray them, selling their lands for his own profit. All of them testified of his "miscariages," which included claiming a "great tract" of land and, in the manner of the English, "marking trees with the letter W" to identify them as his own property. They "did beare witnes against his practise" of "offering to sell those lands," saying that John Wompas was "an evil instrument to disquiet them." Anthony and Thomas Tray declared that John's misdeeds grew out of his selfish and dissolute lifestyle: he had sold their land "to gett mony to be drunke & spend upon his lusts." Other Indians seconded these charges; all demanded that John be prohibited from "medl[ing] any more about those claimes" to Indian land and "withdrew any former Betrustment Committed to him in their Affaires."[13]

The "principall Indians," most a generation older than John Wompas, had made it abundantly clear that they condemned his self-serving actions. Denounced by his kin, John found himself in the position occupied by many mediators between English and Native society—distrusted by both sides. Whether John had the right to sell land was another question. Traditionally, Native sachems had the right to dispose of land, although it was assumed that they would obtain the consent of longtime land users before doing so. But the Hassanamesits' sachem, Wuttasacomponom, was dead—executed by the English on charges of joining with the enemy against them—and there was no evidence that any of his sons or other kin had been recognized as sachem after him. In his stead, the principal men told the court which Nipmucs had rights to particular tracts of land. They asserted that Waban, Piambow, John Awassamog, Anthony Tray, Thomas Tray, and their kin had rights to the land around Hassanamesit. They did not deny that John Wompas was one of those kin, but he was only one: He "could not prove or [demonstrate] any Right hee had in lands there more than other como[n] indians had." In their judgment, John was a "comon indian," not a sachem, and he had sold land without the consent of the other claimants to that land. Daniel Gookin, magistrate at the Indian court, forwarded the court's findings to Governor Leverett, "whereby Wompas his claime was shewed to bee of no great moment or validity." No one recorded John's response to this conclusion, but if his later words and actions are any measure, he was angry, and he had no intention of letting the matter drop.[14]

The elders of the Christian Indians wanted nothing more to do with John Wompas, as their testimony made brutally clear, but the younger Indians were another matter. Many of them had served as soldiers for the English in King Philip's War. Their close kin and companions had died in English service, and they expected that sacrifice to be taken as proof of their faithfulness. Instead, the English lumped them with all other Indians after the war, confining them to a handful of reservations and tightly restricting their freedom, proving that the English distrusted even fellow Christians and comrades in arms. These English actions carried the sting of betrayal to the Indians who had given so much in service of their allies. John Wompas spent considerable time with his Nipmuc kin in the summer of 1677, and he added fuel to their burning resentment. English witnesses would later charge that John Wompas spent the summer "stirring up & dissafecting some Indians his kindred."[15]

One of the Nipmuc men John spent time with that summer was Andrew Pittimee. Pittimee's signature suggests that he, like John, attended an English school; they may have been pupils at the same time in Roxbury or Cambridge. Pittimee shared another characteristic with John: he chafed under English authority. On two separate occasions he had persuaded English servants to run away from their masters and facilitated their escape, and English residents suspected him of "more evill then wittness cann at present convict him of." The war years had brought terrible suffering to Pittimee. The previous summer, while his wife, his sisters, and their children were foraging for berries, they had been set upon and murdered by English soldiers. Pittimee's kinsman, Swagun, attempted to avenge the murders by attacking a passing English colonist, "saying that he must kill an English man." Pittimee's brother made a similar attempt. Although we do not know whether Pittimee himself also tried to avenge the deaths, recounting his losses to John would have stoked both men's anger. Given John's association with him, Pittimee was probably one of those John worked to "dissafect." By doing so, John displayed a growing identification with his fellow Indians in opposition to the English.[16]

The environment of postwar Massachusetts reinforced John Wompas's identity as an Indian, both to the English and to himself. Colonists traumatized by the war regarded all Indians as dangerous enemies, regardless of whether they had sided with Philip Metacom or remained faithful to the English. The renewed restrictions on Indians living in English towns are evidence of English fears, as are court reports of "exceeding feare and dread (of the Indians)." In one incident, Mary Parkes, an English woman from the frontier town of Sherborn, visited a neighbor to collect a debt. While she was there, an Indian entered the house and "tarried there neere about an hour." Unnerved by his presence, Mary declared, "I wished the Indian were gone—I was afraid." Clearly angered by her open expression of dread, the Indian left the house, hid himself behind some bushes near the path, and then sprang up to frighten Mary when she walked by on her way home. Holding a hatchet in his hand and "lookeing most dreadfull fierce, threatning to split [her] downe," the Indian proceeded to play the part Mary had assigned him. He ordered her to follow him into the nearby swamp. While there, he whistled, and when Mary asked why he had done so, he told her he was "signaling to more of his company [which] lay a little way off." Then he declared, "he had killed five English men already & that they lay in the swamp." Not only that, but he claimed his Native companions had "killed [her] husband & children, & neighbours," and he himself had "affrighted & abused other women formerly, killed six Eastern Indians, & one Indian squaw." Having thoroughly terrified her and made her expect "nothing but death at his hands," the Indian man led her out of the swamp, escorted her part of the way to her home, and left her unharmed.[17]

There is no way to positively identify the Indian man in this account, but he sounds a lot like John Wompas. Fluent in English, used to entering English homes and interacting with colonists without hindrance, full of boast and bluster, this man was obviously angry about being treated as if he and all other Indians were savages. Regardless of who intimidated Mary Parkes, similar feelings of frustration over English stereotyping of Indians seem to have animated John Wompas. He had lived most of his life in the English world, he dressed like and carried on business with Englishmen, and he claimed the rights of a subject of the English Crown. But in postwar Massachusetts he was blocked from participating in the English land market, English colonists viewed him with fear and distrust, and his kin had been demoralized, scattered, and killed. At such a time, it is understandable that John Wompas increasingly identified with the Indian cause. In fact, he began to take on the role of a leader —a sachem—of the oppressed Indians of Massachusetts.[18]

Throughout the summer of 1677 John remained in the colony, traveling "up and downe in a vagrant Idle way, among English & Indians," offering to sell Indian land, and delivering pointed critiques of Massachusetts's policies. One of the places he visited on at least two occasions was the home of David and Hannah Meade in Cambridge Village, near Nonantum. In conversations with the Meades, John not only condemned Massachusetts's policies, but he spoke with the confident assurance that his judgments aligned with the king's and would receive royal protection. John's first visit to the Meades, in July 1677, followed closely on the heels of news that colony forces— including two hundred Christian Indians—had been defeated by Wabanaki Indians at Black Point, Maine. After the Massachusetts forces arrived at Black Point, Wabanaki Indians lured them into an ambush. Some of the English soldiers "basely ran away," leaving the rest fatally exposed. Nearly all of the remaining English and twelve of their Indian allies were killed. The disparity between English and Indian deaths was striking. Almost all of the forty English, including both Captain Swett and Lieutenant Richardson, were killed, but only twelve of their two hundred Christian Indian allies were. It seems likely that the Wabanaki attackers practiced what the Christian Indians were earlier accused of—shooting above the heads of the Indians and targeting the English. John lamented the loss of the twelve Christian Indians as if they were his own soldiers, declaring to Hannah Meade "that hee had lost a great many men in this warr." He blamed the loss on English cowardice and mismanagement, saying the English "had acted all one like children."[19]

John's time at Court had made one thing very clear to him: the Massachusetts Colony government was in serious political trouble. John had been present when the king chided Massachusetts agents

William Stoughton and Peter Bulkeley, saying that colony leaders had exceeded their authority by claiming jurisdiction of Maine and New Hampshire, and he may have been present at later meetings between the agents and their antagonists, Robert Mason and Ferdinando Gorges. On both of his visits to the Meades' home, John raised the issue of Massachusetts's illegal intrusion into Maine and New Hampshire, declaring that "the English had nothing to doe to send men to the eastward, it being out of this jurisdiction." John knew the details of the jurisdictional dispute better than most people in the colony. He also knew that Massachusetts's persistence in claiming jurisdiction of Maine offended the king and threatened to undermine the colony's charter authority. John took great satisfaction in sharing this first-hand knowledge with the Meades. When David asked if John had encountered the colony's agents, Stoughton and Bulkeley, in England, John replied that "hee had sene them, & spake with them." He also described the two agents' refusal to meet with the king on the Sabbath day "because it was against their judgment, & contrary to their religion." With obvious relish, Wompas reported, "they had better had gone [on Sunday], for they got nothing by it." John also told of the king's testy reply to the agents' request that he renew their charter: "his grand father had [given] them their pattent but they had forfeited it & acted contrary to it by making lawes to [hang] men for Religion wheras they had no such liberty." The agents were convicted by the words of their own charter, which banned laws contrary to English law. In John's conversations with David and Hannah Meade, he seemed to revel in the humiliation of the colony's representatives, speaking "many words in a desdainfull way of the English: both of the Authority of the country & of the people." The hapless agents were still in London, working to restore favor to the colony, but Wompas doubted anything would come of it. "New England hath lost the day," he declared, and "it is knowne in old england."[20]

David Meade's anxiety to learn the fate of the colony's agents in England is evidence of widely shared fears that Massachusetts's authority was in peril, and those fears would only have been heightened by John Wompas's stories. The investigations carried out by the king's agent Edward Randolph the previous summer, and recent efforts of New York's royal governor Edmund Andros to wrest

Maine from Massachusetts's grip, underlined the real possibility of a royal takeover of colony government. In the disarray following the failed English expedition to Black Point, Andros had shouldered his way into the peace negotiations between Wabanaki Indians and English colonists. In the process, he claimed Maine for the Duke of York and asserted royal control over the region, the very thing John Wompas predicted would happen to Massachusetts. John's public declaration that "New England hath lost the day" suggests he was confident that such political change was coming soon.[21]

John's expectation of royal intervention in Massachusetts may be why he felt justified in selling land despite the Indian court ruling against him in June 1677. Well after that decision, Wompas told David Meade that he had "a great quantyty of land up in the country about Hassannameset & that hee had his majesties letter for it." Another Englishman testified that John broadcasted his right to sell land all over the colony, among both Indians and English, "vapouring of the great quantity of land hee hath, offering to sell that which is other mens possesion or improvement both English & Indians, pretending his majesties letter, to the Gouvnor about his land." In addition to boasting, John continued to sell, register, and mortgage land throughout the summer of 1677. In July or August, John deeded one thousand acres at Quinsigamog Pond in Nipmuc Country to a cooper and fellow mariner from Boston named Benjamin Franklin. On August 16, John appeared at the county court to acknowledge a deed for one thousand acres at Quinsigamog Pond that he had previously sold to John Warner in London. That same day, Wompas signed two additional deeds, one to John Warner mortgaging four thousand acres at Quinsigamog Pond for eighteen pounds and four shillings, and another mortgaging four thousand acres of land in the same area to Benjamin Franklin for ten pounds. John defaulted on both loans, transferring the land to Franklin and Warner.[22]

It is significant that all of these deeds were located in the same area—at or near Quinsigamog Pond in Nipmuc country. This was the location of the new English plantation of Quinsigamog as well as several overlapping English grants, including one held by Ephraim Curtis. John's kin had hired him to dispute these grants in 1672, and in 1674 he had initiated a lawsuit against Curtis, to no avail. John may have felt that his effort to challenge English possession of land at Quinsigamog was rigged against him. The leading promoter of the plantation was Daniel Gookin. Gookin was also on the committee assigned to look into John's complaint from 1672 about English claims to Nipmuc lands and was one of the presiding magistrates at the Middlesex County Court session of 1674 in which John Wompas's case against Ephraim Curtis was scheduled. John did not show up for that hearing, quite possibly because he felt that Gookin's clear conflicts of interest made the effort pointless. John Wompas had good reason to complain as he traveled "up and downe the country" that the English "did wrong them [the Indians] about their lands."[23]

John's fellow Nipmucs apparently shared the sentiment. Shortly after the outbreak of King Philip's War, they targeted Ephraim Curtis's trading post near Quinsigamog Pond, destroying it and looting the trade goods inside. The trading post was one of several buildings near the pond that had been constructed and occupied before the English paid the Indians for the land. The English proprietors of Quinsigamog also built and occupied houses on Nipmuc land years before paying for it in 1677. In December 1675, Nipmucs attacked and destroyed those houses. There was precedent for such a response. In 1664, John Winthrop Jr. wrote: "Experience doth shew us that if any should offer to enter upon any of their [the Indians'] lands without paying and agreeing with them for it, thay are ready to rise up in armes, and to cut them of[f] as they did lately amongst the dutch."[24]

By selling or mortgaging the contested land at Quinsigamog, John Wompas was not dispossessing Indians. They had been pushed off the land long before. Instead, he was challenging English possession of the lands. He knew from long experience that rival claims to the same land would lead to court battles that could significantly hamper settlement. Rival claims could also force the English to negotiate with the Natives and either recognize their title or pay them additional amounts to secure a title that was clear. In fact, the process of unravelling the rival claims to Nipmuc land at Quinsigamog would extend well into the next century.[25]

While John's mortgages and sales of land can be seen as political acts, ways of fighting English wrongs with English weapons, they also served a very practical purpose—providing him with income at a time when he had no other means of support. Apparently, just two months after receiving twenty pounds from the Hewes family in exchange for his Boston house, John Wompas was broke. The known land transactions of the summer of 1677 provided him with at least twenty-eight pounds—more than two years' income for a sailor. How did he run through his cash so quickly? He no longer had a home of his own, so some of the money may have gone toward lodging expenses. Even if friends or relatives put him up for free, John may have returned the favor with gifts or treated his hosts to food or drink. A September 1677 incident at Natick suggests he was doing just that. According to the complaint of Waban, chief ruler of Natick, and its pastor Daniel Takawompait, John Wompas brought an entire barrel of hard cider to Natick at the beginning of September 1677 and proceeded to share its contents with all comers. The result was that "15 or 16 men and women were made drunk" and, no doubt, disorderly.[26]

Public drunkenness had risen alarmingly in the aftermath of the war, among both Indians and English. By freely sharing alcohol with his fellow Indians, John Wompas could only make this growing problem worse and further antagonize the Native elders. His uncles, Thomas and Anthony Tray, had complained the previous June that John sold land "to gett mony to be drunke." They probably saw this incident as further evidence of their charge. John may have seen it differently, however. By procuring a barrel of cider and sharing it with the residents of Natick, he was demonstrating his generosity— his willingness to redistribute his wealth—a quality required of Native leaders. This suggests that John may have been making a bid to be recognized as a sachem. Among the Algonquian-speaking Indians of the Northeast, the office of sachem was hereditary, but maintaining it required the support of elders and followers. Wartime deaths and executions had created a leadership vacuum among area Indians, and John had reason to think he could fill it. He had family connections to Nipmuc sachems. He was kin to the Awassamogs, who were descended from Wuttawushan, a past chief sachem of the Nipmucs, and he would later claim that his father had acted as a sachem during his life. It is not clear whether any claim John had to the sachemship came through matrilineal or patrilineal lines, but the stated connections are at least suggestive, as is John's insistence on continuing to sell Indian land, the traditional prerogative of a sachem. The elders of the Nipmucs did not recognize John as a sachem, but John may have sought the support of the younger generation, people like Andrew Pittimee. His hospitality to the Indians at Natick may have been the tip of the iceberg, one of many times he provided food, drink, or other goods to fellow Indians in an effort to demonstrate his fitness for leadership. Such expenditures would explain why Wompas needed loans from John Warner and Benjamin Franklin so soon after selling his house to the Hewes family.[27]

If John was trying to emulate the qualities of a sachem, it would help make sense of an incident that otherwise seems inexplicable. On September 27, 1677, a report reached Boston that Indians had attacked Sudbury, a frontier settlement twenty-three miles to the west. Given the rout at Black Point the previous May and an Indian raid on Hatfield, Massachusetts, the previous week, the news of the assault was entirely believable. It was a Thursday, the usual day for a midweek sermon, so many men and women were gathered at the Cambridge meetinghouse overlooking Harvard College, and they began to exchange news. John Wompas joined them. The appearance of an Indian at such a time led to obvious discomfort among the townspeople, some of whom stared at him openly. With a sure instinct for the dramatic, John demanded "whether they never saw an Indian before?" When two people replied yes, Wompas intoned darkly, "You shall feel them too."[28]

John Wompas was a Native American in a crowd of colonists who had endured two years of war with their Indian neighbors and feared they were again under attack. In this context, John's claim that the English would soon "feel" as well as see Indians was an alarming threat, delivered—according to English report—in a "surly manner." Openly threatening a people under such fraught circumstances could be highly dangerous. Just two months before, a group of English women in Marblehead, angered over Indians' commandeering of the town's shipping fleet and its English sailing crews, tore two captured Indians apart with their bare hands. John Wompas could easily have met a similar fate. What would lead him to make such a foolhardy threat?[29]

One reason for John's brazen outburst may have been to publicly display his courage and honor. Among Natives of the Northeast, sachems were expected to be eloquent orators, and their speeches served a range of important purposes in community life. One purpose was to provide a ritual way to provoke an enemy to war and, in the process, demonstrate the valor of the speaker. That ritual pattern fits John Wompas's behavior in the late summer and early fall of 1677 in Cambridge and Cambridge Village. John threatened, provoked, and insulted his English neighbors. He derided English soldiers as "all one green hornes." He sneered that English colonists were "not loyal subjects to his majesty," and he predicted imminent Indian attack, as if he could instigate it. By engaging in a traditional Native speech pattern—an exchange of insults with an enemy— John demonstrated that he had the courage and eloquence expected of a leader. Indeed, he boasted of his leadership potential to Hannah Meade, declaring "what great things hee would doe if hee were to leade souldiers against the enemies."[30]

Another possibility is that Wompas felt empowered and protected by the king's letter referring to him as his loyal subject. Indeed, immediately after threatening the English with Indian attack, John proclaimed his status, boasting of his letter from the Crown and declaring himself to be "the kings subject." When some Cambridge villagers declared that "they were his majesties subjects as wel as hee," John scoffed at their pretensions: "hee questioned that . . . [speaking] as if they were not legal subjects to his majestie." The Cambridge villagers' rejection of John's claim and dismissal of his royal letter—"which signifies no more than to doe him Justice touching his right, which is due to all his majesties subjects"— demonstrated that John's status as a subject of the Crown would not protect him. He may have been misled by the obvious power and wealth of Charles II's court at Whitehall into believing that it would. He would not be the first person to make that mistake.[31]

Perhaps John Wompas actually meant to provoke a violent response and dreamed he could lead his people against the English colonists. It is striking that John identified himself as "Indian" at this moment, demanding of the English "whether they never saw an Indian before?" His embrace of the general term "Indian," rather than Nipmuc, may indicate a growing sense of solidarity, not just with his own community, but with all the Indians of New England. There is some linguistic evidence that, as early as 1650, a broader sense of Native identity had developed among the Indians of New England. Abraham Pierson, an English Algonquian speaker, claimed that the term *eansketabaug* referred to all the Algonquian-speaking tribes of the region. In the aftermath of the Pequot War, Indians could not have missed the evidence of English dominance in the region. Some, like the Narragansett sachem Miantonomi, responded by calling for Native unity, saying, "so are we all Indians, as the English are, and Say brother to one another, so must we be one as they are, otherwise we shall be all gone shortly." By embracing the title of Indian, John Wompas, too, could assert the need for Native unity and offer himself as a champion.[32]

Perhaps John's angry speech was merely bravado, which he had in abundance. It certainly succeeded in alarming the colonists. Like Hannah Meade, who saw something sinister in John's claim "that hee had lost a great many men in this warr," the Cambridge colonists found John's performance a credible threat. Some of them would carry their complaints to colony officials, declaring their "fears hee will do some mischief." Wompas's boldness in provoking English fears probably put him in danger, but he may have believed that his vocal insistence on his status as the king's subject would protect him. Perhaps it did. Rather than tear him to pieces, the colonists called for a constable to hustle him off to jail. Prisons protect those inside them as well as those outside.[33]

John sat in Cambridge's town jail for four days. On October 1, 1677, he decided to stop waiting. He escaped from jail and headed west toward Indian country. Town jails in seventeenth-century Massachusetts were notoriously insecure affairs. Later that same year the wooden floorboards of Boston's town jail reached such a state of dilapidation that the prisoners simply broke through them and crawled out underneath. But court records suggest that John Wompas may have relied on his remarkable skills of persuasion, rather than brute force, to win his freedom. On October 2, 1677, Cambridge prison keeper William Healey was ordered to pay the costs of the search party sent out after the escaped John Wompas and "was admonished to be more carefull of his prisoners for the future, on penalty of being turned out of his place, & punished for his offense according to his [deserts]." Perhaps John had convinced Healey that he was

trustworthy, just needed a brisk walk to stretch his legs. Whatever
the cause, Healey allowed John to get away. Samuel Gookin, a resident of Cambridge, was assigned to pursue John Wompas. As the
son of Indian superintendent Daniel Gookin, Samuel may have accompanied his father on visits to Indian towns in the colony and
known the way. Even if he hadn't, his father was a good source of
information on where John Wompas might be likely to go. Within
a short time, Samuel and a companion found John, escorted him
back to Cambridge, and submitted their expenses for the job: twelve
shillings and six pence.[34]

Safely back in custody, John Wompas could face trial at the Middlesex County Court. Like other county courts in Massachusetts, the
Middlesex County Court met four times a year under the supervision of members of the colony's Court of Assistants, who also served
as magistrates, or justices of the peace. At the court's session in October 1677, Daniel Gookin, the same magistrate who had presided
over the Indian court at Nonantum the previous June and John
Wompas's 1674 lawsuit against Ephraim Curtis, sat on the bench,
along with fellow magistrates Simon Bradstreet and Joseph Dudley.
They accepted depositions from David and Hannah Meade about
John Wompas's visits to their home, testimonies from Waban and
Daniel Takawompait about John's getting residents of Natick drunk
the month before, and accounts of John's threats against the Cambridge residents gathered after the Sudbury alarm on September 27.
Other colonists also lined up to testify against John. Grace Oliver, a
resident of Cambridge Village, reported that "upon a very small oc-
asion" John had threatened to "pistoll her" if she was the last woman
on earth. The men who ran him down after his escape from prison
claimed John had "threaten[ed] the death of any man that should
take him."[35]

Wompas had acted the role of an Indian enemy just when the
English were most insecure—threatened by renewed Indian attacks
on their frontier and in danger of losing their charter to Crown in-
vestigators. Although the reported Indian assault on Sudbury proved
a false alarm, colonists were still on edge, fearing renewed attack at
any moment. The magistrates at the Middlesex County Court declared that Wompas's hostile behavior and speeches made him "justly
to be suspected of conspiring with the enemy against us." Indeed,

his escape from prison "argue[d] of his guilt." For these crimes, Wompas was "a person not fitt to have his liberty to live among us." Magistrate Daniel Gookin, who had known Wompas and his relatives for decades, summed up the complaints against him, saying that the witnesses in Cambridge as well as "divers others in the Townes adjacent have observed & seene so much of this wompas Drunkennes & evel carrige" that they begged the council to either imprison John Wompas or send him out of the country. To "send him out of the country" meant just one thing in postwar Massachusetts: to sell him as a slave. It was a fate that hundreds of Indians faced after capture in King Philip's War, as Wompas knew well.[36]

John Wompas's freedom had been restricted before; he had served jail time and paid fines for drunkenness, and colony leaders had prevented land sales that lacked the consent of all his Indian kin. But his freedom to own property in Boston and to travel the region—and the world—had never been questioned. He had never before been threatened with slavery for being, essentially, a "surly" Indian. But the world had changed since Wompas had sailed to England. The Crown might recognize Indians as subjects deserving protection, but in colonial Massachusetts they had no such status. Colony leaders had never considered Indians equal to themselves as subjects of the Crown, but even the inferior status they had accorded Indians as subjects of the colony government was undermined by the war. To the embattled colonists, all Indians had become a potential threat, and that threat needed to be contained through restricted settlements or bound labor.[37]

The county court lacked the authority to make such a "life or limb" decision about selling John Wompas into slavery. Instead, they committed him to the prison in Boston, there to await the next session of the colony's highest tribunal: the Court of Assistants. Wompas was sent to the Boston jail on October 2. The next session of the Court of Assistants was held on October 15, but Wompas did not appear in the records of that session, or in any of the sessions that followed it that winter or spring. Instead, he was released from jail on a bond for good behavior, the early American equivalent of bail. On October 10, 1677, magistrate Joseph Dudley ordered Wompas to post one hundred pounds for his own good behavior, and two friends, or "sureties," to post fifty pounds each to guarantee that good behavior. That made a grand total of two hundred pounds —a vast sum, equal to the entire estate of someone considered a "gentleman" in colonial Boston, and twenty years' worth of John's wages as a sailor.[38]

No record indicates whether John Wompas actually laid down that sum of money, or if he managed to satisfy the court with promises. Joseph Dudley was the only magistrate who signed John's release, and the document reflects a somewhat hurried transaction: Dudley penned initials rather than his full name and wrote the business on the lower half of a paper detailing a completely unrelated case. It is tempting to think that John Wompas presumed on his acquaintance with Dudley to secure his release. He had known Dudley for a very long time. The Dudleys resided in Roxbury for the first few years John lived there, and Joseph attended Corlett's grammar school in Cambridge and Harvard College during some of the same years as John did. Perhaps John promised to let Dudley in on some land deals if he would let him go. There is no documentary evidence that they made such an agreement, but it is striking that Dudley was the only English official involved in Wompas's release. Had Daniel Gookin been present, he is unlikely to have consented. He held a dim view of the reliability of John Wompas's promises, and he was certainly aware of John's illegal land sales, sales that threatened his own undertaking in Quinsigamog. In fact, Joseph Dudley would become a major speculator in Nipmuc lands within the next five years, supervising the surveying and purchase of hundreds of thousands of acres for the colony and securing at least seven thousand acres for himself. How Dudley's and Wompas's speculations intertwined is a complicated story, and one for a later chapter. Suffice it to say that Wompas did not have to stand trial before the entire Court of Assistants. Instead, he found a sympathetic ear—perhaps an interested one—and was soon back to business as usual.[39]

John Wompas's business was selling land. In December 1677, he appeared before magistrate Edward Tyng in Cambridge to acknowledge a deed for one thousand acres to Anthony Mudd, the house builder from England who had assisted him in getting out of debtors' prison. That was John's last recorded appearance in Massachusetts. By spring, he was in Connecticut, looking to sell some of the land he had obtained through his marriage to Ann Prask. He had already sold a portion of that land to several Englishmen from Stonington, Connecticut, sometime in the 1660s. But not all of it. Selling the rest—perhaps to the English who presently occupied it—was precisely what he planned to do when he arrived in Fairfield in May 1678.[40]

John approached the town leaders of Fairfield as boldly as he had approached Governor Leverett of Massachusetts. As before, he cloaked himself in the Crown's authority, asserting that the king's letter required colony officials to do him justice. Remembering the disastrous outcome of his encounter with Leverett, John took additional support along when he went to Fairfield—an unnamed agent and an English witness in his behalf. For the witness, John selected Walter Fyler, a resident of Windsor, a Connecticut town seventy miles northeast of Fairfield. Walter was the father of John Fyler, who had been a student at Harvard during the time John Wompas was studying there himself. The fact that John knew where the elder Fyler lived and felt free to call on him for assistance suggests that he had maintained his connection with John Fyler and his family since their student days.[41]

Walter Fyler's own report of the affair indicates that John Wompas traveled from Boston to Windsor and stayed briefly at Fyler's house. The two of them then journeyed together from Windsor to Hartford, Milford, and finally to Fairfield, all at John's expense. In the end, Walter Fyler was little help to John. Both men tried to convince the town leaders of Fairfield to pay Wompas for the town lands, but they utterly refused. Major Nathan Gold, a prominent citizen of Fairfield and veteran of King Philip's War, seems to have led the opposition. He and "others of Fairfield" refused to acknowledge any right Wompas had in Fairfield lands and declared their unwillingness to accept any evidence based on "the testimony of an Indian." When John Wompas continued to insist on his right, the town leaders of Fairfield locked him in the town jail and sent Walter Fyler packing.[42]

John's exasperation with this latest imprisonment comes through clearly in a second petition to Charles II. He complained "that by the evil practices of major Nathan Gold & others Inhabitants of Fairfeild, Your Petitioner is not only kept out of his just rights, but was also imprisoned by them in May last when he went to demand possession of his Estate according to Your Majestys Order of the 22nd of August 1676." John's words betrayed no sense that his claim to Fairfield was anything less than just. And, in his eyes, it probably was. By English law, John held title to all his wife's property, and a Connecticut court had acknowledged Romanock's deed of Aspetuck to her. (Admittedly, the deed was rather vague about what, precisely, the bounds of Aspetuck were.) English colonists were enjoying possession of Indian land—his land—and he wanted to be paid for it.[43]

If Fairfield's town officials wouldn't listen to him, John knew there were higher courts of appeal. After his stint in prison he traveled upriver to Hartford, the capital of the colony. There, on May 15, 1678, he presented his case for being the true owner of Fairfield to the colony governor and magistrates. Fairfield sent its own representative, a Mr. Burr, to defend the town against John's claims, and Walter Fyler, who by this time was back home in Windsor, sent a letter laying out his reasons for supporting John's claim. In his letter, Fyler complained that Mr. Burr had accused him of having "neither honestie nor witt in standing by the said John Wampus," of wasting John's money by accompanying him to Fairfield, and of angling to get "a great share in the Bootie" John would gain by stripping the English of their just title. Fyler denied these claims. He admitted that his travel expenses had cost John Wompas some eighteen shillings, but John's stay at Fyler's Windsor home had cost Fyler six shillings in turn, and he was "out of hope of ever being paid." More important, he defended his honor, declaring that he always put the "best good of this common wealth" above his own interests. He had not aided John Wompas in order to profit himself, but to save the colony future grief and expense. To his mind, paying John for his land was the wisest thing Fairfield could do, and if "out of penuriousness" the town leaders refused to do it, colony leaders should do it for them.[44]

Why would Fyler go to such trouble to defend John Wompas's claim, an action held up to derision by Burr? If we take him at his word, he feared the colony was in imminent danger, and that fear seems to have been nurtured by his conversations with John Wompas. Fyler had spent at least a week with John, in Windsor and en route to Fairfield. During that time, John had ample opportunity to use his skills of persuasion on the Englishman. He could have shown him the king's letter with its official seal, regaled him with stories of his gracious reception at Whitehall, and warned of the impending loss of Massachusetts's charter, the likelihood of which recent events had underscored. Like Massachusetts's leaders, Connecticut's feared royal interference in their colony government, and with good reason. At the start of King Philip's War, New York's royally appointed governor Edmund Andros laid siege to Saybrook at the mouth of the Connecticut River. In the name of the Duke of York, Andros demanded the surrender of all the land between the Connecticut and Hudson Rivers, where most of Connecticut's major towns were planted. This was, at the core, a question of conflicting grants. The Fairfield dispute was a similar conflict, and John Wompas, like Andros, came backed with the king's authority. If the colony refused to give John Wompas satisfaction, what was to stop him from going to Andros for relief? Wompas could even sell his right to Fairfield's land in New York, and Andros or some other powerful person might come to the colony to enforce that right: "and then if that parsons sword be longer then the sword of fairfield we must be fourced to add our Dagger which may cost manie a thousand pound, which might be prevented now." Standing on his duty as a virtuous citizen, Fyler warned colony leaders that they should respect John Wompas's claims. Apparently, Fyler's willingness to listen to an Indian was something rare in Connecticut. Like Fairfield's town leaders, colony leaders ignored his plea and rejected John Wompas's suit.[45]

John had failed, utterly, in his attempt to secure the right to sell his land in New England, despite the support of the king of England, whose splendid palace at Whitehall and hundreds of courtiers must have made him appear to be the most powerful man in the world. The king had honored John and condemned the Massachusetts agents, but the heady reception John enjoyed at Whitehall was nowhere to be found in the New England colonies. In the aftermath of King Philip's War, in fact, the status of Indians in New England had declined precipitously. John Wompas, an acknowledged subject of the king of England, had been met with nothing but fear and disdain since he returned to New England—jailed twice, declared unfit to give testimony, even threatened with slavery. It is no surprise that, following this most recent failure, John decided to return to England.

Disappointed and angry, he left the court at Hartford and traveled south and west through Connecticut to the colony and town of New York. Like Boston, New York was a busy port, with many ships arriving and departing for England, Spain, Newfoundland, and the Caribbean. An experienced sailor like John Wompas could always secure a berth on a merchant ship, and he probably did not have to wait long to find one bound for London. He saw England as a place where an Indian man was respected, where he could find powerful people with similar grievances against colonial leaders and then return in strength. John Wompas was determined, once again, to appeal to an authority higher than the colonial courts that interpreted law "only for their particular advantage." And this time he would seek relief not only for himself, but for his people, the "other native Indians miserably comprised within the laws made by the English."[46]

CHAPTER NINE

"Royall Protection"

John Wompas, Subject Status, and the

English Crown

His Majesty taking into his gracious consideration the miserable condition of the Petitioner, and declaring his Royall
Pleasure that not only the Petitioner but all such Indians of
New England as are his subjects and submit peaceably and
quietly to his Majesties Government, shall likewise participate
of his Royall Protection.

—LORDS OF THE PRIVY COUNCIL, for King Charles II, 1679

JOHN WOMPAS'S BUSINESS IN Connecticut had ended—disastrously
for him—in May 1678. Imprisoned in both Connecticut and Massachusetts, he chose not to risk returning to either place, decamping
instead to New York, the growing English port town to the southwest. From there he sailed to London, arriving sometime before
March 1679. Renewing his complaint and petition to the king was
his chief purpose in returning, but due to the failure of the king's
letter to recover John's right to sell land he had to rely on his employment as a sailor to get there, which may have required a series

of indirect voyages. The first evidence that John was again resident in London was the registration of a second petition at Whitehall on March 14, 1679, nine months after the fiasco in Connecticut.[1]

John's residence in London allowed him to make new friends and acquaintances and, as he had done before, he drew on them for financial and emotional support and rewarded them with deeds to Native land. John would again find a welcome reception at the court of Charles II, including expressions of support for the rights of the Crown's Native subjects. But the king's supportive words would not translate into deeds, an outcome that reveals much about the English empire's shallow commitment to Native peoples. Resourceful as ever, John managed through his own actions to secure assistance for himself and protection for the lands of his Nipmuc kin.

During his stay in England, John probably made his home in one of the eastern parishes of London such as Allhallowes London Wall. These parishes sat next to Shadwell and the other hamlets of London's east end and shared some of their maritime flavor. The Shadwell Docks are likely where John disembarked from his latest voyage. Its residents were seamen, captains, rope makers, sailmakers, coopers, innkeepers, and other tradesmen catering to the needs of the seafaring population. One such Shadwell tradesman was Edward Pratt, a "victualler," meaning a man licensed to keep an alehouse. Pratt and John Wompas became well acquainted, probably through Pratt's workplace.[2]

Alehouses in seventeenth-century London were considered disreputable establishments, breeders of crime and disorder. Contemporaries associated them with prostitution, and they were known to host card games, dice tossing, and other games of chance. Also known as "tippling houses," they were the lowest tier of the hospitality industry, which had inns catering to the elite, taverns to the poor, and alehouses to the poorest, who had migrated to the city to obtain employment. Alehouses proliferated in the poor suburbs of London, where there were more than three thousand by the early seventeenth century. Many alehouses were simply a room in someone's house, or even a shed or arbor in the back, "the better to obscure idle company" when church wardens came looking for Sabbath violators. Alehouses provided a secondary source of income for

Figure 11. View of Shadwell Docks from the Thames River, London, 1682 [London Metropolitan Archives, City of London]

tradesmen, or a way for a widow to get by without her husband's support. Because the poor ran tippling houses as well as frequenting them, alehouses offered other services aimed at the poor as well, such as providing credit or loans, or accepting pawned merchandise. Owners of alehouses could also rent rooms to lodgers.

Over the course of their friendship, through some combination of loans or other goods or services, John ran up a debt of at least fifty pounds to Edward Pratt. He may have lodged with Pratt for a time during his first or second stay in England, taken his meals and drinks at the alehouse, or run up debts by hosting others there. John also spent a good deal of time in London with John Blake, a fellow sailor from New England. Blake's father owned a house just a few doors from John Wompas's own home in Boston, so Wompas and John Blake may have become acquainted many years before they reconnected in London. They may also have served on ships' crews together. Like Pratt, Blake seems to have provided considerable assistance to John Wompas during his time in London, leaving John in his debt for an unknown amount of money.[3]

The degree of John's obligation to Pratt and Blake was compounded by a political crisis in London from autumn 1678 through 1679, which prevented John from immediately completing his errand at the court. Tension between King Charles II and Parliament had been running high for years. Exiled to France during his young adulthood, Charles had imbibed the absolutist principles of that kingdom, where the king was essentially above the law. At his Restoration in 1660, Charles accepted the Declaration of Breda, which made it clear that in England the law was supreme. But he never abandoned the kind of thinking that had cost his father his life. He insisted on the right to issue edicts without the approval of Parliament, as he did in the Declaration of Indulgence, an act that granted limited religious freedom to Catholics and non-Conformists in England. Parliament was aghast, not only because the king had gone above their heads, but because he had loosened restrictions on a group that many in the country associated with despotism. Hostility toward Catholics had been a staple of English public life since Henry VIII split from the Catholic Church in 1531. Guy Fawkes's attempt to blow up Parliament on November 5, 1605, dubbed the "Gunpowder Plot," merely heightened longstanding fears that Catholics wanted nothing more than to overthrow English liberties, putting the country under the thumb of the Catholic Holy Roman Emperor or his fellow believers on the thrones of Spain and France. The foiling of the Gunpowder Plot was celebrated every year with bonfires and boisterous displays of anti-Catholic propaganda. In 1677, Guy Fawkes Day celebrations featured "mighty bonefires and the burning of a most costly pope . . . and the effigies of 2 divells whispering in his eares, his belly filled full of live catts who squawled most hideously."[4]

This context explains the hysteria that accompanied the revelation of what became known as the "Popish Plot" in early autumn 1678. It was a conspiracy, a Londoner breathlessly reported, "of some eminent Papists for the destruction of the King and introduction of Popery." According to the charges of Titus Oates and Israel Tongue, a vast Jesuit network had laid plans to kill the king and replace him with his Catholic brother James, who would deliver the nation back into Catholic bondage under the yoke of a foreign pope. It was a wild story, and one that King Charles himself never believed. Parliament, however, embraced both the story and its tellers, and as Oates released increasingly lurid accounts of the conspiracy, a tidal wave of anti-Catholic sentiment swept through "the whole Nation."[5]

Responding to public uproar, the king and Parliament began enacting new restrictions on Catholics within the kingdom. On the outskirts of London, where John Wompas was staying, he must have heard the wild rumors circulating and seen evidence of the intensified hatred of Catholics. Londoners deaf to irony defaced the intentionally Catholic-baiting sign of the Pope's Head Tavern, and constables were ordered to search houses for any hidden "priests, jesuits, papists, and persons suspected to be papist" who might be "traytors . . . divelishly affected to the King and government." While the hysteria surrounding the plot heightened tensions throughout the capital, it had personal consequences for John Wompas as well, delaying his efforts to renew his petition to the king. From the first hints of the plot late in the summer of 1678 through the end of the year, the regular business of government ground to a halt while Parliament, the king, and his councils devoted all their energies to uncovering the conspiracy and dealing with its political fallout. If Wompas hoped to have his case heard that year, he was disappointed.[6]

And he was not the only one. Massachusetts's agents to the Crown, William Stoughton and Peter Bulkeley, who had arrived in London in December 1676, were still there in 1678, still in a tug-of-war with Robert Mason and Ferdinando Gorges over the government of Maine and New Hampshire. The longer the case dragged on, the more people with grievances against Massachusetts showed up at Whitehall to present their own complaints. Despite the agents' insistence that they had no authority to speak for the colony in these other cases, the Crown demanded that they appear to answer charges. Exhausted in body and purse, the agents petitioned the king to allow them to return home in July 1678, but he insisted they remain. The Popish Plot, which emerged shortly after their petition was denied, added months more to their ordeal. Not until June 1679 did the council finally allow them to return home, acknowledging that, "owing to the prosecution of a Popish plot," there was "no prospect" of quick resolution of the various issues still in dispute between the Crown and colony.[7]

It is likely that John Wompas had contact with the Massachusetts agents and their detractors, many of whom were at court during March 1679 when John's second petition came before the council. Two of Massachusetts' most bitter opponents were Randall Holden and John Green of Warwick, Rhode Island. Holden and Green's grievances against Massachusetts were similar to John Wompas's, and similarities in their petitions to the Crown suggest that they may have discussed their cases with each other as they waited for justice at Whitehall. Holden and Green had arrived in London in July of 1678 to protest Massachusetts's claim to lands in the King's Province in Rhode Island. They were old hands at appealing to the Crown, having joined with Samuel Gorton in successful royal petitions in both 1644 and 1664. In these earlier appeals, as well as in their petitions and letters of 1678 and 1679, they capitalized on Massachusetts's reputation for disloyalty to the Crown in order to highlight their own status as faithful subjects. They made the same invidious comparisons in a letter to the Lords of Trade in 1678, adding the charge that "the Massachusets Goverment have been the Original occasion of all those miseries that have befallen New England, in the late Warr, by their barbarous usage of the poor Indians . . . which caused those people to fly to Armes to Right themselves." Concluding the letter, they urged the council to "move His Majesty speedily to erect a Supreme Court of Judicature over all the Colonies in New England. And that His Own Royal Authority may bee there soe established that Justice may bee equaly distributed to all." Both the language and the remedy proposed in Holden and Green's letter are strikingly similar to those John Wompas used in his second petition to the king, which read:

> To The King's most Excellent Majesty,
>
> The humble Petition of John Wampus alias White an Indian, Your Majestys subject & Inhabitant of Boston in Your Majesty's Colony of the Massachusets in New england.
>
> That your Petitioner by Marriage of Anne the Daughter of Romanock late Sachim of Aspatuck & Susquanaugh, upon the death of the said Sachim is become sole Proprietor of those Tracks of Land, upon which the Town of Fairfeild in Conecticut Colony is built.
>
> That Your Petitioners Father in Law about nineteen years since delivered up the possession of the said Lands to Your Petitioner, & sometime after the Petitioner sold part thereof to Captain Dennison & Amos Richardson & others of Stonnington in Conecticut Colony for the Sum of 530 £ sterling or thereabouts.
>
> That by the evil practices of major Nathan Gold & others Inhabitants of Fairfeild, Your Petitioner is not only kept out of his just rights, but was also imprisoned by them in May last when he went to demand possession of his Estate according to Your Majestys Order of the 22^d of August 1676, from whence he made his escape to New York, & destitute of money & all necessaries is forced to come to England to seek releif.
>
> Now for as much as Your Petitioner & other native Indians there inhabiting are miserably comprized within the Laws made by the English calculated only for their particular advantage, there being no supreme Courts of Judicature established in that Country, whereunto the oppressed may repair for redress.

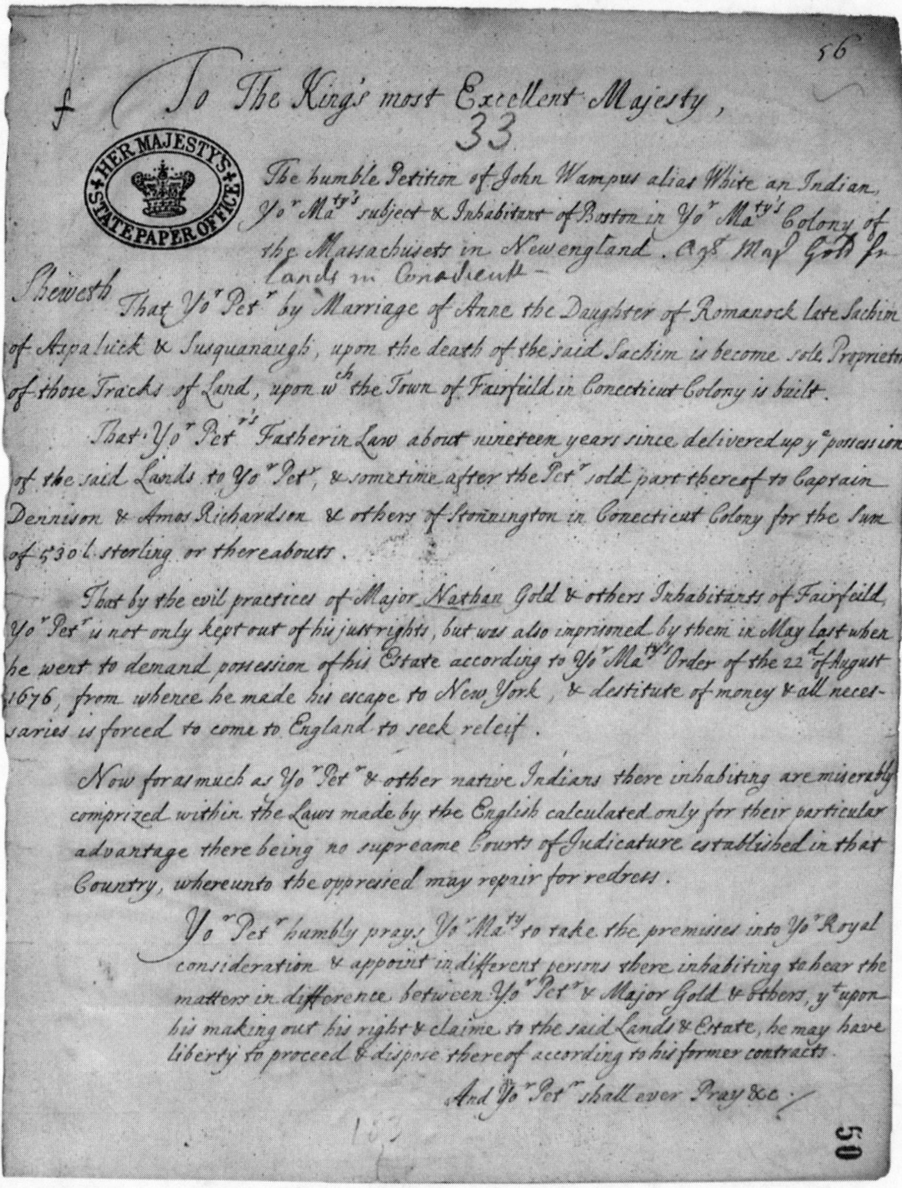

To The King's most Excellent Majesty,

33

The humble Petition of John Wampus alias White an Indian,
Yo.r Ma.ty's subject & Inhabitant of Boston in Yo.r Ma.ty's Colony of
the Massachusets in New england. Ags.t Maj.r Gold for
Lands in Conecticute —

Sheweth That Yo.r Pet.r by Marriage of Anne the Daughter of Romanock late Sachim
of Aspatuck & Susquanaugh, upon the death of the said Sachim is become sole Proprietor
of those Tracks of Land, upon wch the Town of Fairfield in Conecticut Colony is built.

That Yo.r Pet.rs Father in Law about nineteen years since delivered up ye possession
of the said Lands to Yo.r Pet.r, & sometime after the Pet.r sold part thereof to Captain
Dennison & Amos Richardson & others of Stonington in Conecticut Colony for the Sum
of 530 l. storling or thereabouts.

That by the evil practices of Major Nathan Gold & others Inhabitants of Fairfeild,
Yo.r Pet.r is not only kept out of his just rights, but was also imprisoned by them in May last when
he went to demand possession of his Estate according to Yo.r Ma.ty Order of the 22 of August
1676, from whence he made his escape to New York, & destitute of money & all necessaries is forced to come to England to seek releif.

Now forasmuch as Yo.r Pet.r & other native Indians there inhabiting are miserably
comprized within the Laws made by the English calculated only for their particular
advantage there being no supreame Courts of Judicature established in that
Country, whereunto the oppressed may repair for redress.

Yo.r Pet.r humbly prays Yo.r Ma.ty to take the premisses into Yo.r Royal
consideration & appoint indifferent persons there inhabiting to hear the
matters in difference between Yo.r Pet.r & Major Gold & others, yt upon
his making out his right & claime to the said Lands & Estate, he may have
liberty to proceed & dispose thereof according to his former contracts.

And Yo.r Pet.r shall ever Pray &c.

50

Figure 12. John Wompas's second petition to King Charles II [The National
Archives of the UK (TNA), ref. CO1/43 (33)]

Your Petitioner humbly prays Your Majesty to take the premises into Your Royal consideration & appoint indifferent persons there inhabiting to hear the matters in difference between Your Petitioner & Major Gold & others, that upon his making out his right & claime to the said Lands & Estate, he may have liberty to proceed & dispose thereof according to his former contracts

And Your Petitioner shall ever Pray &c.

Like the Rhode Islanders, John lamented the condition of "native Indians" in New England "miserably comprized within the Laws made by the English" and lacking any access to "supreame Courts of Judicature." John begged the king to appoint a neutral court to which he and other Indians could resort for justice. The common proposal of a "supreme court of judicature" in the colonies and the identical phrasing in Holden and Green's and John's letters suggest the possibility that the two Rhode Islanders showed their letter to John before he composed his own. The three shared similar grievances and frequented the same halls of state. It would have been surprising had they not compared notes, particularly once they learned of their mutual antipathy to the Massachusetts government.[8]

It is unclear how long John waited for his petition to the king to be read and considered by the king's council. It was officially marked as received on March 14, 1679. The backlog of business caused by the Popish Plot had certainly slowed things down, but it is also possible that John waited to present the petition until what he deemed was a propitious moment. In fact, Wompas's petition was the last piece of business from New England that the council considered in the month of March, and it came at the end of a month-and-a-half-long series of papers that cast Massachusetts in a very bad light. These included petitions from Robert Mason and Holden and Green, defensive responses from the Massachusetts agents Stoughton and Bulkeley, and proposals from Edward Randolph, shortly to take office as a royal Collector in New England, setting forth what was "necessary towards the reducing that people to their due obedience." By the time the council turned to John's petition, they had reached the limits of their patience with the Bay Colony's trumpeting of its own authority and with the colony agents' severely constrained powers, which prevented them from giving any assurance of future obedience. This parade of Massachusetts's misdeeds would have set the stage for a receptive response to John Wompas's complaints of colonial oppression.[9]

John's petition benefited from the collection of evidence against Massachusetts, even though his specific grievance occurred in the colony of Connecticut. Indeed, his petition seems to be intentionally vague about the exact location where he had been wronged. The first section of John's petition declared his residence in "Boston in Your Majesty's Colony of the Massachusets in New england." The fact that Connecticut was the location of the lands under dispute was buried deeply enough in the document that the council sought clarification, later adding near the top of the petition, in a different hand, the words "against Major Gold for lands in Conadicutt." John attributed the abuses he had suffered to "the Laws made by the English calculated only for their particular advantage." The vague identification of his opponents as "the English" may suggest that John considered the actions of the English officers in Connecticut simply an extension of the same practices in Massachusetts. Certainly, the two colonies' responses to John's claims were strikingly similar. But John's general language also suggests a deliberate strategy. His references to the abuses of "the English" and his own residence in Massachusetts might lead the council to conflate the practices of the two colonies' governments. John probably spent enough time at Whitehall talking with other petitioners, courtiers, scribes, and staff to know that the royal government feared that "the New England disease is very catching." Petitions against neighboring colonies for abuses similar to Massachusetts's had indeed come before the Crown within the previous decade. If court officers believed Connecticut had caught Massachusetts's dangerous disregard for royal authority, all the baggage from Massachusetts's evasion of royal commands, brought to the king and council's attention by the previous months' business, would attach itself to John's plea.[10]

In fact, that is what seemed to happen. Meeting with the council five days after they received John's petition, the king ordered them to write a letter to the Connecticut government in John Wompas's behalf. Like the king's previous letter for John, this one requested "such justice as his case may deserve"—a nebulous direction, open to interpretation for or against John's case. But the letter also addressed the plight of Indians in general, insisting that in the future the Connecticut government "proceed in such manner as his Majesty's subjects may not be forced to undertake so long & dangerous Voyages for obteyning Justice, which his Majesty expects shall be speedily & Impartially administered unto them upon the Place." No such rebuke appears in the king's first letter to Governor Leverett of Massachusetts. It is clear that Connecticut's leaders bore the brunt of the king's displeasure over being presented, once again, with evidence of colonial abuses of an Indian who had now made two "long & dangerous Voyages" to England in pursuit of justice.[11]

As in his previous petition to the king, John Wompas stressed his exotic Indian identity and his status as a subject of the Crown, in order to both pique the king's interest and claim the right of protection the king had extended to Indian subjects. But in the second petition, unlike the first, John broadened his appeal to include all New England Indians, "complayining of the great hardships and miserys he and other Native Indians are subject unto by the Laws of that Colony." Choosing to represent not only himself but all the king's Indian subjects shows John acting the part of a champion of Native interests, and he seems to have had some success in that role. Like John's petition, the Crown's written response was broad in its application of subject status, proclaiming that "not only the Petitioner but all such Indians of New England as are his subjects and submit peaceably and quietly to his Majesty's Government, shall likewise participate of his Royall Protection." John's plea for royal protection for all the Indians of New England may have had a lasting influence. In 1701, the King's Commission for Plantations wrote a letter reproving Massachusetts for its "averseness . . . to establish laws for the relief of its Native American subjects." The similarity of this language to the Crown's 1679 letter in Wompas's behalf suggests that the Commission may have reviewed it before they wrote to Massachusetts in 1701.[12]

The Crown's expressions of support in response to John's petitions go far to explain his confidence in the king's protection, a confidence he earlier displayed by taunting and threatening Cambridge's English residents in September 1677. He thought merely invoking his status as a subject would keep him from harm, and he issued dire predictions that the Massachusetts government's day of power was coming to a close. Indeed, John Wompas's continued granting of deeds for Indian land relied on that prediction, and he seems to have convinced his English friends that a new colonial administration was at hand under which all his promises would be honored. On the strength of John's conviction, John Warner, Anthony Mudd, and Nicholas Warner had already sailed to Massachusetts carrying deeds to three thousand acres in Nipmuc Country that John had given them.[13]

But just what did the king mean by proclaiming that John and all other Indians who had submitted to the Crown were his subjects? Did "royall protection" provide any true benefit to the king's Native subjects across the ocean? Unfortunately for John Wompas and a number of other Indian petitioners, the answer was no. For a succession of Indian appellants from the seventeenth through the end of the eighteenth century, subject status was an empty promise. Royal governments welcomed visiting representatives of Native nations, as well as individuals like John Wompas, acknowledged their status, accepted their gifts and submissions, but left the resolution of their grievances to local colonial governments, which were rarely sympathetic to Native demands. This reality is clear in the Privy Council's letter to Connecticut in response to Wompas's second petition to the Crown. As in their earlier letter to Governor Leverett, the Crown's representatives demanded that the Connecticut government "do the Petitioner such justice as his case may deserve" but insisted that they do so locally—"his Majestie expects [justice] shall be speedily & Impartially administered unto them upon the Place"— not through an appeal to England.[14]

When Indians actually went to England to seek justice, they were welcomed, given letters and respect, but little more. The Crown neither offered to pay John Wompas's way out of prison nor instructed any of its officials to follow up on his case in New England. The council expressed exasperation with colonial governments' forcing Indians "to undertake so long and dangerous voyages for obtaining of Justice," but did not assume the role of a "supreame court of judicature" that John pleaded for. So if the royal government was not willing to ensure the protection of its Native subjects— sending royal officers or ships full of soldiers to defend their rights—

then why bother honoring the Natives who did come? Why administer the oaths of allegiance and supremacy to John Wompas? Why send two separate letters instructing colonial leaders to do him justice?[15]

The answer is that such actions served the empire's interests. The king may have welcomed John Wompas and responded to his petitions for reasons connected to ongoing Crown-colony disputes. In other words, the Crown's attribution of subject status to Indians was largely self-serving. The king defended Native rights when such defense served a larger purpose, such as bringing a recalcitrant colony into line. The most recalcitrant of all the English colonies was Massachusetts, without a doubt. By honoring John Wompas, the king shamed colony leaders and pressured them to conform to his own view of how they should behave. Indeed, the royal tongue-lashing of the messengers from Massachusetts, which John recounted to Cambridge residents on his trip home in 1677, was at its core a conflict between colonial and Crown understandings of what it meant to be a subject of the king of England.

To understand this conflict, we need to briefly review the contentious English history of subject status. As the English jurist Edward Coke explained, subjection at its basic level was an unequal reciprocal relationship in which a subject pledged loyalty to a ruler in exchange for government and protection. But English parliaments had long insisted that subjects had more rights than simply protection and civil order. These included the right to consent to the laws that governed them and to hold their property free from seizure, and these additional rights were inviolable, even by the king. Parliament's fierce defense of the rights of Englishmen culminated in the English Civil War of 1642–1651 and the execution of the king in 1649—an event that sent shivers of horror through all the absolutist monarchies of seventeenth-century Europe. When the English monarchy was restored in 1660, Charles II (who had spent the interregnum in France) was made to understand that French ways would not do in Albion—but the advice didn't stick. Throughout his reign, he pushed to exercise his prerogative, and Parliament pushed back.[16]

Given the extremes of seventeenth-century English politics, it is no surprise that legal theories on the status of subjects occupied a wide spectrum. Within England, most agreed that subjects had fundamental rights that even the king must respect. But there was significant disagreement over whether the rights of Englishmen extended to English colonies or conquered territories. Some theorists claimed that in such places, the king held all authority, granting those privileges necessary to establish order on the periphery of the empire but reserving the right to revoke any privilege—or charter—at will. Other theorists argued that English subjects carried their rights with them wherever they went.[17]

The colonists of Massachusetts Bay adhered to the latter interpretation, declaring in 1664 "that his majesties charter doeth grant unto his subjects here the enjoyment of all the priviledges of any the naturall subjects within any of his dominions." One right they considered inviolable was that of consent to the laws that governed them. The Massachusetts General Court's response in 1678 to the king's demand that they obey the Navigation Acts demonstrated this point: "Wee humbly conceive, according to the usuall saying of the learned in the lawe, that the lawes of England are bounded within the four seas, and doe not reach America. The subjects of his majesty here being not represented in Parliament, so wee have not looked at ourselves to be impeded in our trade by them." The governors of Massachusetts believed that being held liable to laws passed long after they had settled New England would violate their fundamental right of consent and deprive them of the "same liberties as other English subjects." As a show of deference to the king, Massachusetts leaders offered to consider and vote on whether to accept the Navigation Acts as colony law, but they insisted that their vote, not the king's command, was final. Edward Randolph, sent as a royal representative to Massachusetts in 1676 and 1678, expressed his outrage at this state of affairs, blustering to the king that the colony's "Allegiance to Your Majesty seemes only grounded on their Charter . . . and they doe not ground it in naturall obedience, where by right it lyes."[18]

In the king's view, and the view of royal officers like Randolph, a subject's rights were limited by the king's prerogative. For instance, one month before John Wompas's petition was discussed by the Privy Council, the king wrote to the Massachusetts government ordering it to send him a justification of their claim to the conquered territory of Mount Hope, the homeland of the defeated sachem Philip Metacom (King Philip). Massachusetts had presumptuously claimed the conquered land as its own and had even advertised it for sale. The king wrote testily that he "cannot but take notice that no account has been received from them or the other Colonies of the conquest of that country, not doubting but for the future they will be more careful to advertise him or the Privy Council of matters relating to his prerogative and authority." Conquered land was, by definition, the king's, and he expected to exercise his prerogative and authority there.[19]

The petitions of Indian subjects like John Wompas confirmed the royal government's sense that the New England colonies needed to be reined in and may have sped up that process. A court official reported in 1679 that Charles II was "solemnly bent on a general reformation of the abuses in their government." The Dominion of New England—a combined government of the New England colonies and New York under the administration of a royal governor— was the culmination of the king's plan for colonial reform and would be set in place in 1686. Under that administration, the New England colonies' course of self-government would be sharply constrained, consistent with the Crown's view that subjects in the colonies should bring themselves under such royal government as the king deemed appropriate, and that justice should be administered through royal officials directly answerable to him. For Native subjects of the Crown like John Wompas, royally appointed officials who acknowledged and answered to the king promised to be a great improvement over New England's locally elected officials, who had proved unsympathetic to Indian grievances. But in 1679, when John made his second appeal to the king, such a change was still only a promise.[20]

John Wompas had seen how ineffective the king's first letter was in commanding the actions of the governor of Massachusetts. Nevertheless, he interpreted his second letter optimistically, concluding that the "justice" he deserved was the right to sell the disputed land. And sell it he did. In July 1679, John appeared before a justice of the peace in London to acknowledge a deed he had written out to his friend and probable landlord Edward Pratt. In exchange for the substantial sum of fifty pounds, John sold Pratt eight miles square of land "near Quansigamog pond in the Nipmuck Country." The wording of the deed suggests that John sold Pratt this vast acreage to satisfy his debts. The deed notes that John received the fifty pounds both "at & before" the sealing of the contract and states that the sale was "also in recompence & sattisfaccion of the long labor & services performed & done by the said Edward Pratt unto & on the account, of mee the said John Wampas alias White." John had probably earned no income after his arrival in London four to twelve months earlier, so some debt is understandable. But fifty pounds was far more than the average yearly lodging expenses of a single man in late seventeenth-century London. Even spending heavily, John should have been able to get by on less than two pounds a month, which would have consumed only twenty-four pounds if he had been there a full year. John may have lost his money through theft, gambling, or accident, or he may have been engaging in the same kind of status-enhancing displays of generosity as he had in Massachusetts. It may be that the "long labor and services performed" by the alehouse keeper Pratt included bankrolling John's hospitality.[21]

It is curious that John remained in London as long as he did after receiving the king's letter, rather than returning to Connecticut to claim his rights. His debts would certainly have been smaller if he had done so. There are several possibilities as to why he stayed. He may have been waiting until after Edward Randolph, the king's collector of customs for New England, departed. When Randolph did finally leave in the autumn of 1679 he carried with him letters from the council to the governors of Connecticut and the other three New England colonies, as well as the king's picture and royal arms, his seal of office, and a letter attesting to its authenticity. Clearly, he was armed with the trappings of royal power, and John Wompas may have thought waiting until Randolph was in the colonies would improve his chances of success. Indeed, Randolph may have been the person who delivered the letter directing Connecticut leaders to give justice to Wompas. The Connecticut magistrates marked it as "received" in May 1680, which would have been the first time the General Court met after Randolph visited that colony in December 1679.[22]

John's debts to Pratt and others may also have kept him in London, trying to find a way to repay them or, barring that, to satisfy them with land rather than cash. John could be scrupulous about his financial obligations, as demonstrated by his efforts to ensure Boston's jailkeeper received the seventeen shillings he owed him. Pratt may have had no interest in buying land on the other side of the Atlantic Ocean, at least at first, but evidence from the deed suggests that John used his persuasive powers to bring Pratt around. The deed includes several features that make it distinct from the other deeds John gave for Native land. First was the vast amount of land—eight miles in length and breadth. Eight miles square was a common size for a New England town grant, which would have been a strong selling point. The Massachusetts General Court was unlikely to approve a plantation on a plot smaller than eight miles square, as there would be insufficient land for future growth. Having a plot of that precise dimension, then, could speed approval of a new town by the court, after which Pratt could sell individual plots to investors. Second, John included descriptive language in the deed that suggested the land was rich in fur-bearing animals. In addition to the standard language indicating that Pratt's land included meadows, forests, streams, and so on, the deed added "all & singular Moose, deer, furs: Skins . . . privileges, profits, traffiques—tradings." John may have convinced Pratt that the deed positioned him to make a fortune in the fur trade. Finally, John added a claim he had never made previously in a deed—that he was a sachem. He described himself as "John Wampas alias White of Asanamiscock in the Nipmuck country in New England Sachem."

Sachems had the traditional right to convey land. John's kin had denied his right to sell Nipmuc land in the June 1677 court session held near Nonantum, declaring he had no more right to the land than any other common person. John's actions after the court ruling clearly show that he rejected that judgment, and he spent much of his time in Massachusetts stirring up his fellow Nipmucs, convincing them that the "English did wrong them about their lands." He also made efforts to emulate the qualities of a sachem—showing generosity by treating fellow Indians to cider, engaging in ritual insult of the English, and boasting of his potential for leadership. In the leadership vacuum of postwar Massachusetts, Wompas may have been bidding for the role of sachem of his devastated and divided people. In his deed to Edward Pratt from July 1679, he made his claim to leadership explicit. Calling himself a sachem followed logically from John's growing commitment to defending Native rights. It was undoubtedly also a strategic move, meant to override objections to his land sales by either his kin or colony officials, or to assuage any fears Pratt may have expressed that he would not be able to claim the land John sold to him. Regardless of why John named himself a sachem in the deed, it seems to have worked. On November 3, 1679, Edward Pratt registered the deed at the Middlesex County Court, and the county clerk wrote "Assenamiscock all, Nipmuck sachem" in the margins of the court copy. Soon afterward Pratt took up residence in Hassanamesit.[23]

A final reason John remained in London after he received the king's letter, and in fact never returned to the colonies, is that he was too sick to travel. Sometime before September 1679, John became seriously ill. He or his friends hired George Owen, a barber surgeon from the parish of Allhallows London Wall, to care for him, but Owen could not cure him. On September 5, 1679, John made out his will, "being sicke and weake in body but of sound and perfect mynde and memory." Four men, including a notary public, witnessed as John signed and affixed his seal to each of the four pages of the will. Sometime near the end of September, John died. His will was proved before Lord Richard Lloyd at the Prerogative Court of Canterbury in London on October 1, 1679. John Blake was sworn as executor of the will at the same time, with power to serve as co-executor reserved for Edward Pratt "when he should arrive and seek it."[24]

Nothing in the documents surrounding John Wompas's death says what killed him. Being "sicke and weake in body" was standard legal boilerplate, used in most wills. John had spent much of his life among the English of Massachusetts Bay Colony, several years in the metropolis of London, and probably short periods in various other ports of the Atlantic world without falling prey to the European illnesses that had so devastated his Native friends and kin. But the fact that nearly a month elapsed between the signing of the will and its proving at the prerogative court suggests that John may have died of a chronic illness, rather than an acute illness or an accident. He was still a young man of forty-two years, but he had lived a remarkably full life. He had been raised by loving parents who sought to do him good. He had learned the languages, laws, spiritual traditions, and societal structures of two different cultures and received a college education at Harvard. He had married and had a daughter. He had seen much of the Atlantic world through his work as a sailor. He had rubbed shoulders with ordinary laborers and attended an audience with the king of England. He had much to think about, and perhaps much to regret, in the weeks after signing his will, and he evidently decided to resolve some long-unfinished business before dying.

John's last will would serve to complete that work. He apparently intentionally used its careful stipulations and exclusions to protect his homeland for the benefit of his Nipmuc kin. The provisions of the will also put stumbling blocks in the way of the English whose possession of Quinsigamog he had unsuccessfully contested before his first trip to England. John bequeathed "All that My Estate lying and being in New England aforesaid & comonly called or knowne by the name of Assenham East-stock"—Hassanamesit—to his "very loveing kinsmen John a Wonsamock, Pomhammell and Norwaruunt." Notably, John did not include his uncles, Anthony and Thomas Tray, in his bequest. Obviously, he was still smarting from their public condemnation of his actions just two years earlier. A scribe evidently wrote the will to John's dictation, given the anglicization of Hassanamesit to Assenham East-stock, but the transcription also reflects John's word choices and Nipmuc pronunciation. Among Massachusett and Nipmuc speakers in the seventeenth century, both "it" and "ock" were used as place-name endings. "Hassanamesit" appears most often in legal and other documents of the time, but John clearly preferred "Hassanamiscock." That version appears in his deed to Edward Pratt and in his will, in which the scribe's "Assenham East-stock" echoes the "ock" ending. The scribe also recorded "Pomhammell" for the name usually written as "Pomhaman," reflecting John's Nipmuc pronunciation of "l" in place of the Massachusett dialect's "n." Although John Wompas went to live with the Heath family in Roxbury at a young age and spent much of his life speaking English, evidently he never lost his Nipmuc inflections. Reading the will, then, is almost like hearing John speak to us, unconsciously asserting his Nipmuc identity at the same time that he consciously used his will to preserve his Nipmuc homeland.[25]

The will was a legal document binding in English courts, something John knew well, but he was using it to confer Indian land, and
he also knew that the English would look to customary Native law
to confirm the legitimacy of that bequest. To satisfy both legal traditions, John explicitly cast his bequest of Hassanamesit as a transfer
of sachem rights, repeating the claim he made in his deed to Edward
Pratt. In the will, John wrote as a sachem and as the son of a sachem,
passing on to his kinsmen his responsibilities, specifically the obligation of "observing performing fulfilling and keeping all such Articles
and Conditions as my Father and I have or ought to have observed
performed & fulfilled and kept." By bequeathing a sachem's duties
and the territory of the sachemship to John a Wonsamock, Pomhammell, and Norwaruunt, John was legitimizing their claim to the
land in a way that English courts consistently recognized. Interestingly, at least one of the kinsmen to whom John bequeathed sachem
duties claimed a "naturall right, descending . . . from the [Nipmuc]
cheife sachem Wuttawushan," to lands in Nipmuc Country. This
was John Awassamog [a Wonsamock]. John Wompas claimed John
Awassamog as kin, though their exact relationship is unknown. It is
certainly possible that John Wompas was also "nearly related" to
Wuttawushan and that his claim to be a sachem would have been
legitimate had his kin consented to it. On the other hand, the claim
may have been false, another example of John Wompas's strategic
use of Native and English political and legal structures to benefit
himself and, at least in this case, his kin. Regardless of who the legitimate sachem of Hassanamesit actually was in 1679, John Wompas's
claim and his bequest of sachem duties to his kin lent legitimacy to
a transaction that was recorded under English law. Thus he combined English and Indian land ways in an apparent effort to preserve
Indian land.[26]

John also left bequests to Englishmen in his will, including two
of the men who would later claim the right to Hassanamesit. Less
than two months before making out his will, John had sold eight
miles square of Nipmuc land near Quinsigamog Pond to Edward
Pratt. Pratt seems to have thought he had purchased all of Hassanamesit, although there is no evidence that John Wompas ever sold or
mortgaged that specific plot of land. One of the notations in the
margin of the version of the deed registered at the Middlesex County

Court refers to the land as "Assanamiscok *all*." It is likely that this marginal notation by the court recorder reflected Pratt's own claim of where his land was located, but it directly contradicted John's stated intentions in his will. In the deed, which was penned with John present, there is no mention of Hassanamesit. Instead, the deed refers to "8 miles square of land near Quansigamog pond in the Nipmuck Country *or the like quantity elsewhere*." By granting all of Hassanamesit to his kin in his will, John made it clear that Pratt's eight miles square would have to be laid out "elsewhere" than Hassanamesit. Thus, it would have to be either the land at Quinsigamog already deeded to other Englishmen several times over or the land John Wompas claimed at Fairfield, Connecticut—land already occupied by English settlers.[27]

John's bequests to his English friends were limited to those who had provided immediate assistance or friendship in his last months of life. To George Owen, the local surgeon who cared for him, John left four hundred acres of land located next to the property he had deeded to Nicholas Warner near Quinsigamog Pond. To Edward Pratt and John Blake, he left "all the rest and remaynder of my lands"—meaning all the land not otherwise bequeathed in the will—"by what name or names soever the same be called[,] in whose tennure, occupation or possession the same or any part thereof is now or late was in[,] and in what place or places whatsoever in the Countrey of New England or elsewhere." By naming Pratt and Blake his executors and granting them all his remaining lands, John laid the groundwork for significant legal battles. The will granted Pratt and Blake all of Wompas's unbequeathed lands, regardless of whether they were in the "occupation or possession" of someone else. By doing this John Wompas was in effect setting Pratt and Blake on his antagonists: Ephraim Curtis and the Quinsigamog proprietors, the Fairfield townspeople, and any other English colonists who had settled on or purchased land John claimed as his own. He had been unsuccessful in fighting these settlers previously, but through his will and the maze of overlapping deeds he left behind him, John Wompas would manage to carry on the fight over Nipmuc land long after his death.[28]

CHAPTER TEN

"One Piece of Land to
Cling on To"

The Hassanamisco Reservation

The reason why my people still exist is there have always been
people in every generation that kept reminding us who we
were, and that we always had one piece of land to cling on to.

—CHERYLL TONEY HOLLEY, Chief of the Nipmuc Nation and
Hassanamisco Band of Nipmuc Indians, 2014

EDWARD PRATT, THE EXECUTOR of John Wompas's will, wasted no
time attempting to cash in on his acquaintance with the land-rich
Indian sailor. Before John's will had even been proved, Pratt was on
board a ship to Massachusetts. On November 3, 1679, safely landed
in New England, Pratt registered his deed for eight miles square of
Nipmuc land with the Middlesex County clerk. Registering the land
would prove to be the only easy part of the business. Pratt and the
other Englishmen who held deeds to John Wompas's land and benefited from his will battled with colony authorities and John's Nipmuc kin for nearly a quarter of a century, interrupted by wars and
several changes of government. Like John Wompas himself, they

sought to harness the changing political currents for their own advantage, cozying up to royalists like Joseph Dudley in an attempt to subvert the intent of John's will, and lashing out at the defenders of the old charter government and John Wompas's Nipmuc relatives who opposed their efforts. And it was solely their own advantage they were seeking, unlike John, who—at the end of his life if not before—attempted to protect his Nipmuc kin. Despite the self-serving efforts of Pratt and his associates, Hassanamesit remained in Indian possession well into the eighteenth century. A few acres of Hassanamesit—the Hassanamisco Reservation—are still held by Nipmucs in the twenty-first century, and the legal documentation of that possession leads directly back to the will of John Wompas.[1]

When Edward Pratt arrived in Massachusetts around the start of November 1679, he stepped into an unintended gathering of the English beneficiaries of John Wompas. Nicholas Warner and his son John Warner were also in the colony, as was Anthony Mudd, the London house builder who had assisted John in gaining his freedom from debtors' prison. The Warners and Mudd had already begun the process of claiming the land John Wompas sold to them by registering their deeds with the county court. John Warner probably spoke for all of them when he declared that he intended to pay his living expenses "in Land." But to do that, they would have to determine the exact boundaries of the land, divide it up, and find buyers. That is where they began to run into trouble.[2]

The lands John Wompas deeded to Anthony Mudd, Nicholas and John Warner, Edward Pratt, and Massachusetts residents Benjamin Franklin and John Cole all clustered around Quinsigamog Pond and the road to Springfield, which was precisely where the English proprietors of Quinsigamog had laid out their plantation. These proprietors had purchased their lands from Indians other than John Wompas or from fellow Englishmen with previous grants, and they had long since begun to settle those lands or to sell them. If John Wompas's friends tried to lay out or take possession of the land represented in their own deeds, they were likely rebuffed by either Native or English owners and forced to return to Boston to complain to authority. This set up a struggle between Wompas's beneficiaries, who shared his antagonism toward the Bay Colony

government, and the leaders of that government, who had long condemned Wompas's sales as illegitimate. Not surprisingly, these antagonists also diverged over the issue of royal intervention in colony
government. Wompas's beneficiaries hoped for a new royal government to approve their efforts to profit from John Wompas's land.
Daniel Gookin, a magistrate frequently on the bench at the Middlesex County Court, was both an ardent supporter of the old charter
government and the primary force behind the plantation at Quinsigamog, and thus unlikely to offer any assistance to the men whose
deeds conflicted directly with his plantation. Facing such opposition, Wompas's friends were forced to cool their heels in Boston,
waiting for a new government favorable to them to arrive. Nicholas
Warner's frustration with this state of affairs is revealed in an incident from 1678. In October of that year, Boston town officials tried
to warn him out of the town. "Warning out" was an official notifica-
tion from New England town selectmen that a visitor had been denied permission to continue living in the town, usually because he
appeared likely to become a burden to other residents. When Boston's selectmen ordered him to leave, Warner gave a combative
reply, declaring "he will stay in the towne in despite of any or com-
plaine to England." Like John Wompas, Warner was ready to turn
to the Crown for aid, a tactic he likely gleaned from Wompas's experience.[3]

Other Wompas beneficiaries were not as ready to fight as Nicholas Warner. His son John Warner filled his waiting days as a sailor,
shipping out from Boston several times between 1677 and 1679.
Anthony Mudd remained quietly in Boston, where he took the oath
of allegiance administered by Governor Leverett in November
1678. Edward Pratt's arrival in Boston in November 1679 started a
new flurry of efforts to secure Wompas's land. Pratt was a literate
man with some education, enough to allow him to pass as a physi-
cian later in his life. He soon took the lead among the deed holders,
recruiting potential buyers and possibly encouraging some of Wompas's friends to drop their claims. For instance, Anthony Mudd
disappears from New England records shortly after taking his oath
in 1678. There is no evidence of Mudd selling his land, so it is likely
that he conveyed his deed to Pratt or another claimant or simply
abandoned the quest and returned to England. In 1684 John War-

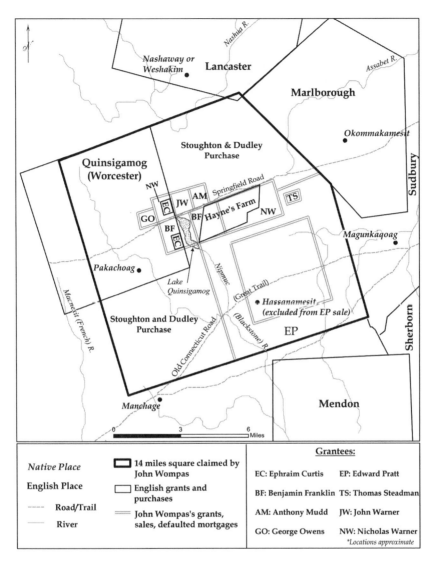

Figure 13. John Wompas's land claims and sales in Nipmuc Country [Map by Jen Macpherson, based on maps in Dennis A. Connole, The Indians of the Nipmuck Country in Southern New England, 1630–1750: An Historical Geography *(Jefferson, N.C.: McFarland, 2001)]*

ner sold his father Nicholas the four thousand acres John Wompas had mortgaged to him and lost in 1677. The younger Warner's last appearance in New England records was in 1684. It is likely that he, too, returned to England. While John Warner and Anthony Mudd dropped out of the land game, Edward Pratt remained, joined within a few months by John Blake, who had returned to Boston from England. Together, they recruited a number of men to buy shares in the vast amount of land they claimed by purchase or bequest from John Wompas. Nicholas Warner did not join Pratt and Blake in this effort. He already had deeds to at least five thousand acres and may have felt little incentive to try for more. In addition, both he and Edward Pratt had strong, combative personalities, which may have discouraged their working together.[4]

On his own, Nicholas Warner continued his attempt to secure his lands, apparently by squatting on the land he considered his property. That land was part of a tract of thirty-two hundred acres near Quinsigamog Pond held by John and Josiah Haynes since 1664, and the brothers brought a lawsuit against the intruder. The case was heard at the Middlesex County Court at Charlestown in June 1681. On the bench was Daniel Gookin, who had spent well over a decade working to untangle the conflicting claims to the area, had previously resolved his own plantation's conflict with the Haynes brothers, and was not about to allow his work to be undone. Nicholas Warner used the court as a stage for his complaints, brandishing a copy of the letter King Charles II had written for John Wompas in 1676 and claiming the protection of the king. Daniel Gookin responded to Warner's dramatics by declaring "his majesty had nothing to doe here, for wee are a free people of our Selves." Warner gave a saucy retort: "If the King hath nothing to doe here, how came I to be arrested in his majestyes name?" In answer to Warner's question, the court ruled in favor of the Haynes brothers and committed Warner to prison. There, Josiah and John Haynes visited him "to take bond . . . for the charges and Costs of Court," which Warner, as the losing party, was responsible for paying. Like Gookin, the Haynes brothers dismissed the authority of the king, telling Warner "thay vallued not the Kings letter at all, for if it were [Warner's] right never soe much [he] should not have it as long as this Government Lasted."[5]

Warner's outspoken antipathy for the Massachusetts government attracted like-minded residents in the Bay Colony. Two of
these were Ann and Thomas Wilkinson, whom a Chelmsford town
officer described as "bad enough, & very prophane . . . as full of
mallice . . . & railing as almost possible may bee." Thomas was continually running up against the civil and religious laws of the colony.
He was charged repeatedly with attempted rape or adultery, he
threatened his neighbors with costly lawsuits to prevent their complaints against him, and he practiced surgery and medicine contrary
to law. In addition, in a pattern that was disturbingly common
among the men who hoped to profit from John Wompas's land, he
was abusive to Indians, being on record as having stolen house mats,
hoes, and three bushels of Indian corn from Jacob, a Christian
Indian of Wamesit. The Wilkinsons attended Warner's trial in
Charlestown, which suggests they were already acquainted with
him, and after Warner was released from prison they joined him in
an appeal to the king. Following John Wompas's example, they
sailed to London and sought an audience with Charles II. Unlike
John, they were not successful, but they did manage to get their
complaints taken down by a scribe, who recorded that Warner and
the Wilkinsons were "ready to depose the matter of fact but no body
will take their depositions." Clearly, their reception at Whitehall was
nothing like the welcome John Wompas had earlier received, whether
because they lacked his charm and persuasiveness or because they
did not have the cachet of his American Indian identity. Nevertheless, their words were recorded and eventually came before the
king's council.[6]

In the process, they may in fact have served their intended purpose: to speed the Crown's overthrow of the Massachusetts Bay government. Thomas Wilkinson's testimony confirmed Warner's account of Gookin's disloyalty, and he added another charge to the
complaint: Thomas Danforth, who was also a judge on the bench at
the county court in June 1681, had failed to reprimand Gookin for
his public expression of contempt for the king's authority. This was
clear evidence of at least two disloyal magistrates, and Ann Wilkinson's testimony asserted that not just magistrates but also their relatives spoke disrespectfully of the king. She reported hearing Jonathan Danforth, brother to Deputy Governor Thomas Danforth, say

that "it was commonly reported in all the taverns and alehowses in London that the King had sixty or seaventy bastards, and that he had given every one of them there portion and sent them away." Scribes at Whitehall recorded these testimonies in 1682, adding them to the growing pile of evidence in support of the efforts of Edward Randolph and others to replace Massachusetts's leaders with a royal governor.[7]

Nicholas Warner later returned to Massachusetts, where he continued to squat on "his Land lying beyond Malbrow not belonging to any Town Ship." There is no evidence that he was able to get a secure enough hold on the land to profit from it, however. By August 1706, Warner was "above 80 years of age and Infirm of body." Apparently destitute, he moved to Boston, where he was twice warned out by the town's selectmen. After that, he disappears from colony records.[8]

Edward Pratt and John Blake had somewhat more success than Nicholas Warner. In 1679, after both had arrived in Massachusetts, Pratt and Blake collected supporters who were willing to buy John Wompas's land or assist them in claiming it. One of them was Joshua Hewes Jr. Another was Richard Thayer. John Wompas had known Hewes for decades and may have known Thayer as well. It is likely that John gave Hewes's name—and perhaps Thayer's—to Pratt and Blake before he died, as there is no evidence either of them knew the men previously. Hewes and Thayer helped Pratt and Blake recruit an additional six men as investors in Wompas's lands. All were Boston tradesmen who lived and worked near Hewes or had known associations with Hewes or Thayer. Once Pratt recruited them, they were drawn together by mutual antipathy toward local and colony leadership. Pratt and Blake had undoubtedly heard of John Wompas's clashes with Massachusetts government during their time together in London. Their own difficulty securing the lands for which they held deeds added fuel to the fire Wompas had kindled. After arriving in Massachusetts, both Pratt and Blake defied colony governors and aligned themselves with representatives of the royal government. When challenged for ignoring a court ruling, Pratt declared "that hee hath freinds lately come over & in power that wil beare him out in it." John Blake, too, was known as "a contemner of the present Athority of this Colony." When challenged for acting contrary to law, Blake retorted, "Law, Law, saith he, a Turd for your Laws! How long do you think your Government and laws will last?"[9]

A number of the men Pratt and Blake recruited as shareholders had a similarly contentious relationship with colony authority. George Danson and William Mumford were Quakers, part of a small group of worshipers who were arrested and whipped through the town for holding an illegal church meeting in 1677. William Harrison also fell outside the dominant Congregationalist pattern of the colony, holding to the Anglican church of the old country and said to be the first man in Boston buried with the Book of Common Prayer. Harrison was also strongly royalist; witnesses in a dispute between Harrison and his next-door neighbor recorded that he exclaimed "that he hoped the Goverment would be changed ere long & then he should have justice." Clearly, a good number of the men seeking to cash in on Wompas's lands openly hoped for a change in government to smooth the way for them.[10]

Some of the men who held shares in John Wompas's lands shared another characteristic as well, a disregard for the rights and welfare of Indians. The most common ways to make money from Indians in early America were to buy their lands and to sell them alcohol. Pratt and Blake did both. Pratt reportedly sold "strong Liquors" to Indians near Hassanamesit. Blake was repeatedly charged with doing the same, "to the greate Disturbans of the neighbours & the Danger of mens lives." Witnesses reported that "tis frequent to see Indians in the street coming from [Blake's] house staggering and smelling strong of Rume, tumbelling Down in the street. Sumtimes one upon a nother, sumtimes abusing one another by fighting, Indangering the lives one of another, sumtimes by laying violent hands on their own parents." Blake's neighbors appealed to colony officials "for sum redress of these evils that so the neighbourhood be not so often disturbed, pore Indians Abused and their lives so frequently hazarded." Another shareholder, Robert Taft, was accused of "irregular trading" with the Indians, a phrase that generally meant selling alcohol without a license. Two other shareholders, John Hayward, who joined the other investors by 1686, and George Danson, owned Indian slaves. Hayward's was a boy formerly owned by the merchant Samuel Shrimpton; Hayward received the boy as partial payment when he sold his Boston house lot to Shrimpton in 1679. There is no evidence concerning Hayward's treatment of the boy, but George Danson's female Indian slave Sarah was unhappy enough to run away in 1679, and she suffered horribly as a result of his efforts to recapture her. Danson hired Henry Eliot, a farmer from Stonington, Connecticut, to bring Sarah back to Boston from Warwick, Rhode Island. Unable to persuade her to go with him voluntarily, Eliot dragged her behind his horse and "was forced to use her so that Shee kep't her bed some daies." Rather than return her to Danson, Eliot tried to employ her in his own harvesting, which she refused, and "at last hee beat her with a whalebone till Shee bled before he could make her work for him." Danson sued Eliot over possession of Sarah, and Eliot agreed to deliver her to him "dead or alive," a condition apparently acceptable to Danson.[11]

Not only did many of these shareholders abuse Indians through illegal alcohol trade or slavery, but by actively seeking to acquire Indian land, they pitted their own self-interest against the well-being of the Indians. At least one of the shareholders—Richard Thayer—participated in a scheme that persuaded Massachusett sachem Josias Wampatuck to deed a large tract of Indian land to him despite the opposition of tribal elders. While many of the sales of Indian land that took place following King Philip's War were made with the consent of Native leaders and traditional landholders, even legitimate sales could be inherently abusive to Indians in times of duress. The mad scramble for Indian lands in postwar Massachusetts was one of those times. After conquering the Indians in the war, many colonists considered Indian lands their just due, whether or not the Native owners had fought against the English. Even the colony government, which had long prohibited sales of Indian land without explicit permission and usually denied such permission when it was sought, relaxed their stance in the aftermath of the war. They seemed to accept the inevitability of a wholesale transfer of Indian lands into English hands. For one thing, the skittish English were not prepared to allow the Indians who remained in the colony to live and travel freely. Restrictions on where Indians could live persisted after the war. In fact, the number of plantations where Indians were permitted to reside was reduced, first from five to four, and then from four to three. With the confinement of Indians to what were essentially reservations, combined with the dramatic decrease in the Indian population through wartime deaths and exile, the English perceived the bulk of Massachusetts Indian country as "empty." Of course, it was not, and even areas where Indians no longer lived were still claimed by Indians, but the English—colonists and leaders alike—saw this as a temporary situation.[12]

Colony leaders moved quickly to lay claim to Indian land in the postwar period. In March 1679, leaders from all the New England colonies met at Plymouth to apportion the territory previously occupied by Indians hostile to the English in the war, which the English defined as conquered land. Next, colony leaders moved to secure unconquered lands that, because of the decreased Native population and the restrictions on where Indians could live, appeared to be open for English settlement. On May 11, 1681, at the request of magistrates Joseph Dudley and William Stoughton, the General Court assigned the two men to visit Nipmuc Country and determine "what titles are pretended to by Indeans or others, and the validity of them, and make returne of what they find therein to this Court." It is significant that one of those who initiated the investigation of Nipmuc lands was Joseph Dudley, who would become a major speculator in Indian lands. Dudley, who was a judge at John Wompas's trial in Cambridge in October 1677, certainly knew about the potential for buying and selling land in Nipmuc Country.[13]

The immediate trigger for Dudley and Stoughton's request was agitation over claims to John Wompas's lands led by Pratt, Blake, and their co-investors. In response to that agitation, Nipmucs living at Natick petitioned colony leaders in May 1681, declaring their right to the Nipmuc Country and requesting compensation for the lands that had been sold there. Among the Indians signing the petition were John Wompas's uncles Thomas and Anthony Tray and others who had protested John's sales at the Indian court in 1677. The Natick petitioners made it clear that they were not asking for compensation for lands sold with the approval of the General Court and the consent of the Indians "that had Right ther unto," nor were they requesting compensation for "the towns & ground [of] the praying Indians in That Country," which they did not intend to sell. No, they wanted compensation for lands sold by men like John Wompas who lacked the right to sell and whose deeds had not been approved by the General Court. In addition to requesting compensation, the Naticks used their petition to make a strong case for their legitimate right to the land, declaring that they were "Subject to his Majesty and his Government in this Jurisdiction" and that they had remained "faithfull to the English Interest" throughout the war. In other words, the English could not claim their land by conquest. They also appealed to the English understanding of natural law, declaring that "wee and our predecessors had & have a naturall Right to much of the Lands Lying in the Nipmuck Country." They knew from past experience that the English acknowledged a natural right to land that was occupied and improved. Both of these approaches demonstrate that these Indians, like John Wompas, understood English justifications for possessing land and could turn them to their own advantage. While current restrictions and wartime depredations had forced them to vacate those lands, they asserted that longstanding ownership and past use gave them a right to compensation.[14]

Dudley and Stoughton had asked the General Court for permission to look into the land controversy raised in the Natick petition, so it is not surprising that they went to work on the assigned task immediately. They sent word for all Indians who claimed lands in the Nipmuc Country to gather in Cambridge in June 1681. Word of this invitation reached Edward Pratt and his partners, and they sent shareholder Richard Thayer to attend the meeting and stake their claim through John Wompas's will. According to Nipmuc Indians Peter Ephraim and John Awassamog, Thayer made "large pretences to the Land of Hassenemeset, by virtue as thay say of a will of John Wampwese," and when the Indians attempted "to make out thare right thay find themselvs interupted & agrieved by said Thayer." Thayer's efforts to claim Hassanamesit indicate that Pratt and his partners had imposed their own interpretation on John Wompas's deeds and his will, certainly not one he intended. John's will made it clear that "All that My Estate . . . knowne by the name of Assenham East-stock [Hassanamiscock]" would pass to his Nipmuc kinsmen John Awassamog, Pomhammell, and Norwaruunt. The eight miles square he sold to Pratt was located elsewhere, "near Quansigamog pond in the Nipmuck country." Pratt assumed this meant Hassanamesit. He had undoubtedly heard John Wompas speak of "Assenamiscock," and John may have allowed Pratt to believe that he had, in fact, purchased the Nipmuc homeland from the sachem authorized to sell it. If that was the case, a reading of the will should immediately have disabused Pratt of the idea. Nevertheless, he and his partners persisted in claiming Hassanamesit as well as "All the rest and remainder" of John's lands "in what place or places whatsoever in the Countrey of New England or elsewhere the same or any part thereof is situate," ignoring the bequest to Wompas's Nipmuc kinsmen.[15]

Thayer's persistence in claiming the praying town land led the Indians who attended the June 1681 meeting to submit a complaint to the governor and council. Because of a general lack of agreement about Native boundaries and rights among the Indians attending the June meeting, Dudley and Stoughton postponed any immediate decision. They directed the Indians to resolve disagreements among themselves and then meet with the Massachusetts Council on September 15, along with Thayer and other shareholders. In preparation for that meeting, Daniel Gookin scheduled a session of the Indian court at Natick on September 14, 1681, where he could take testimony about the claims of John Wompas's executors. Indians attending the court included a number of John's kinsmen and friends—Thomas Tray and Anthony, Nowaruunt, Waban, Jethro, William, Andrew Pittimee, and Peter Ephraim. Gookin took down the Nipmucs' testimony and recorded from memory the testimonies presented at the previous Indian court held in June 1677. Both of the documents Gookin penned focused exclusively on John Wompas's land sales, with every testimony laying out reasons Wompas lacked the right to sell Nipmuc land. As in the June 1677 meeting, the Indians all affirmed that they knew John "from a child" and that he "was no sachem." Thus, he "had no more Right [or] title to Any lands in the Nipmuk Country . . . then other comon Indians." They acknowledged that they had once given John license to act in their name "to declare & endevor to get setled & Recorded, the indians title & Right to those lands." But they denied ever giving him "any power to sell, give, grant or Barter any lands in those parts." Therefore, they "utterly disclaime[d] all his gifts, grants, sales, mortgages or any dispposel of those lands or any part thereof" to Edward Pratt, Nicholas Warner, or any other Englishman. Notably, the Natick Indians did not deny that John Wompas had some right to Nipmuc lands, but they insisted it was a right shared in common, not an exclusive one.[16]

The testimonies recorded by Daniel Gookin were clearly meant to invalidate all of John Wompas's land sales, which had already disrupted Gookin's own enterprise at Quinsigamog. But there was a significant difference between Gookin's accounts of the two Indian courts, in 1677 and in September 1681, and the Natick petition submitted the previous May 1681. In that petition, the Naticks did not repudiate John Wompas's sales; instead, they asked that *all* Indians with a claim to the lands sold be compensated. This request was consistent with past and continuing Native practice. As English settlement expanded and Native lands were surrounded or encroached upon, Indians resigned themselves to the loss of lands they could no longer effectively use, but they sought compensation for those lands, sometimes demanding multiple payments at different times. Again, this reflected Native practice. Indians had long demanded more than one payment for their lands. Initially, this reflected their understanding that they were allowing the English to use the land in exchange for annual tribute. Later, it became clear to Indians that the English saw their payments as absolute purchases, even though the payments were insignificant in comparison with the worth of the land. One way the Indians compensated for this situation was by presenting additional claimants who also expected to be paid, sometimes months, sometimes decades later. The Massachusetts government's efforts to secure the Nipmuc lands presented another situation where Indians accepted the inevitability of some land sales, but they did not accept the reality that only John Wompas or his English beneficiaries would profit from them. They wanted to be compensated too.[17]

Given the fact that the Indians' petition of May 1681 acknowledged John Wompas's sales but asked for compensation for all claimants, why did the testimonies Gookin collected demand a complete repudiation of Wompas's sales? Such repudiation was not necessary for the Indians to receive compensation; they could simply ask for additional payments. However, complete repudiation of the sales was necessary to clear the way for the Massachusetts Bay Colony to purchase the lands. As long as Nicholas Warner, Edward Pratt, and others held deeds to the Nipmuc lands, the colony's purchase of those lands, as well as English occupation of the plantation of Quinsigamog, would be contested. For this reason, it is likely that Gookin, of his own volition or at the request of Dudley and Stoughton, pushed the Natick Indians to disclaim John Wompas's sales.

By September 1681, the Indians had agreed between themselves about the boundaries of their lands in the Nipmuc Country. Dudley and Stoughton, along with the governor and other members of the council, met with the Indians and with Pratt and his associates on September 15, 1681. The council reviewed Pratt's claims, declared them "very uncertain," and directed Dudley and Stoughton to proceed with negotiations to purchase the Nipmuc lands for the colony. The two Englishmen invited some of the "principall claymers" among the Indians to travel with them to Nipmuc Country to point out the boundaries of the land claimed by various Indians. Accepting Dudley and Stoughton's "advise that some compensation be made to the claymers for a full surrender of those lands to the Governor & Company of the Massachusets," the court directed Dudley and Stoughton to "agree with them upon the easiest termes that may be obtained." Setting aside the "uncertaine" claims of John Wompas's English friends and leaving the northern section for later purchase, Dudley and Stoughton secured deeds from Indians with claims to the middle and southern sections, obtaining them on very easy terms indeed. Nipmuc sachem Black James and twenty-nine other Indians signed the southern deed. Waban, Anthony and Thomas Tray, Piambow, John Awassamog, Andrew Pittimee, and sixteen other Nipmucs from Natick signed the middle section deed. All the Indians on both deeds attested to being "Indian natives and naturall descendants of the ancient proprietors and inhabitants of the Nipmug country." The total area of the plot of land Dudley and Stoughton bought from these Natives in behalf of the Massachusetts Bay Colony was fifty miles in length by twenty miles in width— one thousand square miles, or 640,000 acres. The total price the English paid the Nipmucs was fifty pounds—twenty pounds to Black James and his company and thirty pounds to Waban and his company. This price was the equivalent of paying a shilling—one twentieth of a pound—for 640 acres. Once more, the English demonstrated that they would not pay Indians anything close to what they would pay fellow English colonists for unimproved land.

In the same general area and within a year's time, comparable land sold between Englishmen for hundreds of times what they paid the Nipmucs. In October 1682, for instance, a 600-acre plot in Sherborne, which bordered on the Nipmuc lands, was valued at two hundred pounds, or three acres per pound. If it had been valued at the rate Dudley and Stoughton paid for the Nipmuc lands, the plot's total price would have been just under a shilling.[18]

The Massachusetts General Court had urged Dudley and Stoughton to secure "the easiest terms that may be obtained" from the Indian proprietors of the Nipmuc lands. They had good reason to do so. The war had drained the colony treasury. The General Court could not afford to pay the people who did them service in cash, so they paid them in land. Obviously, the court could not pay the Indians with the very land they purchased from them, so they would have to use cash or goods, hence the pitifully small prices they offered for the land. But paying the Indians a pittance for their land did not just reflect the colony's straitened circumstances. It also reflected their attitude that uncivilized Indians did not need the amounts of money that typically changed hands between English buyers and sellers. Indians consistently received insignificant sums, even for "improved" land, a situation paralleled by the salaries of Indian teachers, interpreters, and day laborers like "John Indian," which were one-half of the salaries of Englishmen doing the same jobs.[19]

It is also likely that some of the English approached the negotiations with the Indians with an eye to personal profit. Based on the General Court record, Dudley and Stoughton instigated the Nipmuc land purchases. As magistrates, they also participated in the court's order of October 12, 1681, that all Indians other than apprentices or bond servants confine their residence to Natick, Punkapoag, or Wamesit. Any who failed to do so would be sent to prison. That restriction, passed in the same General Court session in which Dudley and Stoughton were ordered to negotiate with the Indians for a "full surrender" of their lands in the Nipmuc Country, made it impossible for Indians to profit from their lands other than by selling them. This undoubtedly influenced both the Indians' willingness to sell and the low price they received. Dudley's and Stoughton's work in securing deeds to the Nipmuc Country led the General

Court to bestow on them the handsome reward of one thousand acres of land each. As soon as Dudley acquired this land he began selling it, at a considerable profit. Dudley would accumulate more than seven thousand acres of Indian land by his death, and would participate in the founding of a dozen new English towns in Nipmuc Country, two named for himself or his family. Whether Dudley's interest in Indian lands began with a deal to release John Wompas from the large bond keeping him in prison in 1677 or was simply an exaggerated version of what other Englishmen were doing after King Philip's War is impossible to know based on existing records. However, there are tantalizing hints that Dudley was interested not only in John Wompas's Nipmuc lands but also in the Connecticut lands John obtained through his wife Ann. In March 1683 Dudley received a letter from Edward Randolph urging him, "Pray forgett not the Fairefield busines, nor anything else which occurs you, wherein you may serve me and yourselfe." One year later, Dudley officiated at the signing of a power of attorney for Edward Pratt and John Blake, granting their associates the right to take possession of Wompas's Fairfield lands and "grant, bargain, sell, let, set and lease" them for their "utmost profit and best advantage."[20]

Edward Pratt and his partners certainly did not forget the Fairfield business. John's will had left Pratt and Blake "All the rest and remaynder of my lands . . . in what place or places whatsoever in the Countrey of New England or elsewhere." While the will was supremely vague about the locations of these lands, John Wompas seems to have told Pratt and Blake about his failed attempt to take possession of his land in Connecticut. After arriving in Massachusetts, Pratt and Blake hired Richard Thayer to look into claiming this property. Thayer traveled to Fairfield in July 1681 and requested copies of the relevant deeds so that he could lay out the bounds of John Wompas's estate. Fairfield's town clerk admitted that these records existed but refused to turn them over without an explicit order from the Connecticut governor. Frustrated, Thayer wrote to the governor for permission. In his reply, Governor Leete and the magistrates of the colony acknowledged Thayer's right to view the public records but not to lay out bounds: "to suffer strangers to draw lines within townships without order or consent of the town, we

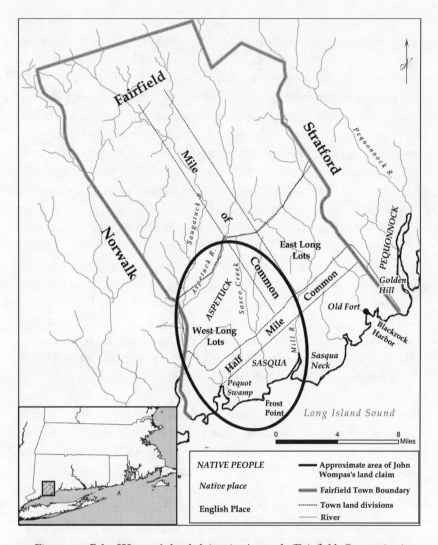

Figure 14. John Wompas's land claims in Aspetuck (Fairfield, Connecticut)
[Map by Jen Macpherson, based on a map in Elizabeth Hubbell Schenk,
History of Fairfield *(New York: The Author, 1889)]*

think not safe to encourage." The town leaders of Fairfield, who had
jailed John Wompas in 1678 after he demanded his land, were not
about to yield to the same demand from Thayer.[21]

Pratt and his partners set aside their efforts to claim land in
Fairfield and the Nipmuc Country for a few years, but in October

1683 news arrived in the colony that must have encouraged them to try again: the king had issued a *quo warranto* against the Massachusetts Colony charter, demanding its surrender to the Crown. This was the first step in the legal process of revoking the colony's charter, preliminary to replacing the colony government with direct rule by the Crown. Word of the quo warranto was brought by the colony's latest agents to the king, Joseph Dudley and John Richards, who arrived in Boston just days before Edward Randolph. Randolph, the royal messenger who had so enraged colony leaders on his previous visit, brought a copy of the quo warranto and a letter from the king and delivered the documents to the General Court assembled for the purpose on November 7, 1683. While the actual revocation of the charter would not occur for another year, Randolph's visit revived the lagging hopes of royalists in the colony enough that they made public shows of support for the magistrates who voted to submit to the king's quo warranto and surrender the charter as commanded. Evidence of sharp divisions between royalists and supporters of the old charter government appeared in the election of May 1684. Three of the magistrates who had supported the king's commands, Joseph Dudley, William Browne, and Bartholomew Gedney, lost their seats on the Massachusetts Council, and when Peter Bulkeley and William Stoughton resigned their own seats in protest of their colleagues' exclusion, seventy of the leading merchants and men of Boston—royalists all—gave Bulkeley and Stoughton the honor of a formal escort on horseback to their homes outside the town.[22]

Randolph's stay in Massachusetts was again brief, but he undoubtedly made time to contact his like-minded friends and declare his intention to return as an officer in the colony's soon-to-be-established royal government. Given Edward Pratt's later declaration "that hee hath freinds lately come over & in power," it is possible that Pratt and Randolph met during this time, if not previously in England. Within a few months of Randolph's arrival, Pratt and company renewed their attempts to secure Wompas's lands in Massachusetts and Connecticut. This time, Pratt decided to focus his own efforts on the Nipmuc lands and let others deal with the land claim in Fairfield. In March 1684, Pratt and John Blake sold their interest in the Fairfield property to a group of Englishmen, most of whom had also bought shares in the Nipmuc lands. Blake does not appear on the records of either the Fairfield or Nipmuc speculations after 1684; he seems to have taken whatever the shareholders paid him ("good causes and considerations") and retired to his home in Wrentham. Joshua Hewes spearheaded the effort in Connecticut in May and June 1684. Taking up where Richard Thayer left off, he and two other men acting as attorneys to the partners sued the Fairfield town leaders for refusing to deliver John Wompas's lands, asking for damages of five thousand pounds.[23]

The Fairfield proprietors responded in force, securing multiple witnesses and employing a lawyer who demolished the partners' case with his learned commentary on English law and his withering mockery of their evidence. The lawyer, William Pitkin, apparently shared Nathan Gold's prejudice against accepting the "testimony of an Indian." He ridiculed Thomas Minor's account of Romanock symbolically conveying land to his daughter, noting the "uncertainty of those dumb signs, if they may be called signs, of turf, twig, stake," and dismissed the value of Native testimonies that supported Minor's account, saying, "If the Indians should say so in Court, yet, when there is so much proved to the contrary, they are not to be believed." The Fairfield proprietors also secured the testimony of a number of local Indians to argue that, according to local Native practice, "the title of land goes by the man and not by the woman," so Ann could not have inherited. It is a wonderful irony that Fairfield's English proprietors used Native legal precedent to fight against the claims of the heirs of John Wompas, an Indian who used English legal practice to support his claim. Finally, Pitkin argued that even if Ann's claim had been valid, she and her father, as well as every other Indian in the region, had been conquered in the Pequot War in 1637. Thus, their lands were forfeit to the English. After hearing all testimonies and arguments, the court, headed by Connecticut's governor Robert Treat, ruled in favor of Fairfield, tossing the sop to Hewes that "they being strangers might not so well understand our laws and methods of practice; therefore, if they saw cause to desire an appeal . . . they had liberty so to do, provided it were done before the Court did break up."[24]

In Massachusetts, the other partners had similarly dismal results. On May 7, 1684, Edward Pratt, John Comer, and William

Mumford, in behalf of all the partners, submitted a petition to the General Court asking for confirmation of a "parsell of Land about eight miles square lying & being scittuate in the Nipmuck Country." They claimed this land by virtue of "the last will & Testament of John Wampus, alias White," and they presented the will—"proved and approved in the Prerogative Court of the Archbishop of Canterbury in the Kingdome of England as may be seen by said will"— to the court as evidence of their right. Someone seems to have advised Pratt and the others that the best way to secure confirmation would be to profess the intention of founding a plantation on the lands. That was the usual pattern: A group of men would petition the General Court for a grant of land eight to nine miles square. These "proprietors" then negotiated with the Indian land owners to purchase their rights to the land. Once the grant was obtained, the proprietors recruited settlers and sold them lots in the new plantation. Thus, Pratt and his partners "pray[ed] this Honered Court's approbation & confirmation of our just & honest Title thereto intending (God willing) with all convenient speed to settle & improve the Same with a competent number of honest Inhabitants which we hope & desire may flourish under the guidance & protection of the Government and wholsome Laws of this jurisdiction here established." It was a nice try, if a somewhat cynical one. A number of the partners had already made it clear that they did not support the "wholsome Laws" of the colony and in fact hoped to flourish under the guidance and protection of an entirely different government as soon as possible. The General Court denied their petition. Pratt and company were not the kind of people they wanted to found plantations. Furthermore, they considered their deeds invalid. The court's reply drew from the testimonies that Daniel Gookin had gathered from the Natick Indians in 1677 and 1681: they "knowe not of any Land that wampas had any . . . legall right unto hee being no sachem but a common person."[25]

Clearly, Pratt and company had been too eager, trying to reap the benefit of political tides that had not yet come in. Chastened, they waited until Randolph returned to Massachusetts before making their next move. The Massachusetts charter was officially revoked in November 1684. The death of King Charles II and succession of his brother James to the throne in February 1685 led to some delays in appointing a new royal governor for Massachusetts. On the suggestion of Edward Randolph, the Crown appointed Joseph Dudley as the president of the Council of New England, a temporary position until Edmund Andros could arrive to take up the office of governor of the newly organized central government for the English colonies of the Northeast—the Dominion of New England. Edward Randolph was appointed deputy governor. Dudley and Randolph sailed from England to Massachusetts in the spring of 1685, arriving in the colony in May. Their arrival emboldened Edward Pratt enough that he moved to Hassanamesit, building a home for himself there "very neare unto [the Indians'] orchards & planting fields," a proximity that seemed intended to provoke them. And it did. They appealed to Daniel Gookin, complaining of Pratt's actions and reporting his boast "that hee hath freinds lately come over & in power that will beare him out in it." Gookin wrote to President Dudley, alerting him to the controversy. No reply exists, but in August 1686, Pratt and his partners signed an agreement with the Native proprietors of Hassanamesit for a division of the lands both of them claimed.[26]

The Indian signers of the agreement included many of the men who had complained against John Wompas in 1677 and 1681. First among them was Thomas Tray, John's uncle. Ironically, considering the Nipmucs' longstanding insistence that John Wompas was no sachem, the agreement they signed declared "the said Wampus their Chiefe and principall in certain Lands lying att Assanamescock in the Nipmugg Country." This was the position John himself had claimed, and his English heirs also used it, undoubtedly to add legitimacy to their demands. But why would John's Nipmuc kin agree to such a description? They probably did so for the same reason Pratt and his partners did: it conferred legitimacy on the agreement, and the agreement benefited not just the partners, but the Nipmucs as well. Although Pratt and his partners had claimed the entire eight-mile-square tract of Hassanamesit, the agreement divided it equally between the Nipmucs and the English. The Indians, of course, had held the land long before the English arrived, and the Massachusetts General Court had previously acknowledged that possession by granting four miles square of land at Hassanamesit to the Indians in 1654. But the Indians had never obtained a legal deed for the land, which would have given much greater security to their claim. Obtaining such a legal deed was one of the reasons the Nipmucs had hired John Wompas before King Philip's War to "endevor to get setled & Recorded, the indians title & Right to those lands." Pratt and his partners also relied on legal documents to secure their claim to Hassanamesit: John Wompas's deed of 1679 to Pratt for eight miles square of Nipmuc land and John's 1679 will. The deed was vague about where the land was located, and the will specifically excluded Hassanamesit from English ownership, reserving it for Wompas's Nipmuc kinsmen, so these documents did as much to bolster the Nipmucs' claims as the English partners' claims. In the end, the 1686 agreement, authorized and signed by Edward Randolph, split the difference. It confirmed the will's bequest of Hassanamesit to John Wompas's Nipmuc kin, providing them with a legal deed of four miles square to Hassanamesit. It also provided a deed of four miles square outside the bounds of Hassanamesit to the English heirs of John Wompas. This was far more than Pratt and his partners had been able to obtain under the old charter government, and that no doubt owed to his having "freinds . . . in power," perhaps Edward Randolph (who signed the agreement) or President Joseph Dudley. But it was far less land than they had hoped for. By submitting his evidence—the deed and the will—to the Massachusetts government, Pratt had unwittingly relinquished his claim to the entirety of Hassanamesit and become the agent for registering the Indians' legal ownership of their homeland.[27]

Pratt and company's success was cut short almost immediately by the very political changes they had longed for. Edmund Andros arrived in Massachusetts in December 1686 as the head of a new royal government, the Dominion of New England. He was not a friend to Pratt, and his legalistic application of Crown policy led him to declare that, upon the loss of Massachusetts's charter, all lands in the colony had reverted to the king. Andros pointedly rejected colonists' claims that land title was based on occupation, improvement, and purchase from the Indians, "villifying the Indian title, saying they were bruits . . . & what Lands the Kings Subject have they are the Kings." Andros insisted that colonists holding land under the old charter apply for new titles and required them to pay a quitrent of two shillings and six pence for every hundred acres. At that rate, Pratt and his partners would have owed over twelve pounds for their four-mile-square plot, and there is no evidence that anyone other than George Danson applied for a new title. Thus, rather than speeding their acquisition of John Wompas's land, the new royal government stalled it.[28]

The Dominion of New England proved to be short lived. In April 1689 news of the Glorious Revolution in England spurred a similarly bloodless revolution in New England. Colonists ousted Andros and his officers, including Randolph and Dudley, and reestablished a government on the pattern of the old charter one. This government was replaced in turn by a new government appointed under the royal charter of 1691. It would be another decade before a governor was appointed who could be said to be a friend to Pratt. In 1702 Joseph Dudley, exiled from Massachusetts after the Glorious Revolution and considered a traitor by the defenders of the old charter, was appointed royal governor of Massachusetts. Pratt and his partners had waited a long time to secure a confirmation of their deed that would allow them to lay out Wompas's lands and occupy or sell them. While they waited, some of the original partners had died, and their heirs or other purchasers had taken their places. In March 1704, the partners—now numbering nine—petitioned Governor Dudley for a confirmation of the lands they had obtained from John Wompas. As in their previous petitions, they requested a full eight-mile-square tract of land that included the four-mile-square plantation of Hassanamesit. At this point, Pratt and his partners' earlier efforts to secure Wompas's land came back to haunt them. In 1686 they had agreed to a division of the disputed lands around Hassanamesit, signing away the central four miles square to John Wompas's uncle Thomas Tray and other Nipmucs in exchange for four miles square encircling the Indian homeland. With this legal deed in evidence, Dudley and the General Court once again confirmed Native ownership of the four-mile-square tract of Hassanamesit, right in the center of the parcel the partners sought for their plantation. In compensation, Governor Dudley tacked an additional four miles square on to the side of the partners' tract, bringing it to the total eight miles square requested. That was the typical size of an English town, and Dudley directed that the tract be named Sutton, probably in honor of an English branch of his family.[29]

After a quarter of a century, three turnovers of government, and two Indian wars, Edward Pratt and his partners finally secured confirmation of their title on March 21, 1704. But that confirmation was contingent on their ability to settle thirty families in Sutton "within seven yeares after the end of the present war with the Indians [Queen Anne's War]." The uncertain deadline acknowledged the difficulty of recruiting settlers during a time when the frontier was under constant threat of attack from the colony's French and Wabanaki Indian foes. Once again, the partners were forced to wait. Edward Pratt returned to Boston. His resources clearly strained, he was twice warned out of the town to prevent him from becoming a burden to the inhabitants. Partners unwilling to wait for the end of the war, including Joshua Hewes, sold their shares immediately. Several more partners died before the war ended in 1713. With the end of the war, the remaining partners were free to recruit settlers, and in little more than a year they reached the required number. In the process, most of the remaining original partners or their heirs sold their shares. Edward Pratt sold his one-tenth share, about 4,100 acres, for two hundred pounds, or about twenty acres per pound, in 1715. This was four times more than he had paid John Wompas for eight miles square of land in 1679, but it had cost him thirty-six years of frustrating labor. The other original partners fared similarly, selling their shares for from sixteen to 102 acres per pound, with an average price of around forty-two acres per pound. Eventually, with the carving up of lots in Sutton into smaller and smaller pieces, some landowners would make a great deal of money, but none of the original purchasers of John Wompas's lands lived long enough to be among them.[30]

The years following King Philip's War were not kind to the Natives of New England. Their population suffered a staggering decline and their land base steadily eroded. The Indians remaining in the colonies—including the Nipmucs—resisted this erosion. Many of them had assisted the English in the war and expected their land rights to be respected. They cited their ancient ownership and their natural right in petitions to the English, as well as their loyalty and military service, and they insisted on being compensated for any lands that were sold. English officials did make some effort to stop or at least slow the loss of Native lands. Twice under the new charter government of 1691, the General Court banned Indian land sales without the express permission of the court, going so far as to declare void sales made without such permission as far back as 1633. When the English obtained large tracts of land from the Indians, as in the Nipmuc Country purchases of the 1680s, they did pay for them; a legitimate legal process was in place. But the prices Natives received for their land cannot be considered fair. Paid only a few pounds for their lands—pounds distributed among many Native claimants—the Indians exhausted the funds quickly and then had nothing left to sell. Military service and the whaling industry offered Nipmuc and other Native men chances to earn incomes to support their families, but these professions had high mortality rates, contributing to the steady diminishment of the Native population.[31]

By the third decade of the eighteenth century, Hassanamesit—the ancient seat of the paramount sachem and home to hundreds of Nipmuc men, women, and children as recently as 1675—had shrunk to just seven families who struggled to make ends meet. In 1727, these Nipmucs agreed to a plan under which their four-mile-square tract of land would become the English town of Grafton, while the plots they lived on would remain in Indian possession. Of the lands the Natives did not currently occupy or use, seventy-five hundred acres would be sold and divided into equal shares for forty English purchasers, who would be responsible for all the costs of the division and for building a meetinghouse and school for the use of the proprietors, both English and Indian. A committee of Englishmen was appointed to assess the seventy-five hundred acres of Hassanamesit land to be sold and determine its value. They reported that a fair value would be 2,500 pounds, or three acres per pound. This appraisal was consistent with the price of land that had been sold between Englishmen in the neighboring town of Sutton since its founding in 1715, and it was significantly higher than the price that any of the original English shareholders of John Wompas's lands had received. Given the long history of English buyers paying Indian sellers ridiculously low prices for their land, this reasonable valuation is surprising. The Massachusetts General Court, which initially rejected the English petition to purchase the Hassanamesit lands, agreed to approve the transaction only after the petitioners met a string of conditions: a committee would determine a fair price for the land, remaining Nipmuc proprietors would retain shares equal in size to English proprietors' shares, and the Nipmucs would enjoy the benefits of all community improvements. Apparently, someone involved in the exchange had come to the realization that the longstanding English practice of purchasing Indian lands for a pittance was morally bankrupt.[32]

One man who held that view was Samuel Sewall, who was appointed by the Massachusetts Council to supervise a land sale at Hassanamesit and to "take Care that the Indians have Justice done them in the said Purchase." Sewall also served as a commissioner of the Society for the Propagation of the Gospel in New England (the New England Company), which oversaw missions to the Christian Indians, and he lamented the long English history of pushing Indians off their lands. Writing to officers of the society in 1700, Sewall proposed safeguarding land for the Eastern Indians recently conquered by the English in King William's War, an action he considered critical to maintaining a "firm and sure" peace: "I should think it Requisite that convenientt tracts of Land be set out to them, and that by plain and natural boundaries, as much as may be, as Lakes, Rivers, Mountains, Rocks—upon which for any English-man to encroach, should be accounted a Crime. Except this be done, I fear their own Jealousies, and the French Friers, will perswade them that the English, as they increase, and think they want more room, Will never leave till they have crowded them quite out of all their Lands. And it will be a vain Attempt for us to offer Heaven to them, if they take up prejudices against us, as if we did grudge them a Living upon their own Earth."[33]

The fact that the English paid the Nipmucs a fair price for their land at Hassanamesit—one consistent with sales of nearby land between English buyers—did not mean the English had come to view the Nipmucs as equals. On the contrary, at the same time the English arranged to purchase Hassanamesit, they placed the Nipmucs in the position of legal dependents. Rather than give them the 2,500-pound payment for Hassanamesit, English officials placed it in a fund from which a legal guardian distributed interest payments to support the small number of Nipmuc families still living in what had become the town of Grafton. Although the principal was diminished by English mismanagement and fraud, these payments would continue well into the nineteenth century—evidence of the persistent presence of Nipmucs in their homeland. Such evidence belied the nineteenth-century trope of the disappearing Indian, which Frederick C. Pierce invoked in his history of Grafton in 1879: "Eliot, nearly two hundred years ago, came here, and first preached the gospel to the Indians. That race, then free and conscious of their rightful possession of the soil, had no suspicion that the day of their extinction was so near at hand;—that their council fires would so soon cease to burn;—that the forests through which they roamed would disappear, and that their hunting and fishing places would be occupied by the habitations and improvements of the white man. The land of their fathers they fondly hoped to leave an inheritance to their children. . . . But in these anticipations they were mistaken. Two centuries have passed—and they have vanished." Contrary to Pierce's lament, the Nipmucs of Hassanamesit had not vanished by the nineteenth century. They had simply become invisible to those whose preconceptions of Indians did not allow for adaptation and mixture with other racial groups—"the complex social practice of Native communities in their survival as Indians." Not only did the Nipmucs survive, but they continued to assert their identity as Indians and maintain their connection with their ancient homeland. Although the Nipmucs were still present, their land base had drastically diminished. Over time, individual Nipmucs sold their allotments for various reasons, to pay a debt, to trade for land elsewhere, to secure the funds to build a house. By the middle of the nineteenth century only a single piece of Native-held land remained—a three-acre parcel, part of the land allotted in 1728 to Moses Printer as a Native proprietor in the new English town of Grafton. Through the unrelenting efforts of his female descendants, particularly Sarah Cisco Arnold, that piece of land eventually became the Hassanamisco Nipmuc Reservation—the only piece of land in the state of Massachusetts that had never passed into the hands of the English. Today it is the site of a museum on the National Register of Historic Places and hosts an annual powwow drawing hundreds to the place Nipmuc scholar Rae

Figure 15. Hassanamesit historical marker, Grafton, Massachusetts

Gould describes as "an important mnemonic device"—a trigger for cultural memory—and a "communal and central place associated with the maintenance of Nipmuc identity."[34]

Even though Hassanamesit persists, the memory of John Wompas scarcely survives outside of the original records that document his deeds. He left no descendants to carry on his name or his story, and soon after the tangle of deeds he left was unwound, the Nipmucs seem to have forgotten him. Interestingly, the English who settled Sutton and Grafton did remember John Wompas, at least when they reflected on the origins of their towns. But they remembered him as he chose to be remembered—as a sachem, one with the authority to distribute Native lands. Edward Pratt and the other partners who sold shares to Sutton had maintained John's practice of calling himself a sachem to legitimize their efforts to obtain his land, declaring their titles were obtained from "an Indian Sachem named John wampas alias White sometime of Hasanamisco in the Nipmugg Country." This tradition passed down to local historians. Writing in 1793 of the origin of the town of Grafton, Rev. Peter Whitney declared that it was "originally purchased by a number of gentlemen of Sachem John Wampus, and his company, Indians, who claimed it." At least four other local historians repeated this story, and it persists to the present. As recently as 2016, the website of the town of Sutton proclaimed its origin through "John Wampus . . . a Nipmuc native american who had inherited the responsibility for this land area from his father, a Nipmuc sachem."[35]

To historians of the larger region who encountered John Wompas's name in the historical records, he was little more than a curiosity. They highlighted one of the unusual facts of his life—his ownership of a home in the heart of Boston, his being one of the handful of Native scholars to attend Harvard College, his petitions to the king of England—and then moved on. In the last decades of the twentieth century, the American Indian Movement awakened Americans to the injustices visited on Indians since European contact, particularly the dispossession of Indian land. Thus, a handful of historians who encountered John Wompas in the documentary record saw him as an "agent for English encroachment" and a "rogue" who, "instead of protecting [Nipmuc] interests . . . had betrayed the community."[36]

It is true that John Wompas sold Nipmuc land without the consent of his kin, violating Native land ways and alienating his uncles and the elders of his tribe. Some of his actions seem to have been driven by selfishness or desperation, and at times he seems to have cared little for the opinion or the interests of his Nipmuc kin. But that changed in the last years of John Wompas's life. Shocked by the impact of King Philip's War on his friends and relatives, he became a harsh critic of colonial governments. In his speech and his petitions he increasingly identified with his Nipmuc heritage and embraced the obligation of preserving and caring for Hassanamesit, a task that he claimed his father Wampooas had "observed performed & fulfilled and kept." This led John—albeit belatedly and at little cost to himself—to fulfill the charge the Nipmucs laid on him in the 1670s to get their lands recorded through legally binding documents acknowledged by English as well as Indians. John's will, in which he portrayed himself as a sachem, encompassed both English and Indian land ways. By claiming sachemship, John invoked the right to convey land, a right the English had long recognized as necessary for legitimate sales of Indian lands. By recording a legal will conveying all the land of Hassanamesit to his Nipmuc kin, John tied the hands of the English beneficiaries of that will. If they used the will as evidence of their ownership, they had to admit the portions of the will that restricted which lands they could claim. As a result, the courts that finally granted John Wompas's lands to Edward Pratt and his partners preserved four miles square—the original boundaries of the praying town of Hassanamesit—for the Nipmucs, long after the lands of other Natives in the colony had passed into English hands. It is hard to avoid the suspicion that that is exactly what John Wompas intended.[37]

Land Transactions of John Wompas and Ann Prask Wompas, 1662–1679

Year and location	Buyer/Grantee	Seller/Grantor	Signers	Price	Source
11 Sept. 1660 Aspetuck (Fairfield, Connecticut Colony)	Ann Prask	Romanock, "late Sachim of Aspatuck & Sasquanaugh"	Original missing	Gift	*CCR*, 3:283. Partial photocopy of original in Humes, "John Wampas"
"Some time after" Aspetuck (Fairfield)	Captain [George] Denison, Amos Richardson, "and others of Stonnington in Conecticut Colony"	John Wompas	Original missing	£530 sterling "or there-abouts"	CO 1/43, no. 33 and CO 5/904, p. 36, TNA
9 July 1662 Pachange, Plymouth Colony	Josias Winslow	Josias Wampatuck	Witnesses (W): Edward Gray [mark], George Wampey [A], and John Wompowes [X]	£21	Bangs, *Indian Deeds*, 125–126
28 Jan. 1666 House and land on Boston Common	"John Wampas an Indian of Boston"	Robert and Sarah Wyard	Signatures (S): Robert Wyard [H], Sarah Wyard [S] W: John Winthrop, James Richards, Thomas Bune, John Waite Acknowledged (A): 28 Jan. 1666, before John Winthrop	£78.4.0 (37.10.0 in hand, 40.10.0 to be paid to John Richards of Boston, assign of Robert and Sarah Wyard, by 29 Sept. 1666 "without fraud or farther delay")	SD, 5:490–491

Year and location	Buyer/Grantee	Seller/Grantor	Signers	Price	Source
			Registered (R): 28 Sept. 1668,* before Edward Rawson		
13 Aug. 1668 Mortgage on Boston home of John and Ann Wompas	John and Ann Wompas	John Richards, agent for Robert Thomson	S: John Wampas [J], Ann Wampas [A] W: William Kileap, John Richards A: 13 Aug. 1668, before John Leveret R: 12 Jan. 1669, before Edward Rawson	£37.5.0 £44.6.0 (8 percent interest "for one whole yeare then Expired"), due 24 Feb. 1669 Discharged: 15 Jan. 1679	SD, 5:540–543
20 Nov. 1671 100 acres of upland ground between Marlborough and Mendon, Massachusetts	Thomas Stedman of New London, Connecticut Colony, mariner	"John Wampus of Boston . . . Indian & seaman"	S: John Wompas [JW and mark] W: Edmund Jaxson, Wm Lytherland, John Ferneside A: 9 June 1674, before Edward Tyng R: 4 Feb. 1675, before Freegrace Bendall	"For & in Consideracon of the great affection & Love which I have & beare unto my well beloved friend . . . As allso for divers other good causes & consideracons"	SD, 8:421

continued

Year and location	Buyer/Grantee	Seller/Grantor	Signers	Price	Source
1675 300 acres in Nipmuc Country	John Cole	John Wompas	Original missing		*MPR*, 9:579
1676? Adjoining to John Warner's land, probably 1,000 acres	Nicholas Warner	John Wompas	Original missing		See John Warner deed, *MD*, 6:86–87
19 Dec. 1676 1,000 acres adjoining to the land of Nicholas Warner, in Quansacomack, Massachusetts Bay Colony	John Warner	John Wompas	S: John Wompas [mark] W: Robert Sergent, Ralph Darlyng, Wm Robinson Sr. A: 16 Aug. 1677, before Simon Bradstreet R: 18 Aug. 1677, before Thomas Danforth	"For and in considerattion of the kindness & maintenance, I had & reserved from Nicholas Warner of Ratleife in the Parish of Stepney . . . when a prisoner in or neere London, as for the loane of severall summes of money—borrowed of the said Nicholas Warner"	*MD*, 6:86–87

Year and location	Buyer/Grantee	Seller/Grantor	Signers	Price	Source
19 Dec. 1676 1,000 acres to be set off from Quinsigamog Pond	Anthony Mud of Ratcliffe in parish of Stepney, London, England	"John Wompos, alias White of Boston in Massachusets bay in New England Marriner now resident in Old England"	S: John Wompos [mark and seal] W: John Warner, Willm Robbinson Sr. A: 12 Dec. 1677: before Edward Ting R: 15 Dec. 1677, before Thomas Danforth	"In gratitude for love, tenderness, and affection shown him by Anthony Mud of Ratcliffe in parish of Stepney . . . while a Prisoner in old England, and in getting my freedom from & out of Prison"	MD, 6:101–102
2 June 1677 Quitclaim of Boston house	Joshua Hews, Mary Lambe, Hannah Hews	"John Wampus als White of Boston in New England Seaman"	S: John Wampus alias John White [JW and mark] W: Richard Woodde, John Hayward Sr. A: 2 June 1677, before Edward Tyng R: 6 June 1677, before Jsa. Addington	£20	SD, 10:111–112
16 Aug. 1677 Mortgage on 4,000 acres of land near Marlborough at Quinsigamog Pond	John Warner of Boston, Tobacconist	"John Wompos, alias White . . . (now resident in old Engld)"	S: John Wompos alias White [mark and seal]	£18.4 To pay John Warner £19.9 by 17 Sept. 1677 to void the deed	MD, 6:82–83

continued

Year and location	Buyer/Grantee	Seller/Grantor	Signers	Price	Source
18 Aug. 1677 Mortgage of 4,000 acres at north and west ends of Quinsigamog Pond	Benjamin Franklin of Boston, Cooper	"John Wampos alias White of Boston in New England"	S: John Wompos alias White [mark and seal] W: John Warner, Peter Goulding A: 16 Aug. 1677, before Simon Bradstreet R: 18 Aug. 1677, before Thomas Danforth	£10 £10.5 due at Benjamin Franklin's new dwelling place 16 Sept. 1677 to void the deed	MD, 6:84–85
17 July 1679 Eight miles square of land near Quinsigamog Pond in the Nipmuc Country	Edward Pratt, of the Parish of St. Paul Shadwell, in the County of Middlesex, victualler	"John Wampas als. White of Asanamiscock in the Nipmuck country in New England Sachem, now ressidt in the citty of London"	S: John Wampas alias White [seal] W: Daniel Wing, George Owen, John Blake, Daniel Shyling Sr. A: 28 July 1679, before Sir George Waterman, Justice of the Peace, City of London R: 3 Nov. 1679, before Thomas Danforth	£50	MD, 7:157–160

Year and location	Buyer/Grantee	Seller/Grantor	Signers	Price	Source
5 Sept. 1679 "All that My Estate . . . by the name of Assenham East-stock" 400 acres in Bedford, Massachusetts, abutting land of Nicholas Warner "All the rest and remaynder of my lands . . . in what place or places whatsoever in the Countrey of New England or elsewhere"	"My very loveing kinsmen John a Wonsamock, Pomhammell, Norwaruunt" "George Owen of the parish of Allhallows London Wall, surgeon" "Edward Pratt of the parish of St Paul Shadwell in the countie of Middlesex, victualler, and John Blake of Plimouth in New-England, husbandman"	"John White alias Wampers late of Boston in New England, Mariner"	S: John White alias Wampers W: Francis Gower, John Barnes, Theep: Haydoste servant to Tho Sumerly, Notary Publique, London Will probated 1 Oct. 1679	Last will and testament	WJW

* SD, 5:490–491 and 540–543 do not include the year format indicating dates that fell between Jan. 1 and March 24 in the old Julian Calendar (e.g., 1665/66). For SD, 5:490–491, I have left the date as 28 Jan. 1666, because the deed also indicates this was in the eighteenth year of Charles II's reign, which was officially counted from 1649. For SD, 5:540–543, I have changed the date of the acknowledgment from 12 Jan. 1668 to 12 Jan. 1669. I assume that Edward Rawson intended the year 1668/69 because the acknowledgment, which precedes registration, took place in August 1668.

Sources: CCR; John Humes, "John Wampas and the Beginning of Sutton," in History of the Town of Sutton, Massachusetts, comp. John C. Dudley (The Town of Sutton, Massachusetts, 1952); TNA; Jeremy Dupertuis Bangs, Indian Deeds: Land Transactions in Plymouth Colony, 1620–1691 (Boston: NEHGS, 2002); SD; MPR; MD; WJW.

People and Places Connected
to John Wompas

* Names of people who purchased or were granted land by John Wompas, or obtained shares in his lands after his death, are marked with an asterisk.

Massachusetts Bay Colony

Hassanamesit (Nipmuc homeland;
Christian Indian town by 1654)

Also spelled Hassanamiscock, Assanamiscock, Assenham East-stock. List includes those who claimed land rights.

Wampooas and wife, parents of John Wompas
> John Wompas (Wampas, Wampus, Wampowess, Wompony, Wompo-
> > nege, Wompos, John White)

Totherswamp (Thomas Tray), brother of Wampooas, uncle of John Wompas
Anthony (Anthony Tray), brother of Wampooas, uncle of John Wompas
Wuttasacomponom (Thomas Wuttasacomponom, Captain Tom), Nipmuc
> sachem
Andrew Pittimee, friend of John Wompas
John Awassamog (John a Wonsamock), kin and heir to John Wompas
Norwaruunt (Nowanit, Nowanont, Norwanont), kin and heir to John
> Wompas
Piambow (Pyam Buckow, Piambohu, Pyamboah)
Pomhammell (Pomhaman, Pomham), kin and heir to John Wompas
Waban, early convert to Christianity

Nonantum (Traditional Native gathering place; Christian Indian town by 1646)

Wampooas and wife
  John Wompas
Totherswamp (Thomas Tray)
Anthony (Anthony Tray)
Waban, early convert to Christianity

Natick (Christian Indian town by 1651)

Waban
Totherswamp (Thomas Tray)
Anthony (Anthony Tray)
Job Nesutan, Native scholar, translator for John Eliot
Piambow (Pyam Buckow, Piambohu, Pyamboah)

Roxbury

Isaac and Elizabeth Heath, friends of John Eliot, supporters of Indian mission
  John Wompas, Native scholar attending grammar school, living with Heaths
Reverend John Eliot, the "Apostle to the Indians"
*George Denison (until 1651), later of Stonington, Connecticut Colony,
  purchaser of land at Aspetuck (Fairfield) from John Wompas
Daniel Weld, schoolmaster
Joshua and Mary Hewes
  *Joshua Hewes Jr.
  Mary Hewes (later Mary Lambe)
  Ann Prask (later Ann Wompas), slave in Hewes household
Native servants/slaves:
  Anthony (Anthony Tray)
  Joan
  Ann Prask (later Ann Wompas)

Boston

John and Ann Wompas; their daughter Anna
Milcah Snow Wright, friend of Ann Wompas
Sarah Ellis, friend of Ann Wompas
Prudence Delany, friend of Ann Wompas
Joshua and Alice Crabtree Hewes (from 1654)
  *Joshua Hewes Jr.
  Mary Hewes (later Mary Lambe)
  Hannah Hewes

*Amos Richardson (from 1673), purchaser of land at Aspetuck (Fairfield)
    from John Wompas
*John Blake, mariner, friend of John Wompas, executor of his will
*Benjamin Franklin, cooper, mariner, friend of John Wompas
John Leverett, governor of Massachusetts Bay Colony

Cambridge

Daniel Gookin, Massachusetts magistrate, superintendent of the Indians,
    supporter of Eliot's missionary work to the Indians, Quinsigamog
    (Worcester) proprietor
Thomas Danforth, Massachusetts magistrate, housed many Native scholars
    in Cambridge
At Harvard between 1665 and 1668:
    President Charles Chauncy
    Joseph Browne, tutor
    Joseph Dudley
    John Filer (Fyler)
    John Stanton
    John Minor
    Joel Hiacoomes
    Caleb Cheesechamauk
    John Wompas

Dorchester

Joseph Dudley, magistrate and governor of Massachusetts Bay Colony
    (1702–1715), speculator in Nipmuc lands
*Paul Dudley

Quinsigamog (Worcester; in Nipmuc Country; received town grant in 1674)

Also spelled Quinsigamond, Quansacomack.

Daniel Gookin, Quinsigamog proprietor
Ephraim Curtis, proprietor of Indian trading house, purchaser of conflicting
    grant to Quinsigamog

Connecticut Colony
Aspetuck and Sasqua (Fairfield)

Also spelled Aspitock, Aspatuck; Sasquanaugh.

Sasqua Indians
Pequonnock Indians
Romanock, father of Prask (Ann Prask, Ann Wompas, Ann White)
Prask (Ann Prask, Ann Wompas, Ann White)
Nathan Gold, opposer of John Wompas's land claims

Milford

Walter Fyler (Filer), acquaintance of John Wompas
John Filer (Fyler), Harvard classmate of John Wompas

Stonington

Thomas Minor, acquaintance of John Wompas
Thomas Stanton, acquaintance of John Wompas
*George Denison
*Amos Richardson (Richeson)

England
Maritime Suburbs of London

*Nicholas Warner, friend of John Wompas
John Warner
*Anthony Mudd, friend of John Wompas
*Edward Pratt, friend of John Wompas
*Dr. George Owen, surgeon to John Wompas

Royal Court

King Charles II
Joseph Williamson, secretary of state
Edward Randolph, royal agent to Massachusetts, later secretary of Massachu-
    setts Colony under royal government
Petitioners:
    John Wompas
    Robert Mason, proprietor of New Hampshire
    Ferdinando Gorges, proprietor of Maine

Randall Holden and John Green, agents for Rhode Island
*Richard Thayer of Braintree, Massachusetts, claimed land leased from
Josias Wampatuck, Massachusett sachem
William Stoughton and Peter Bulkeley, agents for Massachusetts Bay
Colony

Mariners Acquainted with John Wompas

*Thomas Stedman of New London, Connecticut
*John Cole of Charlestown, Massachusetts
*John Blake of Boston, Plymouth, and Wenham, Massachusetts
*John Warner of Ratcliffe, England
*Benjamin Franklin of Boston

Chronology of Key Events

1632 or earlier	Birth of Prask (later Ann Prask Wompas) in Mahican Country
1637 to 1642	Birth of John Wompas in Nipmuc Country
1636–1637	Pequot War
1637 (July)	Prask is taken captive at the end of the Pequot War.
1637	Prask, called Ann by the English, is enslaved in the home of Joshua and Mary Hewes in Roxbury, Massachusetts Bay Colony.
1646 (Nov. 26)	John's father Wampooas offers his son to John Eliot to be "trained up among the English."
1647	Death of John's mother at Nonantum
By 1651	John begins living with Isaac and Elizabeth Heath in Roxbury, attends grammar school.
1651	Founding of Christian Indian community at Natick
1651 (by April 28)	Death of John's father Wampooas at Nonantum
1660 (Sept. 11)	Romanock bequeaths land at Aspetuck (Fairfield, Connecticut) to his daughter Ann Prask.
1661 (May 21)	Ann Prask and John Wompas (John Wompony) married by an English magistrate in Boston, Massachusetts
1664 (Feb. 7)	Birth of Anna, daughter of John and Ann Wompas, in Boston
1665	John begins attending Harvard College.
1667 (Jan. 28)	John and Ann Wompas purchase a home next to Boston Common.
1667 (June)	Probable time of John's sale of part of Aspetuck (Fairfield) to Captain George Denison, Amos Richardson, and others from Stonington, Connecticut, for £530
1668 (by Sept. 10)	John leaves Harvard to take up "some other occupation by sea."

1672	John acts as an agent for the Nipmucs to protest English encroachment on Indian lands.
1674 (after June 9)	John leaves Boston by ship.
1675–1678	King Philip's War in New England
1676 (March)	John is imprisoned for debt "in or neere" London.
1676 (Aug.)	John petitions King Charles II for freedom to sell his lands to pay his debts.
1676 (Aug. 22)	The King's Privy Council writes Governor John Leverett of Massachusetts requesting justice for "our Subject" John Wompas.
1676 (Sept.)	Ann Wompas dies in Boston.
1676 (Dec.)	John is released from debtors' prison in London.
1676 (Dec. 19)	John deeds land to Nicholas and John Warner and Anthony Mudd in England.
1677 (May)	John arrives in Boston.
1677 (June 2)	John quitclaims his Boston home to the Hewes family.
1677 (June)	John presents royal letter to Governor Leverett in Boston. Leverett refers John to an Indian court.
1677 (June)	Indian court denies that John has the right to sell Indian land.
1677 (Aug.–Sept.)	John mortgages 8,000 acres of land in Nipmuc Country to John Warner and Benjamin Franklin and defaults on both mortgages.
1677 (Sept. 27)	John is imprisoned in Cambridge, Massachusetts, for making threatening speeches to a group of townspeople.
1677 (Oct. 10)	John is released from prison on a £200 bond for good behavior.
1678 (May)	John travels to Fairfield, Connecticut, to claim the land Ann inherited from Romanock. He is imprisoned by town leaders. After release, he appeals unsuccessfully to the General Court in Hartford to confirm his ownership of the land at Fairfield.
1678 (summer)	John travels to New York and takes a ship to London.
1679 (March 14)	John petitions King Charles II, complaining of colonial mistreatment of himself and other Indians of New England.
1679 (March 28)	The King's Privy Council writes a letter to the governor and magistrates of Connecticut requesting justice for John Wompas.
1679 (July 17)	John sells Edward Pratt of England eight miles square of land in Nipmuc Country.
1679 (Sept. 5)	John signs his will, leaving land to Edward Pratt, John Blake, and George Owen, but reserving Hassanamesit for his Nipmuc kin.

1679 (late Sept.)	John Wompas dies in London.
1679 (Oct. 1)	John Wompas's will is proved in London.
1679–1704	Litigation over John Wompas's lands in Massachusetts and Connecticut. In 1704 Governor Dudley confirms Edward Pratt and other shareholders' claim to eight miles square but reserves the four-mile-square plot of Hassanamesit for the Nipmuc Indians.
1714	The Town of Sutton is established on lands deriving from John Wompas's sale to Edward Pratt.
1728 (March 19)	Hassanamesit is sold to English investors to create the town of Grafton, with equal shares for seven resident Nipmuc families.
Late 19th century	The last few acres of Hassanamesit, preserved by the Cisco family, come to be considered communal land by the Nipmucs.
1976	The Commonwealth of Massachusetts officially recognizes the Nipmuc tribe.
2004	The federal government denies the Nipmuc Nation status as a federally recognized tribe, ruling that it did not meet four of the seven requirements for recognition laid out by the Bureau of Indian Affairs.
2011	The Hassanamisco Reservation at Hassanamesit is listed on the National Register of Historic Places.

Notes

Abbreviations

AAS	American Antiquarian Society, Worcester, Massachusetts.
AWP	Ann Wompas Inventory and Administration Records, 1676, #830, vol. 12:10, 95, Suffolk County Probate Records, MA.
CCR	J. Hammond Trumbull, ed., *Public Records of the Colony of Connecticut*, 3 vols. (Hartford: F. A. Brown, 1852).
CLM	William H. Whitmore, ed., *The Colonial Laws of Massachusetts, reprinted from the edition of 1672, with the supplements through 1680* (Boston: 1887).
CSL	Connecticut State Library and Archives, Hartford, Connecticut.
CSPC	W. Noel Sainsbury and J. W. Fortescue, eds., *Calendar of State Papers, Colonial Series, America and West Indies*, 16 vols. (Vaduz, Liechtenstein: Kraus Reprint, 1964).
ECR	*Records and Files of the Quarterly Courts of Essex County, Massachusetts* (Salem, Mass.: The Essex Institute, 1913).
EHR	*Records of the Town of East-Hampton*, vol. 1. (Sag Harbor, N.Y.: John H. Hunt, printer, 1887).
ET	Michael P. Clark, ed. *The Eliot Tracts: With Letters from John Eliot to Thomas Thorowgood and Richard Baxter* (Westport, Conn.: Praeger, 2003).
FLR	Fairfield Land Records, CSL, Hartford, Connecticut.
HColl	Daniel Gookin, *Historical Collections of the Indians in New England. MHSC*, 1st ser., 1:141–227.
HAcc	Daniel Gookin, *An Historical Account of the Doings and Sufferings of the Christian Indians in New England, in the Years 1675, 1676, 1677*, in *Archaeologia Americana, Transactions and Collections of the American Antiquarian Society* 2 (1836): 430–532.
HIW	William Hubbard, *The History of the Indian Wars in New England from the First Settlement to the Termination of the War with King*

	Philip, in 1677, ed. Samuel G. Drake, 2 vols. (Baltimore: Genealogical Publishing, 2002 [New York, 1864]).
JAH	*Journal of American History.*
JJW	Richard S. Dunn, James Savage, and Laetitia Yeandle, eds. *The Journal of John Winthrop, 1630–1649* (Cambridge, Mass.: Harvard University Press, 1996).
LMA	London Metropolitan Archives, City of London.
MeHS	Maine Historical Society, Portland, Maine.
MA	Massachusetts State Archives, Columbia Point, Massachusetts.
MAC	Massachusetts Archives Collection, Massachusetts State Archives.
MCR	Nathaniel B. Shurtleff, ed., *Records of the Governor and Company of the Massachusetts Bay in New England*, 6 vols. (Boston: William White, 1854).
MD	Middlesex Deeds, Middlesex County Registry of Deeds, Cambridge, Massachusetts.
MHS	Massachusetts Historical Society, Boston, Massachusetts.
MHSC	*Collections of the Massachusetts Historical Society.*
MPR	*The Acts and Resolves, Public and Private, of the Province of the Massachusetts Bay.* 21 vols. Boston: Wright & Potter, 1869.
NEHGR	*New England Historical and Genealogical Register.*
NEHGS	New England Historical and Genealogical Society, Boston, Massachusetts.
NEQ	*New England Quarterly.*
OED	*Oxford English Dictionary* (online) (Cambridge: Oxford University Press, 2016).
PJW1	Petition of John Wampas alias White, circa 1676, CO 1/37, no. 49, TNA.
PJW2	Petition of John Wampus alias White, received 14 March 1679, CO 1/43, no. 33, TNA.
PCR	David Pulsifer, ed., *Records of the Colony of New Plymouth* (New York: AMS Press, 1968).
RCBR	Robert J. Dunkle and Ann S. Lainhart, trans. *The Records of the Churches of Boston and the First Church, Second Parish, and Third Parish of Roxbury*, CD-ROM (Boston: NEHGS, 2001).
RICR	*Records of the Colony of Rhode Island and Providence Plantations*, 10 vols. (Providence: A Crawford Greene and Brother, 1856).
RRCCB	*Report of the Record Commissioners of the City of Boston*, 39 vols. (Boston: Rockwell & Churchill, 1876–1909).
RWC	Glenn W. LaFantasie, ed., *The Correspondence of Roger Williams*, 2 vols. (Providence: Brown University Press/University Press of New England, 1988).
SGen	James Savage, *Genealogical Dictionary of the First Settlers of New England* (Baltimore: Genealogical Publishing, 1965).

SCF   Suffolk Court Files, Massachusetts State Archives, Columbia Point, Massachusetts.

SCR   *Records of the Suffolk County Court, 1671–1680*, 2 vols., Publications of the Colonial Society of Massachusetts, vols. 29–30 (Boston: Colonial Society of Massachusetts, 1933).

SD   Suffolk Deeds. The first fourteen volumes of the Suffolk Deeds are published as John Tyler Hassam, ed., *Suffolk Deeds* (Boston: 1899). The remaining volumes are in manuscript at the MA.

TNA   The National Archives, United Kingdom.

WJW   Will of John White alias Wampers, 1 October 1679, PROB 11/361, Records of the Prerogative Court of Canterbury, TNA.

WMQ   *William and Mary Quarterly*, 3rd ser.

WFPT   Winthrop Family Papers [transcripts], MHS.

WP   *The Winthrop Papers*, 6 vols. (Boston: Massachusetts Historical Society, 1929–).

YIPP   Paul Grant-Costa and Tobias Glaza, eds., *The New England Indian Papers Series*, Yale University Library Digital Collections, http://findit.library.yale.edu/yipp.

A Note on the Text

1. On the choice to use only Native names, see Julie A. Fisher and David J. Silverman, *Ninigret, Sachem of the Niantics and Narragansetts: Diplomacy, War, and the Balance of Power in Seventeenth-Century New England and Indian Country* (Ithaca, N.Y.: Cornell University Press, 2014), Introduction.

2. James Merrell's "Some Thoughts on Colonial Historians and American Indians," which appeared in 1989, challenged historians to make Indians central to the narrative of early American history and had a powerful influence on my own scholarship (*WMQ* 46, 1 [1989], 94–119). In his assessment in 2012 of how the historical profession had met his challenge in the intervening quarter century, Merrell focused on language, urging historians to be more careful in their use of terms that represent a colonial rather than Native perspective. While his critique prompted me to reevaluate my word choices, I believe that going as far as Merrell suggests actually undermines his original purpose of restoring American Indians to a central position in the mainstream narrative of American history. For instance, replacing colonially imposed names of geographic locations with the original Native ones requires repeated insertions of explanatory phrases ("would later be known as") and unfamiliar terms that baffle and alienate readers not already committed to the project. To make this story accessible to as wide an audience as possible, I use unfamiliar names—both Native and English—sparingly and refer to some locations by their

modern names (James H. Merrell, "Second Thoughts on Colonial Historians and American Indians," *WMQ* 69, 3 [July 2012], 451–512).

Introduction

1. SCF, #1642. I have altered the tense and voice in the first quotation in
   this paragraph to indicate how John Wompas would have spoken. In the
   original document, John's words were reported by an observer, Grindall
   Rawson, who "heard John Wampass ask the people that were there;
   whether they never saw an Indian before."

2. *CCR*, 2:507–508; MAC, 3:330. On the continuation of King Philip's War
   in Maine, see "A Narrative of the Troubles with the Indians in New-
   England, from Pascataqua to Pemmaquid," in *HIW*, vol. 2; Testimony
   against John Wompas, SCF, #1642.

3. On the development of the English empire in relation to colonial Amer-
   ica in this period, see Gregory Evans Dowd, "'Wag the Imperial Dog':
   Indians and Overseas Empires in North America, 1650–1776," in *A Com-
   panion to American Indian History*, ed. Philip J. Deloria and Neal Salisbury
   (Malden, Mass.: Blackwell, 2002); Trevor Burnard, "Empire Matters?
   The Historiography of Imperialism in Early America, 1492–1830," *His-
   tory of European Ideas* 33 (2007): 87–107; Brendan McConville, *The King's
   Three Faces: The Rise and Fall of Royal America, 1688–1776* (Chapel Hill:
   University of North Carolina Press, 2006); James Horn, "The Conquest
   of Eden: Possession and Dominion in Early Virginia," in *Envisioning an
   English Empire: Jamestown and the Making of the North Atlantic World*, ed.
   Robert Appelbaum and John Wood Sweet (Philadelphia: University of
   Pennsylvania Press, 2005); Owen Stanwood, *The Empire Reformed: English
   America in the Age of the Glorious Revolution* (Philadelphia: University of
   Pennsylvania Press, 2011); Richard E. Johnson, *Adjustment to Empire: The
   New England Colonies, 1675–1715* (New Brunswick, N.J.: Rutgers Uni-
   versity Press, 1981); and J. M. Sosin, *English America and the Restoration
   Monarchy of Charles II: Transatlantic Politics, Commerce, and Kinship* (Lin-
   coln: University of Nebraska Press, 1980).

4. John Wood Sweet points out that the English colonizers of Ireland and
   America shared a "guiding colonialist ideology": "The argument was ba-
   sically that in conquering less civilized societies like Anglo-Saxon Britain,
   the Romans had improved them, uplifting them from a primitive state to
   one that was more advanced," and that this same pattern could apply to
   the Irish and Indians, uplifted by the English ("Sea Changes," in *Envisioning an English Empire*, ed. Appelbaum and Sweet, 15). Contemporary
   English colonist Roger Williams wrote of the Indians, "when they heare
   that about sixteen hundred yeeres agoe, England and the Inhabitants
   thereof were like unto themselves, and since have received from God,
   Clothes, Bookes, &c. they are greatly affected with a secret hope con-

cerning themselves" (*A Key into the Language of America* [London: Gregory Dexter, 1643] [Bedford, Mass.: Applewood], "To the Reader"); *MCR* 4, part 2:159.

5. David J. Costa, "The Dialectology of Southern New England Algonquian," in *Papers of the 38th Algonquian Conference* (2007), 101; William Simmons, *Spirit of the New England Tribes: Indian History and Folklore, 1620–1984* (Hanover, N.H.: University Press of New England, 1986), 46–48.

6. Reverend Edmund Brown of Sudbury, Massachusetts, a one-time supporter of Eliot's missionary work, became a bitter critic of the Christian Indians after the war (Jenny Hale Pulsipher, "'Our Sages are Sageles': A Letter on Massachusetts Indian Policy After King Philip's War," *WMQ* 58 [April 2001], 431–448).

   Margaret Newell writes, "The Restoration of Charles II brought heightened scrutiny of all facets of the New England colonies' administration, including their treatment of Native Americans. . . . The desire to restrict local autonomy and rationalize imperial policy played a role in the revocation of Massachusetts Bay's charter and in English efforts to restructure colonial government along more centrally directed lines via the Dominion of New England" (*Brethren by Nature: New England Indians, Colonists, and the Origins of American Slavery* [Ithaca, N.Y.: Cornell University Press, 2015], 194). On the decline of Indian population in New England the decade of King Philip's War, see James D. Drake, *King Philip's War: Civil War in New England* (Amherst: University of Massachusetts Press, 1999), 169.

7. The most comprehensive treatment of John Wompas before the emergence of the New Indian History is John Fred Humes, "John Wampas and the Beginning of Sutton," in *History of the Town of Sutton, Massachusetts*, comp. John C. Dudley (The Town of Sutton, Massachusetts, 1952). Other early works with cameo appearances by Wompas include Justin Winsor, *Memorial History of Boston* (Boston: Ticknor, 1881), 2:xxvi; Frederick William Gookin, *Daniel Gookin, 1612–1687: Assistant and Major General of the Massachusetts Bay Colony* (Privately printed, 1912), 184; Louis B. Wright, *Everyday Life in Colonial America* (New York: G. P. Putnam's Sons, 1965); and Samuel Eliot Morison, *Harvard College in the Seventeenth Century*, 2 vols. (Cambridge, Mass.: Harvard University Press, 1936), 2:356–357. Since the 1990s, Wompas has appeared in a dozen scholarly works, the most extensive treatment being Dennis A. Connole, "Conflict in English and Indian Attitudes Regarding Land Ownership: The Story of John Wampas," in *The Indians of the Nipmuck Country in Southern New England, 1630–1750: An Historical Geography* (Jefferson, N.C.: McFarland, 2001). Shorter discussions of Wompas appear in Alden T. Vaughan, *Transatlantic Encounters: American Indians in Britain, 1500–1776* (New York: Cambridge University Press, 2006), 104–

106; Ann M. Little, *Abraham in Arms: War and Gender in Colonial New England* (Philadelphia: University of Pennsylvania Press, 2007), 2, 42–43; and Coll Thrush, *Indigenous London: Native Travelers at the Heart of Empire* (New Haven, Conn.: Yale University Press, 2016), 62–67.

The earliest contributions to the New Indian History focused on Indians as victims of European colonialism, cultural imperialism, and dispossession of Native lands. Influential examples of this approach include Francis Jennings, *The Invasion of America: Indians, Colonialism, and the Cant of Conquest* (New York: W. W. Norton, 1976 [1975]); Richard Slotkin, *Regeneration Through Violence: The Mythology of the American Frontier, 1600–1860* (Middletown, Conn.: Wesleyan University Press, 1973); Neal Salisbury, *Manitou and Providence: Indians, Europeans, and the Making of New England, 1500–1643* (New York: Oxford University Press, 1982); and James Axtell, *The Invasion Within: The Contest of Cultures in Colonial North America* (New York: Oxford University Press, 1985). Later historians emphasized Indian agency in resisting or adapting to European colonization. See, for example, Daniel K. Richter, *Facing East from Indian Country: A Native History of Early America* (Cambridge, Mass.: Harvard University Press, 2001); David J. Silverman, *Faith and Boundaries: Colonists, Christianity, and Community Among the Wampanoag Indians of Martha's Vineyard, 1600–1871* (New York: Cambridge University Press, 2005); Juliana Barr, *Peace Came in the Form of a Woman: Indians and Spaniards in the Texas Borderlands* (Chapel Hill: University of North Carolina Press, 2007); Pekka Hämäläinen, *The Comanche Empire* (New Haven, Conn.: Yale University Press, 2008); and my own *Subjects unto the Same King: Indians, English, and the Contest of Authority in Colonial New England* (Philadelphia: University of Pennsylvania Press, 2005).

More recently, scholars have focused on the violence of colonialism, an approach that in many ways recapitulates the work of Slotkin and his contemporaries while still attempting to highlight Native action in the face of colonial incursions. See, for example, Ned Blackhawk, *Violence over the Land: Indians and Empires in the Early American West* (Cambridge, Mass.: Harvard University Press, 2006); Peter Silver, *Our Savage Neighbors: How Indian War Transformed Early America* (New York: W. W. Norton, 2008); Patrick Griffin, *American Leviathan: Empire, Nation, and Revolutionary Frontier* (New York: Hill and Wang, 2007); Benjamin Madley, *An American Genocide: The United States and the California Indian Catastrophe, 1846–1873* (New Haven, Conn.: Yale University Press, 2016); and recent works incorporating the paradigm of settler colonialism. See, for example, Wendy Warren, *New England Bound: Slavery and Colonization in Early America* (New York: Liveright, 2016); Bethel Saler, *The Settlers' Empire: Colonialism and State Formation in America's Old Northwest* (Philadelphia: University of Pennsylvania Press, 2015); and Melissa Adams-Campbell, Ashley Glassburn Falzetti, and Courtney Rivard, "Indigeneity and the

Work of Settler Archives," special feature in *Settler Colonial Studies* 5, 2 (2015). In this biography, I emphasize John Wompas's agency but acknowledge that he exercised it under the real and limiting constraints of local English authority, the pressures of an expansionist English population, and the indifference of distant imperial authorities.

The most detailed discussion of John Wompas's land sales appears in Connole, *Indians of the Nipmuck Country*, chapter 8; Jean O'Brien, *Dispossession by Degrees: Indian Land and Identity in Natick, Massachusetts, 1650–1790* (Lincoln: University of Nebraska Press, 2003 [1997], 76–78). Daniel Mandell describes Wompas's land sales as fraud, noting that they became the basis of significant legal conflict and English dispossession of Native land (*Behind the Frontier: Indians in Eighteenth-Century Eastern Massachusetts* [Lincoln: University of Nebraska Press, 1996], chapter 2); Thomas Lewis Doughton, a Nipmuc descendant, has also written about the dispossession of Nipmuc land in "Notes on the Nipmuc Indian Reservation at Hassanamesit or Hassanamisco and the Nipmuc People of Hassanamesit, later Grafton, Massachusetts" (http://massasoit.ocatch. com/grafton1.htm), accessed 28 Oct. 2016.

8. Donna Rae Gould, "Contested Places: The History and Meaning of Hassanamisco," Ph.D. dissertation, University of Connecticut, 2010, 192–193. Cheryll Toney Holley, Chief of the Hassanamisco Nipmuc Indians, notes the distinction between "Hassanamisco," used to refer to Nipmuc people, and "Hassanamesit," which refers to the historic location of the Christian Indian town, now the home of the Hassanamisco Nipmuc Reservation (personal communication, 1 June 2017). Holley has written a short history of the Nipmucs, "A Brief Look at Nipmuc History" (2001; https://native newengland.wordpress.com/2009/09/26/a-brief-look-at-nipmuc-history -by-cheryll-toney-holley), accessed February 2016.

9. For a brief overview of the emergence of the ethnohistorical approach that undergirds the New Indian History, see R. David Edmunds, "Native Americans, New Voices: American Indian History, 1895–1995," *American Historical Review* (June 1995): 724–726. A new generation of scholars, including Josh Reid, Lisa Brooks, Christine DeLucia, and Ashley Falzetti, is combining the ethnohistorical approach with indigenous methodologies such as oral history, indigenous language study, engagement with descendant communities, and indigenous archive construction in an effort to decolonize the narrative of early American history. See, for example, Reid, *The Sea Is My Country: The Maritime World of the Makahs* (New Haven, Conn.: Yale University Press, 2015); Brooks, *Our Beloved Kin: A New History of King Philip's War* (New Haven, Conn.: Yale University Press, 2018); DeLucia, *The Memory Lands: King Philip's War and the Place of Violence in the Northeast* (New Haven, Conn.: Yale University Press, 2018); and Falzetti, "Archival Absence: The Burden of History," *Settler Colonial Studies* 5, 2 (2015): 128–144.

Biographies of early North American Indians include Michael Oberg, *Uncas: First of the Mohegans* (Ithaca, N.Y.: Cornell University Press, 2003); Julie A. Fisher and David J. Silverman, *Ninigret, Sachem of the Niantics and Narragansetts: Diplomacy, War and the Balance of Power in Seventeenth-Century New England and Indian Country* (Ithaca, N.Y.: Cornell University Press, 2014); and Camilla Townsend, *Pocahontas and the Powhatan Dilemma* (New York: Hill and Wang, 2004).

10.   MAC, 30:259a, 260a.

Chapter 1. "The Place of Their Desires"

1.   The epigraphs for this chapter come from *ET,* 403; and Donna Rae Gould, "Contested Places: The History and Meaning of Hassanamisco" (Ph.D. dissertation, University of Connecticut, 2010), 284. John called Hassanamesit "Hassenamiscock" (WJW). Contemporaries, including fellow Nipmucs and English people associated with the Christian Indian movement, used both "Hassanamesit" and "Hassanamiscock." Linguist Frank Siebert associated the use of the place-name suffix "ek/ock," rather than "et/it," with Algonquian speakers living west of the Massachusett Indians, such as the Nipmucs. However, linguist David J. Costa and Nipmuc chief Cheryll Toney Holley argue that both suffixes were used by the Nipmuc as well as the Massachusett Indians (Costa, "The Dialectology of Southern New England Algonquian," in *Papers of the 38th Algonquian Conference* [2007], 100; personal communication with Holley, 1 June 2017). I thank Jessie Little Doe Baird for speaking with me about place-name endings in Massachusett (personal communication, 28 July 2016).

2.   Drawing from the population figures of Daniel Gookin and the analysis of Alfred Crosby, Neal Salisbury estimates a pre-contact Indian population in southern New England of 126,000–144,000. After an estimated 90 percent depopulation brought about by a series of epidemics, the Native population may have declined to around 15,000 by the mid-seventeenth century (Neal Salisbury, *Manitou and Providence: Indians, Europeans, and the Making of New England, 1500–1643* [New York: Oxford University Press, 1982], 30, 105). See also Kathleen Bragdon's analysis of population estimates in *Native People of Southern New England, 1500–1650* (Norman: University of Oklahoma Press, 1996), 23–28. The phrase "widowed land" comes from the paradigm-shattering work of Francis Jennings, *The Invasion of America: Indians, Colonialism, and the Cant of Conquest* (New York: W. W. Norton, 1976 [1975]), chapter 2.

3.   Frank G. Speck, "A Note on the Hassanamisco Band of Nipmuc," *Bulletin of the Massachusetts Archaeological Society* 4 (1944): 49–56. Daniel Gookin describes Native wigwams in *HColl,* 150. Kathleen Bragdon notes that the word "wigwam" arose from the Native word *weekuwout,*

meaning "in his house" (*Native People*, 108, 253, note 3). Andrew Lipman argues that "wigwam" came from the Eastern Abenaki language but, through "contact languages" or "trade pidgins," it came into use in regions further west (*The Saltwater Frontier: Indians and the Contest for the American Coast* [New Haven, Conn.: Yale University Press, 2015], 103). On Native houses, see also Mary Lynn Rainey, "Native American Architecture on Nantucket Island, Massachusetts," in *Nantucket and Other Native Places: The Legacy of Elizabeth Alden Little*, ed. Elizabeth S. Chilton and Mary Lynne Rainey (Albany: State University of New York Press, 2010), 26–30, 56; Bert Salwen, "Indians of Southern New England and Long Island: Early Period," in *Northeast*, ed. Bruce Trigger, vol. 15 of *Handbook of North American Indians* (Washington, D.C.: Smithsonian Institution, 1978), 160–176; and Harral Ayres, *The Great Trail of New England* (Boston: Meador, 1940), 91–92. An Indian woman called Mary mentioned "hilling time" in 1675 in reference to when she traveled, demonstrating how the agricultural calendar structured time and travel among Natives of the region (MA 30·184a); *HColl*, 184.

Native naming patterns are evident in the names of John Wompas and his father. Children frequently took as a last name the first or only name of a parent. Among the Hassanamesit Nipmuc, for instance, Sarah Boston was the daughter of Boston Phillips (Thomas Doughton, personal interview, Worcester, Massachusetts, 28 July 2016); Mrs. Arthur Taft, "The Last of the Aborigines of Grafton," MS circa 1958, Grafton Public Library, Grafton, Massachusetts, 1–2; Ayres, *Great Trail*, 103, 233–235; Dennis A. Connole, *The Indians of the Nipmuck Country in Southern New England, 1630–1750: An Historical Geography* (Jefferson, N.C.: McFarland, 2001), 20–22; *HColl*, 185.

4. Speck, "A Note on the Hassanamisco," 50. Karen O. Kupperman notes that some scholars have dismissed primary documents that claim "American Indian polities were hierarchically organized with a hereditary elite and strong chiefs." However, more recent interdisciplinary scholarship supports the presence of hierarchy and status-consciousness among Native communities: "Hereditary elites apparently did exist broadly across indigenous American polities" (foreword to Robert Appelbaum and John Wood Sweet, eds., *Envisioning an English Empire: Jamestown and the Making of the North Atlantic World* [Philadelphia: University of Pennsylvania Press, 2005], xiv). John Eliot wrote in 1673 that the man he appointed as ruler over the new praying towns in Nipmuc Country, Wuttasacompanom (Captain Tom), was "their ancient Sachem" ("An Account of Indian Churches in New England" [1673], in *MHSC*, 1st ser., 1:10:128); see also Richard W. Cogley, *John Eliot's Mission to the Indians Before King Philip's War* (Cambridge, Mass.: Harvard University Press, 1999), 156. On paramount sachems, see Kathleen Joan Bragdon, "Another Tongue Brought In: An Ethnohistorical Study of Native Writings in Massachusett" (Ph.D.

dissertation, Brown University, 1981), 46, 122, 128; and Bragdon, *Native People*, chapter 5.

On Indian perceptions of early European visitors, see William S. Simmons, *Spirit of the New England Tribes: Indian History and Folklore, 1620–1984* (Hanover, N.H.: University Press of New England, 1986), chapter 3; and *Johnson's Wonder-Working Providence, 1628–1651*, J. Franklin Jameson, ed. (New York: Barnes & Noble, 1952), 48–49. My description here draws particularly from Phineas Pratt's Relation (*MHSC*, 4th ser., 4:488). Basque, French, Spanish, and English visitors to the New England coast well before 1620 are evidenced by the coins, brass, and other European objects present among the Natives when later English voyagers arrived (*JJW*, 55; Louis B. Wright, ed., *The Elizabethans' America: A Collection of Early Reports by Englishmen on the New World* [Cambridge, Mass.: Harvard University Press, 1965], chapters 6, 16–18; and Bruce J. Bourque and Ruth H. Whitehead, "Trade and Alliances in the Contact Period," in Emerson W. Baker et al., *American Beginnings: Exploration, Culture and Cartography in the Land of Norumbega* [Lincoln: University of Nebraska Press, 1994]). On Native adaptations of European goods, see Christopher L. Miller and George R. Hamell, "A New Perspective on Indian-White Contact: Cultural Symbols and Colonial Trade," *JAH* 73 (1986): 311–328; and Daniel K. Richter, *Facing East from Indian Country: A Native History of Early America* (Cambridge, Mass.: Harvard University Press, 2001), chapter 2. On northeastern Native seasonal patterns, see Bragdon, *Native People*, chapter 1; Roger Williams, *A Key into the Language of America* (Bedford, Mass.: Applewood, n.d. [London: Gregory Dexter, 1643]), 47–48.

5. J. S. Marr, J. T. Cathey, "New Hypothesis for Cause of an Epidemic Among Native Americans, New England, 1616–1619," *Emerging Infectious Diseases*, Feb. 2010 (http://www.cdc.gov/EID/content/16/2/281.htm), accessed 1 June 2016. Jessie Little Doe Baird, a Mashpee Wampanoag, recounts a vision in which her ancestors spoke in *Wôpanâôt8âôk* (Wampanoag), saying, "We've been killed by the yellow thing" (Kathleen Burkhalter, "Three Stories About the Wampanoag People," a Harvard Journalism Capstone Project, 2012 [https://medium.com/@mizkathleen/three-stories-about-the-wampanoag-people-20d7df96081b#.sncfizpj4], accessed 31 May 2016). See also the entry for "pestilence" in James Hammond Trumbull, *Natick Dictionary* (Washington, D.C.: Government Printing Office, 1903). Dwight B. Heath, ed., *Mourt's Relation: A Journal of the Pilgrims at Plymouth* (Bedford, Mass.: Applewood, 1963), 50–52, 28–34; Rev. Higgeson, "New England's Plantation, 1629," in *MHSC*, 1st ser., 1:117–124; *Boston News-Letter*, March 19–26, 1730, cited in Annie Haven Thwing, *The Crooked and Narrow Streets of the Town of Boston, 1630–1822* (Boston: Marshall Jones, 1920), 7.

6. *HColl*, 148–149; Salisbury, *Manitou and Providence*, 26–30, 101–105; *ET,*

94. Adaptive immunity is acquired through previous exposure to a specific pathogen; innate immunity refers to the biological mechanisms—cells and proteins—that fight all disease. David S. Jones, "Virgin Soils Revisited," provides a useful reminder that Native susceptibility to European diseases was not simply a result of "no immunity." Like all humans, Native peoples possessed innate immunity. Rather, social and environmental factors and a lack of the adaptive immunity that previous disease exposure would have provided increased their vulnerability to the devastating epidemics (*WMQ* 60 [Oct. 2003]: 703–742). Phineas Pratt, who settled at Weymouth on Massachusetts Bay in 1622, claimed that local Indians reported "half" of their people died in the first wave of disease. *Mourt's Relation* gives Samoset's report that "all the inhabitants" of Patuxet died in an "extraordinary plague" around 1616 (Herbert U. Williams, "The Epidemic of the Indians of New England, 1616–1620, with Remarks on Native American Infections," *Johns Hopkins Hospital Bulletin* 20 [1909]: 346, 345).

    Important contributions to the longstanding debate over Native population numbers before European settlement include Sherburne F. Cook, "Interracial Warfare and Population Decline Among the New England Indians," *Ethnohistory* 20, 1 (1973): 1–24, and "The Significance of Disease in the Extinction of the New England Indians," *Human Biology* 45 (Sept. 1973): 485–508; Dean Snow and Kim M. Lanphear, "European Contact and Indian Depopulation in the Northeast: The Timing of the First Epidemics," *Ethnohistory* 35, 1 (1988): 351–383; Henry F. Dobyns, with the assistance of William R. Swagerty, *Their Number Become Thinned: Native Population Dynamics in Eastern North America* (Knoxville: University of Tennessee Press, 1983); Alfred Crosby, "Virgin Soil Epidemics as a Factor in the Aboriginal Depopulation in America," *WMQ* 33 (April 1976): 289–299, and *The Columbian Exchange: Biological and Cultural Consequences of 1492* (Praeger, 2003); and Russell Thornton, "Health, Disease, and Demography," in *A Companion to American Indian History*, ed. Philip J. Deloria and Neal Salisbury (Malden, Mass.: Blackwell, 2002). There is wide but not universal consensus that Native American depopulation in the wake of European contact exceeded 90 percent. For a contrary view, see David P. Henige, *Numbers from Nowhere: The American Indian Contact Population Debate* (Norman: University of Oklahoma Press, 1998).

7.   William Bradford, *Of Plymouth Plantation, 1620–1647*, ed. Samuel Eliot Morison (New York: Knopf, 1952), 87. The process of amalgamation among survivor communities is referred to in the scholarly literature as ethnogenesis, a term introduced in 1971 by William Sturtevant (Alexandra Harmon, "Wanted: More Histories of Indian Identity," in *Companion to American Indian History*, ed. Deloria and Salisbury, 252–253); Heath, ed., *Mourt's Relation*, 60–61, 66; William Wood, *New England's Prospect* (1634), ed. Alden T. Vaughan (1977), 115; *JJW*, 47–49; *ET*, 60, 272, 382.

8. Contemporary English colonists knew very little about inland Native groups, so information on their population and the impact of disease is fragmentary. Thomas Dudley, assistant governor of Massachusetts Bay Colony, wrote in 1632 that the Nipmucs' "numbers exceed any but the Pecoates and the Narragansets." This quote suggests that the epidemic of 1616–1618 bypassed the Nipmucs as well as the Pequots and Narragansetts (Thomas Dudley to the Countess of Lincoln, March 12, 1631/32, in Alexander Young, ed., *Chronicles of the First Planters of the Colony of Massachusetts Bay, from 1623 to 1636* [Boston: Charles C. Little and James Brown, 1846], 306). Bragdon, "Another Tongue Brought In," 103; *HColl*, 147–148; Williams, *Key*, 140; *JJW*, 33–38; Walter W. Woodward, *Prospero's America: John Winthrop, Jr.: Alchemy and the Creation of New England Culture, 1606–1676* (Chapel Hill: University of North Carolina Press, 2010), 167; Bernard Bailyn, *The Barbarous Years: The Conflict of Civilizations, 1600–1675* (New York: Knopf, 2012), 372; *Boston News-Letter*, 29 August 1723, cited in Thwing, *Crooked and Narrow Streets*, 6–7.

9. Salisbury, *Manitou and Providence*, 48–49, 57; Daniel K. Richter, *Ordeal of the Longhouse: The Peoples of the Iroquois League in the Era of European Colonization* (Chapel Hill: University of North Carolina Press, 1992), 22; Bragdon, *Native People*, 132–135; Jean M. O'Brien, *Dispossession by Degrees: Indian Land and Identity in Natick, Massachusetts, 1650–1790* (Cambridge: Cambridge University Press, 1997), 20; David Murray, *Indian Giving: Economies of Power in Indian-White Exchanges* (Amherst: University of Massachusetts Press, 2000), 19–20; Katherine A. Hermes, "'Justice Will Be Done Us': Algonquian Demands for Reciprocity in the Court of European Settlers," in *The Many Legalities of Early America*, ed. Christopher L. Tomlins and Bruce H. Mann (Chapel Hill: University of North Carolina Press, 2001); *MAC* 30:146. The perception that peace and trade were inseparable was common among Algonquian speakers as well as the neighboring Houdenesaunee (Iroquois) (Timothy Shannon, *Iroquois Diplomacy on the Early American Frontier* [New York: Penguin, 2008], 22).

10. *JJW*, 101. William Wood's 1633 map of Massachusetts shows the location, by name, of the communities of Sagamore John, Sagamore James, and Chickatabut, as well as Passaconaway of the Pennacooks (*New England's Prospect*); *JJW*, 108–109, 105.

11. Thomas Dudley to the Countess of Lincoln, 12 March 1631/32, in *Chronicles of the First Planters*, ed. Young, 306. Eliot mentions smallpox epidemics among the Indians in 1650 and 1651 ("A Letter from New-England, from Mr. Eliot, preacher of the Word there," YIPP). My thanks to Paul Grant-Costa for alerting me to this document and providing a transcription.

12. *ET*, 74, 94. See also *Johnson's Wonder-Working Providence*, 41, 48. Many of the Puritan colonists of New England saw themselves as seventeenth-century versions of the children of Israel, guided by God to a new land

of promise. At the same time, some Puritans, including John Eliot, initially believed the Indians were descendants of Israel and saw their missionary work as a way to restore these lost Israelites to the truth (Michael Hoberman, *New Israel/New England: Jews and Puritans in Early America* [Amherst: University of Massachusetts Press, 2011], 13–16).

13. Other Algonquian-speaking people used the names Cautantouwit and Keihtan for the benevolent god and Abbomocho for the malevolent god; *HColl*, 154; Bragdon, *Native People*, 188–190; Simmons, *Spirit of the New England Tribes*, chapter 3, 121. For contemporary English accounts of Indian religion, see Williams, *Key*, 123–139; Wood, *New England's Prospect*, 96–101, 112; John Josselyn, *A Critical Edition of Two Voyages to New-England* [London, 1674], ed. Paul J. Lindholt (Hanover, N.H.: University Press of New England, 1988), 95–96; see also Bragdon, *Native People*, chapters 8–10; Clara Sue Kidwell, "Native American Systems of Knowledge," in *Companion to American Indian History*, ed. Deloria and Salisbury, 97; and William S. Simmons, "Conversion from Indian to Puritan," *NEQ* 52, 2 (June 1979): 197–218.

14. Cogley, *John Eliot's Mission*, appendix 4, 259. Nineteenth-century historian John C. Crane claimed that Waban was born near Concord, Massachusetts ("The Nipmucks and their Country," *Proceedings of the Worcester Society of Antiquity* 16 [1898]: 101–117). On James Printer, see Jill Lepore, *The Name of War: King Philip's War and the Origins of American Identity* (New York: Knopf, 1998), 136–149. I surmise that Totherswamp and Thomas Tray were the same person because one of the pronunciations of Totherswamp is "Todorsway," which is very similar in sound to "Thomas Tray" (Cogley, *John Eliot's Mission*, 254). The last documented use of "Tutteswamp" in the records occurs in 1668 (MAC 30:156a) and the first documented use of "Thomas Tray" in 1679 (*MCR* 5:228). Wampooas's and Totherswamp's younger brother is called Anthony in early records, but usage shifts to "Anthony Tray" as early as 1672, likely to associate him with his older brother (*MCR* 4, part 2:537). Identification of Anthony, Totherswamp, and Wampooas as brothers rests on multiple accounts. In one account of Anthony's conversion, he claims his "brothers" died, and in another that his "brother" died. Both recount the same story, so one is likely a mistranscription (*ET*, 292, 364–365, 382; Cogley, *John Eliot's Mission*, 254, appendix 2; MAC 30:156a, 158, 159, 247); *ET*, 370. Evidence of the impact of Waban's example appears in the conversion narratives recorded in preparation for gathering a Native church at Natick (*ET*, 96, 122, 292–293, 365, 372). While Waban was clearly a man of influence, within the Eliot Tracts he is both described as a sachem and said not to be a sachem (*ET*, 96, 122).

15. Governor Cradock to John Endicott, 16 Feb. 1629, in *Chronicles of the First Planters*, ed. Young, 133–134. For criticism of the Massachusetts colonists' failure to teach religion to the Indians in the first years of coloni-

zation, see *ET,* 1, 93, 150; Thomas Lechford, *Plain Dealing: Or, Newes from New-England* [1642], *MHSC,* 3rd ser., 3:80–88. Francis Jennings claims Eliot and his colleagues began preaching to the Indians only when material and political incentives pushed them to do so (*Invasion of America,* chapter 14). For a rebuttal of Jennings's arguments see Richard Cogley, "Idealism vs. Materialism in the Study of Puritan Missions to the Indians," *Method & Theory in the Study of Religion* 3, 2 (1991): 165–182. Certainly, compared with the Spanish and French colonizers, the Puritans did relatively little missionary work. One of the reasons for this was structural: unlike Catholics, who had celibate religious orders exclusively dedicated to proselytizing, Protestant clerics were attached to specific congregations. Any missionary work they did had to come on top of their obligations to their congregations and families. *ET,* 226, 262, 303.

16. See the Indian conversion narratives in "Tears of Repentance" and "Late and Further Manifestation" in *ET.* For an excellent analysis of Native conversion narratives, see Richter, *Facing East,* chapter 4. The Society for the Propagation of the Gospel in New England was referred to as "the Corporation" until 1664, when, under Parliament's recharter, it became known as "The Company for Propagation of the Gospel in New England and Parts Adjacent in America," shortened to the "New England Company" (*ET,* 11–14). New England Company Records indicate that "Company" began to replace "Corporation" in official records in 1668 (Corporation for New England Records [photostats], 1653–1685, MHS).

Much of the recent scholarship on Indian conversion narratives cautions against using them to determine Native motivations for accepting Christianity, noting that the narratives were translated and recorded by Englishmen for their own purposes, and pointing out the mediated nature of the confession form itself, which conformed to English Puritan expectations, not Native ones (Jacqueline M. Henkel, "Represented Authenticity: Native Voices in Seventeenth-Century Conversion Narratives," *NEQ* [March 2014]: 10). Other scholars see "danger in assuming that [missionary] documents *could not* and *did not* record the individual and collective actions of Native Americans or the reactions of other Native people and non-Natives," arguing that "excluding the written record categorically as a tool to help understand Native histories is itself a form of colonialism" (Stephen A. Mrozowski et al., "Magunkaquog Materiality, Federal Recognition, and the Search for a Deeper History," *International Journal of Historical Archaeology* 13 [2009]: 435). Scholars who similarly wrestle with the "authenticity" of Native conversion narratives and the challenges of interpreting mediated documents include Hilary E. Wyss, *Writing Indians: Literacy, Christianity, and Native Community in Early America* (Amherst: University of Massachusetts Press, 2000); Joshua David Bellin, "'A Little I Shall Say': Translation and Interculturalism in the John Eliot Tracts," in *Reinterpreting New England Indians and the Colonial Experience,* ed. Colin G. Calloway and Neal Salisbury (Boston: The Colonial Society of Massachusetts, 2003); Kristina Bross, *Dry Bones and Indian Sermons: Praying Indians in Colonial America* (Ithaca, N.Y.: Cornell University Press, 2004); Kristina Bross and Hilary E. Wyss, ed., *Early Native Literacies in New England: A Documentary and Critical Anthology* (Amherst: University of Massachusetts Press, 2008); and Linford D. Fisher, *The Indian Great Awakening: Religion and the Shaping of Native Cultures in Early America* (New York: Oxford University Press, 2012).

17. *ET,* 269, 292–293. Other Indians who mentioned visiting English homes and being urged to "pray to God" include Nipmuc sachem Thomas Wuttasacomponom, Nipmuc Indian Montunkquanit, Massachusett Indian Ponompam, and early Nipmuc convert Waban (*ET,* 269, 271, 272, 292–293, 371, 373, 389); John Eliot to Richard Baxter, 7 Oct. 1657, in "Some Unpublished Correspondence of the Rev. Richard Baxter and the Rev. John Eliot, 'The Apostle to the American Indians,' 1656–1682," *Bulletin of the John Rylands Library* 15 [1931]: 157–160. Examples of Indians who claimed to "hate" English speaking of Christianity appear in *ET,* 182, 273, 276, 290, 292–293, 363, 389, 392.

18. For the view that Indians converted out of sincere belief, see Cogley, *John Eliot's Mission* and "Idealism vs. Materialism"; Alden T. Vaughan, *New England Frontier: Puritans and Indians, 1620–1675,* 3rd ed. (Norman: University of Oklahoma Press, 1995 [1965]); Richter, *Facing East,* 90; and James Axtell, "Were Indian Conversions Bona Fide?" in *After Columbus: Essays in the Ethnohistory of Colonial North America* (New York: Oxford University Press, 1988). For the view that Indians converted for material reasons, see Jennings, *Invasion of America*; Neal Salisbury, "Red Puritans: The 'Praying Indians' of Massachusetts Bay and John Eliot," *WMQ* 31, 1 (January 1974): 27–54; Dane Morrison, *A Praying People: Massachusett Acculturation and the Failure of the Puritan Mission, 1600–1690* (New York: Peter Lang, 1995). Linford Fisher suggests that the neutral terms "affiliation" or "religious engagement" may be more accurate than "conversion" when discussing American Indian Christianity, arguing against "conceiving of religious change in terms of a wholesale renunciation of one set of ideas in favor of another." He also notes the challenge of interpreting Native actions in the presence of a power disparity: "Contemplating the proffered religion becomes considerably more complicated as the balance of power tips less and less in the favor of the indigenous population" (*Indian Great Awakening,* 8, 5). On the numbers of Natives who accepted Christianity, see Vaughan, *New England Frontier,* 303. Eliot's account of Wampooas's and his wife's conversions depicts them as among the most ardent of the Christian proselytes, whose faith motivated their decisions. Unfortunately, we do not have first-person accounts from either of John Wompas's parents. Cheryll Toney Holley, the sachem of the Hassanamisco Nipmucs, believes that her ancestors chose to ac-

cept Christianity as a strategy for cultural survival (personal communication, 4 Sept. 2017).

19. An example of seeking these signs appears in *ET,* 175. I have listed four key steps in conversion that appear in the Christian Indian tracts, but other scholars have listed as many as ten separate steps. See, for example, Richter, *Facing East,* 124; and Charles Lloyd Cohen, *God's Caress: The Psychology of Puritan Religious Experience* (New York: Oxford University Press, 1986), 202–212.

20. *ET,* 179. On Native oratory, see Kathleen J. Bragdon, "Vernacular Literacy and Massachusett World View, 1650–1750," in Peter Benes, ed., *Algonkians of New England: Past and Present,* The Dublin Seminar for New England Folklife Annual Proceedings, 1991 (Boston University Press, 1993), 33; and *ET,* 150; Constance A. Crosby, "The Algonkian Spiritual Landscape," in *Algonkians of New England,* ed. Benes, 36; Christina Hodge, "Faith and Practice at an Early-Eighteenth-Century Wampanoag Burial Ground: The Waldo Farm Site in Dartmouth, Massachusetts," *Historical Archaeology* 39, 4 (2005): 79–80. On metaphor in Native ritual speech, see Bragdon, *Native People,* 190–193, 229, 236; Clara Sue Kidwell, "Native American Systems of Knowledge," in *Companion to American Indian History,* ed. Deloria and Salisbury, 89. Abenaki writer Joseph Bruchac notes that metaphor is a constant feature of Native storytelling, explaining that "Being able to think in metaphor and to see the spirit that exists in all things may be a necessary requirement for the kind of relationships that American Indian people have to their traditional stories" (*Our Stories Remember: American Indian History, Culture, and Values Through Storytelling* [Golden, Colo: Fulcrum, 2003], 51, 63).

21. David Silverman, *Faith and Boundaries,* 71; on the claim that Christianity simply revived ancient Indian teachings, see *ET,* 119, 150, 153, 164, 165, 180, 245; Bragdon, *Native People,* 189–191; Fisher, *Indian Great Awakening,* 15–19; Cogley, *John Eliot's Mission,* 243; *ET,* 395, 115–116, 137, 183.

22. *ET,* 281, 269, 289, 370, 375, 385.

23. Ann Marie Plane provides a richly detailed discussion of Native and English dream practices in *Dreams and the Invisible World in Colonial New England: Indians, Colonists, and the Seventeenth Century* (Philadelphia: University of Pennsylvania Press, 2014). Robert Cushman, cited in William S. Simmons, "Conversion from Indian to Puritan," *NEQ* 52, 2 (June 1979): 200; Plane, *Dreams,* 49–50; *ET,* 137; Simmons, *Spirit of the New England Tribes,* 263; Kathleen J. Bragdon, "The Material Culture of the Christian Indians of New England, 1650–1775," in *Documentary Archaeology in the New World,* ed. Mary Beaudry (Cambridge: Cambridge University Press, 1988), 130. Archaeologists found English items used in distinctly Native ways in their excavation of the Christian Indian town of Magunkaquog and concluded, "If the evidence from Magunkaquog is indicative of similar communities throughout Southern New England, then even the

most ardent of converts retained their belief in Native spirituality" (Mrozowski et al., "Magunkaquog Materiality," 453, 457); *ET*, 180, 183.

24. Primary accounts of New England powwows include *ET*, 97–98; Williams, *Key*, 195–200; Wood, *New England's Prospect*, 93–101; *HColl*, 154. For scholarly discussion of powwows, see Bragdon, *Native People*, 203–208; Simmons, *Spirit of the New England Tribes*, 55–58; and Richter, *Facing East*, 63. *ET*, 364; *HColl*, 154.

25. Simmons, *Spirit of the New England Tribes*, 121. On English perceptions that Indians prayed to the devil, see Williams, *Key*, 129. Algonquian-speaking groups of New England used the names Chepi, Mattand, and Hobbomock for the mischievous god, and Cautantouwit, Keihtan, and Mannit for the benevolent one (*HColl*, 154; Bragdon, *Native People*, 188–190); *ET*, 63, 95, 96, 125, 149, 153, 239, 374, 393. See also William S. Simmons, "Cultural Bias in the New England Puritans' Perception of Indians," *WMQ* 38, 1 (Jan. 1981): 56–72; and David S. Lovejoy, "Satanizing the American Indian," *NEQ* 67, 4 (Dec. 1994): 603–621. For contemporary English accounts of Indian religion, see Williams, *Key*, 123–139; Wood, *New England's Prospect*, 96–101, 112; Josselyn, *A Critical Edition of Two Voyages*, 95–96; see also Bragdon, *Native People*, chapters 8–10. On the possibility that powwows' failure to cure epidemic disease promoted acceptance of Christianity, see Kidwell, "Native American Systems," 97; and Simmons, "Conversion from Indian to Puritan"; *JJW*, 105.

26. Simmons, "Conversion from Indian to Puritan," 200. Following the Pequot War, the Puritan minister Increase Mather reported that "the Lord . . . put a fear and dread of us into the hearts of the Indians round about us; and many of them did voluntarily put themselves under the government of the English" ("Capt. Roger Clap's Memoirs," in *Chronicles of the First Planters of the Colony of Massachusetts Bay*, ed. Alexander Young [Boston: Charles C. Little and James Brown, 1846], 364; see also *ET*, 9). *ET*, 138, 269; MAC 30:6, 15; quoted in Cogley, *John Eliot's Mission*, 57.

   On differing Indian and English systems of land distribution, see O'Brien, *Dispossession by Degrees*; Bragdon, *Native People*, 43, 138–145; Emerson W. Baker, "'A Scratch with a Bear's Paw': Anglo-Indian Land Deeds in Early Maine," *Ethnohistory* 36, 3 (1989): 235–256; Virginia DeJohn Anderson, "King Philip's Herds: Indians, Colonists, and the Problem of Livestock in Early New England," *WMQ* 51 (Oct. 1994) and *Creatures of Empire: How Domestic Animals Transformed Early America* (New York: Oxford University Press, 2004); and chapter 4 of this book. On Christian Indians giving up claims to other lands, see Fisher, *Indian Great Awakening*, 24. On the General Court's grant to Nonantum, see E. Jennifer Monaghan, *Learning to Read and Write in Colonial Massachusetts* (Amherst: University of Massachusetts Press, 2005), 52. Cogley describes the protected status of Christian Indian land and restrictions on Indian land sales in *John Eliot's Mission*, 2–5, 30–33, 231–237. On land taken from

Dorchester for the use of the praying town of Punkapoag, see "Communications from the Town Clerk of Dorchester," *MHSC*, 1st ser., 1:98–100.

27.   *ET*, 183, 138.

28.   Ayres, *Great Trail*, 91; *ET*, 135.

29.   Ola E. Winslow, *John Eliot: Apostle to the Indians* (Boston: Houghton Mifflin, 1968), 96; Cogley, *John Eliot's Mission*, 49–51; Linford D. Fisher and
Lucas Mason-Brown, "By 'Treachery and Seduction': Indian Baptism
and Conversion in the Roger Williams Code," *WMQ* 71, 2 (April 2014):
184–186; *ET*, 160, 83–84.

    Cockenoe was taken captive in the Pequot War in 1637. After several
years as a slave in the household of Richard Colicott of Dorchester,
Cockenoe seems to have been freed. By 1646 he had become John Eliot's
first Indian interpreter and continued to assist him until about 1649 when,
to Eliot's regret, he returned to live on Long Island. Indians on Long Island spoke the Algonquian language of Mohegan/Pequot/Montauk, which
was closely related to Nipmuc and the other Southern New England Algonquian languages. Cockenoe was probably very familiar with the Massachusett and Nipmuc languages, having lived in Massachusetts and
worked with Eliot and his Nipmuc and Massachusett converts for nearly
a decade (William Wallace Tooker, *John Eliot's First Indian Teacher and
Interpreter, Cockenoe-de-Long Island* [New York: Francis P. Harper, 1896],
15–16; David J. Costa, "The Dialectology of Southern New England Algonquian," in *Papers of the 38th Algonquian Conference* [2007], 81–127).

30.   *ET*, 87–88.

31.   *ET*, 95–96, 117. On Shepherd as the author of this Christian Indian tract,
The Clear Sun-shine of the Gospel (London, 1648), see David D. Hall, *A
Reforming People: Puritanism and the Transformation of Public Life in New
England* (New York: Alfred A. Knopf, 2011), 187.

32.   *ET*, 97–98, 115–116, 127. Neal Salisbury argues that such responses as
weeping are evidence of cultural breakdown among Natives and help explain their willingness to accept a new religious tradition ("Red Puritans"). Archaeologists Stephen A. Mrozowski, Holly Herbster, David
Brown, and Katherine L. Priddy contend that adopting Christianity "did
not involve the erasure of Native spirituality, but rather its being symbolically interwoven into a hybrid cultural fabric that represented a dynamic
interpretation of religious practice. . . . We see this new spiritual reality
as an indigenous product rather than something developed out of resistance to English, religious doctrine" ("Magunkaquog Materiality," 433).

    Contemporary Europeans noted the "universal male dominance" in
Algonquian-speaking societies, as did later scholars. Eleanor Leacock
challenged the Native origin of the pattern of male dominance, arguing
that it was an artifact of colonization (Betty Bell, "Gender in Native
America," in *Companion to American Indian History*, ed. Deloria and Salisbury, 308–311; Nancy Shoemaker, ed., *Negotiators of Change: Historical*

Perspectives on Native American Women [New York: Routledge, 1995], 2–12). Others, like Andrew Lipman, accepted it as a Native pattern: "However distorted the colonial gaze was, though, there is ample evidence that in Algonquian households men were dominant over women" (*Saltwater Frontier*, 32). A number of Indian women held the office of sachem during the fifty years after English settlement. This may have been an anomaly connected with the dramatic depopulation brought on by European diseases, or it may indicate that matrilineality played a role in the inheritance of political office (Bragdon, *Native People*, 160–161). Despite the presence of some female sachems, women in New England Indian societies were generally subordinate to men, particularly those in the coastal region, where the development of the wampum trade may have decreased women's status (Bragdon, *Native People*, 49–53, chapter 6; see also Kathleen J. Bragdon, "Island Queens: Women Sachems on Martha's Vineyard and Nantucket in the Colonial Period," in *Nantucket and Other Native Places*, ed. Chilton and Rainey, 87–100).

33. Vaughan, *New England Frontier*, 303; *ET*, 136, 272, 392–393; Neal Salisbury, ed., *The Sovereignty and Goodness of God, by Mary Rowlandson, with Related Documents* (Boston: Bedford, 1997), 21, 41, 71, 75, 97; Jenny Hale Pulsipher, "Massacre at Hurtleberry Hill: Christian Indians and English Authority in Metacom's War," *WMQ* 53 (July 1996): 459–486; *ET*, 392–393, 390; Cogley, *John Eliot's Mission*, 55.

34. *ET*, 151–152. Eliot would later publish *The Dying Speeches of Several Indians* (Boston, 1685). For scholarly interpretation of these dying speeches, see Kristina Bross, "Dying Saints, Vanishing Savages: 'Dying Indian Speeches' in Colonial New England Literature," *Early American Literature* 36, 3 (2001): 325–352; and Erik R. Seeman, "Reading Indians' Deathbed Scenes: Ethnohistorical and Representational Approaches," *JAH* 88, 1 (2001): 17–47.

Plane, *Dreams*, 159–164. Plane also notes that Indian converts engaged in dialogue with their Christian mentors over the meaning of dreams. By asking such questions as "if a man dream that he seeth God, doth his soule then see him?" they indicated their continuing belief in the value of dreams for conveying spiritual knowledge (51). Kristina Bross analyzes Christian Indian Samuel Ponampam's confession as an example of crafting a Native Christian identity "that served their needs and through which they performed a Native Christianity potentially unrecognizable to their English proselytizers" ("Temptation in the Wilderness: Samuel Ponampam's Confession," in *Early Native Literacies*, ed. Bross and Wyss, 118).

35. *ET*, 95, 222–223. Eliot described the four children Wampooas presented to him in 1646 as Wampooas's "owne sonne and three more Indian children to bee trained up among the English, one of the children was nine yeares old, another eight, another five, another foure" (*ET*, 94). Because

Wampooas's son John is listed first, I have assumed that the first listed age pertains to him. However, he may have been as young as four in 1646 and nine in 1651. Cheryll Toney Holley, sachem of the Hassanamisco Nipmucs, acknowledges the evidence that Nipmuc children went to live among the English, but she does not believe that their parents would have surrendered them voluntarily: "Knowing that it would prevent the culture from continuing . . . why would they give those beloved children away?" (personal communication, 4 Sept. 2017).

36. Gookin claimed Indian "men and women are very loving and indulgent to their children" (*HColl*, 149). See also *ET*, 89; Karen Ordahl Kupperman, *Settling with the Indians: The Meeting of English and Indian Cultures in America, 1580–1640* (Totowa, N.J.: Rowman and Littlefield, 1980), 136. J. Patrick Cesarini, "John Eliot's 'A Breif History of the Mashepog Indians, 1666,'" *WMQ* 65 (Jan. 2008): 117; and Sydney V. James Jr., ed., *Three Visitors to Early Plymouth: Letters About the Pilgrim Settlement in New England During Its First Seven Years* (Plymouth, Mass.: Plimoth Plantation, 1963), 17.

   ET, 95, 151. Sixteen miles from Nonantum was not far enough to reach Hassanamesit, so Wampooas and his family must have been living, or at least "planting," in another area at this time. John Wompas later claimed the right to fourteen miles square of land between Marlborough and Mendon, close to the present location of Hassanamesit (Grafton, Massachusetts) (SD, 8:421). He also specifically claimed Assenham Eaststock (Hassanamiscock) in his will, indicating that was the place from which his family originally came (WJW).

37. *ET*, 373; Edmund S. Morgan, *The Puritan Family: Religion and Domestic Relations in Seventeenth Century New England* (New York: Harper and Row, 1966), chapter 4.

38. *ET*, 269, 295, 365, 389, 392, 222.

39. *ET*, 222–223; see also Williams, *Key*, 95–96.

Chapter 2. "Prask That Was Wife to John Wompas"

1. This chapter's epigraph is from Trumbull Papers, *MHSC*, 9th ser., 5:118. Estimates of the number of Pequot dead vary, from Captain John Mason's claim of 600–700, to Captain John Underhill's of 400, and John Winthrop's of 300 (John W. De Forest, *History of the Indians of Connecticut from the Earliest Known Period to 1850* [Hartford: William James Hammersley, 1851], 133). Alfred Cave, whose *The Pequot War* provides the most comprehensive recent treatment of the war, thinks the true figure is closer to Mason's estimate (Amherst: University of Massachusetts Press, 1996, 151). I have estimated "over five hundred" residing at the fort based on these figures.

2. Cave, *Pequot War*, 59–60, 69, 136–148; *WP*, 3:177, 284–285; John Mason,

A Brief History of the Pequot War (Ann Arbor, University Microfilms, 1966 [Boston, 1736]), ix, 14; John Underhill, *Newes from America* (New York: Da Capo Press, 1971 [London, 1638]), 39.

Primary accounts of the war include those by John Mason and John Underhill; Lion Gardiner, *Relation of the Pequot Warres* (1660), *MHSC*, 3rd ser., 3:131–160; a primary account embedded in William Hubbard's *The History of the Indian Wars* (*HIW*, 2:5–38); and Philip Vincent, *A True Relation of the Late Battell Fought in New England* (Norwood, N.J.: Walter J. Johnson, 1974 [London, 1637]). Scholarly treatments of the war include Cave, *The Pequot War;* Laurence M. Hauptman and James D. Wherry, eds., *The Pequots in Southern New England: The Fall and Rise of an American Indian Nation* (Norman: University of Oklahoma Press, 1990); Adam J. Hirsch, "The Collision of Military Cultures in Seventeenth-Century New England," *JAH* 74, 4 (March 1988): 1187–1212; Ronald Dale Karr, "'Why Should You Be so Furious?': The Violence of the Pequot War," *JAH* 85, 3 (Dec. 1998): 876–909; Michael L. Fickes, "'They Could Not Endure that Yoke': The Captivity of Pequot Women and Children After the War of 1637," *NEQ* 73, 1 (2000): 58–81; Andrea Robertson Cremer, "Possession: Indian Bodies, Cultural Control, and Colonialism in the Pequot War," *Early American Studies* 6, 2 (Fall 2008): 295–345; Andrew Lipman, "'A Meanes to Knit Them Togeather': The Exchange of Body Parts in the Pequot War," *WMQ* 65, 1 (Jan. 2008): 3–28; and Katherine A. Grandjean, "The Long Wake of the Pequot War," *Early American Studies* 9, 2 (Spring 2011): 379–411.

3.   The estimated size of Sassacus's army that marched to Mystic Fort on the morning of the massacre comes from the work of archaeologist Kevin McBride and his colleagues at the Mashantucket Pequot Museum and Research Center ("Pequot War Interactive Timeline" [http://www.tiki -toki.com/timeline/entry/480305/The-Pequot-War-Era], accessed 2 December 2016).

4.   Mason, *Brief History*, 10–11. After the destruction of Mystic Fort, fighting continued for much of the day between the English (77, plus 250 Indian allies) and the Pequots (300–400). Kevin McBride and his colleagues estimate that over the course of the Mystic campaign, 150 Pequot soldiers and 400 noncombatants were killed, while two English soldiers were killed and forty or more wounded (Pequot War Interactive Timeline; "Battlefields of the Pequot War" [http://pequotwar.org], accessed 13 Aug. 2016; Michael Souza, "Battlefield Archaeology Sheds New Light on the Pequot War," *The Westerly Sun*, 13 March 2014, and Brian Hallenback, "Digging for the Truth About the Pequot War," *The Day*, 16 March 2014 [http://pequotwar.org/media-center/press-room], both articles accessed 13 Aug. 2016).

5.   *MCR*, 4, part 2:229–235. Captain John Mason claimed similarly that the Pequots "were ere while a TERROR to all that were round about them,

who resolved to Destroy all the ENGLISH and to Root their very Name out of this Country" (*Brief History*, 14).

6. Underhill, quoted in Cave, *Pequot War*, 153; David H. Dye, *War Paths, Peace Paths: An Archaeology of Cooperation and Conflict in Native Eastern North America* (New York: Alta Mira Press, 2009), 102; Underhill, *Newes*, 43.

    Daniel Richter notes that the pattern of adopting captives was practiced by most of the nations the Iroquois fought, including the Algonquians of New England (*Ordeal of the Longhouse: The Peoples of the Iroquois League in the Era of European Colonization* [Chapel Hill: University of North Carolina Press, 1992], 70, and chapters 2–4; see also Evan Haefeli and Kevin Sweeney, *Captors and Captives: The 1704 French and Indian Raid on Deerfield* [Amherst: University of Massachusetts Press, 2003], chapter 8). On adoption of captives among American Indians, see Daniel K. Richter, "War and Culture: The Iroquois Experience," *WMQ* 40 (Oct. 1983): 528–559; Jose Antonio Brandao, *Your Fyre Shall Burn No More: Iroquois Policy Toward New France and Its Native Allies to 1701* (Lincoln: University of Nebraska Press, 1997), chapters 3–4; James F. Brooks, *Captives and Cousins: Slavery, Kinship, and Community in the Southwest Borderlands* (Chapel Hill: University of North Carolina Press, 2002); and Pauline Turner Strong, "Transforming Outsiders: Captivity, Adoption, and Slavery Reconsidered," in *A Companion to American Indian History*, ed. Philip J. Deloria and Neal Salisbury (Malden, Mass.: Blackwell, 2002), 339–356.

7. Roger Williams (RW) to Sir Henry Vane and John Winthrop (JW), 15 May 1637, *WP*, 3:414. On Williams, see Edmund S. Morgan, *Roger Williams: The Church and the State* (New York: Harcourt, Brace & World, 1967); and Linford D. Fisher and Lucas Mason-Brown, "By 'Treachery and Seduction': Indian Baptism and Conversion in the Roger Williams Code," *WMQ* 71 (April 2014): 175–202; Cave, *Pequot War*, 135.

    Ronald Dale Karr argues that the Pequots' probing may have been an attempt to "establish a mutual understanding over the rules of warfare." Challenging Adam Hirsch's claim that the clash of English and Indian cultures combined to create a previously unknown level of violence in the Pequot War, Karr notes that in wars against Christian enemies, Europeans observed the laws of warfare that spared surrendering captives and civilians from violence. However, in wars against "illegitimate" foes—non-Christians, rebels, or heretics—there were no restraints on warfare. Thus, the violence of the Pequot War arose from English perceptions that the Pequots were illegitimate foes who needed to be brought into subjection to English authority (Karr, "'Why Should You Be so Furious?'; Hirsch, "The Collision of Military Cultures").

8. John W. De Forest summarizes estimates of the number killed at Mystic Fort in *History of the Indians*, 133; see also Cave, *The Pequot War*, 151; Underhill, *Newes*, 44; Mason, *Brief History*, 15.

9. *HIW*, 2:33. On Native hospitality, see *HColl*, 153; *ET*, 126; De Forest,

History of the Indians, 32; James Axtell, *The Invasion Within: The Contest of Cultures in Colonial North America* (New York: Oxford University Press, 1985), 166.

10. *HIW*, 2:31, 30, 33; RW to JW, 21 June 1637, *RWC*, 2:86; JW to William Bradford, 28 July 1637, *WP*, 3:456.

11. *MHSC*, 5th ser., 9:122, 130. On Native practices of polygamy and "wife lending," see William A. Starna, *From Homeland to New Land: A History of the Mahican Indians, 1600–1830* (Lincoln: University of Nebraska Press, 2013), 73; and Susanah Shaw Romney, *New Netherland Connections: Intimate Networks and Atlantic Ties in Seventeenth-Century America* (Chapel Hill: University of North Carolina Press, 2014), 138.

My estimate of Prask's age is based on several circumstances. First, Prask gave birth to a child in February 1664, so she was likely not much older than forty at that point, making thirteen the oldest she could have been at the time of the Swamp Fight in 1637. The fact that Prask remained living with the English after most other captives ran away suggests that the time she spent at Sasqua was insufficient to learn the local dialect and develop ties to Sasqua Indians. In addition, Sasqua Indians testified that Prask was five years old when her father brought her to Sasqua to live. It seems likely that they would have updated that age when speaking of her capture if she had been significantly older at that time. For these reasons, I believe Prask was not much older than five in 1637. On the possibility that Sasqua was Prask's ancestral home, see *MHSC*, 5th ser., 9:132.

12. JW to William Bradford, 20 May 1637, in William Bradford, *Of Plymouth Plantation, 1620–1647*, ed. Samuel Eliot Morison (New York: Alfred A. Knopf, 1952), 394; *JJW*, 221, 226–227; *HIW*, 2:19; *MCR*, 1:192, 195.

13. *HIW*, 2:35; Mason, *Brief History*, 16–18; JW to William Bradford, 28 July 1637, in *WP*, 3:456–457. On Stanton's qualifications as an interpreter, see Cave, *Pequot War*, 101; and Julie A. Fisher, "Speaking 'Indian' and English: The Bilinguals of Seventeenth-Century New England, 1636–1680," Ph.D. dissertation, University of Delaware, 2016.

14. Richter, "War and Culture"; Karr, "Why Should You Be so Furious?" 884–886; Fickes, "'They Could Not Endure,'" 61; *JJW*, 218–220, 225–227; *HIW*, 2:30.

15. Mason, *Brief History*, 17. My claim that Romanock escaped is based on the fact that he survived the Swamp Fight and lived at least until 1660 (*CCR* 3:282–283). Captured male combatants were killed following both major battles of the Pequot War, a fact that explains why male soldiers chose not to surrender. Hubbard claimed that only twenty to thirty Natives escaped from the swamp (*HIW*, 2:36).

16. The Pequot captives sent to the West Indies were intended for Bermuda but ended up on Providence Island, a Puritan colony, instead (Patrick Copeland to JW, 4 Dec. 1639, *WP* 4:157); *HIW*, 2:36–37; *PCR* 1:97; *JJW*, 227–228.

17. *HIW*, 2:21; Israel Stoughton to JW, 28 June 1637, *WP*, 3:435; Richard Davenport to Hugh Peter, 17 July 1637, *WP*, 3:453–454.

　　Within Native kinship systems, children who lost their parents could rely on other relatives and fellow tribe members as an extension of their natal family. Abenaki writer Joseph Bruchac explains that widespread Native American stories about wolves, who all "take part in feeding, watching over, and playing with the young," reinforce proper child-rearing: "That is how it should be in a human village, where no child should ever be without caring adults" (Joseph Bruchac, *Our Stories Remember: American Indian History, Culture, and Values Through Storytelling* [Golden, Colo.: Fulcrum, 2003], 159). Prask's unique circumstances—her recent arrival at Sasqua, her age at capture, her presumed inability to speak the local dialect, and the disruptions brought on by the war—probably interfered with this normal extension of care. On Native kinship systems, see Jay Miller, "Kinship, Family Kindreds, and Community," in *A Companion to American Indian History*, ed. Deloria and Salisbury; on the Mahican language, see Starna, *Homeland*, 74–76.

18. RW to JW, 10 July 1637, *WP*, 3:446–448; *JJW*, 218, 225–227; *WP*, 3:435, 450; *WP*, 4:157–159; *WP*, 5:164–165; *RWC*, 1:88–89, 117. On Pequot War captives escaping from the English, see Mason, *Brief History*, 17; *WP*, 3:509, 511–512; *RWC*, 1:168, 206. Rhode Islander William Harris declared of captives in King Philip's War a generation later: "Many are kept as servants and well treated in Rhode Island, but they will run away as soon as peace is concluded as in the Pequot war 40 years since" (William Harris to [Sir Joseph Williamson], 12 Aug. 1676, TNA, CO 1–37, no. 47).

　　The historiography of Indian slavery in North America, long neglected, has enjoyed a recent resurgence. For nearly a century, the standard work on the subject was Almon W. Lauber, *Indian Slavery in Colonial Times Within the Present Limits of the United States* (Columbia University Press, 1913). At the turn of the twenty-first century, James F. Brooks's *Captives and Cousins* and Alan Gallay's *The Indian Slave Trade: The Rise of the English Empire in the American South, 1670–1717* (New Haven, Conn.: Yale University Press, 2002) revitalized the field, followed by such works as Ned Blackhawk, *Violence over the Land: Indians and Empires in the Early American West* (Cambridge, Mass.: Harvard University Press, 2006); Juliana Barr, *Peace Came in the Form of a Woman: Indians and Spaniards in the Texas Borderlands* (Chapel Hill: University of North Carolina Press, 2007); Carl Ekberg, *Stealing Indian Women: Indian Slavery in the Illinois Country* (Champaign: University of Illinois Press, 2007); Pekka Hämäläinen, *The Comanche Empire* (New Haven, Conn.: Yale University Press, 2008); Alan Gallay, ed., *Indian Slavery in Colonial America* (Lincoln: University of Nebraska Press, 2009); Christina Snyder, *Slavery in Indian Country: The Changing Face of Captivity in Early America* (Cambridge, Mass.: Harvard

University Press, 2010); Brett Rushforth, *Bonds of Alliance: Indigenous and Atlantic Slavery in New France* (Chapel Hill: University of North Carolina Press, 2012); and Andrés Reséndez, *The Other Slavery: The Uncovered Story of Indian Enslavement in America* (Boston: Houghton Mifflin Harcourt, 2016). One important contribution of the most recent histories of Indian slavery is the argument that, while slavery existed in pre-contact Native societies, European involvement in the slave trade transformed it from a culturally based practice that functioned to replenish populations and strengthen alliances to a commodity-based trade that was destructive to alliances as well as to Native populations.

On New England Indian slavery, see Margaret Ellen Newell, *Brethren by Nature: New England Indians, Colonists, and the Origins of American Slavery* (Ithaca, N.Y.: Cornell University Press, 2015); and Wendy Warren, *New England Bound: Slavery and Colonization in Early America* (New York: Liveright, 2016). Shorter treatments of Indian slavery in New England include Ethel Boissevain, "Whatever Became of the New England Indians Shipped to Bermuda to Be Sold as Slaves," *Man in the Northeast* 11 (Spring 1981): 103–114; Fickes, "'They Could Not Endure,'" 58 81; chapter 6 of Jill Lepore, *The Name of War: King Philip's War and the Origins of American Identity* (New York: Alfred A. Knopf, 1998); Lipman, "'A Meanes to Knit Them Togeather'"; Michael Oberg, *Uncas: First of the Mohegans* (Ithaca, N.Y.: Cornell University Press, 2003), chapters 3 and 7; Linford D. Fisher, "'Dangerous Designes': The 1676 Barbados Act to Prohibit New England Indian Slave Importation," *WMQ* 71 (Jan. 2014): 99–121, and "'Why Shall Wee Have Peace to Bee Made Slaves': Indian Surrenderers During and After King Philip's War," *Ethnohistory* 64, 1 (2017): 65–90.

19. On the Massachusetts slavery law of 1641, see Newell, *Brethren by Nature*, 6; *CLM*, 53. On slavery in seventeenth-century New England, see Edmund S. Morgan, *The Puritan Family: Religion and Domestic Relations in Seventeenth Century New England* (New York: Harper and Row, 1966, chapter 5. On the post-seventeenth-century racial basis of slavery, see Kathleen Brown, "Beyond the Great Debates: Gender and Race in Early America," *Reviews in American History* 26, 1 (1998): 96–123; Joyce E. Chaplin, "Race," in *The British Atlantic World, 1500–1800*, ed. David Armitage and Michael J. Braddick (New York: Palgrave Macmillan, 2002); Carl H. Nightingale, "Before Race Mattered: Geographies of the Color Line in Early Colonial Madras and New York," *The American Historical Review* 113, 1 (Feb. 2008): 48–71; George Lee Haskins, *Law and Authority in Early Massachusetts: A Study in Tradition and Design* (New York: Macmillan, 1960), 124–129; Gallay, ed., *Indian Slavery*, 38.

20. "An Answer to the Propositions presented by the honored French Agent to the President and Commissioners for the English United Colonies [1651]," in Thomas Hutchinson, *The Hutchinson Papers*, 2 vols. (Albany,

N.Y.: Publications of the Prince Society, 1865), 1:271. The sermon delivered by the ministers in Hartford prior to Mason's expedition against the Pequots declared it a "just warre" (Edward Johnson, *Johnson's Wonder-Working Providence, 1628–1651*, ed. J. Franklin Jameson [New York: Barnes & Noble, 1952], 166). According to just war ideology, conquerors had "Just right" to the land of their foes by conquest (WFPT, 11 March 1657/58); Morgan, *Puritan Family*, 110–111; Newell, *Brethren by Nature*, 26–30; Captain Richard Morris to John Winthrop Jr., *WP*, 5:164–165; Hugo Grotius, *De Jure Belli ac Pacis* (1625), reprinted in London as *The Rights of War and Peace* (London, 1682): book 3, VII. See also Francisco de Vitoria, "On the Law of War," in Francisco de Vitoria, *Political Writings*, ed. and trans. Anthony Pagden and Jeremy Lawrance (New York: Cambridge University Press, 1991): 293–328. Colonial New English discussions of just war ideology appear in RW to the Massachusetts General Court, 5 Oct. 1654, in *RICR*, 1:295–296; *MCR*, 4, part 1: 141–144; *JJW*, 676–677. Scholarly discussions of just war ideology appear in Francis Jennings, *The Invasion of America: Indians, Colonialism, and the Cant of Conquest* (New York: W. W. Norton, 1976 [1975]), 4–6; Wilcomb E. Washburn, *Red Man's Land, White Man's Law: The Past and Present Status of the American Indian*, 2nd ed. (Norman: University of Oklahoma Press, 1995), 57; Lepore, *The Name of War*, 105–113; Olive Patricia Dickason, "Old World Law, New World Peoples, and Concepts of Sovereignty," in David B. Quinn et al., *Essays on the History of North American Discovery and Exploration: The Walter Prescott Webb Memorial Lectures*, ed. Stanley H. Palmer (College Station: Texas A&M University Press, 1988); Karr, "Why Should You Be so Furious?" 879–881; and Newell, *Brethren by Nature*, 26–31.

    Captives consigned to perpetual slavery could be bought and sold, as evidenced by Roger Williams's letter to Richard Callicot concerning two runaway children he had returned to him: "if you be minded to put either of them away [sell them], I desire to give you your desire: otherwise I wish you much Comfort in the keeping of them" (*WP*, 3:496).

21. *MCR*, 5:115, *CCR*, 2:351; *CLM*, 251–252; *MCR*, 5:136. While the Massachusetts General Court referred the issue of how to dispose of the "Indian squaws" to the Council, their decision is absent from the records (*MCR*, 1:201). For examples of term slavery—English and Indian—see *CLM*, xxix; *MCR*, 1:246, 5:25; *ECR*, 3:376; *RICR*, 2:549.

    On enslavement of Indians in King Philip's War, see Morgan, *Puritan Family*, 110–112; *MCR*, 5:136; *CLM*, 251–252; Fisher, "'Why shall wee have peace,'" 8, 12, 21. Margaret Newell argues that, in some cases, the status of King Philip's War slaves was passed on to their children (*Brethren by Nature*, 174).

22. RW to JW, ca. 21 June 1637, *WP*, 3:446–447. The Narragansett messenger's reluctance to speak reveals his superiors' diplomatic strategy of as-

certaining English wishes before declaring their own. In this way, they preserved the right to speak last, the traditional prerogative of one with superior status (Bragdon, *Native People*, 173–174). On killing male captives in the Pequot War, see Newell, *Brethren by Nature*, 31, 38; Strong, "Transforming Outsiders," 343.

23. RW to JW, 10 July 1637, *RWC*, 1:95; RW to JW, 15 July 1637, *RWC*, 1:101, 109; RW to JW, ca. 21 June 1637, *WP*, 3:446–447; RW to JW, 31 July 1637, *WP*, 3:459; RW to JW, 10 July 1638, *WP*, 3:459.

24. Patrick Copeland to JW, 4 Dec. 1639, *WP*, 4:157.

25. Fickes, "'They Could Not Endure,'" 65–68; Israel Stoughton to JW, ca. 28 June 1637, *WP*, 3:435. John Winthrop wrote in his journal that of eighty Pequot prisoners taken, forty-eight women and children were sent to Boston, "disposed of to particular persons in the country" (*JJW*, 225); RW to JW, 30 June 1637, *RWC*, 1:88–89. For other requests for captives, see Israel Stoughton to JW, ca. 28 June 1637, *WP*, 3:435; RW to JW, ca. 30 June 1637, *WP*, 3:436; Hugh Peter to JW, ca. 15 July 1637, *WP*, 3:450.

26. Eben Putnam, ed. and comp., *Lieutenant Joshua Hewes: A New England Pioneer and Some of His Descendants* (Privately printed, 1913), 19, 91–107; *MCR*, 1:192.

27. *CLM*, 91; Morgan, *Puritan Family*, 116–118; First Church of Roxbury Records, *RCBR*, 7 Aug. 1646. One captive, probably Cockenoe, joined the church in Dorchester (*ET*, 160).

 Ann Prask Wompas's "A," copied carefully by the Suffolk County Clerk, appears in *Suffolk Deeds* 5:540–543. In colonial New England, the skill of reading was almost universal, taught to boys and girls so that both could read the Bible. Writing was a separate skill, taught later if at all. The document containing Ann's initial "A" is connected to a deed and, like all such documents, is a copy rather than an original (originals would have been retained by the parties to the exchange). However, the clerk making this copy took care to reproduce the signatures and marks on this and other documents as they originally appeared. They are distinct from each other and from the clerk's own hand. The fact that Ann's "A" shows signs of writing practice suggests that her education went beyond the basic level of reading (Ross W. Beales Jr., "Literacy and Reading in Eighteenth-Century Westborough, Massachusetts," in *Early American Probate Inventories*, The Dublin Seminar for New England Folklife Annual Proceedings, 1987, ed. Peter Benes [Boston: Boston University Press, 1987], 41.)

28. *JJW*, 1:260–261, Feb. 1638; Constance A. Crosby, "The Algonkian Spiritual Landscape," in *Algonkians of New England: Past and Present*, The Dublin Seminar for New England Folklife Annual Proceedings, 1991, ed. Peter Benes (Boston University Press, 1993), 36.

29. RW to JW, 10 Nov. 1637, *RWC*, 1:131; *PCR*, 1:64; Morgan, *Puritan Family*, chapter 5.

30. RW to JW, 10 Nov. 1637, *WP*, 3:509; *JJW*, 1:225–226, 6 July 1637; RW
to JW, 31 July 1637, *WP*, 3:458–459; RW to JW, 12 Aug. 1637, *WP*,
3:479–480; RW to JW, *RWC*, 1:110. For inquiries about Reprieve, see
RW to JW, 26 Oct. 1637, *WP*, 3:502; RW to JW, 10 Nov. 1637, *WP*,
3:508; RW to JW, 20 Nov. 1637, *WP*, 3:511; RW to JW, 23 July 1638,
RWC, 1:168; RW to JW, 21 July 1640, *RWC*, 1:202; and RW to JW, 7
Aug. 1640, *RWC*, 1:206. For English demands for the return of runaways,
see RW to JW, 31 July 1637, *WP*, 3:459; RW to JW, 12 Aug. 1637, *WP*,
3:479–480; Israel Stoughton to the Governor and Council of Massachusetts,
14 Aug. 1637, *WP*, 3:480–482; RW to JW, 20 Aug. 1637, *WP*, 3:488; RW
to JW, 26 Oct. 1637, *WP*, 3:500; RW to JW, 10 Nov. 1637, *WP*, 3:508–
509; and RW to JW, 23 July 1638, *RWC*, 1:168–169. Margaret Newell
speculates that Narragansett claims that some runaways had died may
have been "a ruse to foil their recapture" (*Brethren by Nature*, 104).

31. On continuing efforts to retrieve runaways, see *JJW*, 225–226; RW to
JW, 10 July 1637, *WP*, 3:446–448; RW to JW, ca. 12 Aug. 1637, *RWC*,
1:110; RW to JW, 20 Aug. 1637, *RWC*, 1:113–115 (note); RW to JW, 10
Jan. 1637/8, *WP*, 4:6–7; RW to JW, ca. 1 Aug. 1638, *WP*, 4:48–50; RW to
JW, 30 Dec. 1648, *WP*, 4:88; RW to JW, 21 July 1640, *WP*, 4:269; RW
to JW, 7 Aug. 1640, *WP*, 4:273.

　　　On the decision to allow Pequots to continue living with the Mohegans and Narragansetts, see RW to JW, 14 June 1638, *RWC*, 1:164. *PCR*,
9:97–101; *PCR*, 10:134. Nathaniel Morton, writing in 1664, summarized
the situation: "The Pequots have since been taken under the immediate
government of the English colonies, and live in their own country, being
governed by such of their own, as are by the English substituted and appointed for that purpose" ("New England's Memorial," in *Chronicles of the
Pilgrim Fathers*, ed. John Masefield [New York: E. P. Dutton, 1936], 133).
See also Kevin A. McBride, "The Historical Archaeology of the Mashantucket Pequots, 1637–1900: A Preliminary Analysis," and Jack Campisi,
"The Emergence of the Mashantucket Pequot Tribe, 1637–1975," in *The
Pequots in Southern New England*, ed. Hauptman and Wherry. On Cassacinamon's role in the survival of the Pequots as a nation, see Kevin A.
McBride, "The Legacy of Robin Cassacinamon: Mashantucket Pequot
Leadership in the Historic Period," in *Northeastern Indian Lives, 1632–
1816*, ed. Robert S. Grumet (Amherst: University of Massachusetts Press,
1996).

32. First Church of Roxbury Records, *RCBR*, August 6–7, 1646; *WP*, 3:450;
Joseph Barlow Felt, *A Memoir, or Defence of Hugh Peters* (Boston, 1851),
16–17; *WP*, 5:164–165; *PCR*, 1:64; *RWC*, 1:117; *ET*, 160; William Wallace Tooker, *John Eliot's First Indian Teacher and Interpreter, Cockenoe-
de-Long Island, And the Story of His Career from the Early Records* (New
York: Francis P. Harper, 1896), 16–17.

33. AWP. On Stockholm Syndrome, see James T. Turner, "Factors Influenc-

ing the Development of the Hostage Identification Syndrome," *Political Psychology* 6, 4 (1985): 705–711; *PCR*, 10:167.

Chapter 3. "To Bee Trained Up Among the English"

1. This chapter's epigraphs come from *ET*, 95 and 373. William Wood, *New England's Prospect* (1634), ed. Alden T. Vaughan (Amherst: University of Massachusetts Press, 1977), 58; Charles M. Ellis, *The History of Roxbury Town* (Boston: Samuel G. Drake, 1847), 143.

2. John Eliot was called the "apostle to the Indians" in his own lifetime by his ministerial colleagues Thomas Thorowgood and Richard Baxter (N. H. Keeble and G. Nuttall, eds., *Calendar of the Correspondence of Richard Baxter*, 2 vols. [Oxford: Oxford University Press, 1991], 2: #793; Linford D. Fisher and Lucas Mason-Brown, "By 'Treachery and Seduction': Indian Baptism and Conversion in the Roger Williams Code," *WMQ* 71, 2 [April 2014], n. 13). Later writers adopted the phrase, which has become almost inseparable from his name. See, for example, Samuel Eliot Morison, "John Eliot, Apostle to the Indians," in *Builders of the Bay Colony* (Boston: Houghton Mifflin, 1958); Ola E. Winslow, *John Eliot: "Apostle to the Indians"* (Boston: Houghton Mifflin, 1968); see also E. Jennifer Monaghan, *Learning to Read and Write in Colonial Massachusetts* (Amherst: University of Massachusetts Press, 2005), 49.

3. On Eliot's belief that civility must precede conversion, see Richard W. Cogley, *John Eliot's Mission to the Indians Before King Philip's War* (Cambridge, Mass.: Harvard University Press, 1999), 6–7, 107. Recent scholars have devoted considerable attention to the subject of Native literacy and its impact—positive and negative—on Native peoples. See, for example, Margaret Connell Szasz, *Indian Education in the American Colonies, 1607–1783* (Albuquerque: University of New Mexico Press, 1988); Bernd C. Peyer, *The Tutor'd Mind: Indian Missionary-Writers in Antebellum America* (Amherst: University of Massachusetts Press, 1997); Hilary E. Wyss, *Writing Indians: Literacy, Christianity, and Native Community in Early America* (Amherst: University of Massachusetts Press, 2000); Monaghan, *Learning to Read*; Jill Lepore, "Dead Men Tell No Tales: John Sassamon and the Fatal Consequences of Literacy," *American Quarterly* 46, 4 (Dec. 1994): 479–512; Kristina Bross, *Dry Bones and Indian Sermons: Praying Indians in Colonial America* (Ithaca, N.Y.: Cornell University Press, 2004). In addition, scholars have explored the concept of Native *literacies*, different ways Native peoples have interacted with and understood the written word in the context of their own traditions of knowledge and meaning. See Lisa Brooks, *The Common Pot: The Recovery of Native Space in the Northeast* (Minneapolis: University of Minnesota Press, 2008); Hilary E. Wyss, *English Letters and Indian Literacies: Reading, Writing, and New England Missionary Schools, 1750–1830* (Philadelphia: University of Penn-

sylvania Press, 2012); Kristina Bross and Hilary E. Wyss, eds., *Early Native Literacies in New England: A Documentary and Critical Anthology* (Amherst: University of Massachusetts Press, 2008); Jace Weaver, *American Indian Literary Nationalism* (Albuquerque: University of New Mexico Press, 2006); Drew Lopenzina, *Red Ink: Native Americans Picking Up the Pen in the Colonial Period* (Albany: State University of New York Press, 2013); Birgit Brander Rasmussen, *Queequeg's Coffin: Indigenous Literacies and Early American Literature* (Durham, N.C.: Duke University Press, 2012); and John Demos, *The Heathen School: A Story of Hope and Betrayal in the Age of the Early Republic* (New York: Vintage, 2014).

   "A Letter from New-England, from Mr. Eliot, preacher of the Word there, of the glorious progresse of the Gospell among the Heathen there," YIPP. The Records of the United Colonies Commissioners contain examples of efforts to instill English skills as well as education in Native youth and adults. For instance, in September 1662 Daniel Gookin requested and received ten pounds to teach spinning "or other manifactury" to Natick Indians (*PCR* 10: 280).

4. Accounts of the founding of Natick appear in *ET,* 11, 15–16, 303–305; and *HColl,* 180–184; *MCR,* 4, part 1:75. John Eliot wrote that "Civil Government" began at Natick in 1650 (*ET,* 402). *ET,* 224–226.

5. Peter Benes, *Meetinghouses of Early New England* (Amherst: University of Massachusetts Press, 2012), 34–38. On the process of gathering a church in seventeenth-century New England, see David D. Hall, *The Faithful Shepherd: A History of the New England Ministry in the Seventeenth Century* (Chapel Hill: University of North Carolina Press, 1972), 79–118; Charles Lloyd Cohen, *God's Caress: The Psychology of Puritan Religious Experience* (New York: Oxford University Press, 1986); Edmund S. Morgan, *Visible Saints: The History of a Puritan Idea* (Ithaca, N.Y.: Cornell University Press, 1965).

6. *ET,* 303. The Natick Church was finally gathered in 1660 (Cogley, *John Eliot's Mission,* chapter 5, 137; *ET,* 305). Dane Morrison argues that the failure of the Natick Church to be approved on its first attempt is evidence of English racism (*A Praying People: Massachusett Acculturation and the Failure of the Puritan Mission, 1600–1690* [New York: Peter Lang, 1995], 99–119). Strictness was not limited to Native converts, however. Dorchester also failed to receive approval at its first attempt to gather a church, and the founders of New Haven took a year to scrutinize prospective members before gathering a church in 1639 (*ET,* 42, note 43; Stephen Foster, *The Long Argument: English Puritanism and the Shaping of New England Culture, 1570–1700* [Chapel Hill: University of North Carolina Press, 1991], 157).

7. Examples of Eliot counseling with Heath appear in *ET,* 204, 304–308.

8. Quoted in Jean M. O'Brien, *Dispossession by Degrees: Indian Land and Identity in Natick, Massachusetts, 1650–1790* (Lincoln: University of Nebraska

Press, 2003 [1997]), 34. On conflict between Dedham and Natick, see O'Brien, *Dispossession*, 31–42; and *The Early Records of the Town of Dedham, Massachusetts, 1659–1673* (Dedham, Mass., 1894), 4: appendix; *ET*, 305, 379.

9. Natick's schoolmaster Monequasson confessed that when he was called "to make a Church at *Natick*, I loved *Cohannet*" (*ET*, 275, 304). Cogley, *John Eliot's Mission*, 118, 259; Szasz, *Indian Education*, 113–114.

10. *ET*, 14, 306.

11. *ET*, 306; Roger Williams, *A Key into the Language of America* (1643) (Bedford, Mass.: Applewood), 29–30. For English perceptions of Native child-rearing, see Sydney V. James Jr., ed., *Three Visitors to Early Plymouth: Letters About the Pilgrim Settlement in New England During Its First Seven Years* (Plymouth, Mass.: Plimoth Plantation, 1963), 17; *HColl*, 149, 182; Karen Ordahl Kupperman, *Indians and English: Facing Off in Early America* (Ithaca, N.Y.: Cornell University Press, 2000), 153–155. Massachusetts leaders' warnings against "sinfull indulgence in family goverment" reflected the ideal, not the actuality. The failure of the English to adhere to the ideal is one of the chief reasons Eliot and others gave for separating Indians into "praying towns" where they could be away from evil influences, Indian and English (*MCR*, 4, part 2:34–27; *ET*, 40, note 24).

12. *ET*, 304–308. This punishment—public humiliation and lashing—was also meted out to English colonists convicted of repeated drunkenness, although they could pay a fine instead of being whipped. Paying a fine does not seem to have been an option in the case of Totherswamp's son (*CLM*, 82). My thanks to Julie Fisher for pointing out parallel English punishments for drunkenness.

13. *ET*, 307.

14. *ET*, 306.

15. JWJ to Robert Boyle, 25 Sept. 1664, WFPT. Daniel Gookin called for placing as many Indian children as servants in English families as possible. Girls would be trained in "good housewifery of all sort," and boys would be taught their master's trade. Both boys and girls would also be taught to read and write in English, at the charge of their masters (*HColl*, 235). Indian parents' reluctance to turn their children over for English child-rearing prevented the realization of Gookin's plan. Jean M. O'Brien argues that Indian adoption of English culture was "selective . . . in order to resist their complete effacement by an aggressive and expansive English presence" ("'Our Old and Valluable Liberty': A Natick Indian Petition in Defense of Their Fishing Rights, 1748," in *Early Native Literacies*, ed. Bross and Wyss, 125).

16. *ET*, 95; Cogley, *John Eliot's Mission*, 118, 259; Szasz, *Indian Education*, 113–114; *ET*, 256. John Endecott reported in 1651 that Monequasson wrote in English "true and very legibl[y]," and John Wilson wrote the same year that the Indian schoolmaster at Natick "doth read and spell

very well" (Cogley, *John Eliot's Mission*, 118; *ET*, 231). The United Colonies records for 1656 noted that Daniel Weld was paid for teaching nine Indian youths, eight boys and one girl (*PCR*, 10:167). See also *ET*, 365, 373. Ellis, *History of Roxbury*, 136, 30.

17. *ET*, 95, 364–365. On Indians and guns, see David J. Silverman, *Thundersticks: Firearms and the Violent Transformation of Native America* (Cambridge, Mass.: Harvard University Press, 2016).

18. Williams, *Key into the Language*, 53. Richard A. Bailey claimed that English people "imagined the essential spiritual natures of their red and black neighbors as inferior to their own," drawing from such evidence as John Eliot condemning the "diabolical" actions of unbelieving Indians, and other English referring to Indians as "beasts." But such arguments fail to acknowledge that these terms were applied equally to unbelieving or disobedient English people and that the terms described people's actions, not their essential natures (*Race and Redemption in Puritan New England* [New York: Oxford University Press, 2011], 49, 72). This is not to say that English people were not racist in their attitudes toward Indians, only that linguistic evidence for that racism is problematic. *ET*, 364–365.

19. John Dane, *A Declaration of Remarkable Providences in the Course of my Life. By John Dane, of Ipswich* (1682) (Boston, 1854), 12. On colonial responses to Indian "nakedness," a term the English used for Indians wearing loincloths, aprons, and mantles, see Williams, *Key into the Language*, 118–119; Kupperman, *Indians and English*, 48–53; and Robert F. Berkhofer Jr., *The White Man's Indian: Images of the American Indian from Columbus to the Present* (New York: Knopf, 1978), 7. Colony records and contemporary writings are rife with examples of Indians being charged with "insolence." See *MCR*, 4, part 2:233; *MAC*, 30: 208a; *PCR*, 9:3–6, 71; *HIW*, 2:40, 98, 161, 182. On English expectations of deferential language and behavior toward social superiors, see Jane Kamensky, *Governing the Tongue: The Politics of Speech in Early New England* (New York: Oxford University Press, 1997), 7–8, 18–19, 64–65; Ellis, *History of Roxbury*, 21.

20. Oliver N. Bacon, *A History of Natick* (Boston: Damrell and Moore, 1856), 13–14. Indians also applied the phrase "poor Indians" to themselves, suggesting that they heard it often (*PCR*, 5:66). On "pity" for the Indians' status as non-Christians, see Jacqueline M. Henkel, "Represented Authenticity: Native Voices in Seventeenth-Century Conversion Narratives," *NEQ* 87 (March 2014), 26; Laura Stevens, *The Poor Indians: British Missionaries, Native Americans, and Colonial Sensibility* (Philadelphia: University of Pennsylvania Press, 2004); and Cogley, *John Eliot's Mission*, 247; *HColl*, 147.

21. *SGen* (Heath); J. Wingate Thornton, *Lives of Isaac Heath, and John Bowles* (Roxbury, Mass.: [s.n.], 1850); Ellis, *History of Roxbury*, 17. At Isaac Heath's death in 1660, his estate was valued at 671 pounds (*Suffolk County*

Wills: Abstracts of the Earliest Wills upon Record in the County of Suffolk, Massachusetts [Baltimore: Genealogical Publishing, 1984], 184–185); *ET*, 223.

22. On the strictness of New England child-rearing, see Edmund S. Morgan, *The Puritan Family: Religion and Domestic Relations in Seventeenth Century New England* (New York: Harper and Row, 1966), chapters 3–4; John Demos, *A Little Commonwealth: Family Life in Plymouth Colony* (New York: Oxford University Press, 1970), chapters 4–5, 9; Karin Calvert, *Children in the House: The Material Culture of Early Childhood, 1600–1900* (Boston: Northeastern University Press, 1992), chapters 1–2. On family government, see Roger Thompson, *Sex in Middlesex: Popular Mores in a Massachusetts County, 1649–1699* (Amherst: University of Massachusetts Press, 1986), preface; James, ed., *Three Visitors*, 17; *HColl*, 149, 182; Williams, *Key into the Language*, 29–30; Kupperman, *Indians and English*, 153–155.

23. Charles Hambrick-Stowe, *The Practice of Piety: Puritan Devotional Disciplines in Seventeenth-Century New England* (Chapel Hill: University of North Carolina Press, 1982), xv, 143–150; Morgan, *Puritan Family*, chapter 4; James Axtell, *The School upon a Hill: Education and Society in Colonial New England* (New Haven, Conn.: Yale University Press, 1974), 23. Eliot also composed a catechism specifically for the children of Natick which was in use in manuscript form in 1651 and in print by 1654. There is no evidence that Isaac or Elizabeth Heath could read or speak the Massachusett language, so it is unlikely they used that catechism (*ET*, 225; *PCR*, 10:123); Cogley, *John Eliot's Mission*, appendix 5; Axtell, *School upon a Hill*, 37–44, 174; Rev. John Eliot's Records, *RCBR*, 6 December 1674.

24. Hambrick-Stowe, *The Practice of Piety*, 99; Benes, *Meetinghouses*, 2, 29, 64; Morgan, *Puritan Family*, 102; Ola Elizabeth Winslow, *Meetinghouse Hill, 1630–1783* (New York: W. W. Norton, 1972 [1952]), 145; Alice Morse Earle, *The Sabbath in Puritan New England*, 5th ed. (New York: Charles Scribner's Sons, 1892), chapter 5; John Winthrop Platner, "The Congregationalists," in *The Religious History of New England* (Cambridge, Mass.: Harvard University Press, 1917), 23; *PCR*, 10:165, 207.

25. Monaghan, *Learning to Read*, 29; *PCR*, 10:138, 140.

26. Eben Putnam, ed. and comp., *Lieutenant Joshua Hewes: A New England Pioneer and Some of His Descendants* (Privately printed, 1913), 44–45; John Langdon Sibley, *Biographical Sketches of Graduates of Harvard University* (Cambridge, Mass.: Charles William Sever, 1873), 1:11; Monaghan, *Learning to Read*, 39; John W. Ford, ed., *Some Correspondence Between the Governors and Treasurers of the New England Company* (London: Spottiswoode, 1896), 14.

27. Axtell, *School upon a Hill*, 171–173; *PCR*, 10:167. Waban's son apparently attended school in Dedham in the early 1640s, before Eliot began preaching to the Indians, but all the Indians who later attended English schools seem to have done so in Roxbury or Cambridge (*ET*, 83). *MHSC*, 5th ser., 1:409; Szasz, *Indian Education*, 126; Samuel Eliot Morison, *Harvard Col-*

lege in the Seventeenth Century (Cambridge, Mass.: Harvard University Press, 1936), 1:353; Daniel Weld to John Winthrop Jr., 4 Oct. 1665, WFPT. Weld, who was teaching Roxbury's grammar school by 1652, probably earned twenty-two pounds per year as a base salary, like the schoolmaster teaching immediately before him (Charles Knapp Dillaway, *A History of the Grammar school, or, "The free schools of 1645 in Roxburie"* [Roxbury, 1860], 8, 27).

28. Monaghan, *Learning to Read*, 39–44. On female teachers of "dame schools," see *ET*, 187; *The Diary of Samuel Sewall, 1674–1729*, ed. M. Halsey Thomas (New York: Farrar, Straus and Giroux, 1973), 1:164; Axtell, *School upon a Hill*, 175; Morgan, *Puritan Family*, 101.

29. Morison, *Harvard College in the Seventeenth Century*, 1:353–354. Szasz claims there were forty Indian students over the whole period (*Indian Education*, 126). David Adams Wallace, *Education for Extinction: American Indians and the Boarding School Experience, 1875–1928* (Lawrence: University Press of Kansas, 1995).

30. Rev. John Eliot's Records, *RCBR*, 1645, 1647, 1649, 1659, 1660, 21 Jan. 1660/61; Thornton, *Lives*, 93.

31. *ET*, 396, 67; *PCR*, 10:190; Szasz, *Indian Education*, 126.

32. *HColl*, 172–173. On apprenticeships, see Morgan, *Puritan Family*, 68–78, 120–122; Axtell, *School upon a Hill*, 113–119; Daniel Vickers with Vince Walsh, *Young Men and the Sea: Yankee Seafarers in the Age of Sail* (New Haven, Conn.: Yale University Press, 2005), 106. For a comparison with maritime apprenticeship in England, see *Barlow's Journal of His Life at Sea in King's Ships, East & West Indianmen & Other Merchantmen from 1659 to 1703*, tr. Basil Lubbock (London: Hurst & Blackett, 1934), 1:15, 18, 37.

33. *PCR*, 10:244–245, 251, 280, 310–311, 397–398. On wages for seventeenth-century English laborers, see Gloria L. Main, "Gender, Work, and Wages in Colonial New England," *WMQ* 41, 1 (Jan. 1994), 51–60.

34. For complaints to the Crown against Massachusetts, see *CSPC*, 5: #16–18, 33, 45, 49–51, 53, 64, 78, 89–90, 519, 548, 929. *MCR*, 4, part 2:158–164, 34.

35. *MCR*, 4, part 2:25; George Cartwright to Samuel Gorton, 26 May 1665, *CSPC*, 5: #999; Robert Carr, George Cartwright, and Samuel Maverick to Sec. Lord Arlington, 27 May 1665, *CSPC*, 5: #1000.

36. *MCR*, 4, part 2:159, 182, 187. On the Narragansett submission to the Crown, see Jenny Hale Pulsipher, *Subjects unto the Same King: Indians, English, and the Contest of Authority in Colonial New England* (Philadelphia: University of Pennsylvania Press, 2005), 55–59.

37. The Governor and Council of the Massachusetts to the Chief Saggamakers of the Mohawk Indians, Boston, 9 Sept. 1665, CO 1/19, no. 104, TNA.

38. *CSPC*, 5: #1000, 1103, 1197; *RWC*, 2:577–579, note 4; William Leete and Robert Chapman to the Governor and Assistants of Connecticut, 30

June 1665, *MHSC*, 4th ser., 7:556; James Noyes to JWJ, 1 Jan. 1666/67, WFPT; MAC, 30:131–132, 72, 73, 275a; Jeremy Dupertuis Bangs, *Indian Deeds: Land Transactions in Plymouth Colony, 1620–1691* (Boston: NEHGS, 2002), 314–316. On the petitions of Josias Wampatuck, John Wompas, and Richard Thayer, see MAC, 30:131–132; PJW1; PJW2; MAC, 3:34–35; and chapters 8–9 in this book.

39. SCF, #516, 16 Oct. 1662.
40. *MCR*, 2:195–197; "A Declaration of the Generall Court of his Majesties Colony in the Massachuse[tts]," CO 1/19, no. 62, TNA.
41. *MCR*, 4, part 2:210–211.
42. Samuel Eliot Morison, *The Founding of Harvard College* (Cambridge, Mass.: Harvard University Press, 1935), 415; Christina J. Hodge, "'A Small Brick Pile for the Indians': The 1655 Harvard Indian College as Setting," in *Archaeologies of Mobility and Movement*, ed. M. C. Beaudry and T. G. Parno (New York: Springer Science + Business Media, 2013), 217–236; Dick Hoefnagel, "The Dartmouth Copy of John Eliot's Indian Bible (1639): Its Provenance," *Dartmouth College Library Bulletin*, April 1993 (http://www.dartmouth.edu/~library/Library_Bulletin/Apr1993/LB-A93-Hoefnagel.html?mswitch-redir=classic), accessed 11 Aug. 2016.

Archaeological digs in Harvard Yard have been taking place regularly since 2005. The 2009 and 2011 digs uncovered the foundation trench of the Indian College and found several pieces of lead printing type from the press (Peabody Museum of Archaeology and Ethnology, "Digging Veritas" [http://www.peabody.harvard.edu/DV-online], accessed 12 Feb. 2016). For links to published articles on the digs at Harvard Yard, see Peabody Museum of Archaeology and Ethnology, "Research and Teaching Resources" (https://www.peabody.harvard.edu/node/309), accessed 11 Aug. 2016.

43. *ET*, 11; Morison, *Harvard College*, 1:342–343; *ET*, 353, 396; Robert Boyle to John Winthrop Jr., 21 April 1664, in *Proceedings of the Massachusetts Historical Society* (1862), 5:376–377.
44. PCR, 10:128–129, 228, 252, 265, 289; quoted in Morison, *Harvard College*, 1:342, 358.
45. Morison, *Harvard College*, 1:353–354, 356, note 2; Szasz, *Indian Education*, 126, 114; HColl, 172; *ET*, 21; Ford, ed., *Some Correspondence*, 27–31.
46. *ET*, 353, 396; Morison, *Harvard College*, 1:169.
47. HColl, 173; Ford, ed., *Some Correspondence*, 9, 14.
48. Sibley, *Biographical Sketches*, vol. 2 (1668); Morison, *Harvard College*, 1:14–15, 44–46, 329, 359; Ford, ed., *Some Correspondence*, 14.
49. Morison, *Harvard College*, 1:94–100, 48.
50. Morison, *Harvard College*, 1:91.
51. Morison, *Harvard College*, 1:100; Axtell, *School upon a Hill*, 219. The buttery was the place where "butts" of beer were stored; it also stored other food supplies, including those that parents sent as payment in kind (Mor-

ison, *Harvard College*, 1:58, 90). For a sociocultural analysis of the buttery based on recent archaeological digs in Harvard Yard, see Christina J. Hodge, "Consumerism and Control: Archaeological Perspectives on the Harvard College Buttery," *Northeast Historical Archaeology* 42 (2013): 54–74.

52. Morison, *Founding*, 252, chapter 20, 281; Morison, *Harvard College*, 1:49, 46, 85.

53. Morison, *Harvard College*, 1:58.

54. Short biographies of Gookin, Gerrish, and Treat appear in Sibley, *Biographical Sketches*, vol. 3; Morison, *Founding*, 248; Ford, ed., *Some Correspondence*, 34; Samuel Eliot Morison, *Builders of the Bay Colony* (Boston: Houghton Mifflin, 1958), 289. Daniel Gookin acknowledged—and demonstrated—the prejudice that kept English ministers from willingly serving among Indian Christians, "by reason of the poverty and barbarity, which cannot be grappled with, unless the person be very much mortified, self denying, and of a publick spirit, seeking greatly God's glory; and these are rare qualifications in young men" (*HColl*, 183).

55. Southern New England Algonquian (SNEA) languages include Massachusett, Narragansett, Nipmuc, Mohegan-Pequot-Montauk, and Quiripi. Algonquian linguist Ives Goddard states that similarities among geographically contiguous Eastern Algonquian languages would have made "partial bilingualism easy" ("Eastern Algonquian Languages," in *Northeast*, ed. Bruce Trigger, vol. 15 of *Handbook of North American Indians* [Washington, D.C.: Smithsonian Institution, 1978], 70).

   More properly, the Wôpanâak or Wompanoag language is written as *Wôpanâôt8âôk* (Jessie Little Doe Baird, telephone interview and email message, 29 July 2016 and 11 August 2016). In 1993 Jessie Little Doe Baird, a MacArthur Fellowship–winning linguist, co-founded the Wôpanâak Language Reclamation Project (http://www.wlrp.org/project-history.html, accessed 11 August 2016). On her ongoing work, see Jessie Little Doe Baird, "How Did this Happen to My Language?" in *Bringing our Languages Home: Language Revitalization for Families*, ed. Leanne Hinton (Berkeley, Calif.: Heyday, 2013); Rucha Chitnis, "From Extinction to Existence: The Wôpanâak Language," *Cultural Survival Quarterly*, 14 January 2016 (https://www.culturalsurvival.org/news/extinction-existence-wopanaak-language), accessed 10 August 2016; and Kathleen Burkhalter, "Three Stories About the Wamponoag People," a Harvard Journalism Capstone Project, 2012 (https://medium.com/@mizkathleen/three-stories-about-the-wampanoag-people-20d7df96081b#.sncfizpj4), accessed 31 May 2016. I thank Jessie Little Doe Baird for helping me understand some of the distinctions between Algonquian languages, including Nipmuc and Massachusett; and Thomas Doughton, a Nipmuc descendant and historian, for speaking with me about his research on the Nipmuc Indians. Doughton disputes whether the language being reclaimed by modern Nipmuc descendants is actually Nipmuc, because it is based on a Loup A manuscript that is not incontrovertibly connected to Nipmuc people. In addition, he believes the lack of documented political acts by a recognizable Nipmuc paramount sachem in the historical period suggests that English colonists may have mislabeled Hassanamesit and Natick Indians as Nipmuc when they were actually inland Massachusett Indians. The term Nipmuc, he believes, should properly apply only to those Natives living on the west side of the Blackstone (Nipmuc) River (Thomas Doughton, interview by author, Worcester, Mass., 28 July 2016). For Nipmuc language reclamation efforts, see http://www.nipmuclanguage.org/, accessed 3 March 2017.

Scholarly works on the Eastern Algonquian languages include Jessie Little Doe Fermino, *An Introduction to Wampanoag Grammar*, M.S. thesis, Massachusetts Institute of Technology (MIT), 2000; Ives Goddard, "Eastern Algonquian Languages," in *Northeast*, ed. Trigger, 70–77; Ives Goddard and Kathleen J. Bragdon, eds., *Native Writings in Massachusett* (Philadelphia: American Philosophical Society, 1989); and David J. Costa, "The Dialectology of Southern New England Algonquian," in *Papers of the 38th Algonquian Conference* (2007), 81–127. "Some Unpublished Correspondence of the Rev. Richard Baxter and the Rev. John Eliot, 'The Apostle to the American Indians,' 1656–1682," *Bulletin of the John Rylands Library* 15 (1931): 454.

56. "Some Unpublished Correspondence," 454. John Wompas traveled through Massachusetts and Connecticut colonies as far as Manhattan Island in New York Colony; such travel would have been aided by familiarity with other Algonquian dialects than Nipmuc. United Colonies Commissioners to Edward Winslow, 24 Sept. 1653, in Ebenezer Hazard, *Historical Collections* (Philadelphia: T Dobson [for the Author], 1792), 2:299.

57. Ford, ed., *Some Correspondence*, 9.

58. Patrick Griffin, *American Leviathan: Empire, Nation, and Revolutionary Frontier* (New York: Hill and Wang, 2007), 43–49; *ET*, 86.

59. A search of the database *Early English Books Online* from 1600–1700 showed fifteen printed works containing both "Indian" and "savage." In all but three of the fifteen sources, the terms were used together—"Indian savage" or "savage Indian"—as if they were one term, suggesting that savagery and Indian identity were inseparable in the minds of these writers. Examples of colonial English attitudes toward Indians appear in *RWC*, 2:693, 704, 708; *RICR*, 2:132–138; and *ET*, 104. See also Ronald Takaki, "The Tempest in the Wilderness: The Racialization of Savagery," *JAH* 79 (Dec. 1992): 892–912; Neal Salisbury, ed., *The Sovereignty and Goodness of God, by Mary Rowlandson, with Related Documents* (Boston: Bedford, 1997), 3–4; Roy Harvey Pearce, *Savagism and Civilization: A Study of the Indian and the American Mind* (Baltimore: Johns Hopkins Press, 1953 [reprinted 1965]); Richard Slotkin, *Regeneration Through Violence: The My-*

thology of the American Frontier, 1600–1860 (Middletown, Conn.: Wesleyan University Press, 1973).

60. This copy of Cicero's *De Officiis* is held at the MHS. Morison describes the sketch and the title page in Morison, *Harvard College*, 1:356. Albert Matthews discusses the signature of another Native scholar, Joel Hiacoomes, in "Comenius and Harvard College," *Publications of the Colonial Society of Massachusetts, Transactions*, 21:186. Samuel Eliot Morison speculated that a classmate wrote the caption on the sketch as a joke (*Harvard College*, 1:356). After comparing John Wompas's signature on the title page of *De Officiis* with the writing on the facing page and elsewhere in the book, I believe that the caption accompanying the drawing was written by Wompas himself.

   Morison, *Harvard College*, 1:48. For the location of the Cambridge meetinghouse and other public sites, see Lucius Robinson Paige, *History of Cambridge, Massachusetts, 1630–1877* (Boston: H.O. Houghton, 1877); Marian Card Donnelly, *The New England Meeting Houses of the Seventeenth Century* (Middletown, Conn.: Wesleyan University Press, 1968), 45; Morison, *Harvard College*, 1:48; Benes, *Meetinghouses of Early New England;* Ellis, *History of Roxbury*, 28. For more on the structure and social hierarchy of New England churches, see Ola E. Winslow, *Meetinghouse Hill, 1630–1783* (New York: Macmillan, 1952); and Hall, *Faithful Shepherd*. Daniel Gookin noted that, at the founding of Natick, about one hundred Indians gathered and selected rulers according to the Old Testament pattern Eliot suggested. Because they chose only one ruler over a hundred, two over fifty, and ten over ten, there must have been approximately one hundred people in the community at that time (*HColl*, 180–181). Gookin describes wigwams as large as one hundred feet long and thirty feet wide (*HColl*, 150); *ET*, 268.

   Ministers' salaries in New England were determined by individual congregations and ranged from about forty to over one hundred pounds per year. Watertown records indicate that their minister was paid 120 pounds per year in 1654, while their schoolmaster was paid thirty pounds per year (*Watertown Records* [Watertown, Mass.: Press of Fred G. Barker, 1891], 2:35–37). The New England Company paid John Eliot and Thomas Mayhew fifty pounds per year for their work with the Christian Indians. English assistants in the work, such as Peter Folger and Richard Bourne, received twenty to thirty pounds per year; Daniel Gookin, the Indian superintendent responsible for holding court among the Indians twice yearly, received fifteen to twenty pounds per year. Indian rulers, appointed to govern the praying towns, received twenty pounds per year. Indian teachers who preached to their fellow Indians received five to ten pounds per year, as did Indian schoolmasters and interpreters, including Sassamon, Monequason, Job, and Hiacoomes. English schoolmasters employed to teach Indians received twenty pounds per year (*PCR*, 9:163, 167, 189–190, 205–207, 296–297, 317, 330, 356).

61. My thanks to Glen Cooper for this translation.
62. Joseph Browne was the only fellow commoner at Harvard during John Wompas's years there. Fellow commoners were students whose parents paid double fees (Morison, *Harvard College*, 1:63). Thus, he took precedence over every other undergraduate, sitting at the fellows' table for meals even when he was a first-year student. When he graduated with his B.A. in 1666, he immediately became a tutor—evidently, John Wompas's tutor (Sibley, *Biographical Sketches*, vol. 2 [1666]).
63. Commissioners of the United Colonies, Boston, to Hon. Robert Boyle, 10 Sept. 1668, in *Some Correspondence*, ed. Ford, 21. The phrases "of those Indians at the colledge" and "one of them" suggest that at least one of the six Native students still in the Roxbury and Cambridge grammar schools when John entered Harvard in 1665 had joined him at the college by 1668 (*Some Correspondence*, ed. Ford, 14); SD, 8:421.

Chapter 4. "My Proper Right & Inheritance"

1. This chapter's epigraphs come from SD, 8:421 and Commissioners' return regarding Indian sachems' petitions, 13 May 1680, YIPP. Many thanks to Paul Grant-Costa for helping me locate the letter from Owaneco on the back of this return. Eben Putnam, ed., *Lieutenant Joshua Hewes: A New England Pioneer and Some of His Descendants* (Privately printed, 1913), 29–30, 44–45, 53–59. SD, 5:540–543 includes the clerk's tracing of Ann Wompas's elegantly formed "A."
2. In December 1656 Joshua Hewes married the widow Alice Crabtree in Boston (Putnam, *Lieutenant Joshua Hewes*, 72); PCR, 9:190; Samuel Eliot Morison, *The Founding of Harvard College* (Cambridge, Mass.: Harvard University Press, 1935), 192.
3. PCR, 2:280; CCR, 3:283. At the time *CCR* was printed, Romanock's original deed to Ann Prask was at the Connecticut State Library and Archives (CSL) in Colonial Records of Deeds &c, I: 290. As of 2014, this document was missing. Proof that it did exist as late as 1952 is a partial photograph of it in John Humes, "John Wampas and the Beginning of Sutton," in *History of the Town of Sutton, Massachusetts*, comp. John C. Dudley (The Town of Sutton, Massachusetts, 1952), 29. For Fairfield's bounds, see FLR, 670–669, CSL. John Wompas's claim that he sold part of the land for 530 pounds appears in his second petition to King Charles II in 1679 (PJW2).
4. WP, 5:164–165; Harral Ayres, *The Great Trail of New England* (Boston: Meador, 1940); Katherine Grandjean, *American Passage: The Communications Frontier in Early New England* (Cambridge, Mass.: Harvard University Press, 2015).
5. Minor and Stanton were well known to the Commissioners of the United Colonies, who needed good translators for much of their business (PCR,

10:105, 128, 141, 187–188; *CCR*, 2:17; Frances Manwaring Caulkins, *History of New London, Connecticut: From the First Survey of the Coast in 1612, to 1852* [New London, Conn.: Published by the Author, 1852], 103). In a 1684 trial, Minor testified to meeting Romanock and John Wompas (*MHSC*, 5th ser., 9:123–140). For Stanton's education with the Indian scholars at Roxbury and Cambridge, see *PCR*, 10:128, 189–190, 205–207, 228, 252, 262, 288–289, 292, 296–297.

6. *RRCCB*, 9:81; *The Diary of Thomas Minor, Stonington, Connecticut, 1653 to 1684* (New London, Conn.: Day, 1899), 21. On blue, see *OED*, blue, *adj.*, 4c; "Ganglion Cyst of the Wrist and Hand" (http://orthoinfo.aaos.org/topic .cfm?topic=a00006), accessed 17 Aug. 2016; "Ganglion Cyst" (http://www .ehealthstar.com/conditions/ganglion-cyst), accessed 17 Aug. 2016. Sasquage means "the country of the Sasquas" (*MHSC*, 5th ser., 9:123–140).

7. *MHSC*, 5th ser., 9:123–140.

8. Brian P. Owensby and Richard J. Ross, eds., *Meanings of Justice in British and Iberian America: Settler and Indigenous Law as Counterpoints, 1600–1825* (New York: New York University Press, forthcoming).

John's 1679 petition to King Charles II refers to Romanock as "late Sachim of Aspatuck & Susquanaugh" (PJW2). Romanock's status as a sachem and the legitimacy of female land ownership in Native society were disputed by Indian witnesses in the 1684 trial in which John Wompas's English heirs attempted to wrest possession of the land at Fairfield, Connecticut, from its English residents. Whether the Algonquian-speaking peoples of New England were matrilineal—passing land and the right to political office through the female line—or patrilineal is still debated. Amy E. Den Ouden argues that New England Natives were matrilineal but were driven to adopt patrilineal practices by pressure from the dominant English culture (*Beyond Conquest: Native Peoples and the Struggle for History in New England* [Lincoln: University of Nebraska Press, 2005], 83, 246–247 n. 18). This pressure may explain why the Indians in the 1684 trial affirmed that "according to their custom, the title of lands goes by the man and not by the woman" (*MHSC*, 5th ser., 9:122–123). While the question of whether land passed through matrilineal or patrilineal lines (or both) in New England is unresolved, there is ample evidence that Indian women were able to own land. Their names appear on multiple deeds, and Indian men also claimed land "in right of their wives" (Indian Deed, New Plymouth, 1676/77, Folder 5, Ayers MS, Newberry Library, Chicago, Ill.; "Hearing of Uncas's complaints," 13 Nov. 1665, WFPT; *CCR*, 3:283). For examples of Natives claiming right to land and/or political office through patrilineal lines, see MAC, 30:326a and John Wompas's last will and testament (WJW).

Romanock's turf and twig ceremony appears in *MHSC*, 5th ser., 9:132–134. Malcolm Gaskill cites a similar ceremony in Virginia in 1654

(*Between Two Worlds: How the English Became Americans* [New York: Basic, 2014], 203). See also *OED*, turf, *n.*, 1d.

John Wompas's known connection to Joshua Hewes, Ann Prask's master and one of the English purchasers on the land deed for which a "John Indian" served as interpreter in 1659, increases the likelihood that Wompas was "John Indian" (Deed of Quinebaug Lands, 28 April 1659, WFPT). On Thomas Minor, see *SGen*. On John Wompas and Thomas Minor carving their initials into tree trunks, see MAC, 30:259a; and *Diary of Thomas Minor*, 205. For other Natives using the English system of marking property bounds, see William A. Starna, *From Homeland to New Land: A History of the Mahican Indians, 1600–1830* (Lincoln: University of Nebraska Press, 2013), 114–115.

9. *Diary of Thomas Minor*, 41; *CCR*, 1:265; Caulkins, *History of New London*, 129; *PCR*, 10:128, 141. On Algonquian-language speakers in seventeenth-century New England, see Julie A. Fisher, "Speaking 'Indian' and English: The Bilinguals of Seventeenth-Century New England, 1636–1680," Ph.D. dissertation, University of Delaware, 2016.

10. On English claims of land by conquest, see *MHSC*, 9th ser., 5:118; and the Testimony of Thomas Stanton, 1683, William Samuel Johnson Papers, Connecticut Historical Society, Hartford, Conn. Indians, too, claimed rights to land by conquest, reclaiming land they had formerly sold to the Dutch after conquering them in war (Richard Nicolls to John Winthrop Jr., 6 June 1666, WFPT).

    If Romanock did obtain a deed before 1660, it no longer exists. Deeds of Indian land to the inhabitants of Fairfield appear in the Fairfield Land Records (FLR), CSL, and in YIPP. They include the earliest deed of 20 March 1656/57 (FLR, 671), followed by deeds on 20 March 1661 (FLR, 673), 11 April 1661 (FLR, 672), and 18 May 1681 (FLR, 667), as well as confirmations on 14 June 1680 (Trumbull Papers, 135a, CSL), 6 Oct. 1680 (FLR, 669–670), and 27 May 1686 (FLR, 662).

    While there is no evidence that the English paid the Indians for Fairfield land before 1657, they did pay for Pequot lands elsewhere in Connecticut as early as 1638. However, they acknowledged that their payment was small enough to be considered a "gratuity" in exchange for the Indians' "gift" of land (*MHSC*, 5th ser., 9:118); FLR, 671, 20 March 1656/57, CSL.

11. My supposition that John Wompas helped Romanock obtain a deed would explain why Romanock did not sign any of the deeds from 1657 on but was still able to grant "Aspitock" to his daughter in 1660 (*CCR*, 3:282–283).

12. On coverture, see Cornelia Hughes Dayton, *Women Before the Bar: Gender, Law, and Society in Connecticut, 1639–1789* (Chapel Hill: University of North Carolina Press, 1995); and Marylynn Salmon, *Women and the Law*

of Property in Early America (Chapel Hill: University of North Carolina Press, 1986). The Privy Council's letter in response to John's petition gives the payment amount as 350 pounds. This was clearly a clerical error, as the petition itself says "530 £ sterling or thereabouts" (PJW2; CO 5:904, pp. 36–37, TNA). The claim that 530 pounds may have been the highest price paid for Indian land in seventeenth-century New England is based on my survey of land sales in Massachusetts, Plymouth, and, to a lesser extent, Connecticut. While I have looked at as many deeds as possible within the course of researching this book, I have not seen all of them.

13. The same law that guaranteed a woman one-third of her husband's estate at his death guaranteed one-third of the estate to a woman after a divorce, as long as she was not the guilty party (Dayton, *Women Before the Bar,* 111–112; George Lee Haskins, *Law and Authority in Early Massachusetts: A Study in Tradition and Design* [New York: Macmillan, 1960], 181, 195); Samuel Eliot Morison, *Harvard College in the Seventeenth Century* (Cambridge, Mass.: Harvard University Press, 1936), 1:356; John Blake and Edward Pratt's Letter of Attorney, *MHSC,* 5th ser., 9:123–127.

14. Major Humphrey Atherton was the Indian Superintendent in 1661, but he was acting in his capacity as a magistrate when he officiated at John and Ann Wompas's marriage (*RRCCB,* 9:81).

15. On the role of marriage in reinforcing status, wealth, and power, see Kathleen J. Bragdon, *Native People of Southern New England, 1500–1650* (Norman: University of Oklahoma Press, 1996), 161; and David Hackett Fischer, *Albion's Seed: Four British Folkways in America* (New York: Oxford University Press, 1989), 283; *RRCCB,* 9:89.

16. *PCR,* 3:192 describes the Native practice of taking a new name at a significant life stage. See also William S. Simmons, *Spirit of the New England Tribes: Indian History and Folklore, 1620–1984* (Hanover, N.H.: University Press of New England, 1986), 46–48; and Patricia E. Rubertone, *Grave Undertakings: An Archaeology of Roger Williams and the Narragansett Indians* (Washington, D.C.: Smithsonian Institution Press, 2001), 148.

"Wompi" means "it is white" in Massachusett and Narragansett. In Loup, which a number of scholars consider to be Nipmuc, "wonbai" means "it is white" (David J. Costa, "The Dialectology of Southern New England Algonquian," in *Papers of the 38th Algonquian Conference* [2007], 101). The use of "white" to denote English people did not become widespread until after 1700, but it does appear occasionally in colonial English records in the previous century. For instance, Massachusetts governor John Leverett reported in 1673 that in a distant earthquake "one negro [was] kild and a whytes arme broake" (John Leverett to John Winthrop Jr., 31 March 1673, WFPT). Although skin color began to replace religion and nationality to designate difference in this era, color was not yet indelibly associated with race. See Carl H. Nightingale, "Before Race

Mattered: Geographies of the Color Line in Early Colonial Madras and New York," *The American Historical Review* 113, 1 (Feb. 2008): 62–63. See also Nancy Shoemaker, "How Indians Got to Be Red," *American Historical Review* 102, 3 (June 1997): 625–644. On changes in racial attitudes following King Philip's War, see Jenny Hale Pulsipher, "'Our Sages are Sageles': A Letter on Massachusetts Indian Policy After King Philip's War," *WMQ* 58 (April 2001), 431–448, and "Playing John White," in *Native Acts: Indian Performance in Early North America*, ed. Joshua Bellin and Laura Mielke (Lincoln: University of Nebraska Press, 2011), 196–220.

17. Francis Jennings, *The Invasion of America: Indians, Colonialism, and the Cant of Conquest* (New York: W. W. Norton, 1976 [1975]), chapters 5, 8, 11. For other scholarly treatments of Indian land transfer in New England, see Neal Salisbury, *Manitou and Providence: Indians, Europeans, and the Making of New England, 1500–1643* (New York: Oxford University Press, 1982), chapter 6; William Cronon, *Changes in the Land: Indians, Colonists, and the Ecology of New England* (Hill and Wang, 1983); Yasuhide Kawashima, *Puritan Justice and the Indian: White Man's Law in Massachusetts, 1630–1763* (Middletown, Conn.: Wesleyan University Press, 1986), 51–71; Jeremy Dupertuis Bangs, *Indian Deeds: Land Transactions in Plymouth Colony, 1620–1691* (Boston: New England Historical and Genealogical Society, 2002); Stuart Banner, *How the Indians Lost Their Land: Law and Power on the Frontier* (Cambridge, Mass.: Harvard University Press, 2005); Emerson W. Baker, "'A Scratch with a Bear's Paw': Anglo-Indian Land Deeds in Early Maine," *Ethnohistory* 36, 3 (1989): 235–256; Daniel R. Mandell, "Selling the Praying Towns: Massachusett and Nipmuck Land Transactions, 1680–1730," *Northeast Anthropology* 70 (2007): 15, and *Behind the Frontier: Indians in Eighteenth-Century Eastern Massachusetts* (Lincoln: University of Nebraska Press, 1996); John Frederick Martin, *Profits in the Wilderness: Entrepreneurship and the Founding of New England Towns in the Seventeenth Century* (Chapel Hill: University of North Carolina Press, 1991); and Jean M. O'Brien, *Dispossession by Degrees: Indian Land and Identity in Natick, Massachusetts, 1650–1790* (Lincoln: University of Nebraska Press, 2003 [1997]), which gives a nuanced description of Indian land loss at Natick "through the excruciating workings of business as usual" (8–9).

David J. Silverman notes other instances of Indians employing English law to turn "literacy from the colonists' advantage into their own," in "'We Chief Men Say This': Wampanoag Memory, English Authority, and the Contest over Mittark's Will," in *Early Native Literacies in New England: A Documentary and Critical Anthology*, ed. Kristina Bross and Hilary E. Wyss (Amherst: University of Massachusetts Press, 2008); Alan Taylor, *American Colonies: The Settling of North America* (New York: Penguin, 2001), 380; Richard White, "Creative Misunderstandings and New Understandings," *WMQ* 63 (Jan. 2006), 9–14.

18. The "uplands" land use pattern of the Nipmuc Indians is not as well understood as the coastal and riverine patterns Kathleen Bragdon describes in *Native People*. Uplands Indians seem to have combined some of the seasonal "circumscribed movements" of coastal dwellers with those of the more sedentary agricultural riverine dwellers (*Native People*, 59–75, chapter 4). See also O'Brien, *Dispossession by Degrees*, chapter 1; Kathleen Joan Bragdon, "Another Tongue Brought In: An Ethnohistorical Study of Native Writings in Massachusett," Ph.D. dissertation, Brown University, 1981, 93–94, 106–108; Baker, "'A Scratch with a Bear's Paw,'" 240; Roger Williams, *Key into the Language of America* (1643; Bedford, Mass.: Applewood), 94–96; Transcriptions of two depositions by Indians relating to the lands that formerly belonged to King Philip, Mar. 1687 and Dec. 1686, Indian miscellaneous manuscripts, ca. 1675–1889, Mss col 1501, box 2: subjects and states, New York Public Library Archives and Manuscripts, New York, N.Y.

     On a sachem's need for consent to alienate land, see MAC, 30:275a; Bragdon, *Native People*, 138. Yasuhide Kawashima acknowledged that sachems distributed land to particular families or individuals and that the land remained theirs to use until "that family died out," at which time the land would revert to the sachem. Such a pattern is similar to the English legal practice of life estate, in which land was held by an individual and/or his heirs, but they lacked the right to alienate that land to others (*Puritan Justice and the Indian*, 42–43, note). Bethel Saler describes the Native pattern of shared use of territory, arguing that it reflected kinship ties through generations of intermarriage between tribes as well as an understanding that use rather than purchase conveyed ownership (*The Settlers' Empire: Colonialism and State Formation in America's Old Northwest* [Philadelphia: University of Pennsylvania Press, 2015], 106–107).

19. Baker, "'A Scratch with a Bear's Paw,'" 235–256; David J. Silverman, *Faith and Boundaries: Colonists, Christianity, and Community Among the Wampanoag Indians of Martha's Vineyard, 1600–1871* (New York: Cambridge University Press, 2005), 95, 125. Virginia DeJohn Anderson notes that the English persistently allowed joint use of land by Indians and English ("King Philip's Herds: Indians, Colonists, and the Problem of Livestock in Early New England," *WMQ* 3rd ser., 51 [Oct. 1994], 610; *Creatures of Empire: How Domestic Animals Transformed Early America* [New York: Oxford University Press, 2004]).

20. On gifts given to sachems by the English, see *JJW*, 45–47. For examples of English paying Indians tribute, see Bangs, *Indian Deeds*, 72, 257, 258; and Jenny Hale Pulsipher, "'Dark Cloud Rising in the East': Indian Sovereignty and the Coming of King William's War in New England," *NEQ* 80 (Dec. 2007): 593–595. On the continuing strength of the northeastern Indians, which allowed them to maintain significant political influence over the English colonists, see Emerson W. Baker and John G. Reid,

"Amerindian Power in the Early Modern Northeast: A Reappraisal," *WMQ* 61 (Jan. 2004), 77–106. Some might argue that "rent" better describes what the English regularly paid to the Indians for use of their land; of course, through "creative misunderstanding," the terms rent and tribute could coexist (Bangs, *Indian Deeds*, 29).

21. *CCR*, 2:473–474; *MCR*, 3:280; Genesis 1:28. The colony's first governor, John Winthrop, explained this thinking in his journal: "The Indians having only a natural right to so much land as they had or could improve, so as the rest of the country lay open to any that could and would improve it" (*JJW*, 284). On English debates over the right to land by royal grant, conquest, or purchase, see Craig Yirush, *Settlers, Liberty, and Empire: The Roots of Early American Political Theory, 1675–1775* (New York: Cambridge University Press, 2011), 65–73; Lauren Benton, *A Search for Sovereignty: Law and Geography in European Empires, 1400–1900* (New York: Cambridge University Press, 2010), chapter 1; and Jeffrey Glover, *Paper Sovereigns: Anglo-Native Treaties and the Law of Nations, 1604–1664* (Philadelphia: University of Pennsylvania Press, 2014), 131.

"Reasons and Considerations Touching the Lawfulness of Removing," in *Mourt's Relation: A Journal of the Pilgrims at Plymouth*, ed. Dwight B. Heath (Bedford, Mass.: Applewood, 1963), 92–93. Evidence that Cushman's view existed in old as well as New England appears in Thomas More's *Utopia*, which justified war "when any people holdeth a piece of ground void and vacant to no good or profitable use: keeping others from the use and possession of it, which, notwithstanding, by the law of nature, ought thereof to be nourished and relieved" (cited in Wilcomb E. Washburn, *Red Man's Land, White Man's Law: The Past and Present Status of the American Indian*, 2nd ed. [Norman: University of Oklahoma Press, 1995], 40).

22. *JJW*, 107; Emerson W. Baker, "Salem as Frontier Outpost," in *Salem: Place, Myth and Memory*, ed. Dane Morrison and Nancy Schultz (Boston: Northeastern University Press, 2004), 29. Although these laws were enacted in 1634, Massachusetts did not publish them until 1648 (*CLM*, 74; see also *MCR*, 3:280). In conformance to the law, the deed to John Winthrop's 3,000-acre farm exempted 100 acres of "improved" Indian land (*MCR*, 4, part 2:108); in another case, the Massachusetts General Court confirmed a land grant, "the just right of any Indian to any part of this land always excepted" (*MCR* 3:189). For other laws restricting sale of Indian lands, see *RICR*, 1:236, 404; *PCR* 11:41, 183. Jean O'Brien describes Indians using English justifications for possession of land in *Dispossession by Degrees*, 75.

23. Evarts B. Greene and Virginia D. Harrington, *American Population Before the Federal Census of 1790* (Baltimore: Genealogical Publishing, 1993 [1932]), 8–10; Neal Salisbury, *Manitou and Providence: Indians, Europeans, and the Making of New England, 1500–1643* (New York: Oxford University Press, 1982), 30, 105; Bragdon, *Native People*, 23–28.

24. Deed of Quinebaug Lands, 28 April 1659, WFPT; MAC, 30:131–132; Bangs, *Indian Deeds*, 125–126. Some Indians even attempted to secure legal injunctions against the sale of their land to any Englishman ever (Bangs, *Indian Deeds*, 205).

25. MAC, 30:260a; Ephraim Curtis Bill of Costs against John Wampas, Middlesex Court Folios, 68-5, 7 April 1674, MA; Middlesex County Court Records, Pulsifer Transcript, 3:87, MA.

26. Notably, Massachusetts officials included Indians among those to whom they were willing to grant land, and a number of Indians took advantage of this provision to secure lands threatened by English encroachment (see *MCR*, 3:246; *MCR*, 4, part 2:94–95; MAC, 30:19, 19a, 21, 69, 136). Daniel Gookin gave three reasons why Indians should obtain grants for their own lands from the English: 1) to prevent future conflict over ownership, 2) to secure the land for their children, "this being a provision in all those grants, that they shall not sell or alienate any part of those lands unto any Englishman without the general court's consent," and 3) to provide a place where Christian Indians could dwell together, "without which neither religion or civility can well prosper" (*HColl*, 179).

27. *CLM*, 74; William Lincoln, *History of Worcester, Massachusetts* (Worcester: Charles Hersey, 1862), 20, 16. Sagamore John of Pakachoog and other Nipmucs sold a 3,200-acre parcel near Quinsigamog Pond to the English in 1665. However, this piece was located on the east side of the pond, so it did not include the land granted by the General Court to Quinsigamog plantation or the land on which Ephraim Curtis's trading house was built. Curtis obtained his land from Mary Noyes, widow of Thomas Noyes, who in turn purchased it from the heirs of Rev. John Norton, who received a grant to the land from the General Court. No record of Norton's purchase from the Indians exists, and it may never have occurred (MD, 4:72–74, 7:194–195).

28. Lincoln, *History of Worcester*, 9–17; MD, 8:317–318; *JJW*, 107. For deeds associated with Quinsigamog, see appendix: Land Transactions of John Wompas and Ann Prask Wompas, 1662–1679; MD 3:69–70, 4:72–74, 7:194–195, 8:317–318; *MCR* 4, part 2:111–112. Samuel Gorton, another critic of Massachusetts policy, declared that the king expected his colonists to take no lands from the Indians "without giving satisfaction for them" (*MHSC*, 4th ser., 7:627); Bangs, *Indian Deeds*, 222–223; Commissioners' return regarding Indian sachems' petitions, 13 May 1680, YIPP; Nathaniel Saltonstall, "The Present State of New-England with Respect to the Indian War, by N.S., 1675," in Charles H. Lincoln, ed., *Narratives of the Indian Wars, 1675–1699* (New York: Barnes & Noble, 1952 [1913]), 26.

29. Bethel Saler notes that "gift" and "commodity" are defining metaphors for Native and English society and that exchange in the former "turns objects and persons into social relations" (*Settlers' Empire*, 128–130); Deed to Tunxis Sepos, 9 April 1650, YIPP. The amount that the magis-

trates previously paid the chief sachem Sequason is not stated. Other startling examples of low prices paid for Indian land include the 1648 sale of five square miles in Sudbury for five pounds (SD, 1:93), and the 1668 sale of twenty square miles of Wabanaki land for two large Indian blankets, two gallons of rum, two pounds of powder, four pounds of musket balls, and twenty strings of wampum (Coll. S-1262, Misc. box 59/27, 2965, MeHS). A number of scholars, including Yasuhide Kawashima, Peter Leavenworth, and David Konig, have noted the very low monetary value English colonists assigned to "waste" or wilderness land (Kawashima, *Puritan Justice*, 59; Peter S. Leavenworth, "'The Best Title That Indians Can Claim': Native Agency and Consent in the Transferal of Pawtucket Land in the Seventeenth Century," *NEQ* 72 [June 1999]: 290). However, even unimproved land sold for much higher prices between Englishmen. In 1732–1733, land recently purchased from Nipmuc Indians sold between Englishmen for an average price of three pounds per acre (Worcester County Registry of Deeds, Worcester, Massachusetts, vol. 3:2–3, 4, 9, 11–12, 14–16, 18–20, 22, 25).

30. Deed to Tunxis Sepos, 9 April 1650, YIPP. I thank Tamar Herzog for pointing out Giovanni Levi's discussion of need as a factor in the fair price of land among early modern Europeans (*Inheriting Power: The Story of an Exorcist*, trans. Lydia G. Cochrane [Chicago: University of Chicago Press, 1988], 80–94).

31. PJW2.

32. In 1671 the Wampanoag sachem Philip used confirmation to secure a payment of sixteen pounds for land that his father Massasoit had long since sold to the colony (SD, 7:272–273); see also Haynes to Winthrop, 1643, in *MHSC*, 4th ser., 6:355–356. Harry Andrew Wright, ed., *Indian Deeds of Hampden County* (Springfield, Mass., 1905), 33. Sachems' rights included "the skin of every blacke woolfe and the skin [of] every deere killed in the River," moose skins, and the right to grant permission for strangers to hunt on or pass through their land (Roger Williams to John Winthrop Jr., 20 March 1649/50, WFPT); Deed of Quinabaug Lands, 28 April 1659, WFPT; Hearing of Uncas's complaints, 13 Nov. 1665, WFPT; Richard Nicolls to John Winthrop Jr., 6 June 1666, WFPT. On English exclusions of specific Native rights from land deeds, see *PCR*, 9:144. Other examples of exclusion include Matthew Gilbert to John Winthrop Jr., 3 Oct. 1660, WFPT. For English courts voiding illegal sales of Indian land, see MAC, 30:129, 275a, 279b; see also O'Brien, *Dispossession by Degrees*, 38.

33. The deed would have to be recorded and confirmed before the land could be resold, so it is likely John Wompas sold Fairfield land to the Englishmen from Stonington shortly after the 1667 confirmation date. SD, 8:421, 10:111–112. For a sampling of Native marks and signatures, see MAC, 30:1, 3, 4, 73, 78, 87, 102, 113, 133a, 134, 136, 136a, 146, 169, 182, 191, 191a, 229, 257, 257a, 260a, 262a, 267, 269, 275a, 276, 277a, 279a, 280, 305.

34. SD, 8:421; *ET,* 222.

35. On Indians challenging land sold without proper consent, see MAC, 30:275a, which discusses a case from 1666 (MAC, 30:131–132). On Native demands for additional payments, see Deed to Tunxis Sepos, 9 April 1650, YIPP.

36. MD, 6:86–87, 101–102, 82–83, 84–85; MD, 7:157–160; MD, 8:317–318; SD, 12:297–299, 378–380. English deeds provided a documentary record of land sales, and these were retained by the buyer and the seller, with the transaction later recorded and confirmed by county clerks. Clerks' transcriptions of deeds were far more likely to survive than the deeds held by buyers and sellers. Some of the evidence of John Wompas's land sales appears only in petitions, demonstrating that the deeds of those sales did not survive and may never have been recorded. So Wompas may actually have sold much more land than sixty-six square miles in Massachusetts and a large tract in Fairfield, Connecticut.

37. MAC, 30:259a. For an account of Nipmuc demands for payment for the same land Wompas sold, see the final chapter in this book.

Chapter 5. "I Cherish a Desire to Be at Sea"

1. This chapter's epigraphs come from Commissioners of the United Colonies to Hon. Robert Boyle, 10 Sept. 1668, in John W. Ford, ed., *Some Correspondence Between the Governors and Treasurers of the New England Company* (London: Spottiswoode, 1896), 21. For the Nipmuc Nation's ongoing project to recover and restore historic *mishoons,* see http://project mishoon.homestead.com. In August 2015, twelve rowers from six New England tribes paddled a newly constructed thirty-six-foot mishoon from Mystic, Connecticut, to Noank (Martha's Vineyard), an effort sponsored by the Mashantucket Pequot Museum and Research Center (http://www .theday.com/local/20150808/corrected-northeastern-tribes-partner-to -paddle-on-mishoons-maiden-voyage); Daniel Vickers with Vince Walsh, *Young Men and the Sea: Yankee Seafarers in the Age of Sail* (New Haven, Conn.: Yale University Press, 2005), 14.

   On Indians and Atlantic seafaring, see Matthew R. Bahar, "People of the Dawn, People of the Door: Indian Pirates and the Violent Theft of an Atlantic World," *JAH* 101 (Sept. 2014): 401–426; Nancy Shoemaker, *Native American Whalemen and the World: The Contingency of Race* (Chapel Hill: University of North Carolina Press, 2015); Kelly K. Chaves, "Before the First Whalemen: The Emergence and Loss of Indigenous Maritime Autonomy in New England, 1672–1740," *NEQ* (March 2014): 46–71; Jason Mancini, "Beyond Reservation: Indians, Maritime Labor, and Communities of Color from Eastern Long Island Sound, 1713–1861," *Connecticut History Review* 54, 1 (Spring 2015): 143–163; and Andrew Lipman, *The*

Saltwater Frontier: Indians and the Contest for the American Coast (New Haven, Conn.: Yale University Press, 2015), chapter 2.

2. The homes of John and Ann Wompas and their neighbors, as well as Harrison's ropewalk, public buildings, and taverns are identified on Samuel Clough's map of Boston (1676), Massachusetts Maps, MHS, available online at http://masshist.org/online/massmaps/img-viewer.php?item_id =1737&mode=small&nmask=16&img_step=5#imgnav. Phyllis Whitman Hunter, *Purchasing Identity in the Atlantic World: Massachusetts Merchants, 1670–1780* (Ithaca, N.Y.: Cornell University Press, 2001), 25–27; Vickers, *Young Men*, 59–60, 44. Sir William Petty and Dr. Taylor gave Boston's population as 1,500 families in 1675, based on conversations with two New England merchants. They also surveyed the number and size of New England's shipping fleet (*The Petty Papers: Some Unpublished Writings of Sir William Petty*, edited from the Bowood Papers by the Marquis of Lansdowne, 2 vols. [Boston: Houghton Mifflin, 1927], 2:100). Gary Nash estimated the population of Boston in 1690 to be 6,000 (*The Urban Crucible: The Northern Seaports and the Origins of the American Revolution* [Cambridge, Mass.: Harvard University Press, 1986], 6). Annie Haven Thwing, *The Crooked and Narrow Streets of the Town of Boston, 1630–1822* (Boston: Marshall Jones, 1920), 26; Walter Muir Whitehill, *Boston: A Topographical History*, 2nd ed. (Cambridge: Harvard University Press, 1968), 20–23; Barry Levy, *Town Born: The Political Economy of New England from its Founding to the Revolution* (Philadelphia: University of Pennsylvania Press, 2009), 155, 161.

3. SD, 5:490–491.

4. Nathaniel Ingersoll Bowditch in *RRCCB*, 5:23–25.

5. SD, 5:490–491; *CCR*, 3:283.

6. SD, 5:490–491, 540–543; SD, 10:111–112. Given the fact that John seemed unable to apply more than thirty-seven pounds to the purchase price of his home, the Stonington men may have given him only a portion of the agreed price for the land, promising the rest once they were able to secure title. But it is also possible that John managed to spend all 530 pounds before 1667.

7. Peter Kemp, *The British Sailor: A Social History of the Lower Deck* (London: J. M. Dent & Sons, 1970), 31; Ralph Davis, *The Rise of the English Shipping Industry in the Seventeenth and Eighteenth Centuries* (London: Macmillan, 1962), 120; Vickers, *Young Men*, 80–85, 88; Edmund S. Morgan, *The Puritan Family: Religion and Domestic Relations in Seventeenth Century New England* (New York: Harper and Row, 1966), 119; *Petty Papers*, 100–108. Boston merchant Robert Gibbs paid English day laborers two to two and a half shillings a day in the 1670s. He paid less to servants (one and a half shillings/day), women (one shilling/day), and Indians (one shilling/day) (Robert Gibbs Account Book, Robert Gibbs Business Records, AAS).

The Massachusetts government also paid a wage of a shilling a day to Indian laborers (*CSPC*, 9: #721). Records of Native sailors serving on English vessels are extremely rare before 1700. In one surviving example, an "Indian, servant to Tho. Clowter" received twenty shillings per month in 1679; in another "the Indian" received twenty-two shillings per month in 1690 (*SCR*, 2:1092; John Walley Papers, Manuscripts, NEHGS).

8. The phrase "very loveing freind" comes from John Wompas's will and reflects the formulaic language used in most wills to designate beneficiaries (WJW). While the phrase is formulaic, it still indicates that John Wompas placed Blake in a special category relative to other acquaintances. For the Three Doves tavern, see Samuel Clough, Map of Boston, 1676, MHS. Milcah Wright was previously married to Thomas Snow. After his death, she married Captain William Wright, who moved into the Snow home. Milcah's son Samuel Snow ran the Three Doves tavern out of this home. See Samuel C. Clough, "Remarks on the Compilation of the Boston Book of Possessions," *Colonial Society of Massachusetts Publications* 27 (1932): 5; SD, 6:302; *RRCCB*, 2:61–62. Milcah Wright and Sarah Ellis mentioned conversations with Ann "often in her lifetime" (AWP).

    Evidence of John Wompas's relationships with other mariners appears in SCF, #1809. On the seafarers' community in Boston and other urban ports, see Steven J. J. Pitt, "Cotton Mather and Boston's 'Seafaring Tribe,'" *NEQ* 85, 2 (June 2012): 222–252; Robert Lee, "The Seafarers' Urban World: A Critical Review," *International Journal of Maritime History* 25, 1 (June 2013): 23–64; and Isaac Land, "Humours of Sailortown: Atlantic History Meets Subculture Theory," in *City Limits: Perspectives on the Historical European City* (Montreal: McGill-Queen's University Press, 2010).

9. Commissioners of the United Colonies to Hon. Robert Boyle, 10 Sept. 1668, in *Some Correspondence*, ed. Ford, 21; *PCR*, 2:244, 310–311; John Hull Letter Book, transcription, 18 Sept. 1677, p. 355, AAS.

10. James Axtell, *The School upon a Hill: Education and Society in Colonial New England* (New Haven, Conn.: Yale University Press, 1974), 113–121; Morgan, *Puritan Family*, chapter 5; Vickers, *Young Men*, 106. For an example of a formal apprenticeship, see Peter Edward Pope, *Fish into Wine: The Newfoundland Plantation in the Seventeenth Century* (Chapel Hill: University of North Carolina Press, 1994), 244.

11. Vickers, *Young Men*, 115; SD, 8:421; MD, 7:157–160; WJW; Davis, *The Rise of the English Shipping*, 154–155. Nancy Shoemaker found many Native men serving as officers in the nineteenth-century New Bedford whaling industry, although only one who served as master. Pay was based on experience and skill, not race, although race could impact social relations in the larger maritime community ("Mr. Tashtego: Native American Whalemen in Antebellum New England," *Journal of the Early Repub-*

lic 33 [Spring 2013]: 115–116, 121). The scarcity of seventeenth-century records, particularly of Native seamen, makes it difficult to draw firm conclusions about relative wages or the role of race in advancement in that century.

12. Based on the small number of surviving records, Indians were unusual in English crews until the rise of the whaling industry at the end of the seventeenth century (David J. Silverman, "The Impact of Indentured Servitude on the Society and Culture of Southern New England Indians, 1680–1810," *NEQ* 74, 4 [Dec. 2001]: 622–666; Mark A. Nicholas, "Mashpee Wampanoags of Cape Cod, the Whalefishery, and Seafaring's Impact on Community Development," *American Indian Quarterly* 26, 2 [Spring 2002]: 165–197; John A. Sainsbury, "Indian Labor in Early Rhode Island," *NEQ* 48, 3 [Sept. 1975]: 378–393; and Chaves, "Before the First Whalemen").

Indian whalers at Easthampton on Long Island were paid in half shares of whale blubber and bone. Like Indian sailors of eighteenth-century Nantucket, these Natives quickly ran into debt and worked "from yeare to yeare till all old debts bee discharged." Long before joining English whaling enterprises, Indians harvested whales that washed ashore or lured whales into shallow bays where they beached themselves (*EHR*, 1:379, 382–383, 407; Daniel Vickers, "The First Whalemen of Nantucket," in *After King Philip's War: Presence and Persistence in Indian New England*, ed. Colin G. Calloway [Hanover, N.H.: University Press of New England, 1997]; Shoemaker, *Native American Whalemen;* Mancini, "Beyond Reservation"; Elizabeth Alden Little and J. Clinton Andrews, "Drift Whales at Nantucket: The Kindness of Moshup," in *Nantucket and Other Native Places: The Legacy of Elizabeth Alden Little*, ed. Elizabeth S. Chilton and Mary Lynne Rainey [Albany: State University of New York Press, 2010]).

On Native expertise in English sailing technology, see Bruce J. Bourque and Ruth H. Whitehead, "Trade and Alliances in the Contact Period," in *American Beginnings: Exploration, Culture, and Cartography in the Land of Norumbega*, ed. Emerson W. Baker et al. (Lincoln: University of Nebraska Press, 1994), 136–139; Martin Moore, *Memoirs of the Life and Character of Rev. John Eliot, Apostle of the N. A. Indians* (Boston: Published by T. Bedlington, Flagg & Gould, Printers, 1822), 126. On Native piracy, see James Axtell, "The Vengeful Women of Marblehead: Robert Roules's Deposition of 1677," *WMQ* 31 (Oct. 1974): 647–652; Bahar, "People of the Dawn"; MAC, 60:277a, 61:222. On the coastal trade, see Barbara Rumsey, "Waldron vs. Smith: Shipwreck at the Eastward, 1671," *Maine History* 39, 2 (2000), 68–93; and Faith Harrington, "Sea Tenure in Seventeenth Century New Hampshire: Native Americans and Englishmen in the Sphere of Coastal Resources," *Historical New Hampshire* 40 (1985): 1–2; *EHR*, 1:271, 378–383, 407.

Documented Indian sailors in the English fleet during the seven-
teenth century appear in MAC, 60:277a; MAC, 30:195; John Romeyn
Brodhead, ed., *Documents Relative to the Colonial History of the State of
New-York* (Albany, N.Y.: Weed, Parsons, 1853), 3:168–169; SD, 8:421,
EHR, 1:379, 382–383; SCR, 2:778, 1092; John Whalley Papers, NEHGS;
Natick Petition, ca. 1700, Manuscripts, NEHGS; Vickers, *Young Men*, 20.

13. ET, 69; Vickers, *Young Men*, 88; *Barlow's Journal of His Life at Sea in King's
Ships*, 2 vols., tr. Basil Lubbock (London: Hurst & Blackett, 1934), 1:62;
Christopher Lloyd, *The British Seaman, 1200–1860: A Social Survey*
(Rutherford, N.J.: Fairleigh Dickinson University Press, 1970), 54.

14. Peter Wilson Coldham, *English Adventurers and Emigrants: Abstracts of
Examinations in the High Court of Admiralty with Reference to Colonial Amer-
ica*, 2 vols. (Baltimore: Genealogical Publishing, 1985), 1:151, 2:25–26;
MAC, 60:33.

15. Quoted in Davis, *English Shipping*, 154–155, 156; Thwing, *Streets of Boston*, 35–39; Coldham, *English Adventurers*, 1:144, 2:25–26; SCR, 1:250–
252. Wars between European countries made shipmasters leery of ven-
turing to sea without the protection of a convoy of other ships, and
waiting for such a convoy to assemble could take months. At the height
of the wars, some ship owners directed their captains to dismiss their
sailors and remain in port (John Hull Letter Book, p. 164, AAS).

On English taken captive by pirates, see Linda Colley, *Captives: Britain, Empire, and the World, 1600–1850* (London: Jonathan Cape, 2002),
43–44; Nabil Matar, *Britain and Barbary, 1589–1689* (Gainesville: University Press of Florida, 2005), 55. Boston sailor William Condy spent six
months in an Algerian prison in 1680/81 (Coldham, *English Adventurers*,
2:29). New England merchant Abraham Browne was captured and enslaved in 1655; his father had been enslaved before him and held for three
years before being redeemed for 150 pounds by his wife (Stephen T.
Riley, "Abraham Browne's Captivity by the Barbary Pirates, 1655," in
Seafaring in Colonial Massachusetts [Boston: The Colonial Society of Massachusetts, 1980], 31–32). For lurid tales and allusions to Barbary captivity, see John Josselyn, "Chronological Observations of America, 1673," in
MHSC, 3rd ser., 3:355; and ECR 3:142–143.

16. Lloyd, *British Seaman*, 43–46; Vickers, *Young Men*, 108.

17. Quoted in Vickers, *Young Men*, 107; Levy, *Town Born*, 217; *Barlow's Journal*, 1:83, 89.

18. Vickers, *Young Men*, 74; Coldham, *English Adventurers*, 1:63, 106–107,
2:3. The *Constant Martha* traveling from Maryland to Bristol, which normally took six–seven weeks, took sixteen weeks to make the journey "because of adverse winds" (Coldham, *English Adventurers*, 2:23).

19. See Laurel Thatcher Ulrich's discussion of "deputy husbands" in *Good
Wives: Image and Reality in the Lives of Women in Northern New England,
1650–1750* (New York: Vintage, 1991 [1980]), chapter 2; and Lisa Nor-

ling, *Captain Ahab Had a Wife: New England Women and the Whalefishery, 1720–1870* (Chapel Hill: University of North Carolina Press, 2000), 37–42. For more on mariners' wives, see Elaine Forman Crane, *Ebb Tide in New England: Women, Seaports, and Social Change, 1630–1800* (Boston: Northeastern University Press, 1998); and Margaret S. Creighton and Lisa Norling, eds., *Iron Men, Wooden Women: Gender and Seafaring in the Atlantic World, 1700–1920* (Baltimore: Johns Hopkins University Press, 1996).

20. Crane, *Ebb Tide in New England*, 103; Norling, *Captain Ahab*, 158–159. Isaac Land notes that sailors regularly shared rooms with the same companions in the same lodging houses. His essay focuses on eighteenth- and nineteenth-century sailor life, as do most scholarly treatments of sailors, but evidence such as the Warner-Franklin lawsuit of 1679 in Suffolk County Court suggests that the same pattern held in seventeenth-century Boston (Land, "Humours of Sailortown," 336; SCF, #1809).

21. See appendix, Land Transactions of John Wompas and Ann Prask Wompas, 1662–1679; SCF, #1809.

22. The interactions of all of these people are discussed in SCF, #1809.

23. On ships laid up for the winter, see *Barlow's Journal*, 1:39. William Thomson to John Winthrop Jr., 15 Jan. 1660/61, WFPT; Lloyd, *British Seaman*, 56, 90. Contrary to Marcus Rediker and Peter Linebaugh's depiction of sailors as an emerging proletariat, Paul Gilje argues that the liberty sought by sailors had less to do with ideology and collective identity than with individual freedom (Paul A. Gilje, *Liberty on the Waterfront: American Maritime Culture in the Age of Revolution* [Philadelphia: University of Pennsylvania Press, 2004], 175, 179; Peter Linebaugh and Marcus Rediker, *The Many-Headed Hydra: Sailors, Slaves, Commoners, and the Hidden History of the Revolutionary Atlantic* [Boston: Beacon Press, 2000]).

24. William Leete to John Winthrop Jr., 7 Feb. 1660/61, WFPT; quoted in Davis, *English Shipping*, 116; quoted in Hunter, *Purchasing*, 44.

25. The stereotypical association of Indians with alcohol was promoted by such nineteenth-century writers as Harriet Forbes, who claimed that "like all the Indians . . . [the Nipmucs] spent their time making baskets, and drinking up the profits from the sale of them" (quoted in Donna Rae Gould, "Contested Places: The History and Meaning of Hassanamisco," Ph.D. dissertation, University of Connecticut, 2010, p. 154). Peter C. Mancall's excellent study, *Deadly Medicine: Indians and Alcohol in Early America*, examines both the stereotype and the history of Indians and alcohol (Ithaca, N.Y.: Cornell University Press, 1995, chapter 1). The "Notes and Sources" section of *Deadly Medicine* contains an exhaustive bibliography of the historical, anthropological, sociological, psychological, and medical literatures on Native American alcohol consumption. Most of these literatures accept the argument that there is a substantial ethnocultural component to drinking behaviors, and the role alcohol use

and dependence played in Native America cannot be separated from this context. See also Gilbert Quintero, "Making the Indian: Colonial Knowledge, Alcohol, and Native Americans," *American Indian Culture and Research Journal* 25 (2001): 57–71.

On differences between Native and English drinking behaviors, see Mancall, *Deadly Medicine*, 14–27, 68–75; Michael Goode, "Dangerous Spirits: How the Indian Critique of Alcohol Shaped Eighteenth-Century Quaker Revivalism," *Early American Studies* 14, 2 (Spring 2016): 258–283.

26.   Samuel Stow to John Winthrop Jr., 29 April 1673, WFPT; *MCR*, 1:106; *MCR*, 4, part 2:297 (May 1666), 564 (Oct. 1673).

27.   Court records from all of the New England colonies are rife with examples of illegal sales of alcohol to Indians. See, for example, John Pynchon to JWJ, 10 May 1671, WFPT; *SCR*, 1:404; Middlesex Court Folios, 1663-35-4, MA; *PCR*, 5:59; and Mancall, *Deadly Medicine*, 103–106. Captain Wyborne's testimony about the penalty of ten days' labor for drunkenness was given in London in support of charges against Massachusetts Bay Colony for abusing its charter, so the possibility of bias must be considered (*CSPC*, 9: #721). *MCR*, 4, part 2:564.

28.   *MCR*, 5:61–62; *Diary by Increase Mather* (Cambridge, Mass.: John Wilson and Son, University Press, 1900), 27 Jan. 1675/76, p. 23; "John Eliot's Records," *RCBR*, April 1677. In May 1679, colony officials prohibited the selling of strong drink on militia training days as a consequence of the disorder prevalent among English and Indians (*MCR*, 5:211).

29.   *SCR*, 1:267, 330; MAC, 30:259a; Daniel Gookin, in Depositions of David and Hannah Meade, Collection 77, Autographs of Special Note, Box 1, MeHS. Anna White is not mentioned in Ann Wompas's wishes for the disposal of her estate, and John Wompas's uncles Anthony and Thomas Tray asserted after their nephew's death that he had no living children (AWP; MAC, 30:260a).

30.   MAC, 30:259a. John Wompas mentioned the magistrates' prohibition on his land sales in the petition he sent to King Charles II in 1676 (PJW1). Because John was absent from the Massachusetts Bay Colony from around June 1674 until June 1677, the ban on land sales must have begun before his 1674 departure.

31.   *SCR*, 1:267, 330.

32.   *SCR*, 1:267. On legal procedure in the early Massachusetts Courts, see Bradley Chapin, *Criminal Justice in Colonial America, 1606–1660* (Athens: University of Georgia Press, 1983), especially chapter 2.

33.   *SCR*, 1:330.

34.   Depositions of David and Hannah Meade, MeHS; AWP.

35.   It is not clear if John did all the work for Gibbs himself or whether he received the credit for work done by several people. All of the credits fall in a two-week period between 14 May 1674 and 31 May 1674, for a total

credit of one pound, thirteen shillings, and nine pence (Robert Gibbs Account Book, Robert Gibbs Business Records, AAS); *CSPC*, 9: #721.

On wages in seventeenth-century New England, see Gloria L. Main, "Gender, Work, and Wages in Colonial New England," *WMQ* 41, 1 (Jan. 1994), 51–60; Gloria Main reports that the average wage for male farm laborers in rural Massachusetts from 1630 to 1674 was thirteen pence, but wages at the end of this period and in Boston seem to have been higher, as evidenced by the rates of two shillings per day, two shillings and six pence per day, and eighteen pence per day (for servants) paid by Robert Gibbs (Main, "Gender, Work, and Wages," 48; Robert Gibbs Account Book, AAS). In Nov. 1675, the Massachusetts General Court set a wage of one shilling and six pence, or eighteen pence, for laborers hired to do the farm labor of men impressed to serve in King Philip's War (*MCR*, 5:65). In 1687, a French visitor to Boston reported that Indians were paid eighteen pence per day for labor in the fields, while English workmen required a minimum of twenty-four pence per day (*Report of a French Protestant Refugee, in Boston, 1687*, trans. E. T. Fisher [Brooklyn, N.Y.: 1868], 20).

36. Samuel Clough, Map of Boston, 1676, MHS; Robert Gibbs Account Book, AAS. The prices of fabric in the Gibbs account book range from six pence per yard for "black scrit" to eight shillings per yard for fine kersey, but the bulk of fabrics sold for between twenty-one and thirty pence per yard. Woolen frieze, a coarse, napped fabric, fell in this range, at twenty-two pence per yard. John paid more for the white cloth he purchased—two shillings and eight pence (thirty pence) per yard. Formal wear at the time included white collars and cuffs with a black suit, as demonstrated by contemporary portraits (Louise Dresser, "Portraits in Boston, 1630–1720," *Archives of American Art Journal* 6, 3–4 [July–Oct. 1966]: 1–34). Skilled male craftsmen earned around eighteen pence a day in this period, although tailors were on the lower end of the craft wage scale. Female seamstresses earned about 40 percent of a male wage (Main, "Gender, Work, and Wages," 43–44, 48). A "gown" was "a loose flowing upper garment worn as an article of ordinary attire." The term was used for men's as well as women's attire through the seventeenth century (*OED*).

Chapter 6. "New England Hath Lost the Day"

1. This chapter's epigraph comes from Depositions of David and Hannah Meade, Box 1, Autographs of Special Note, Collection 77, MeHS. Jill Lepore, *The Name of War: King Philip's War and the Origins of American Identity* (New York: Knopf, 1998), chapter 2. On the spread of news in seventeenth-century London, see Leslie Shepard, *The History of Street*

Literature (Newton Abbot, U.K.: David & Charles, 1973), 14; and Ian Atherton, "The Itch Grown a Disease: Manuscript Transmission of News in the Seventeenth Century," in *News, Newspapers, and Society in Early Modern Britain*, ed. Joad Raymond (London: Frank Cass, 1999), 39–40.

2. *MCR*, 4, part 2:58; Gavin Weightman, *London's Thames: The River that Shaped a City and Its History* (New York: St. Martin's, 2004); Constance A. Crosby, "The Algonkian Spiritual Landscape," in *Algonkians of New England: Past and Present*, ed. Peter Benes, The Dublin Seminar for New England Folklife Annual Proceedings, 1991 (Boston: Boston University Press, 1993), 36; William S. Simmons, *Spirit of the New England Tribes: Indian History and Folklore, 1620–1984* (Hanover, N.H.: University Press of New England, 1986), 97–98.

3. Lisa Brooks, noting that waterways are central to northeastern Native space, cited Indian use of the phrase "the river to which I belong" (*The Common Pot: The Recovery of Native Space in the Northeast* [University of Minnesota Press, 2008], 176 and map 1). Coll Thrush evocatively imagines how indigenous visitors to London would have interpreted the city from a Native perspective in "The Iceberg and the Cathedral: Encounter, Entanglement, and Isuma in Inuit London," *Journal of British Studies* 53, 1 (Jan. 2014): 59–79, and *Indigenous London: Native Travelers at the Heart of Empire* (New Haven, Conn.: Yale University Press, 2016).

   Magunkaquog, Nonantum, Natick, and Hassanamesit were all set on hills. Dwelling and communal spaces were usually placed on the leeward slopes, with the flat hilltop reserved for planting (Stephen A. Mrozowski et al., "Magunkaquog Materiality, Federal Recognition, and the Search for a Deeper History," *International Journal of Historical Archaeology* 13 [2009]: 440, 446; H. F. Keith, "Early History of Hassanamisco [or Keith Hill]," 1886, pp. 7–9, Indian Folder, Grafton Historical Society, Grafton, Massachusetts).

   On London's population, see Patrick Morrah, *Restoration England* (London: Constable, 1979), 53. Arthur Bryant claims a population of 500,000 to 600,000 in *The England of Charles II* (London: Longmans, Green, 1934), 13. For an analysis of population estimates, see Vanessa Harding, "The Population of London, 1550–1770: A Review of the Published Evidence," *The London Journal* 15, 2 (1990): 111–128. The figure of 12,000 for Boston comes from *The Petty Papers: Some Unpublished Writings of Sir William Petty*, 2 vols. (Boston: Houghton Mifflin, 1927), 2:100; Hugh Morrison, *Early American Architecture from the First Colonial Settlements to the National Period* (New York: Oxford University Press, 1952), 88–89. For the history of the monument to the Great Fire of London, see http://www.themonument.info/history/introduction.html.

4. John Spurr, *England in the 1670s: "This Masquerading Age": A History of Early Modern England* (Oxford: Blackwell, 2000), 159; Thrush, "Iceberg

and the Cathedral," 71; Bryant, *England of Charles II*, 18 (quote), 16–17; Liza Picard, *Restoration London* (New York: St. Martin's, 1997), 66.

5. *Simon Bradstreet's Journal, 1664–83*, in *NEHGR*, 9 (1855): 45–46; Morrah, *Restoration England*, 55, 140, 142.

6. Picard, *Restoration London*, 8–9; Bryant Lillywhite, *London Signs: A Reference Book of London Signs from Earliest Times to About the Mid-Nineteenth Century* (London: George Allen and Unwin, 1972); Bryant, *England of Charles II*, 14–16.

7. "An exact survey of the streets, lanes and churches contained within the ruins of the city of London" (London: Old House, 2006); James W. P. Campbell, *Building St. Paul's* (London: Thames & Hudson, 2007), 23; Simon Bradley and Nikolaus Pevsner, *London: The City Churches* (New Haven, Conn.: Yale University Press, 2002 [1998]), 24; A. E. W. Mason, *The Royal Exchange: A Note on the Occasion of the Bicentenary of the Royal Exchange Assurance* (London, 1920), 27–35; Peter Burman, *St. Paul's Cathedral: The New Bell's Cathedral Guides* (London: Bell and Hyman, 1987).

8. For the monument's inscriptions, see http://www.themonument.info/history/inscriptions.html. Lois Green Carr, Russell R. Menard, and Lorena S. Walsh, *Robert Cole's World: Agriculture and Society in Early Maryland* (Chapel Hill: University of North Carolina Press, 1991), 157–161; Campbell, *Building St. Paul's*, 37; Spurr, *England in the 1670s*, 143.

9. Spurr, *England in the 1670s*, 133.

10. Peter Clark, "The Alehouse and the Alternative Society," in *Puritans and Revolutionaries: Essays in Seventeenth-Century History presented to Christopher Hill* (Oxford: Clarendon Press, 1978); Mark Hailwood, *Alehouses and Good Fellowship in Early Modern England* (Woodbridge, U.K.: Boydell & Brewer, 2014); Brian Weiser, *Charles II and the Politics of Access* (Woodbridge, U.K.: The Boydell Press, 2003), 27, 37, 38, 45, 74; Anna Keay, *The Magnificent Monarch: Charles II and the Ceremonies of Power* (London: Continuum, 2008), 171–173.

11. John Winthrop Jr. lodged in Coleman Street while in London (Lucy Downing to John Winthrop Jr., 17 Dec. 1648, in Rosell L. Richardson, *Amos Richardson of Boston and Stonington* [New York: Published by the author, 1906], 17). Bernard Bailyn, *The New England Merchants in the Seventeenth Century* (New York: Harper Torchbooks, 1955), 36–37; J. M. Sosin, *English America and the Restoration Monarchy of Charles II: Transatlantic Politics, Commerce, and Kinship* (Lincoln: University of Nebraska Press, 1980), 15.

12. Samuel Angell, *An Historical Sketch of the Royal Exchange, chiefly compiled from Stowe and other authorities* (London, 1838), 1–6, 9, 20; Effingham Wilson, *Wilson's Description of the New Royal Exchange* (London, 1844), 20–22, 31; Picard, *Restoration London*, 5.

13. Hannah Farber, "The Rise and Fall of the Province of Lygonia, 1643–

1658," *NEQ* 82 (Sept. 2009): 490–513. Farber quotes a letter illustrating the ambulatory business style at the Exchange: "I having noe desire to speake with Mooreton alone, putt him of[f] a turne or 2 on the exchange" (496). *CSPC*, 9: #889.

14. Michael Power, "Shadwell: The Development of a London Suburban Community in the Seventeenth Century," *The London Journal* 4, 1 (1978): 36–37.

15. LMA/Middlesex County Records, Calendar of Sessions Books, Sessions book 355, Hicks Hall, August 1678, p. 40.

16. Joanna Innes, "The King's Bench Prison in the Later Eighteenth Century: Law, Authority, and Order in a London Debtors' Prison," in *An Ungovernable People: The English and Their Law in the Seventeenth and Eighteenth Centuries* (New Brunswick, N.J.: Rutgers University Press, 1980), 250–298, 264. While Innes focuses on rents in the late eighteenth century, late seventeenth-century rents were comparable; see Gregory Clark, "Housing Rents, Housing Quality, and Living Standards in England and Wales, 1640–1909" (1999), 26 (http://faculty.econ.ucdavis .edu/faculty/gclark/papers/housecost.pdf), accessed 18 Oct. 2016. For rents in the parishes of London, see Tai Liu, *Puritan London: A Study of Religion and Society in the City Parishes* (Newark: University of Delaware Press, 1986), 211. For food prices, see Jeremy Boulton, "Food Prices and the Standard of Living in London in the 'Century of Revolution,' 1580–1700," *Economic History Review* 53, 3 (2000): 455–492.

   English seamen with no rank or special skill received wages of twenty-two to forty shillings per month (*SCR*, 1:137, 143, 2:930, 1059; John Foye Account Book, Manuscripts, NEHGS; Robert Sedgwick Ledger, Manuscripts, NEHGS). Native sailors received twenty to twenty-two shillings per month (*SCR*, 2:1092; John Walley Papers, Manuscripts, NEHGS). Based on these very limited examples, Native mariners received pay comparable to that of the least experienced English sailors.

17. Bryant, *England of Charles II*, 35, 40, 103; Morrah, *Restoration England*, 56–57, 106; Clark, "The Alehouse," 50–53. For an example of John treating fifteen people to cider in Natick, Massachusetts, see SCF, #1642, #1644.

18. *MPR*, 9:579; PJW1.

19. LMA, Middlesex Sessions Calendar, Sessions Book 328, Westminster, Oct. 1675, pp. 57, 55–73. On debtors' prisons in early modern England, see Philip Woodfine, "Debtors, Prisons, and Petitions in Eighteenth-Century England," *Eighteenth-Century Life* 30, 2 (Spring 2006): 1–31; Innes, "The King's Bench Prison"; and Anthony Babington, "Newgate in the Eighteenth Century: The Life in Prison of Felons, Debtors, and Rebels," *History Today* 21, 9 (Sept. 1971): 650–657.

20. LMA/MJ/SD-1, Debtors' Petitions; LMA/CLA/047/LJ/13/1677/004.

21. Simon Wood, *Remarks on the Fleet Prison* (London: printed and sold by the author, 1733), 15–16.

22. Copy of fees charged by the Keeper of New Prison, Clerkenwell, LMA/MJ/SP/1671/002, quoted in Richard H. Condon, "The Fleet Prison," *History Today* 14, 7 (July 1964): 453–460; Alexander Harris Pitofsky, *Misplaced in the Prison-House: Prison Reform and the Novel in Eighteenth-Century England* (Ph.D. dissertation, University of Virginia, 2000), 27; R. B. Pugh, "Newgate Between Two Fires," *Guildhall Studies in London History* 3, 3 (1978): 138; LMA, Middlesex Sessions Calendar, Sessions Book 328, Westminster, Oct. 1675.

23. Debtors' sessions were held "according to a late act of Parlamt, for the reliefe and release of poore distressed prissoners" (LMA/MJ/SD/001, Debt Cases). Surviving records show that debtor sessions were held in 1671 and again in 1678–1679, but nothing indicates that they were held during Wompas's year in prison (LMA/Middlesex County Records, Sessions book 358, Hicks Hall; LMA/Middlesex County Records, Calendar of Sessions Books, vols. 301–361, with index; LMA/Middlesex Sessions Calendar for 1678–1679).

24. MD, 6:101–102, 86–87. While "liberty prisons" were intended for debtors only, court orders banning persons charged with criminal misdemeanors from these prisons suggest that intent was not always fulfilled (LMA, Sessions Book 328, Westminster, Oct. 1675, pp. 47–49). Wood, *Remarks on the Fleet Prison*, 8, 10–11, 15–16; Pitofsky, *Misplaced in the Prison-House*, 25–28.

25. Brian Weiser, "Access and Petitioning During the Reign of Charles II," in *The Stuart Courts* (Stroud, U.K.: Sutton, 2000), 203. PJW1; PJW2; "Was Gov. Leverett a Knight?" *NEHGR* 35: 272–275.

26. Weiser, "Access and Petitioning," 203–204; Depositions of Nicholas Wardner, Thomas Wilkison, and Anne Wilkison (1682), CO 1/48, no. 116, TNA.

27. Sosin, *English America*, 172; Colonial Entry Book, vol. 93:150, CO 389/4, TNA; PJW1.
    On American Indian petitions and visits to the British Crown (most of which took place in the eighteenth century), see Eric Hinderaker, "The 'Four Indians Kings' and the Imaginative Construction of the First British Empire," *WMQ* 53 (July 1996): 487–526; Camilla Townsend, *Pocahontas and the Powhatan Dilemma* (New York: Hill and Wang, 2004); Alden T. Vaughan, *Transatlantic Encounters: American Indians in Britain, 1500–1776* (New York: Cambridge University Press, 2006); Craig Yirush, "'Chief Princes and Owners of All': Native American Appeals to the Crown in the Early Modern British Atlantic," in *Indigenous Versus European Land Claims, 1500–1914*, ed. Saliha Belmessous (Oxford University Press, 2011); Jace Weaver, *The Red Atlantic: America Indigenes and the Mak-*

ing of the Modern World, 1000–1927 (Chapel Hill: University of North Carolina Press, 2014); and Thrush, *Indigenous London.*

28. MAC, 30:132–333, 72–73; *CSPC*, 5: #1103; Jonathan Beecher Field, *Errands into the Metropolis: New England Dissidents in Revolutionary London* (Hanover, N.H.: University Press of New England, 2009), chapter 3; Harry M. Ward, *The United Colonies of New England,1643–1690* (New York: Vantage, 1961), chapter 7. For another example of an Indian petition benefiting an English ally (Rhode Island), see "Petition of Weeounkbass, Queen in the Niantick country, to the king," *CSPC*, 10: #1338. On Richard Thayer's efforts to use royal appeal to secure Indian land, see MAC, 30: 275a; and William S. Pattee, MD, *A History of Old Braintree and Quincy* (Quincy: Green & Prescott, 1878), 40–54.

29. Jeremy Dupertuis Bangs, *Indian Deeds: Land Transactions in Plymouth Colony, 1620–1691* (Boston: NEHGS, 2002), 314–316.

30. Administering oaths of allegiance to the colony rather than the Crown took place as late as October 1677 (10 October 1677, MHS Photostats, MHS). On the failure of Massachusetts Bay Colony officials to administer the oaths of allegiance and supremacy to the king in the colony, see *CSPC*, 9: #848; 10: #667–668. After arriving in England, Stoughton and Bulkeley expressed their willingness to receive the oaths, and they were administered in April 1677 (*CSPC*, 10: #653, #675). In April 1678, King Charles II again sent a letter requesting that colony leaders give the oath as administered in England, and in October 1678, the Court complied (*MCR*, 5:193); PJW1.

31. *MCR*, 4, part 2:58; William Shakespeare, *The Tempest*, II.ii.31–33; PJW1. Walter Woodward notes that John Winthrop sent specimens of exotic New World creatures to Charles II, including a starfish, which the king was so taken with that he ordered it to be "engraven and printed" (*Prospero's America: John Winthrop, Jr: Alchemy and the Creation of New England Culture, 1606–1676* [Chapel Hill: University of North Carolina Press, 2010], 295). The king's taste for the exotic was shared by many of his subjects. Diarist John Evelyn wrote in October 1677 that "I went with Mrs. Godolphin and my wife to Blackwall, to see some Indian curiosities" (*Diary and Correspondence of John Evelyn, F.R.S.*, ed. William Bray, Esq. [London: Henry Colburn, publisher, 1850], vol. 2, 9 Oct. 1677). See also Christian F. Feest, "The Collecting of American Indian Artifacts in Europe, 1493–1750," in *America in European Consciousness, 1493–1750*, ed. Karen Ordahl Kupperman (Chapel Hill: University of North Carolina Press, 1995).

32. Colonial Entry Book, vol. 93:150, CO 389/4, TNA; *MCR*, 4, part 2:58.

33. The copy of the king's letter in Governor Leverett's papers carries an endorsement indicating that it was received 2 June 1677, just after John Wompas arrived back in Massachusetts ("Was Gov. Leverett a Knight?").

34. MD, 6:101–102, 86–87.

35. *SCR*, 1:267 (see also 1:330); MAC, 30:224a.

36. The boy from Hassanamesit was Joseph, the eleven-year-old son of Anaweekin (Neal Salisbury, ed., *The Sovereignty and Goodness of God, by Mary Rowlandson, with Related Documents* [Boston: Bedford, 1997], 144); MAC, 30:224a; *HColl*, 174–175; *MHSC*, 4th ser., 2:283–284.

37. *CSPC*, 9: #506; Orders in Council, 1660–1692, in *MHSC*, 4th ser., 2:287; *CSPC*, 9: #838. On the political crisis facing Massachusetts in this period, see Stephen Saunders Webb, *1676: The End of American Independence* (New York: Knopf, 1984); Robert M. Bliss, *Revolution and Empire: English Politics and the American Colonies in the Seventeenth Century* (Manchester, U.K.: Manchester University Press, 1990); and Pulsipher, *Subjects unto the Same King*.

38. On the relationship between Randolph and Mason, see Charles Wesley Tuttle, *Capt. John Mason, the Founder of New Hampshire* (Boston: The Prince Society, 1887), 102. Robert Noxon Toppan, *Edward Randolph, Including His Letters and Official Papers*, 7 vols. (Boston: The Prince Society, 1898), 1:48; *MCR*, 5:106–113.

39. *CSPC*, 9: #797, #1070; *MHSC*, 4th ser., 2:286; Edward Randolph to Sec. Coventry, 17 June 1676, in *CSPC*, 9: #953. See also *CSPC*, 9: #847, #848, #945, #1037, #1067, #1158.

40. John Winthrop Jr.'s English contacts informed him that "no busynesse can be done here at Court without [he hath] some Interest" (Woodward, *Prospero's America*, 256). See also Linda Levy Peck, "Benefits, Brokers, and Beneficiaries: The Culture of Exchange in Seventeenth Century England," in *Court, Country, and Culture: Essays on Early Modern British History in Memory of Perez Zagorin* (Rochester, N.Y.: University of Rochester Press, 1992). *CSPC*, 9: #1186; Governor Leverett to Sir Joseph Williamson, 13 Oct. 1676, *CSPC*, 9: #1070; Letter of instructions to the colony agents, 6 Sept. 1676, in *MCR*, 5:115.

41. The king likely invited the Massachusetts agents to visit him on Sunday, 17 Dec. 1676, the first Sunday following the reading of the colony's papers before the Privy Council. John Wompas's report of their visit the following Monday appears in the Depositions of David and Hannah Meade, MeHS.

42. Simon Thurley, *The Whitehall Palace Plan of 1670*, London Topographical Society Publication No. 153 (London, 1998), 20; Keay, *Magnificent Monarch*, 173, 137, 101, 96; Weiser, *Politics of Access*, 27, 75.

43. Derek Wilson, "Was Hans Holbein's Henry VIII the Best Piece of Propaganda Ever?" *Daily Telegraph*, 23 April 2009 (http://www.telegraph.co.uk/news/uknews/5206727/Was-Hans-Holbeins-Henry-VIII-the-best-piece-of-propaganda-ever.html), accessed 4 Oct. 2016.

44. Keay, *Magnificent Monarch*, 101; Morrah, *Restoration England*, 52; "News Foreign and Domestick," *Universal Magazine*, July 1761, 52; *MCR*, 5:156.

45. At least eight short accounts of King Philip's War were printed as bulle-

tins in London in 1675 and 1676 (Charles H. Lincoln, ed., *Narratives of the Indian Wars, 1675–1699* [New York: Barnes & Noble, 1952], 21–22).

46. Depositions of David and Hannah Meade, MeHS.

47. Depositions of David and Hannah Meade, MeHS; *CSPC*, 5: #230; 7: #1397, #1408, #1420; 9: #412–413, #1186–1187; 10: #4, #9–10, #170.

48. SCF, #1642; Depositions of David and Hannah Meade, MeHS.

Chapter 7. "Hee Had Lost a Great Many Men in the Warr"

1. This chapter's epigraphs come from Hannah Meade's deposition, Box 1, Collection 77, Autographs of Special Note, MeHS and AWP (as reported by Milcah Wright). King Philip's War prompted nearly thirty primary accounts (Jill Lepore, *The Name of War: King Philip's War and the Origins of American Identity* [New York: Alfred A. Knopf, 1998], 241–244). Among those was Daniel Gookin's *An Historical Account of the Doings and Sufferings of the Christian Indians in New England*, which focuses on the wartime experiences of Christian Indians (*HAcc*). Douglas Leach's *Flintlock and Tomahawk: New England in King Philip's War* (New York: Macmillan, 1958) remained the standard study of the war until the turn of the twenty-first century. New treatments of the war include Lepore, *The Name of War*; James D. Drake, *King Philip's War: Civil War in New England* (Amherst: University of Massachusetts Press, 1999); Jenny Hale Pulsipher, *Subjects unto the Same King: Indians, English, and the Contest of Authority in Colonial New England* (Philadelphia: University of Pennsylvania Press, 2005); Kyle Zelner, *A Rabble in Arms: Massachusetts Towns and Militiamen During King Philip's War* (New York: New York University Press, 2009); Daniel R. Mandell, *King Philip's War: Colonial Expansion, Native Resistance, and the End of Indian Sovereignty* (Baltimore: Johns Hopkins University Press, 2010); and Julie A. Fisher and David J. Silverman, *Ninigret, Sachem of the Niantics and Narragansetts: Diplomacy, War, and the Balance of Power in Seventeenth-Century New England and Indian Country* (Ithaca, N.Y.: Cornell University Press, 2014).

2. Alden T. Vaughan, *New England Frontier: Puritans and Indians, 1620–1675*, 3rd ed. (Norman: University of Oklahoma Press, 1995 [1965]), Appendix III, p. 342; *HColl*, 179. Eight Nipmuc sachems submitted to the English in 1668 also, in order to secure protection from Narragansett attacks (Richard W. Cogley, *John Eliot's Mission to the Indians Before King Philip's War* [Cambridge, Mass.: Harvard University Press, 1999], 30–33, 155); MAC, 67:214–217; Leach, *Flintlock and Tomahawk*, 73–74; Dennis A. Connole, *The Indians of the Nipmuck Country in Southern New England, 1630–1750: An Historical Geography* (Jefferson, N.C.: McFarland, 2001), 163–164.

3. *HColl*, 177, 193; *HAcc*, 468, 449, 534–535; Kathleen Joan Bragdon, "Another Tongue Brought In: An Ethnohistorical Study of Native Writings

in Massachusett" (Ph.D. dissertation, Brown University, 1981), 74; MAC, 30:198b.

4. *HAcc*, 450–451.

5. Pulsipher, *Subjects unto the Same King*, 151–153, 140; *HAcc*, 458, 473.

6. "The Examination and Relation of James Quannapaquait," in *The Sovereignty and Goodness of God, by Mary Rowlandson*, ed. Neal Salisbury (Boston: Bedford, 1997), 120–121; *HAcc*, 473, 485. In 2010, descendants of the Christian Indians and their supporters staged a commemorative "sacred run and paddle" to Deer Island (Christine DeLucia, "The Memory Frontier: Uncommon Pursuits of Past and Place in the Northeast After King Philip's War," *JAH* (March 2012): 975; MAC, 30:200a.

7. *HAcc*, 475.

8. On Thomas Wuttasacomponom's status, see *HColl*, 192. The Massachusetts Council ordered English soldiers to destroy the corn in the towns of Christian Indians who had defected to Philip, but soldiers also destroyed some of the fields of friendly Indians (*HAcc*, 467; MAC, 67:220). Several Christian Indians from Magunkaquog attributed their attack on the Eames farmstead, which led to the death of several members of that family, to their suspicion that Thomas Eames had stolen their corn (MAC, 30:211, 173).

   Colonist Thomas Walley reported that the Indians "take great notice of the severeity showed towards the squaws that are sent a way, some of them much greived others I feare pro[vo]ked" (Thomas Walley to Rev. John Cotton, 17 April 1676, John Davis Papers, #30, MHS). Beginning in May 1676, the colonies offered mercy to Indians who surrendered to English authority; some of those who surrendered were also sent out of the country as slaves (Linford D. Fisher, "'Why Shall Wee Have Peace to Bee Made Slaves': Indian Surrenderers During and After King Philip's War," *Ethnohistory* 64, 1 [2017]: 65–90, and "'Dangerous Designes': The 1676 Barbados Act to Prohibit New England Indian Slave Importation," *WMQ* 71 [Jan. 2014]: 99–121); DeLucia, "Memory Frontier"; Virginia Bernhard, *Slaves and Slaveholders in Bermuda, 1616–1782* (University of Missouri Press, 1999), chapter 2; Margaret Ellen Newell, *Brethren by Nature: New England Indians, Colonists, and the Origins of American Slavery* (Ithaca, N.Y.: Cornell University Press, 2015), chapters 6 and 7; and Wendy Warren, *New England Bound: Slavery and Colonization in Early America* (New York: Liveright, 2016); Rev. John Eliot's Records, *RCBR*, June 1676; *HAcc*, 477–480.

9. *HAcc*, 477; MAC, 30:188, 188a. William Torrey, for the Deputies to the General Court, concurred with the magistrates' demand, writing, "We desire you to obtain those false messengrs of cruelty to the praying Indians . . . that they may receive condigne punishment" (MAC, 30:189).

10. Roger Williams to John Leverett, 14 Jan. 1675, *MHSC*, 4th ser., 6:307; "The Examination and Relation of James Quannapaquait," in *Sovereignty*,

ed. Salisbury, 121, 125. On captured Indians sent to Barbados and Bermuda as slaves, see Fisher, "'Dangerous Designes.'"

11. "A True Account of the most Considerable Occurrences that have hapned in the Warre between the English and the Indians in New-England" (London, 1676 [reprinted by The New England & Virginia Company, Salem, Mass.]), 2, 7. On the impact of Canonchet's death, see Pulsipher, *Subjects unto the Same King*, 202–203; *CCR*, 2:474–477, 480; *PCR*, 5:173–174, 207; MAC, 30:216–217.

12. MAC, 30:172; Salisbury, ed., *Sovereignty*, 137–138; SD, 13:202–204; Rev. John Eliot's Records, *RCBR*, 21–22 June 1676.

13. Daniel Gookin reported Job Nesutan's wartime death; however, a Middlesex County Court in 1678 called for a Job Nesutan and his wife to appear to give evidence in a case, suggesting that he may actually have survived (*HAcc*, 444; Middlesex Court Folios, 1678-78-4-c, MA). On the sale of Joseph Tuppakuwillin into slavery, see MAC, 30:198. Three Christian Indians were executed 21 Sept. 1676, in connection with the murder of the Eames family (MAC, 30:210a, 211, 212, 215b, 216–217; *HAcc*, 532). Three other Indians were executed 26 Sept. 1676 (*The Diary of Samuel Sewall, 1674–1729*, ed. M. Halsey Thomas [New York: Farrar, Straus and Giroux, 1973], 22–23); *HColl*, 195; *HAcc*, 533.

14. MHS Photostats, 27 June 1675, MHS; *MCR*, 5:57, 46–47.

15. Jenny Hale Pulsipher, "Massacre at Hurtleberry Hill: Christian Indians and English Authority in Metacom's War," *WMQ* 53 (July 1996): 459–486. Until the late seventeenth century, racial identity had less to do with color than culture; prejudice certainly existed between cultural others, but behavior and beliefs divided them much more than skin. See, for example, Nancy Shoemaker, "How Indians Got to Be Red," *American Historical Review* 102, 3 (June 1997): 625–644; Joyce E. Chaplin, "Race," in *The British Atlantic World, 1500–1800*, ed. David Armitage and Michael J. Braddick (New York: Palgrave Macmillan, 2002); Cogley, *John Eliot's Mission*, 7–9; Ivan Hannaford, *Race: The History of an Idea in the West* (Baltimore: Johns Hopkins University Press, 1996), xii–xv, chapters 6–7; and Vaughan, *New England Frontier*, 20, 62–63, 324 and *Roots of American Racism: Essays on the Colonial Experience* (New York: Oxford University Press, 1995), chapters 1–2, 8.

16. George Madison Bodge, *Soldiers in King Philip's War*, 3rd ed. (Baltimore: Genealogical Publishing, 1997 [1906], 67–68); *HAcc*, 455–458; *The Diary of Samuel Sewall*, 1:18–19, 21–23; see also MAC, 30:183a, 221b. John Hull recorded the sale of seventy-seven captive Indians in Boston on 24 August 1676 and 109 more on 23 September 1676 (Salisbury, ed., *Sovereignty*, 145–147). Samuel Shrimpton reported purchasing nine captives in July 1676. Indians were also sent out of the country as slaves in 1675 (MHS Photostats, 8 July 1676, 13 Aug. 1675, MHS; MAC, 30:184a).

17. *CCR*, 2:481–482; *MCR*, 5:114–115; MAC, 30:226, 228, 184a; Morgan

Lodge to Sir Joseph Williamson, Deal, 17 Nov. 1675, YIPP; A List of Slaves Belonging to His Majesty's Bagnio at Tangiers, 20 Feb. 1677, YIPP; Letter from Captain Thomas Hamilton to the Admiralty Board, 16 Dec. 1675, YIPP; *CLM*, 251–252; *CCR*, 2:288–290, 379, 385.

18. On the commodification of captives of King Philip's War, see Newell, *Brethren by Nature*, chapter 6; Salisbury, ed., *Sovereignty*, 145–147; AWP.

19. Vickers and Walsh, *Young Men and the Sea*, 83–85, 146, 153; Peter Pope, "The Practice of Portage in the Early Modern North Atlantic," *Journal of the Canadian Historical Association* 6, 1 (1995): 24–25, 31–32.

20. AWP. Patricia Trautman provides an excellent overview of clothing styles, class, and sumptuary law in "Dress in Seventeenth-Century Cambridge, Massachusetts: An Inventory-Based Reconstruction," in *Early American Probate Inventories*, The Dublin Seminar for New England Folk Life Annual Proceedings, 1987, ed. Peter Benes (Boston: Boston University Press, 1987), 51–73.

21. AWP. Ann's inventory is one of only a handful of probate records or wills of Native people from early America. For other examples, see WJW; the will of Mary Mecumpas, in *A Digest of the Early Connecticut Probate Records*, comp. Charles William Manwaring (Hartford, Conn: R. S. Peck, 1904), 5: 487–488; Katherine Hermes, "By Their Desire Recorded: Native American Wills and Estate Papers in Colonial Connecticut," *Connecticut History* 38, 2 (1999): 150–173; and Elizabeth A. Little, "Probate Records of Nantucket Indians" (Nantucket, Mass.: Archaeology Dept., Nantucket Historical Association, 1980).

22. Ann Wompas's household goods are similar to those listed in the inventory of Alice Catlin, widow of a merchant from Lynne, before her remarriage to Evan Thomas (AWP; SD, 3:448–449). To compare Ann's clothing with that of seventeenth-century female colonists from Cambridge, see Trautman, "Dress in Seventeenth-Century Cambridge," 59.

23. Milcah Wright and Sarah Ellis both testified of the events surrounding Ann Wompas's death (AWP). Rebecca J. Tannenbaum notes that "a sick person was never alone—there was always at least one watcher," usually female if the sick person was a woman ("The Housewife as Healer: Medicine as Women's Work in Colonial New England," in *Women's Work in New England, 1620–1920*, Dublin Seminar for New England Folklife, ed. Peter Benes [Boston: Boston University Press, 2003], 162). SCR, 1:123, 259; Samuel C. Clough, "Remarks on the Compilation of the Boston Book of Possessions," *Colonial Society of Massachusetts Publications* 27 (1932): 5; SD, 6:302; 11:82–84; *RRCCB*, 2:61–62; Samuel Clough, Map of Boston, 1676, MHS; SD, 10:73–74; AWP.

24. AWP.

25. Cornelia Hughes Dayton, *Women Before the Bar: Gender, Law, and Society in Connecticut, 1639–1789* (Chapel Hill: University of North Carolina Press, 1995), 19–20.

26. Cornelia Dayton notes that "in the North American colonies, ending an unhappy marriage through mutual agreement or desertion was not infrequent. . . . Communities appear to have protected abandoned women by sanctioning their self-support through industry or remarriage, under the collective pretense that the husbands were dead. Nonetheless, the property and status of such family units lacking a legitimate male head were inevitably precarious, being continually subject to legal challenge or the husband's surprise return" (Dayton, *Women Before the Bar,* 110).

27. James T. Turner, "Factors Influencing the Development of the Hostage Identification Syndrome," *Political Psychology* 6, 4 (1985): 705–711. For an example of a seventeenth-century English child assimilating to an Indian family and culture, see John Demos, *The Unredeemed Captive: A Family Story from Early America* (New York: Knopf, 1994). Hewes spent years working to ensure the well-being of his uncle's widow and orphan. The fact that he was elected as sergeant and later lieutenant of Roxbury's militia, deputy to the General Court, and town selectman is a measure of the esteem of his fellow citizens (Eben Putnam, ed. and comp., *Lieutenant Joshua Hewes: A New England Pioneer and Some of His Descendants* [Privately printed, 1913], 14, 39, 41–42, 48); AWP.

28. AWP; *CLM,* 53.

29. While it is possible that Joshua Hewes Sr.'s efforts in behalf of his uncle's heirs diminished his own fortunes, they were already diminishing before Foote's death (SD, 1:166, 214). On Joshua Hewes Sr.'s wealth, see Charles M. Ellis, *The History of Roxbury Town* (Boston: Samuel G. Drake, 1847), 36–37, 69–70. On his business relationship with Joshua Foote, see Bernard Bailyn, *The New England Merchants in the Seventeenth Century* (New York: Harper Torchbooks, 1955), 35, 51, 101; and Putnam, *Lieutenant Joshua Hewes,* 28–30, 63–66, 86–87. On Hewes's marriage to Alice Crabtree, see *RRCCB,* 9:58; AWP.

Chapter 8. "The English Did Wrong Them About Their Lands"

1. This chapter's epigraph comes from SCF, #1642, 1642a, 1644; and Deposition of Hannah Meade, Box 1, Collection 77, Autographs of Special Note, MeHS. Samuel Clough, Map of Boston, 1676, MHS. The best candidate I have found for the ship that carried John Wompas from London to Boston was Captain Anderson's, which arrived in Boston on 15 May 1677 (*The Diary of Samuel Sewall, 1674–1729,* ed. M. Halsey Thomas [New York: Farrar, Straus and Giroux, 1973], 43). John Warner, the eighteen-year-old son of Nicholas Warner, arrived in Boston and began lodging with Benjamin Franklin on that day. Wompas had made out a deed for 1,000 acres of land to John Warner in gratitude for the services Nicholas Warner had done for him in England, and it is likely they came to

Boston together, Wompas to clear the way for selling his land, and Warner to redeem his deed (SCF, #1804).

2. Alarms could be signaled by lighting a beacon, discharging a musket three times in succession, continually beating a drum, or sending a messenger to nearby towns (*MCR*, 2:25, 28–29, 43, 115, 120, 223; 5:242). For the location of Boston's beacon, see Walter Muir Whitehill, *Boston: A Topographical History* (Cambridge, Mass.: Harvard University Press, 1959), 7; *CLM*, 225; *Diary by Increase Mather*, Samuel A. Green, ed. (Cambridge, Mass.: John Wilson and Son, University Press, 1900), 54. The General Court issued orders to regulate rebuilding in the aftermath of the fire on 24 May 1677 (*MCR*, 5:140).

3. Rev. John Eliot's Records, *RCBR*, 1677; *CLM*, 223, 225, 345.

4. Morgan Lodge to Sir Joseph Williamson, 17 Nov. 1675, YIPP; Morgan Lodge to Sir Joseph Williamson, 8 Dec. 1675, YIPP. Wompas's continuing contact with New Englanders visiting London would likely have kept him apprised of the major news from home, including the progress of King Philip's War (*MPR*, 9:579). Eben Putnam, ed. and comp., *Lieutenant Joshua Hewes: A New England Pioneer and Some of His Descendants* (Privately printed, 1913), 91–92.

5. *CLM*, 223; *MCR*, 5:136.

6. SD, 5:540–543. Robert Thomson, a resident of England who held the Wompases' loan, was one of the governors of the New England Company. It is possible that his support for the Indian mission and for Natives like John and Ann who had received English education made him decline to foreclose on the loan. The Hewes family remained in possession of the house until 1726, when it was sold for 210 pounds (Putnam, *Lieutenant Joshua Hewes*, 100).

7. *CSPC*, 9: #1023; a transcription of the letter, including an endorsement indicating that Leverett received it on 2 June 1677, appears in *NEHGR*, 35:272–275; Michael G. Hall, *The Last American Puritan: The Life of Increase Mather* (Middletown, Conn.: Wesleyan University Press, 1988), 113, 188; SD, 5:541–543.

8. CO 389/4, p. 150, TNA; Middlesex Court Folios, 1676, 93-2-b, MA.

9. Because the oaths of allegiance and supremacy were not regularly administered in Massachusetts, John must have taken his oaths at Whitehall. On the meaning of subject status within the English empire, see Craig Yirush, *Settlers, Liberty, and Empire: The Roots of Early American Political Theory, 1675–1775* (New York: Cambridge University Press, 2011), chapters 1 and 2; Lauren Benton, *A Search for Sovereignty: Law and Geography in European Empires, 1400–1900* (New York: Cambridge University Press, 2010), chapter 2; Brendan McConville, *The King's Three Faces: The Rise and Fall of Royal America, 1688–1776* (Chapel Hill: University of North Carolina Press, 2006), 232–238. For evidence that the contents of John Wompas's letter from the king had spread in the colony, see SCF, #1642.

10. *HAcc*, 518.

11. Gookin said that the Court was held "at [Cowesit] neare the Lower falls of Charles River" (MAC, 30:259a); Richard W. Cogley, *John Eliot's Mission to the Indians Before King Philip's War* (Cambridge, Mass.: Harvard University Press, 1999), 229–230.

12. Brubaker and Cooper, "Beyond Identity," *History and Society* 29, 1 (Feb. 2000): 1, 19. On the complicated nature of identity, especially in cross-cultural figures like John Wompas, see James H. Merrell, "'The Cast of His Countenance': Reading Andrew Montour," in *Through a Glass Darkly: Reflections on Personal Identity in Early America*, ed. Ronald Hoffman, Mechal Sobel, and Frederika J. Teute (Chapel Hill: University of North Carolina Press, 1997); I thank Greg Nobles for pointing out John Wompas's similarity to Andrew Montour. See also James A. Clifton, *Being and Becoming Indian: Biographical Studies of North American Frontiers* (Chicago: Dorsey, 1989); Marge Bruchac, "Musings on Northeastern Indian Identity" (http://www.avcnet.org/ne-do-ba/his_mb03.html), accessed 18 Nov. 2016; Liza Black, "The Predicament of Identity," *Ethnohistory* 48, 1–2 (2001): 337–350; and Eva Marie Garroutte, *Real Indians: Identity and the Survival of Native America* (Berkeley: University of California Press, 2003).

13. I base my assertion that Waban, Piambow, and John Awassamog were John Wompas's kinsmen on the 1681 testimony of a number of "principal Indians" that, in addition to Thomas and Anthony Tray, they were the legal holders of the land "adjoining Hassanamisco" which John Wompas claimed as his inheritance (MAC, 30:262a); Cogley, *John Eliot's Mission*, appendix 3. Thomas Tray was known as "Totherswamp" or "Tottesway" in the 1660s and earlier. MAC, 30:259a.

14. On the challenges of intercultural brokerage, see Margaret Connell Szasz, ed., *Between Indian and White Worlds: The Cultural Broker* (Norman: University of Oklahoma Press, 1994); James H. Merrell, *Into the American Woods: Negotiators on the Pennsylvania Frontier* (New York: Norton, 1999); Clara Sue Kidwell, "Indian Women as Cultural Mediators," *Ethnohistory* 39 (1992): 97–107; Eric Hinderaker, "Translation and Cultural Brokerage," in *A Companion to American Indian History*, ed. Philip J. Deloria and Neal Salisbury (Malden, Mass.: Blackwell, 2002); Louise A. Breen, "Praying with the Enemy: Daniel Gookin, King Philip's War, and the Dangers of Intercultural Mediatorship," in *Empire and Others: British Encounters with Indigenous Peoples, 1600–1850*, ed. Martin Daunton and Rich Halpern (Philadelphia: University of Pennsylvania Press, 1999); and Frederick Fausz, "Middlemen in Peace and War: Virginia's Earliest Indian Interpreters, 1608–1632," *Virginia Magazine of History and Biography* 95 (1987): 41–64; MAC, 30:262a, 259a; SCF, #1642.

15. SCF, #1642, 1642a, 1644.

16. Andrew Pittimee used a number of different marks or initials for his sig-

nature, but several of them include cursive English letters (MAC, 30:276, 279a, 280; Ayer NM MS 23, Vault Box, Newberry Library, Chicago, Ill.). John Hammond to John Winthrop Jr., 4 Oct. 1666, WFPT; Jenny Hale Pulsipher, "Massacre at Hurtleberry Hill: Christian Indians and English Authority in Metacom's War," *WMQ* 53 (July 1996): 459–486, and "'Our Sages are Sageles': A Letter on Massachusetts Indian Policy After King Philip's War," *WMQ* 58 (April 2001), 445; SCF, #1642.

17. MAC, 30:199, 121. The report of this incident is undated. Archivists indexed it in 1663, but it appears to be connected to two other documents dated 1682, suggesting that the incident occurred around that time (MAC, 30:272a, 272b).

18. SCF, #1642a.

19. SCF, #1642; *HIW*, 2:235–236; SCF, #1596; *Diary by Increase Mather*, 48; Depositions of David and Hannah Meade, MeHS.

20. Depositions of David and Hannah Meade, MeHS.

21. CO 1-37, no. 70, TNA; Pulsipher, *Subjects unto the Same King*, 233–236.

22. Depositions of David and Hannah Meade, MeHS; SCF, #1642; MD, 6:82–83, 11:80–81, 6:101–102, 6:86–87, 6:84. It is notable that Franklin struck a much better bargain than Warner for the same amount of land. Wompas seems to have had some difficulty convincing Franklin to make him the loan. Wompas sweetened the deal by claiming the land included direct access to the well-traveled Connecticut highway and all the potential easements and trade benefits that might accrue from that location.

23. MAC, 30:260a; Middlesex Court Records, 3:86, MA; William Lincoln, *History of Worcester, Massachusetts* (Worcester, Mass.: Charles Hersey, 1862), 10–12; SCF, #1642.

24. Massachusetts Council to Major Pynchon, 10 July 1675, Winthrop Papers [MS], MHS; MD, 4:72–74, 7:194–195. Nipmuc Indians had good reason to oppose Ephraim Curtis's continued settlement at Quinsigamog. He headed a group of Englishmen sent to destroy corn at the towns of Christian Indians who had defected to the enemy, contributing to Indian starvation during the winter of 1676. He also antagonized Christian Indians loyal to the English by seizing guns from Natick Indians (MAC, 67:256a, 30:179a). Peter Leavenworth and Alice Nash also note examples of Indians attacking English-occupied property that they perceived as illegitimately obtained or whose occupants had offended local Indians (Peter S. Leavenworth, "'The Best Title That Indians Can Claim': Native Agency and Consent in the Transferal of Pawtucket Land in the Seventeenth Century," *NEQ* 72 [June 1999]: 278, 288; Alice M. Nash, "Quanquan's Mortgage," in *Cultivating a Past: Essays on the History of Hadley, Massachusetts*, ed. Marla Miller [University of Massachusetts Press, 2009], 39). John Winthrop Jr. to Thomas Willys, 26 July 1664, WFPT.

25. Dennis A. Connole, *The Indians of the Nipmuck Country in Southern New England, 1630–1750: An Historical Geography* (Jefferson, N.C.: McFar-

land, 2001), chapter 8; Jean M. O'Brien, *Dispossession by Degrees: Indian Land and Identity in Natick, Massachusetts, 1650–1790* (Lincoln: University of Nebraska Press, 2003 [1997]), 74–78.

26. *HColl*, 71; MAC, 30:276.

27. Rev. John Eliot's Records, *RCBR*, 1677; MAC, 30:259a; Kathleen J. Bragdon, *Native People of Southern New England, 1500–1650* (Norman: University of Oklahoma Press, 1996), chapter 5; O'Brien, *Dispossession by Degrees*, 81; WJW.

28. *CCR*, 2:507–508; MAC, 3:330; SCF, #1642a.

29. James Axtell, "The Vengeful Women of Marblehead: Robert Roules's Deposition of 1677," *WMQ* 31 (Oct. 1974): 647–652.

30. Kathleen J. Bragdon, "Emphatical Speech and Great Action: An Analysis of Seventeenth-Century Native Speech Events Described in Early Sources," *Man in the Northeast* 33 (1987): 101–111, 106. Ann M. Little views Wompas's insults as an attempt to emasculate the English (*Abraham in Arms: War and Gender in Colonial New England* [Philadelphia: University of Pennsylvania Press, 2007], 42); Deposition of Hannah Meade, MeHS; SCF, #1642.

31. SCF, #1642. Robert Child and Samuel Gorton were two notable examples of colonists whose appeals to the Crown failed to protect them from colonial antagonists (David S. Lovejoy, *Religious Enthusiasm in the New World* [Cambridge, Mass.: Harvard University Press, 1985], chapter 3; Jonathan Beecher Field, *Errands into the Metropolis: New England Dissidents in Revolutionary London* [Hanover, N.H.: University Press of New England, 2009], chapter 3).

32. Katherine A. Hermes, "Jurisdiction in the Colonial Northeast: Algonquian, English, and French Governance," *The American Journal of Legal History* 43, 1 (Jan. 1999): 53; Lion Gardiner, *Relation of the Pequot Warres* (1660), *MHSC*, 3rd ser. 3:131–160.

33. SCF, #1642a; Depositions of David and Hannah Meade, MeHS.

34. Middlesex Court Records 3:195, MA.

35. SCF, #1642, #1644; Middlesex Court Records, 3:195, MA.

36. Middlesex Court Records, 3:193, MA; SCF, #1642; Depositions of David and Hannah Meade, MeHS; Margaret Ellen Newell, *Brethren by Nature: New England Indians, Colonists, and the Origins of American Slavery* (Ithaca, N.Y.: Cornell University Press, 2015), 116, 129.

37. SCF, #1642a; Margaret Newell notes that "contestation for control between local governments in English North America and imperial officials in London meant that Indians' citizenship in the empire remained an occasional question rather than a consistently implemented policy" (*Brethren by Nature*, 58).

38. John Noble, ed., *Records of the Court of Assistants of the Colony of the Massachusetts Bay, 1630–1692*, 3 vols. (Boston: County of Suffolk, 1901), 1:106; SCF, #1644, paper #14; *CLM*, 5.

39. SCF, #1644, paper #14; John Langdon Sibley, *Biographical Sketches of Graduates of Harvard University* (Cambridge, Mass.: Charles William Sever, 1881), vol. 2 (Joseph Dudley, 1665).

40. MD, 6:101–102; *CSPC*, 10: #928; *CCR*, 3:221–222.

41. PJW2; Sibley, *Biographical Sketches*, vol. 2 (John Filer, 1666).

42. Testimony of Walter Fyler, 15 May 1678, YIPP (many thanks to Paul Grant-Costa for bringing this document to my attention); Connole, *Indians of the Nipmuck Country*, 129.

43. PJW2; *CCR*, 3:282–283.

44. Testimony of Walter Fyler, YIPP.

45. On overlapping grants, see Pulsipher, *Subjects unto the Same King*, 130–131; testimony of Walter Fyler, YIPP.

46. PJW2.

Chapter 9. "Royall Protection"

1. This chapter's epigraph comes from CO 5:904, p. 36–37, TNA. See also "From the Lords of the Council, to the Governor and Magistrates," *CCR*, 3:281–282, appendix 22; PJW2.

2. In John Wompas's 1679 deed of land to Edward Pratt he declared himself a resident of the City of London, which usually meant within the city walls (MD, 7:157–160). The surgeon who attended John in his final illness was a resident of the London parish of Allhallowes London Wall, which increases the likelihood that John lived there or nearby (WJW); Sydney Mattocks, "Shadwell," in *The Copartnership Herald* 2, 23 (Christmas 1932–January 1933).

   Shadwell held just over 600 households in 1650. Three-quarters of the male heads of household were employed in sea or river trades, with about 53 percent mariners, 11 percent involved in related trades such as shipbuilding or sailmaking, and 7 percent watermen or lightermen plying their trade on the Thames (Michael Power, "Shadwell: The Development of a London Suburban Community in the Seventeenth Century," *The London Journal* 4, 1 [1978]: 29–32); for victuallers' licenses, see LMA, Middlesex County Records, Calendar of Sessions Books, vols. 301–361: Middlesex Court Sessions, Sessions book 337, Westminster, Oct. 1676, p. 43.

3. LMA, Middlesex County Records, Calendar of Sessions Books, vols. 301–361: Middlesex Court Sessions, Sessions Book 363, Hicks Hall, July 1679, p. 55. For an example of a tobacconist selling ale from his house, see LMA/MJ/SP/1667/02/001. Peter Clark, "The Alehouse and the Alternative Society," in *Puritans and Revolutionaries: Essays in Seventeenth-Century History Presented to Christopher Hill* (Oxford: Clarendon Press, 1978).

   On John Blake, see Almira Torrey Blake, *The Ancestry and Allied Families of Nathan Blake 3rd and Susan (Torrey) Blake: Early Residents of East*

Corinth, Vermont (Boston: Stanhope Press, published by author, 1916), 10–14. In John Wompas's will, John Blake is referred to as "of Plimouth in New-England" (WJW). SCF, #2426 refers to Blake as "late of Sandwich and now of Wrentham."

Samuel Clough, map of Boston, 1676, MHS; Blake, *Ancestry and Allied Families*, 8; WJW; MD, 7:157–160.

4. *The Hatton Correspondence*, 22 Nov. 1677, cited in Sheila Williams, "The Pope-Burning Processions of 1679, 1680 and 1681," *Journal of the Warburg and Courtauld Institutes* 21, 1–2 (Jan.–June 1958): 105.

5. Evelyn reported on 15 Nov. 1678 that Oates "grew so presumptuous, as to accuse the Queen of intending to poison the King" (*Diary and Correspondence of John Evelyn, F.R.S.*, ed. William Bray, Esq., 4 vols. [London: Henry Colburn, publisher, 1850], 2:125–126, 127); Stephen Coote, *Royal Survivor: A Life of Charles II* (New York: Palgrave, 2001), 329–330; Narcissus Luttrell, *A Brief Historical Relation of State Affairs, from September 1678 to April 1714* (Oxford, at the University Press, 1857), 9. See also John Spurr, *England in the 1670s: "This Masquerading Age": A History of Early Modern England* (Oxford: Blackwell, 2000), chapter 9.

6. Luttrell, *A Brief Historical Relation*, 2–4, 9; LMA, Middlesex County Court, Sessions book 361, Westminster, April 1679, pp. 45–46.

7. *CSPC*, 10: #1028.

8. Opponents of Massachusetts present during John Wompas's second sojourn in London included Edward Randolph, Robert Mason, and Ferdinando Gorges, Richard Thayer of Braintree, Massachusetts, and Randall Holden and John Green of Warwick, Rhode Island; *MCR*, 3:95–97; *MCR*, 4, part 2:253–255; *CSPC*, 1:325–326, 5: #1170, 10: #766, see also 5: #999; Reply of Randall Holden and John Greene, Deputies for Warwick, to the Answer of William Stoughton and Peter Bulkeley, Agents for the Massachusetts, CO 1/42, No. 115, 30 July 1678, TNA; PJW2.

9. *CSPC*, 10: #870, #872, #877–878, #880, #893, #904–905, #906, #912–913, #917, #921, #922, #927–928.

10. PJW2; quoted in Richard E. Johnson, *Adjustment to Empire: The New England Colonies, 1675–1715* (New Brunswick, N.J.: Rutgers University Press, 1981), 36; *CSPC*, 7: #352; 11: #1316.

11. Foreign Correspondence, ser. 1, vol. 1:14a, CSL; see also *CCR*, 3:281–282, appendix 22; PJW2.

12. PJW2; Lords of the Council to the Governor and Magistrates, *CCR*, 3:281–282. The 1701 letter is cited in Margaret Ellen Newell, *Brethren by Nature: New England Indians, Colonists, and the Origins of American Slavery* (Ithaca, N.Y.: Cornell University Press, 2015), 194.

13. MD, 6:86–87, 101–102.

14. Lords of the Council to the Governor and Magistrates, *CCR*, 3:281–282. On American Indian petitions to and visits to the British Crown, see Eric Hinderaker, "The 'Four Indians Kings' and the Imaginative Construc-

tion of the First British Empire," *WMQ* 53 (July 1996): 487–526; Alden T. Vaughan, *Transatlantic Encounters: American Indians in Britain, 1500–1776* (New York: Cambridge University Press, 2006); Craig Yirush, "'Chief Princes and Owners of All': Native American Appeals to the Crown in the Early Modern British Atlantic," in *Indigenous Versus European Land Claims, 1500–1914*, ed. Saliha Belmessous (New York: Oxford University Press, 2011), and "Claiming the New World: The Mohegan Case and Amerindian Rights in Eighteenth-Century British America," *Law and History Review* 29, 2 (May 2011): 333–373; Jace Weaver, *The Red Atlantic: America Indigenes and the Making of the Modern World, 1000–1927* (Chapel Hill: University of North Carolina Press, 2014); and Coll Thrush, *Indigenous London: Native Travelers at the Heart of Empire* (New Haven, Conn.: Yale University Press, 2016). I have previously described Indians using royal appeal to raise themselves to an equal status with colonists as subjects of the king, thus removing themselves from direct colonial authority, in *Subjects unto the Same King: Indians, English, and the Contest of Authority in Colonial New England* (Philadelphia: University of Pennsylvania Press, 2005).

The Crown took the same approach with Natives of the colony of Virginia, accepting their submission and declaring them to be "his Majestys subjects" who deserved his protection. But like the Natives of New England, they were required to seek that relief locally, "address[ing] themselves to the governor for relief" (Articles of Peace in Virginia, *Acts of the Privy Council of England, Colonial Series*, vol. 1, 1613–1680, ed. W. L. Grant and James Muro [Liechtenstein: Kraus Reprint, 1966 (1908)], 1: #1169).

15. Lords of the Council to the Governor and Magistrates, *CCR*, 3:281–282.

16. Craig Yirush, *Settlers, Liberty, and Empire: The Roots of Early American Political Theory, 1675–1775* (New York: Cambridge University Press, 2011), 67–74. On Charles II's political struggles with Parliament, see Brian Weiser, *Charles II and the Politics of Access* (Woodbridge, U.K.: Boydell, 2003); and George Macaulay Trevelyan, *The English Revolution, 1688–1689* (London: Oxford University Press, 1938).

17. This section draws from Craig Yirush's excellent discussion "English Rights in an Atlantic World," in *Settlers, Liberty, and Empire*, chapter 1; see also Lauren Benton, *A Search for Sovereignty: Law and Geography in European Empires, 1400–1900* (New York: Cambridge University Press, 2010).

18. *MCR*, 4, part 2:197; *MCR*, 5:200; *MCR*, 5:201; *MCR*, 4, part 2:168–173; *Acts of the Privy Council*, 1: #1216.

19. *CSPC*, 10: #890.

20. CO 1/43, no. 31, TNA.

21. *MD*, 7:157–160. The typical rent for an artisan in London was two shillings six pence per week, the same rent that a debtor in the "state house" (the finest lodging in debtor's prison) paid. The regular rent on the mas-

ter's side of debtor's prison was one shilling six pence per week, and on the common side it was one shilling per week (Joanna Innes, "The King's Bench Prison in the Later Eighteenth Century: Law, Authority, and Order in a London Debtors' Prison," in *An Ungovernable People: The English and Their Law in the Seventeenth and Eighteenth Centuries* (New Brunswick, N.J.: Rutgers University Press, 1980), 250–298, 264; Gregory Clark, "Housing Rents, Housing Quality, and Living Standards in England and Wales, 1640–1909" (1999): 26 (http://faculty.econ.ucdavis .edu/faculty/gclark/papers/housecost.pdf), accessed 18 Oct. 2016; SCF, #1642.

22. *CSPC*, 10: #1130; Robert Noxon Toppan, *Edward Randolph, Including His Letters and Official Papers*, 7 vols. (Boston: The Prince Society, 1898–), 1:120–121, 3:54.

23. For John's efforts to pay Boston's jailer, see SCF, #1809. On the size of a town grant, see MD, 8:317–318. MD, 7:157–160; SCF, #1642. On Pratt's residence near Hassanamesit, see Daniel Gookin to Governor Dudley, 1686, in possession of JW Thornton, Esq., of Boston, *NEHGR* (April 1864): 178.

24. In seventeenth-century England a chirurgeon, also called a barber surgeon, practiced not just surgery but also medicine. G. A. Auden cites a 1608 entry in guild records admitting to practice a man who was "a traviler, a chirurgeon, being skilful, namelie esspeciallie as he saieth in fowre diseases" ("The Gild of Barber Surgeons of the City of York," *Proceedings of the Royal Society of Medicine* [1 Feb. 1928], 1403); WJW.

25. The strategy of using English documents and law to defend Native rights was used by other Natives as well. Jean O'Brien argues that "New England Indians in Natick and elsewhere resisted the aggressions of their neighbors by understanding and using the power of literacy in English and using English forms of deference to push for individual and collective Indian rights" ("'Our Old and Valluable Liberty': A Natick Indian Petition in Defense of Their Fishing Rights, 1748," in *Early Native Literacies in New England: A Documentary and Critical Anthology*, ed. Kristina Bross and Hilary E. Wyss [Amherst: University of Massachusetts Press, 2008], 129).

The scribe recorded the names of John's kinsmen as he heard them: John a Wonsamock was usually recorded as John Awassamog, Norwaruunt was Nowanit, and Pomhammell was likely Pomhaman, who was a ruler at the new Christian Indian town of Mugunkaquog near Hassanamesit in 1671 (WJW; Richard W. Cogley, *John Eliot's Mission to the Indians Before King Philip's War* [Cambridge, Mass.: Harvard University Press, 1999], 254, 256). Alice Nash notes the "internal colonialism" that made Englishmen impose Massachusett pronunciation on Nipmuc speech ("Quanquan's Mortgage," in *Cultivating a Past: Essays on the History of Hadley, Massachusetts*, ed. Marla Miller [Amherst: University of Massachusetts Press, 2009], 31); David J. Costa, "The Dialectology of Southern New England Algonquian," in *Papers of the 38th Algonquian Conference* (2007), 100.

26. MAC, 30:260a; Jean M. O'Brien, *Dispossession by Degrees: Indian Land and Identity in Natick, Massachusetts, 1650–1790* (Lincoln: University of Nebraska Press, 2003 [1997]), 75, 81; see also David J. Silverman, *Faith and Boundaries: Colonists, Christianity, and Community Among the Wampanoag Indians of Martha's Vineyard, 1600–1871* (New York: Cambridge University Press, 2005), 124, 134; WJW; Nash, "Quanquan's Mortgage," 30.

27. MD, 7:157–160 (italics added).

28. WJW.

Chapter 10. "One Piece of Land to Cling on To"

1. This chapter's epigraph comes from Suzanne Benally, "Sanctioned Theft: Tribal Land Loss in Massachusetts," in "We Are Still Here: Tribes in New England Stand Their Ground," *Cultural Survival Quarterly* 38, 2 (June 2014) (https://www.culturalsurvival.org/publications/cultural-survival-quarterly/sanctioned-theft-tribal-land-loss-massachusetts), accessed 1 June 2016. MD, 7:157–160.

2. The Warners and Anthony Mudd had been in the colony for one or two years already. John Warner seems to have arrived about the same time as John Wompas in late May 1677 (MD, 6:86–87). Mudd was in Massachusetts by December of the same year (MD, 6:101–102), and Nicholas Warner by the fall of 1678 (*RRCCB*, 10:57, 7:123); SCF, #1809; SD, 13:292, 383.

3. Dennis A. Connole, *The Indians of the Nipmuck Country in Southern New England, 1630–1750: An Historical Geography* (Jefferson, N.C.: McFarland, 2001), 149–155; William Lincoln, *History of Worcester, Massachusetts* (Worcester: Charles Hersey, 1862), 9–11, 35; *RRCCB*, 7:123. On the warning out system, see Cornelia H. Dayton and Sharon V. Salinger, *Robert Love's Warning: Searching for Strangers in Colonial Boston* (Philadelphia: University of Pennsylvania Press, 2014).

4. SCF, #1809 (John Warner); *SCR*, 2:966 (Anthony Mudd); MAC, 70:466 (Edward Pratt); MD, 7:187–188, 6:82–83 (John Warner).

5. MD, 3:69–70; Lincoln, *History of Worcester*, 14–15; CO 1/48, no. 116, TNA. Warner seems to have been wielding the king's letter as a token of power, not actually reading it aloud. If he had read it, Gookin, Danforth, and the Haynes brothers would surely have commented on the absence of any clear royal command to confirm John Wompas's right to the land.

6. Middlesex Court Records, David Pulsifer transcription, 3:105, 175, 332, MA; Middlesex Court Folios 1677-76-2-b, MA; Ayer MS 329, Vault box, Newberry Library, Chicago, Illinois. On Wilkinson's behavior, see Roger Thompson, *Sex in Middlesex: Popular Mores in a Massachusetts County, 1649–1699* (Amherst: University of Massachusetts Press, 1986), 133–135, 143–145, 171, 174; Ann Wilkinson's charge against Jonathan Danforth

may have been intended as revenge against him for spearheading complaints against Thomas Wilkinson (CO 1/48, no. 116, TNA).

7. CO 1/48, no. 116, TNA.

8. *RRCCB*, 11:57, 113.

9. Thayer acted as a lawyer for Pratt and Blake, probably on the promise of future payment or shares. He is named on Pratt and Blake's 1684 Letter of Attorney, and he sold a full one-eighth share in John Wompas's Nipmuc lands to James Brading and Joseph Peirce of Boston before 1686 (*MHSC*, 5th ser., 9:123–127; SD, 15:33). Men recruited to purchase shares in Wompas's Nipmuc lands included George Danson, John Hayward, John Comer, Joshua Hewes, William Mumford, John Pittom, John Jackson, William Harrison, and Robert Taft (SD, 14:1, 16:89, 39:79). Daniel Gookin to Governor Dudley, 1686, *NEHGR* (April 1864): 178; MAC, 36:407, 410.

10. Danson was convicted of "vilifying Constable Willys in the Execution of his office" and sentenced to pay a fine of forty shillings (*SCR*, 2:867–868). On Mumford, see Mrs. Harriette M. Forbes, "William Mumford, Stone Cutter," *Old Time New England* 13, 3 (1926): 138–149. On Danson, see *SGen* and *SCR*, 2:867–68, 917. Another friend of John Wompas, John Cole, also had Quaker associations. His wife Ursula was frequently punished for meeting with fellow Quakers such as Benanuel Bowers (Middlesex Court Records, Pulsifer transcript, 1:296, MA). On Harrison, see *SGen* and SCF, #2377, paper 13).

11. Daniel Gookin to Joseph Dudley, n.d., *NEHGR* (April 1864): 178; MAC, 36:406–407; Lewis Alexander Leonard, *Life of Alphonso Taft* (New York: Hawke, 1920), 247; *SGen* (Taffe); SD, 11:227 (Hayward); *SCR*, 2:1086–1092.

12. On the Massachusetts government selling Indian land after King Philip's War, see MAC, 30:259; *MCR*, 5:328, 378–379; *HAcc*, 450–451; *MCR*, 5:136.

13. On the rush to acquire Indian land in the postwar period, see John Frederick Martin, *Profits in the Wilderness: Entrepreneurship and the Founding of New England Towns in the Seventeenth Century* (Chapel Hill: University of North Carolina Press, 1991); and Peter S. Leavenworth, "'The Best Title That Indians Can Claim': Native Agency and Consent in the Transferal of Pawtucket Land in the Seventeenth Century," *NEQ* 72 (June 1999): 275–300; MAC, 69:203a; *MCR*, 5:315.

14. MAC, 30:257.

15. MAC, 30:276a; WJW; MD, 7:157–160.

16. *MCR*, 5:328–329; MAC, 30:276a is undated. Archivists placed it on the calendar in 1683, but internal evidence indicates that it was written between June and September 1681; MAC, 30:260a. Daniel Gookin's June 1677 meeting with the Christian Indians, in which they rejected John Wompas's right to sell Indian land, appears in MAC, 30:259a.

17. For example, Natick Indians successfully challenged the sale of land to

Ensign Grout that had been made without their knowledge. After the Court voided the sale, they immediately sold it to a different Englishman, Mathew Rice (MAC, 30:276).

18. *MCR*, 5:329; *MCR*, 5:365–369, 361–365; see also *MCR*, 5:341–342. Dennis Connole maps these sales and makes a similar calculation of the relative price of land sold by Indians and by English in *Indians of the Nipmuck Country*, 236, 246; SD, 12:289.

19. *MCR*, 5:329; *PCR*, 10:180–190, 218; Robert Gibbs Account Book, Gibbs Business Records, AAS.

20. *MCR*, 5:327–329, 365. As an example of Dudley's profit, he purchased one-half of five miles square (8,000 acres) of Nipmuc land for ten pounds in 1682 (SD, 12:297–299); one year later, he sold a mere 2,000 acres of that land for 250 pounds (SD, 12:378–380); Martin, *Profits in the Wilderness*, 92–95. Edward Randolph, the relentlessly snarky royal agent to New England, complained repeatedly of Dudley, Stoughton, and other Council members "Sharing the Country amongst themselves and laying out Large tracts of lands" (Robert Noxon Toppan, *Edward Randolph, including his letters and official papers*, 7 vols. [Boston: The Prince Society, 1898], 6:187–188, 211, 217, 221). Towns named for Dudley include Dudley and Sutton, for the Sutton-Dudleys of England (Edward Randolph to Joseph Dudley, March 1683, in George Adlard, *The Sutton-Dudleys of England and the Dudleys of Massachusetts: From the Norman Conquest to the Present Time* [London: Printed for the Author, 1862]), 69; John Blake and Edward Pratt's Letter of Attorney, *MHSC*, 5th ser., 9:123–127. If Randolph was the man who delivered the Crown's letter in response to John Wompas's second petition to the Connecticut Colony government on his visit there in December 1679, he would have known about Wompas's claim to Fairfield land (Toppan, *Edward Randolph*, 1:120–121, 3:54).

21. WJW; *CCR*, 3:282–283.

22. *CSPC*, 11: #1541; Toppan, *Edward Randolph*, 1:256; *CSPC*, 11: #1808.

23. Randolph requested the position of secretary and the king's Council approved it in November 1683 (Toppan, *Edward Randolph*, 6:162–163); *CSPC*, 11: #1928; Gookin to Dudley, 178; the Englishmen holding shares in the Connecticut lands were John Comer, John Pittom, John Jackson, George Danson, Joshua Hewes, William Harrison, William Mumford, Richard Thayer, John Smith, and Robert Taft (John Blake and Edward Pratt's Letter of Attorney).

24. Connole, *The Indians of the Nipmuck Country*, 129; *MHSC*, 5th ser., 9:122–123, 127–140. Accounts of these events can also be read in Thomas J. Farnham, *Fairfield: The Biography of a Community, 1639–1989* (West Kennebunk, Maine: Published for the Fairfield Historical Society by Phoenix Pub., 1988); and Elizabeth Hubbell Schenk, *History of Fairfield* (New York: The Author, 1889–1905).

25. MAC, 16:337.

26. *CSPC*, 11: #1928; 12: #319; *The Diary of Samuel Sewall, 1674–1729,* ed. M. Halsey Thomas (New York: Farrar, Straus and Giroux, 1973), 1:94–95. Randolph would later be secretary to Governor Edmund Andros (*CSPC*, 12: #1717); Daniel Gookin to Joseph Dudley, 178; SD, 16:89.

27. SD, 16:89. Other men who appeared on the agreement as well as on at least one of the previous complaints included Zachary Abram, Peter Ephraim, Simon Sassomit, and James Rumneymarsh. Indians who had signed earlier but were missing from this list included Waban, Anthony, Norwaruunt, John Awassamog, Piambow, and Eliazer Pegun. Taking the places of those who had died were kin such as Benjamin Tray and Samuel Awassamog, and other Hassanamesit Indians such as James Printer; MAC, 30:260a; Daniel Gookin to Joseph Dudley, 178.

28. John Langdon Sibley, *Biographical Sketches of Graduates of Harvard University, In Cambridge, Massachusetts* (Cambridge, Mass.: Charles William Sever, 1881), 2:167–168; MAC, 35:145; Craig Yirush, *Settlers, Liberty, and Empire: The Roots of Early American Political Theory, 1675–1775* (New York: Cambridge University Press, 2011), 65–72. Danson asked for title to 390 acres in Worcester, considerably less land than his one-ninth share of four miles square entitled him to, perhaps to avoid paying the quitrent on that many acres. It is possible that the land confirmed to him was not part of the Wompas lands, but a separate transaction ("Land Warrants Issued Under Andros, 1687–1688," *Publications of the Colonial Society of Massachusetts,* 21:303–304); Lincoln, *History of Worcester,* 36, 47; Theodore B. Lewis, "Land Speculation and the Dudley Council of 1686," *WMQ* 31 (April 1974): 267.

29. Owen Stanwood, *The Empire Reformed: English America in the Age of the Glorious Revolution* (Philadelphia: University of Pennsylvania Press, 2011); *MPR*, 21:729–730. Paul Dudley, the oldest son of Joseph Dudley, became a shareholder by 1713 (SD, 27:285). The grant for the new town of Sutton is also reprinted in Rev. William A. Benedict and Rev. Hiram A. Tracy, *History of the Town of Sutton, Massachusetts, From 1704 to 1876* (Worcester: Sanford, 1878), 10–12; Adlard, *The Sutton-Dudleys of England.*

30. *MPR*, 21:729–730; *RRCCB*, 11:57, 68; SD, 29:250. Partners who died before 1716 included George Danson (1696), Joshua Hewes (1704), John Pittom (1699), and William Harrison (1686) ("Land Warrants Issued Under Andros"; *SGen* [Hewes]; Thomas Bridgman, *Epitaphs from Copp's Hill Burial Ground, Boston: With Notes* [Boston: 1851], 9; *SGen* [Harrison]). Records of sales, purchases, deeds, and bequests of shareholders in the land John Wompas sold or bequeathed to Edward Pratt appear in SD, 14:1, 15:33, 16:89, 22:473, 22:515, 27:285, 27:286, 27:297–298, 28:2, 28:76–77, 28:109, 29:250, 30:102, 30:165, 32:69, 33:32, 33:216, 34:38, 34:99, 35:233, 38:72, 39:79, 41:163. James Smith came closest to making "a great deal" of money, but he was not one of the original purchasers. He

married Prudence Harrison, widow of William Harrison, thereby obtaining Harrison's share. He purchased more shares from other partners and lived long enough to benefit from the successive divisions of land in Sutton. By 1724, he had earned 670 pounds from sales of shares and land in Sutton (SD, 29:250, 30:102, 32:69, 34:38, 38:72).

31.   Daniel R. Mandell, "Selling the Praying Towns: Massachusett and Nipmuck Land Transactions, 1680–1730," *Northeast Anthropology* 70 (2007): 15; MAC, 30:348–349; MAC, 30:474–475; SD, 13:202–204; Jean M. O'Brien, *Dispossession by Degrees: Indian Land and Identity in Natick, Massachusetts, 1650–1790* (Lincoln: University of Nebraska Press, 2003 [1997]), chapters 5–6; Daniel R. Mandell, *Tribe, Race, History: Native Americans in Southern New England, 1780–1880* (Baltimore: Johns Hopkins University Press, 2008), chapters 1–3.

32.   Frederick Clifton Pierce, *History of Grafton, Worcester County, Massachusetts* (Grafton, Mass.: C. Hamilton, 1879), 34–46.

33.   *MPR*, 9:617; Judith S. Graham, "Samuel Sewall," *Oxford Dictionary of National Biography* (www.oxforddnb.com); Extract of a letter From Samuel Sewall to the honorable Sir William Ashurst, 3 May 1700, LMA/CLC/540/MS07955/001, Records of the New England Company.

Few English officials shared Sewall's commitment to doing justice to the Indians. For instance, in 1763, the Dudley family purchased 440 of the 640 acres remaining to the Nipmucs near the town of Dudley for fifty pounds, then immediately sold the same land to an Englishman for 650 pounds. The Indian guardians of the time reasoned that, because the Nipmucs living on the remaining 200 acres were "mostly Females," the "Land is not like to be of great use to them hereafter" (quoted in Connole, *Indians of the Nipmuck Country*, 237–238).

34.   Thomas L. Doughton, "Unseen Neighbors: Native Americans of Central Massachusetts, a People Who Had 'Vanished,'" in *After King Philip's War: Presence and Persistence in Indian New England*, ed. Colin G. Calloway (Hanover, N.H.: University Press of New England, 1997); Pierce, *History of Grafton*, 78. On English mismanagement and fraud, see Donna Rae Gould, "Contested Places: The History and Meaning of Hassanamisco" (Ph.D. dissertation, University of Connecticut, 2010), 206–211, 220–224.

The trope of the vanishing Indian appears in countless nineteenth-century histories, newspaper articles, and works of literature and art. For historical discussion and repudiation of this myth, see Doughton, "Unseen Neighbors," 218; Jean M. O'Brien, *Firsting and Lasting: Writing Indians Out of Existence in New England* (Minneapolis: University of Minnesota Press, 2010); Gould, "Contested Places"; Stephen A. Mrozowski et al., "Magunkaquog Materiality, Federal Recognition, and the Search for a Deeper History," *International Journal of Historical Archaeology* 13 (2009): 441–443; Jason Mancini, "'In Contempt and Oblivion': Censuses, Ethnogeography, and Hidden Histories in Eighteenth-Century Southern New England," *Ethnohistory* 62, 1 (January 2015): 62–64, and "Beyond Reservation: Indian Survivance in Southern New England and Eastern Long Island, 1713–1861," Ph.D. dissertation, University of Connecticut, 2009.

For a detailed account of the loss of Hassanamesit land and an analysis of its meaning and place in modern Nipmuc identity, see Gould, "Contested Places." For Hassanamesit's listing on the National Registry of Historic Places, see http://home.nps.gov/nr/feature/indian/2011/Hassanamisco_Reservation.htm, accessed 18 February 2017; Gould, "Contested Places," 192–193, 85. On the role of memory in Native American identity, see Christine DeLucia, "The Memory Frontier: Uncommon Pursuits of Past and Place in the Northeast After King Philip's War," *JAH* (March 2012): 975–997, and *Memory Lands: King Philip's War and the Place of Violence in the Northeast* (New Haven, Conn.: Yale University Press, 2018).

35. SD, 29:250; Rev. Peter Whitney, *The History of the County of Worcester, Massachusetts* (1793). Other local histories that describe John Wompas as a sachem include Pierce, *History of Grafton*, 25; Mary DeWitt Freeland, *The Records of Oxford Massachusetts* (Albany, N.Y.: Joel Munsell's Sons, 1894), 13; John Warner Barber, *Historical Collections* (Worcester, Mass.: Warren Lazell, 1844), 609; Abijah P. Marvin, *History of Worcester County, Massachusetts*, 2 vols. (Boston: C. F. Jewett, 1879), 1:22. Wompas also appears as a sachem in Bernd C. Peyer, *The Tutor'd Mind: Indian Missionary-Writers in Antebellum America* (Amherst: University of Massachusetts Press, 1997), 49; Sutton, Massachusetts town website (http://www.suttonmass.org/history/suttonname.html), accessed 13 Jan. 2016.

36. Nathaniel Ingersoll Bowditch, in *RRCCB*, 5:23–25; John Andrew Doyle, *The English in America: The Puritan Colonies* (London, 1887), 2:269; Annie Haven Thwing, *The Crooked and Narrow Streets of the Town of Boston, 1630–1822* (Boston: Marshall Jones, 1920), 158; Allan Forbes, *Some Indian Events of New England* (Boston: Printed for the State Street Trust Company, 1934), 70; Justin Winsor, *The Memorial History of Boston* (Boston: Ticknor, 1881), 2:xxvi; Samuel Eliot Morison, *Harvard College in the Seventeenth Century*, 2 vols. (Cambridge, Mass.: Harvard University Press, 1936), 1:356–357; Louis B. Wright, *Everyday Life in Colonial America* (New York: G. P. Putnam's Sons, 1965), 146; O'Brien, *Dispossession by Degrees*, 76–78, 90; Mandell, "Selling the Praying Towns," 12; see also Daniel R. Mandell, *Behind the Frontier: Indians in Eighteenth-Century Eastern Massachusetts* (Lincoln: University of Nebraska Press, 1996), 43–45.

37. WJW. For another example of people subject to a dominant race employing the tools of literacy to secure rights, see Rebecca J. Scott and Jean M. Hebrard, *Freedom Papers: An Atlantic Odyssey in the Age of Emancipation* (Cambridge, Mass.: Harvard University Press, 2012).

Of all the references to John Wompas by nineteenth- and twentieth-century historians, only one, John C. Crane, shares my contention that Wompas intentionally used English legal deeds to protect Nipmuc land. Writing in 1898, Crane declared: "Wampus seems to have been a man of executive ability, and had the foresight to reserve the plantation of Hassanamisco for his brethren" ("The Nipmucks and their Country," *Proceedings of the Worcester Society of Antiquity* 16 [1898]: 107).

Index